THE SUPREME COURT ON CHURCH & STATE

THE SUPREME COURT
ON CHURCH & STATE

edited by Joseph Tussman

New York

OXFORD UNIVERSITY PRESS 1962

FOREWORD

This volume grows out of a long-held and widely shared conviction that the work of the Supreme Court needs to be made more easily available for a variety of educational purposes. I am grateful to University College of Syracuse University not only for the opportunity it provided to experiment with the use of Supreme Court cases in a program of adult education but also for the encouragement and financial support which made it possible for me to produce this manuscript. I am especially indebted to Alexander N. Charters, Dean, Clifford L. Winters, Jr., Associate Dean, and to Mr. Roy J. Ingham, Program Administrator—all of University College. I profited greatly from continuous discussion with Joel Berke, Howard Lentner, and Richard Newman—graduate students at Syracuse University. And I was greatly stimulated and encouraged by the way in which the members of the "Issues of the 20th Century" program read and discussed these cases.

PREFACE

"Preoccupation by our people with the constitutionality, instead of with the wisdom, of legislation or executive action is preoccupation with a false value."

These words of Justice Frankfurter, emerging, as they do, from a lifetime of involvement with the theory and practice of government in America pose something of a challenge to anyone who sets about to increase that preoccupation. No one, I suppose, would argue that we should not be concerned with the wisdom of our actions, and perhaps the warning is only against excess. But when all allowances are made the suggestion still remains that constitutional-mindedness is something of a spiritual disorder.

This, of course, raises some questions about the place of the Supreme Court in American life, and I think it would not be unfair to Justice Frankfurter's position to see in it the suggestion that if, indeed, all were well with us the Supreme Court would be a far less interesting and significant institution than it is.

But questions of wisdom and of constitutionality are not so easily separated, and it is because he is aware of this that Justice Frankfurter is also a leading advocate of judicial "self-restraint." The relation of constitutionality to wisdom is a complex problem. Some degree of folly is "legitimate" and the remedy is not the court but the "political" process. But it is also the case that, on occasion, what we think wise may be unconstitutional; and there we chafe at the restraint of rule and principle, robe and parchment. Here is all our twentieth-century electronic equipment, there the encumbering legacy of the eighteenth century. Are we then, where we are concerned with constitutionality, preoccupied with a false value?

In the end the answer to this question takes us to the heart of the theory of the state and the theory of moral behavior. And it is because it takes us there that the study of the Supreme Court is especially rewarding.

Foreign observers, Tocqueville among them, have been struck with our constitutional preoccupation. It is a fact of American life. But its significance has not always been grasped. Some countries seem old countries even when their governments are new. But ours seems young even as it ages. Put shortly, they have traditions; we have a charter. We are a people of the Text and the Gloss.

It is not through perversity or accident that constitutionality looms large in our lives. It is a reflection of the fact that our political life has not floated easily on a stable, homogeneous cultural foundation. We have not had the deep-rooted moral consensus based in centuries of a common history; we have not had an established church. The result is that we have had to pay more explicit attention to the moral basis of political life.

The constitution, the idea of constitutionality, has thus come to occupy a crucial position. It stands somewhere between the daily products of political machinery and the moral sense of a culture; it is a peculiar merging of the political and the moral, and it gives to our politics a moral flavor and to our moral controversies a political form. On the one hand it keeps politics always subject to moral demands and prevents it from moving off on its own into a condition in which it would need to rest more heavily on sanction or coercion. On the other hand, providing the common ground on which our political life is played, it makes less urgent the drives for religious and moral orthodoxy and sustains such separation as is possible of church and state.

The constitution is thus both a political and a moral charter and, seen in this light, our preoccupation with it is hardly an addiction to a false value. There are, to be sure, diseases into which it is all too easy to fall. We can worship the letter at the expense of the spirit or presume too much in the name of the spirit. We can disguise our self-serving as law-mindedness or can develop casuistry to the point of shamelessness and hypocrisy. These are tendencies to which moral life is always prone, and it is just at this point that the Supreme Court has a special, guiding role.

We look to the court as the arbiter of constitutionality. Whether intended or not, it has established this position and holds it against recurrent challenge and even, at times, its own misgivings. Day in, day out it faces the question of whether the actions of government are within the bounds of constitutional propriety. The particular problem may be about the meaning of free speech, or double jeopardy, or equal protection or due process, and this is interesting enough. But as it deals with these problems it must also deal with questions about the nature of rules and principles, the proper art of interpretation, and the role of a constitution in a democratic society. Thus the court deals not only with the principles of the constitution but also with the principles of constitutionalism; and I know of no better way of coming to grips with the fundamental problems of political life than by sharing in these preoccupations of the court.

I am not sure that the Supreme Court is not more important as an educational institution than as a governing tribunal. It is, of course, important for what it does. But it is even more important for what it thinks and says as it does it. Decade after decade some of our most powerful minds have grappled with the most urgent and perplexing issues of American life. Its judicial character—although it is far from being simply a "court"—brings it within the tradition of adversary proceedings and requires that it support its decisions with carefully stated opinions. These are subjected to a powerful barrage of criticism and analysis, professional and amateur, from many points of view. The court must give reasons for what it does. It must display its wisdom. It must demonstrate capacity to grasp the baffling details of a concrete situation, give meaning to principles which seem applicable, make difficult consequential decisions —and do all this with the awareness of the implications of its activity for the theory of the state and for democratic political life. Moreover, the tradition of dissenting opinions makes publicly apparent the conflicting strains within the court, develops counterargument of great power, and pushes the court into greater depth of analysis—to everyone's profit.

In the course of its way of life the Supreme Court produces a body of literature quite unique in quality and significance. It welds fact and theory in a context of action. The study of this literature is exciting and rewarding. Unfortunately, however, several things contribute to the fact that it remains, for most people, an unexplored domain.

First, because it is a court its activity brings it within the purview of the legal profession which, to some extent, guards it as a mystery which only the elect can approach. It is of special concern to lawyers, and they study it in a special way. But it is not entirely *their* oracle, although the habit of seeing it this way tends to warn others off.

Political scientists also deal with the court, generally in the form of the study of "constitutional law"; and it is in this form that most non-lawyers who read or have read opinions come to do so. In spite of the variety of approaches, it is a testimony to the intrinsic quality of Supreme Court opinions that such courses almost invariably stand as a high-point in college education. But even here, the dominance of a professional attitude does little to dispel the technical and professional aura which shrouds the court. So that it is generally assumed, incorrectly I believe, that only after hard technical training can one understand what the court is talking about or profitably read its opinions.

Second, not unrelated to what has just been said, is the astonishing unavailability of Supreme Court opinions. There are, of course, complete sets of Supreme Court reports—in three different editions—available in law libraries and even general libraries. But these are forbidding to the nonexpert and are not really available for convenient and leisurely perusal. In addition, there are various collections of opinions or of selections from opinions, volumes of "great" or "leading" decisions or the collected opinions of some Justice of unusual stature or interest. These are all useful, especially for the particular purpose for which they have been created. But they do not serve the general purpose at which this series aims.

Suppose, for example, that one would want to read the great controversy over the Smith Act as it bears on the communication activities of communists; or the great case involving the use of public funds to pay transportation costs for parochial school children. These are generally available only in fragments in extant collections. One is driven to the sets of complete reports, and these, as I said, are generally inaccessible and forbidding. The Dennis and Everson cases do not deserve this fate and we cannot afford this form of burial.

It is the intention of this series to help remedy this situation. The plan is to bring together in a single volume the significant opinions of the court on a problem of interest and importance. We begin, in this volume, with the problem of "church and state."

Since those who read this have the volume in hand it is only necessary to comment on a few of its features.

1. Generally, the opinions are presented in full. The exceptions are some of the earlier opinions, important historically, in which some detail and parts not relevant to the problems of church and state have been omitted. In some of the modern cases omission is made of some unnecessary detail or of material of a purely technical nature. Such omissions are indicated.

2. All of the important cases are included—indeed almost all of the religious cases are found here. The exception is in the area of the regulation of proselytizing in streets or parks. The chief cases are here, but not all.

3. Citations and footnotes have been omitted. As for the citations, they are of use only for technical purposes of legal research, and anyone engaged in such research will be working with the regular sets of reports. The footnotes have been omitted for the same reason. Some have purely technical import. Some do contain material of general interest, but they have been judged by the opinion writers themselves as not an integral part of the opinion.

The Introduction is not intended as a brief for a particular interpretation of the First Amendment. It is a general sketch of the problems involved. It is believed that, with the background it provides, the volume will present no technical difficulties even to the adult who has never read an opinion before.

CONTENTS

INTRODUCTION

"Congress shall make no law respecting an establishment of religion, or prohibiting the free exercise thereof . . ."

These, the opening words of the First Amendment of the Constitution of the United States, sought to avoid, not to borrow trouble. But they have troubled us a great deal and the storm has not yet passed. For they touch upon the relation of the religious to the secular life; and all attempts at either separation or integration of these spheres or aspects of human culture seem to exact a price we are pained to pay.

To state the problem as that of keeping religion and politics separate is already to take some answers for granted. Religion—although I attempt no definition here—involves a complex of belief, attitude, and practice; so, too, does politics. How these are related, in a single person or in a society, is a question not, perhaps, adequately solved by a judgment of Solomon cleaving the spirit from the flesh. Is it altogether improper for religious character to express itself in social life or for politics to draw sustenance from the moral fruits of religious insight?

It has not always seemed so, and the sense of continuity has found expression historically in demands for the subordination of politics to religion and of religion to politics. "Separation" is but one position among others—whether stated in terms of religion and politics or, more concretely, of church and state.

The First Amendment in its attractive brevity leaves much unstated and seems to take much for granted. Even its spirit is elusive. Is it the practical expression of "a religious people"? Or is it a tolerant statement of commitment to a secular experiment? Does it indeed put us "under God"? What is "establishment" and what is an "exercise" of religion? The Amendment does not explain itself. As we begin our analysis we make several preliminary observations:

First, the religious clauses of the First Amendment are only part of the First Amendment, itself only a part of the Bill of Rights attached to the Constitution. They are not isolated statements to be interpreted without relation to context. Specifically, other parts of the First Amendment protect the freedom of speech, press, and assembly against abridgment, and these, in the absence of a religious clause, would seem to provide adequate protection for the freedom of religious belief, worship, proselytizing, and criticism. Is the religious clause, then, redundant or should it be interpreted as having a narrower scope in protecting something not protected by other clauses?

Second, the Amendment speaks of action by Congress. At the time of its adoption some of the states had religious establishments and the Amendment seems, in part, to protect state establishments against Congressional action. In fact the entire Bill of Rights was regarded as a limitation only upon the power of the federal government. However, after the Civil War the Fourteenth Amendment was adopted and it is now generally accepted that, as a result, the First Amendment limits action by state government also.

Third, the Amendment speaks of two different things—"establishment" and "free exercise." The problems arising under each will be separately analyzed, but they are not altogether unrelated and the interpretation of the one has a bearing on the interpretation of the other. The freedom to worship as one thinks best seems to be intrinsically valuable; but it is not necessarily incompatible with the existence of a religious establishment. England has an established church, but there is also freedom of worship outside the establishment and freedom for nonbelievers as well. Are we against establishment, nevertheless, because of the threat it poses to freedom of worship—so that the establishment clause is instrumental to the end expressed in the free exercise clause? Or does the point of the establishment clause lie beyond its contribution to religious freedom and in its expression of the ideal of a secular society, with freedom of worship thrown in as a boon to believers? Much turns on which clause we emphasize. Aid to parochial schools, for example, seems to facilitate the free exercise of religion; it is also held to threaten the separation of church and state. In this controversy those seeking aid generally stand on the free exercise clause; those opposing, on the establishment clause. My point is simply that the twofold character of the religious part of the First Amendment poses some problems.

Fourth, the Amendment does not speak specifically of churches, but of religion. And "religion," we may assume, has a broader scope than "organized religion." The Amendment is not simply a charter for churches. It bears upon the freedom of nonbelievers as well as of believers; and the prohibition of establishment may reach beyond the prohibition of an official church to the denial of the preferred status of any doctrine or creed.

ESTABLISHMENT

The spirit of establishment is both the spirit of the inside-track and the spirit of partnership. Even where most members of a body politic adhere to a single religion or to the same church, establishment has its critics. In this case the objection is to some of the features of partnership of church and state—to the exchange of material support for spiritual comfort, to the loss of critical independence, to theocratic aspirations, to the concentration of power, to the policeman at the service of the priest. Where there is religious diversity, to these are added the objections to the preferred position of a favored church—proselytizing handicaps, invidious distinctions between orthodox and heterodox, and, inevitably, the fears of persecution.

Behind the American rejection of establishment lies both the earlier experience of colonial establishments and the fact of multiplicity and diversity. And whatever one might believe to be the healthy or proper relation between church and state, our situation is inescapably one of *churches* and state—thus adding to the already difficult questions of partnership or co-operation the exacerbations of the problems of favor and discrimination.

But the rejection of establishment is not necessarily the rejection of religion. It is one thing to hail "no discrimination," quite another to insist on "no aid or co-operation." Both are aspects of "no establishment" but they seem to be alternative rather than complementary interpretations. Those who oppose all aid to religion seem, a fortiori, to oppose favoritism or discrimination. But there are those who find the meaning of "no establishment" exhausted in the demand for equal treatment and find no barrier in the Amendment to various forms of governmental aid to, or co-operation with, the religious life of the community. We are, it is said, "a religious people," and however puzzling this phrase may be it is pressed in the service of the view that it is altogether appropriate for our government to treat sympathetically the demands of religious life, to aid in furthering the spiritual development of the people—as it furthers material and intellectual development—provided that it does so with an even hand, without intrusion or control, and without coercion of non-believers.

Thus, everyone agrees that under the First Amendment there can be no official church nor even, short of that, a specially favored church. The issues lie beyond this consensus; they turn on the question of aid and co-operation, on the question of whether the government is furthering a legitimate public purpose when it acts to encourage, support, or aid the institutions of religious life or whether it is precisely the point of the "no establishment" clause that it precludes government action to this end.

Although it does not appear in the Constitution, discussion of establishment leans heavily on "a wall of separation between church and state." This phrase of Jefferson was first quoted by the Court in the Mormon polygamy case. It reappeared in the Everson case (parochial school bus fares) and shortly the metaphor comes in for heavy treatment. Justice Black says the wall may not be breached; Justice Frankfurter admonishes that a wall is not a fine line easily overstepped; Justice Jackson fears that the wall may become as winding as Jefferson's famous serpentine wall at the University of Virginia and later declares that it has become even more warped and twisted than he expected; and Justice Reed concludes that a rule of law should not be drawn from a figure of speech. That Justice Black upholds the use of public funds to reimburse parents sending children to parochial schools in the same opinion in which he resurrects the unbreachable wall of separation may come as a surprise.

But it is not my purpose to trace what may be found in the cases. It is, rather, to call attention to some of the complexities concealed behind familiar phrases. The "wall of separation" is suggestive, whether it recalls the Maginot Line or reminds us that there is something in the ground that hates a wall or that good fences make good neighbors. But the figure of speech tells us little about the ways in which what is separate may be related. We also speak, for example, of the "separation of powers" in our government, and this suggests differing jurisdictions and a measure of independence. But does it also preclude all forms of co-operation and support? I do not argue the case for "aid"; I simply point out that "separation" does not settle the question even if "separation" is taken as canonical.

The current position, promulgated by Justice Black for the Court in the Everson case, is that neither a state nor the federal government can "pass laws which aid one religion, aid all religions, or prefer one religion over another." Since it is granted on all sides that aiding one or preferring one over another is improper, the issue is over the bar to aiding all religions. The Everson doctrine has been bitterly assailed but has not, so far, been repudiated. I call attention to some of the questions it must face:

1. How does this doctrine square with the policy of tax-exemption for church property and church schools? This seems to be a form of financial aid, apparently constitutional, and, in principle, to all churches.

2. How significant is the distinction between aid to the individual and aid to the religious institution? Is a free lunch program or a free transportation program, extended to parochial school children, unobjectionable because it is thought of as helping children (or parents) rather than as helping the church?

3. If we reject this distinction as a device which undermines the "wall," do we then stand in danger of denying to citizens, because of their religious commitments, the benefits of general welfare legislation?

Apart from various forms of financial aid there are other problems of co-operation. Is "released-time" for religious instruction a violation of the principle of separation? Or the adjusting of schedules for religious holidays? Or Sunday (*The* Sabbath?) closing laws? Or censorship of blasphemy? Does "no establishment" really forbid all forms of co-operation?

In addition to such questions of aid and comfort there are still other aspects to the problem. The separation of church and state, we often hear, requires the separation of religion and politics. We are to keep politics out of religion and religion out of politics; government should not meddle with religious matters nor should churches concern themselves with politics.

To keep politics out of religion seems to mean that government should concern itself neither with questions of religious doctrine nor with the internal affairs of religious organizations. As for religious doctrine, no one, I suppose, would regard it as consistent with the First Amendment for government to attempt to pass judgment on disputed doctrinal matters or to concern itself with the truth of religious beliefs or claims. The Ballard case (The Great I AM) stands for the principle of *caveat emptor* where prophets are concerned. It is not for government to decide whether organized religion is, as Jehovah's Witnesses claim, the greatest racket ever invented; or whether faith heals better than penicillin; or whether skepticism is pernicious—although, as we shall see when we consider the "free exercise" of religion, the regulation of religiously motivated action is another matter.

"If there is any fixed star in our constitutional constellation," writes Justice Jackson in the Barnette case, "it is that no official, high or petty, can prescribe what shall be orthodox in politics, nationalism, religion, or other matters of opinion or force citizens to confess by word or act their faith therein." This has not prevented Congress from inserting "under God" into the pledge of allegiance, but this, I suspect, testifies less to the government's desire to intervene in religion than to the pressure of sanctimonious zeal unrestrained by constitutional scruple.

Nor has it always been possible for government to keep out of the internal affairs of religious organizations. Two cases illustrate this. In Watson v. Jones the court was called upon to decide which of two groups, divided over slavery, had control over disputed church property. And in the modern Kedroff case the court had to decide whether St. Nicholas Cathedral belonged to an "American" group or to a group recognizing the authority of the Moscow patriarch. While these involved property claims, the court had to plunge into questions of internal church organization. The court deals with such matters unavoidably and with reluctance. It can be said, on the whole, that our government treads warily on religious ground and respects the independence of religion, doctrinally and organizationally.

But keeping religion out of politics is another matter, and it is not so clear that it is always reasonable to do so. Let us consider several variations on this theme:

THE USE OF GOVERNMENT TO FURTHER RELIGIOUS ENDS

Churches are not always free of the temptation to tap the public purse and to call in the police to further or protect the faith. Zeal for salvation is not easily balked. The aid-to-parochial-school and released-time movements are seen as attempts by religious groups to win the support and co-operation of public authority and public resources for religious ends. Whether, under the establishment clause, this is a legitimate public purpose is a question I have already posed.

There is also the tendency to call in the secular arm to remove temptation and supplement internal discipline. Thus, one might regard the views of a church about the sinfulness of gambling or drinking or Sunday golf, or reading forbidden literature or seeing proscribed films, or practicing birth control, with relative equanimity and with such agreement or disagreement as is involved in one's own religious position. And if churches

xvii

were content with the freedom to spread their views and accepted the challenge of educating their members and maintaining their own discipline some bitterness would disappear from political life. But, alas! We call on the lawmaker and the police to ban the film, to stop the sale, to revoke the license. And the retort is, of course, "Guard your own flock, but don't try to impose your rules on us!"

THE POLITICALLY MINDED CHURCH

But the problem is broader than that of enlisting the aid of the secular arm for such religious purposes. In an age in which government determines so much of the character of our lives it is quite natural to turn to politics as a means of improving or reshaping the world. To reshape it by eradicating games of chance may seem an odd ambition. But what of reshaping it in ways that satisfy a religious conception of human brotherhood—eradicating racial and economic injustice? May a church not condemn segregation or exploitation? May it not urge legislators to curb what it takes to be evil? Does it really make sense to say that we may lobby and vote our pocketbooks but must, as we enter the political arena, carefully divest ourselves of our deepest moral or religious convictions about the shape of the good life and the good society? This, I think, is an absurd demand. Does population policy merit less political attention than crop control? Not every question on which a church has a position is a purely religious question, not to be raised in the political forum.

I regret as much as anyone the excesses of ruthlessness, insensitivity, and irrationality of churches in the militant mood. But I do not see how we can really exclude, in the name of the First Amendment, religiously motivated political action. It begs too many questions about the scope of religious concern to "separate" churches in this way from the concerns of this world.

THE RELIGIOUS TEST OF THE CANDIDATE

Even before the adoption of the First Amendment the Constitution provided that "no religious Test shall ever be required as a Qualification to any Office or public Trust under the United States." This is formally the case, but we are surely aware that the religion of a candidate for public office is a matter of considerable interest. Is it legitimately so? Or is this another way in which we should keep religion out of politics?

The difficulties are obvious. No one wants to add religious sectarianism to political partisanship. Few will defend expressions of religious animosity or prejudice. But if in choosing representatives and officials we are guided in part by our judgment of character how can we ignore the candidates' philosophy or religion? May it not be as significant as his family life, his hobbies, or the details of his latest operation? The fact is, I think, that people do regard the religion of a candidate as relevant. And it is difficult to see why they should not do so.

The prohibition of laws respecting an establishment of religion, the implied separation of church and state, poses, as we have seen, a number of difficulties. We do not want, in Justice Jackson's phrase, "a state-ridden church in a church-ridden state." But neither is it clear that government is required to be indifferent to the demands of religious life or that it may not, if it avoids discrimination, support the spiritual quest of the citizen. The metaphor of "separation" does not solve everything.

FREE EXERCISE

The First Amendment also provides against laws which prohibit the free exercise of religion. Unless this is purely gratuitous it means more than that government should not legislate about what is so inner or private or spiritual that it is in any case beyond the power of government to reach. Something is protected which is vulnerable to invasion, and "free exercise" must refer in part to actions on the public stage.

But the "exercise of religion" is also a phrase whose seeming clarity turns into baffling obscurity. For once it is recognized that it deals with more than some sort of "inner" freedom it is seen to involve us in relations between belief and action. Actions, however, especially as they involve others, are generally subject to the demands of social order and control, and the question quickly becomes "When does the demand of government as it regulates action constitute a prohibition of or interference with the free exercise of religion?"

It should be noted that the variety of religions and churches adds to the difficulty of giving broad scope to conduct which claims to be an exercise of religion. When there is an established church recognized as the instrument of the exercise of religion the problem of the freedom of its exercise is worked out between church and state as the two organizations create their modes of co-operation and their spheres of jurisdiction and autonomy. The free exercise of religion may come to mean simply authority of *the* church over matters which are recognized as falling within its domain. But when the claims of religion are no longer voiced by a single authoritative church, government has greater difficulty in accommodating itself to those claims.

In the light of this situation I begin by stating what the guarantee of free exercise cannot be taken to mean. It cannot mean that any person must be permitted to do anything which seems to him to be required by his religion; nor can he decline with impunity to do what is required by law if it conflicts with his religious views. "The free exercise of religion" does not put all religiously motivated action beyond the authority of law.

The problems of "free exercise" must be worked out, therefore, without the easy acceptance of either the doctrine of a purely "inner" or spiritual freedom or of an anarchic enthronement of the religious conscience of each individual as the supreme law of the land. Belief and action are both involved; but not *mere* belief, nor *all* action claiming the sanction of religion. The cases present us with a variety of situations in which the free exercise of religion is at stake. It is not my purpose to sum them up but rather to sketch some of the dilemmas we face.

FREEDOM OF BELIEF

In a simpler age men consoled themselves with the belief that while external powers might coerce the body into the required posture, the mind at least was beyond reach, private and inviolable. Galileo's fabled mutter, "but it moves," as he rose from his knees seemed to epitomize the ultimate futility of any attempt to control the mind. But in our age of advertising we are no longer so sure that what inhabits our mind is either a native product or carries our official visa. If "freedom of belief" is not to mean simply unawareness of the conditioning we are undergoing it must carry with it some control over the conditions which nourish, dwarf, or warp the mind.

Of course, the freedom of religious belief means at least that there is no governmentally certified creed which the citizen must believe or which he must say he believes. But the principle may require more of us. It is hardly enough to say "believe what you will" and then to expose to pressure or embarrassment those who do not share a dominant view. Those who are outside a popular consensus must always pay a price. But is it for government to add weight to this burden? What, for example, did we do when we added "under God" to the pledge of allegiance? What about those who do not believe in God or in the kind of God we can be said to be under? Are they excluded from the circle of allegiance? Is this a religious test for membership? Or is the nonbeliever expected to lie? To deliberately create a situation in which a citizen must either refrain from participation in a public ceremony or express a religious belief he may not share is certainly not to show much devotion to or understanding of the principle of freedom of belief.

But the problem goes beyond that of compulsory avowal or disavowal of belief and the embarrassment that makes for intellectual conformity. It involves more broadly the right—of parents, for example—to provide or maintain a general environment conducive to the development of desired moral and intellectual attitudes and beliefs. And this takes us into the problem of education, of public and parochial schools, of released-time, of curricula dealing with religious controversy, and, of course, of censorship and freedom of communication and criticism. Protection of the freedom of belief requires that we pay attention not only to the cruder attempts at coercion but to subtler forms of control and influence as well.

FREEDOM OF WORSHIP

While it may be misleading to attempt to distinguish sharply between belief, worship, the performance of religious duties, and religiously motivated actions, each emphasizes a different aspect of the exercise of religion, and, recognizing that they are also interrelated, I turn now to freedom of worship, understood as generally "ceremonial."

We proclaim the freedom to worship as one pleases or not to worship at all. We facilitate this freedom by refraining from taxation of the house of worship. We do not require attendance at church (although compulsory chapel attendance in our military academies, a practice of dubious constitutionality, is apparently well established).

But two sorts of difficulties have arisen even in this area. First, there are ceremonial occasions which we do not generally think of as "religious" which may, to some, seem idolatrous or in conflict with their ceremonial attitude or commitments. Thus, the case of Jehovah's Witnesses and the flag salute, or of Quakers and the taking of oaths. We are prone to ceremony and ritual as part of public celebration or solemn public occasion. This may not be a vice, but in a society like ours it poses difficulties. For our public ritual must be either nondenominational or interdenominational, or "secular." No one is quite happy with yankee-pagan, or with anything else. And it is self-defeating to open wounds as we attempt, on solemn occasions, to achieve a mood of unity and common dedication.

Second, there are also problems of limits to the ritual freedom of sects. Without parading horrifying ritualistic possibilities—not unknown to history—it is clear that the freedom of worship does not take under its protection the ritualistic performance of actions which would otherwise be criminal.

FREEDOM TO PROSELYTIZE

The freedom to preach to the unconverted, to spread the faith, is a valued part of the free exercise of religion. This freedom to communicate would appear to be included in the broad protection of freedom of speech, press, and assembly found in other parts of the First Amendment. I touch here only on the question of whether "religious" communication is subject to special considerations.

To what extent is the general freedom of speech or advocacy hobbled or limited by the fact that religion is involved? There are, obviously, some general taboos observed among us, protecting religious views from irreverent, gloves-off treatment. Atheism is fair game for the sniper, and overtones of "blasphemy" and "sacrilege" still linger in a society in which *lèse-majesté* has lost its force. But the recent case of "The Miracle" has given blasphemy short shrift and evoked from Justice Clark, speaking for the court, the remark that "It is not the business of government in our nation to suppress real or imagined attacks on a particular religious doctrine, whether they appear in publications, speeches, or motion pictures." There is some feeling, I believe, that the church is a privileged sanctuary and that ideas which take refuge there enjoy some freedom from attack. But this is due more to private pressures and the force of custom than to direct governmental action.

On the other hand, we seem at times to verge on what I have come to think of as the "piggy-back" doctrine—the view that after religious communication has ridden to the normal limits of freedom of speech it goes an additional distance on its own steam. Some of the opinions on the proselytizing activities of Jehovah's Witnesses raise this suggestion. The question is whether the addition of religious freedom to freedom of speech gives to religious communication greater freedom from regulation than is enjoyed by political or commercial communication.

The First Amendment protects the right to proselytize, but if we look to it to protect the freedom to criticize we can hardly expect that it will also serve to protect us against criticism.

RELIGION AND FREEDOM OF ACTION

Religion is not always or only a matter of belief and worship; it may require of its adherents that they act in certain ways. I shall not linger over such actions as are closely related to worship and constitute religious duties in a narrow sense—the observance of special holidays, for example. I turn, rather, to religious commands or prohibitions which require actions contrary to the law of the state. Mormons, for example, regarded plural marriage not as a pleasant option but as a religious duty; but bigamy is, for us, a secular crime. Military service is a legal requirement; but bearing arms violates the religious convictions of some citizens. Does the guarantee of the free exercise of religion mean that the law cannot require actions contrary to religious conviction or the religious conscience?

The further we get from questions of belief and worship into the realm of action the less does this seem to be the case. We are not surprised that an early court dealt curtly with Mormon polygamy; but one searches later cases in vain for the vindication of claims of conscience or religious belief as overriding the demands of law. The notable exception is the Barnette case, reversing the flag-salute holding of the Gobitis case; but there the action was of a ceremonial character and required that children be compelled to utter "what was not in their mind."

Thus, in spite of all the talk about respect for conscience, conscientious objection has only as much protection as policy-making bodies are moved to grant. There is no constitutional elevation in the First Amendment, as interpreted by the court, of the demands of conscience over the laws of the state where the state acts impartially to promote a legitimate public purpose. The free exercise of religion does not mean that religiously motivated action is above the law. Where religion is a "private" matter this position is inescapable; the alternative is anarchy.

SECULARISM AND NEUTRALITY

It should be noted that while government is barred from prohibiting the free exercise of religion nothing is said in the free exercise clause about government action designed to aid or facilitate the free exercise of religion. If there is a limitation on this score it is to be found in the establishment clause, so interpreted as to see in the idea of separation of church and state a prohibition of impartial aid to religion. Taken together in this way the Amendment can be summed up as meaning "no aid—no hindrance." But the "no aid" interpretation of the establishment clause is strongly challenged, and the alternative view sums up the Amendment as "no partiality—no hindrance." Thus is posed the fundamental issue between those who would see us as a tolerant but secular society and those who find in the conception of a secular state a denial of our history as "a religious people." The latter see the establishment clause not as a dis-establishment of "religion" but only as the recognition of the legitimate diversity of religious faith and the denial of special status to any religion —not as a requirement of neutrality as between religion and irreligion but only as between one religion and another.

The "no-hindrance" feature, common to both interpretations, would seem unquestionably to apply to the nonreligious or irreligious as well as to the religious among us. Government may not coerce the unbeliever to belief or worship.

But the question of aid is more difficult. Consider the public school question. If we can distinguish "nonreligious" from both "religious" and "irreligious" then it can be argued that the public schools should simply be nonreligious—leaving the issue between religion and irreligion to parents and churches, while the school is neutrally nonreligious. But many insist that a school that is not religious is simply irreligious in spirit. The choice, they say, is between godliness and godlessness, and the choice is an inescapable one.

If this dichotomy is accepted, religion cannot be simply put aside without prejudice to its claims; religion is either in or out, and "out" carries with it the overtones of rejection. To keep religion out of state-supported public education is, in this view, to put the state on the side of godlessness in spite of the claim that, in the words of Justice Douglas, "we are a religious people whose institutions presuppose a Supreme Being." The First Amendment, it is argued, does not require that govern-ment be netural "against religion."

The tendency of partisans to deny that there is a neutral position is a familiar one. Where is neutral ground in the struggle between good and evil? Indifference? That itself is evil. Is it possible, then, to maintain a neutral position for public education which does not fall into this difficulty?

There seem to be two possibilities. First, in the face of the conflict between religious and irreligious positions the school is to attempt to be fair. It may attempt to present the "facts" as to a jury; or impartially to present each "opinion," refraining from judgment; or to develop canons of judgment by which the controversial positions may be tested. In one way or another it is to claim or develop "objectivity." But this attempt itself must be philosophically based and issues reappear as metaphysical or methodological ones—not to be resolved by administrative ukase.

Second, there is the path of "avoidance," by which we attempt to ignore the problems or issues with which religion is concerned. But the question here is what such avoidance does to the scope and character of public education. It may leave it technical or narrowly vocational, and it would take the heart out of any attempt to deal with "the whole man." It may be doubted that such avoidance is either possible or desirable.

The conception of the neutral, nonreligious school is not so simple as we sometimes think. Neither "objectivity" nor "avoidance" altogether voids the claim that the "nonreligious" school may, in effect, be "irreligious." * And if this is so, it is not clear that taxing religious parents to support irreligious education is less objectionable in principle than taxing the irreligious to support the teaching of religious doctrine. The case for "no aid" to parochial schools or to released-time programs depends on the possibility of maintaining a real distinction between nonreligious and irreligious.

I am not sure we have succeeded in doing so. If we have not, the charge that public education in its secular form is irreligious may have some substance. As a nonbeliever I may find this convenient. But I am not sure that it is altogether fair or that it justifies, in the name of "neutrality," the rejection of the claims of our religious citizens to public support for their efforts at providing education that is religious in spirit. The neutrality of the public school should not, I suggest, be considered beyond challenge. And "no partiality" may, in the end, turn out to be a more appropriate slogan than "no aid."

The two religious clauses of the First Amendment present us with two major problems. First, to what extent does the guarantee of the free exercise of religion require deference to religiously motivated action? While it seems impossible to recognize the religious conscience of each individual as the supreme law of the land the court's general denial of the constitutional status of the claims of conscientious action or objection may come as something of a surprise.

Second, is the establishment clause to be understood as prohibiting all forms of aid or co-operation between churches and the state or as merely prohibiting discriminatory treatment? This question is far from settled and promises to be bitterly contested.

It is, I hope, hardly necessary to add, as we try to understand and deal wisely with the problems of religious freedom, that the freedom and dignity of the nonbeliever—the agnostic or the atheist—is as precious and as much to be protected as that of the believer. Earlier, we would have called ourselves a "Christian nation." More recently the phrase is a "religious nation." Someday, perhaps, we may come to think of ourselves as a spiritual nation, deeply involved in the quest for truth about the nature of the universe and man's place in it.

---

* The case is hardly better if schools avoid the "irreligious" charge by developing a vague religiosity—a loose united front against atheism. Whatever such a position might be called, it is only nonreligious in the sense that it is nondenominational. It is hardly nonreligious or neutral as between religion and irreligion.

THE SUPREME COURT ON CHURCH & STATE

TERRETT v. TAYLOR   9 Cranch 43 (1815)

"But the free exercise of religion cannot be justly deemed to be restrained by aiding with equal attention the votaries of every sect to perform their own religious duties . . ."

Mr. Justice Story

In 1801 the Virginia Legislature asserted its right to all the property of the Protestant Episcopal churches in the parishes of the state and directed that certain lands be sold, the proceeds to be used for the support of the poor of the parish. The Legislature asserted that its own act of 1776 which confirmed the rights of the church to all its lands and other property was inconsistent with the bill of rights and constitution of Virginia and was, therefore, void. (Part of the Court's opinion is omitted.)

MR. JUSTICE STORY DELIVERED THE OPINION OF THE COURT.

. . . This summary view of so much of the Virginia statutes as bears directly on the subject in controversy, presents not only a most extraordinary diversity of opinion in the legislature as to the nature and propriety of aid in the temporal concerns of religion, but the more embarrassing considerations of the constitutional character and efficacy of those laws touching the rights and property of the Episcopal Church.

It is conceded on all sides that, at the revolution, the Episcopal Church no longer retained its character as an exclusive religious establishment. And there can be no doubt that it was competent to the people and to the legislative to deprive it of its superiority over other religious sects, and to withhold from it any support by public taxation. But, although it may be true that "religion can be directed only by reason and conviction, not by force or violence," and that "all men are equally entitled to the free exercise of religion according to the dictates of conscience," as the bill of rights of Virginia declares, yet it is difficult to perceive how it follows as a consequence that the legislature may not enact laws more effectually to enable all sects to accomplish the great objects of religion by giving them corporate rights for the management of their property, and the regulation of their temporal as well as spiritual concerns. Consistent with the constitution of Virginia the legislature could not create or continue a religious establishment which should have exclusive rights and prerogatives, or compel the citizens to worship under a stipulated form or discipline, or to pay taxes to those whose creed they could not conscientiously believe. But the free exercise of religion cannot be justly deemed to be restrained by aiding with equal attention the votaries of every sect to perform their own religious duties, or by establishing funds for the support of ministers, for public charities, for the endowment of churches, or for the sepulture of the dead. And that these purposes could be better secured and cherished by corporate powers, cannot be doubted by any person who has attended to the difficulties which surround all voluntary associations. While, therefore, the legislature might exempt the citizens from a compulsive attendance and payment of taxes in support of any particular sect, it is not perceived that either public or constitutional principles required the abolition of all religious corporations.

Be, however, the general authority of the legislature as to the subject of religion as it may, it will require other arguments to establish the position that, at the revolution, all the public property acquired by the Episcopal churches, under the sanction of the laws, became the property of the state. Had the property thus acquired been originally granted by the state or the king, there might have been some color (and it would have been but a color) for such an extraordinary pretension. But the property was, in fact and in law, generally purchased by the parishioners, or acquired by the benefactions of pious donors. The title thereto was indefeasibly vested in the churches, or rather in their legal agents. It was not in the power of the crown to seize or assume it; nor of the parliament itself to destroy the grants, unless by the exercise of a power the most arbitrary, oppressive and unjust, and endured only because it could not be resisted. It was not forfeited; for the churches had committed no offense. The dissolution of the regal government no more destroyed the right to possess or enjoy this property than it did the right of any other corporation or individual to his or its own property. The dissolution of the form of government did not involve in it a dissolution of civil rights, or an abolition of the common law under which the inheritances of every man in the state were held. The state itself succeeded only to the rights of the crown; and, we may add, with many a flower of prerogative struck from its hands. It has been asserted as a principle of the common law, that the division of an empire creates no forfeiture of previously-vested rights of property. And this principle is equally consonant with the common sense of mankind and the maxims of eternal justice. Nor are we able to perceive any sound reason why the church lands escheated or devolved upon the state by the revolution any more than the property of any other corporation created by the royal bounty or established by the legislature. The

4

revolution might justly take away the public patronage, the exclusive cure of souls, and the compulsive taxation for the support of the church. Beyond these we are not prepared to admit the justice or the authority of the exercise of legislation. . .

VIDAL v. GIRARD'S EXECUTORS
2 Howard 205 (1844)

> "No fault can be found with Girard for wishing a marble college to bear his name forever, but it is not valuable unless it has a fragrance of Christianity about it."
> —Daniel Webster, challenging Girard's will before the Court

Stephen Girard, a wealthy resident of Philadelphia, died in 1831 leaving a will which, among other things, provided for the establishment of a college for orphans. Among detailed instructions for the regulation of the college Girard provided that:

"They shall be instructed in the various branches of a sound education, comprehending reading, writing, grammar, arithmetic, geography, navigation, surveying, practical mathematics, astronomy, natural, chemical, and experimental philosophy, the French and Spanish languages (I do not forbid, but I do not recommend the Greek and Latin languages), and such other learning and science as the capacities of the several scholars may merit or warrant. I would have them taught facts and things, rather than words or signs; and especially, I desire that by every proper means a pure attachment to our republican institutions, and to the sacred rights of conscience, as guaranteed by our happy constitutions, shall be formed and fostered in the minds of the scholars."

Girard added, however, a crucial provision:

"I enjoin and require that no ecclesiastic, missionary, or minister of any sect whatsoever, shall ever hold or exercise any station or duty whatever in the said college; nor shall any such person ever be admitted for any purpose, or as a visitor, within the premises appropriated to the purposes of the said college.

"In making this restriction, I do not mean to cast any reflection upon any sect or person whatsoever; but, as there is such a multitude of sects, and such a diversity of opinion amongst them, I desire to keep the tender minds of the orphans, who are to derive advantage from this bequest, free from the excitement which clashing doctrines and sectarian controversy are so apt to produce; my desire is, that all the instructors and teachers in the college shall take pains to instil into the minds of the scholars the purest principles of morality, so that, on their entrance into active life, they may, from inclination and habit, evince benevolence towards their fellow-creatures, and a love of truth, sobriety, and industry, adopting at the same time such religious tenets as their matured reason may enable them to prefer."

"A cruel experiment," said Webster, "is to be made upon these orphans, to ascertain whether they cannot be brought up without religion." The Court considers whether this provision invalidates Girard's will. (Part of the opinion, which deals with other issues, is omitted.)

MR. JUSTICE STORY DELIVERED THE OPINION OF THE COURT.

. . . The case, then, according to our judgment, is completely closed in by the principles and authorities already mentioned, and is that of a valid charity in Pennsylvania, unless it is rendered void by the remaining objection which has been taken to it.

This objection is that the foundation of the college upon the principles and exclusions prescribed by the testator, is derogatory and hostile to the Christian religion, and so is void, as being against the common law and public policy of Pennsylvania; and this for two reasons: First, because of the exclusion of all ecclesiastics, missionaries, and ministers of any sect from holding or exercising any station or duty in the college, or even visiting the same, and second, because it limits the instruction to be given to the scholars to pure morality, and general benevolence, and a love of truth, sobriety, and industry, thereby excluding, by implication, all instruction in the Christian religion.

In considering this objecton, the court are not at liberty to travel out of the record in order to ascertain what were the private religious opinions of the testator (of which, indeed, we can know nothing), nor to consider whether the scheme of education by him prescribed, is such as we ourselves should approve, or as is best adapted to accomplish the great aims and ends of education. Nor are we at liberty to look at general considerations of the supposed public interests and policy of Pennsylvania upon this subject, beyond what its constitution and laws and judicial decisions made known to us. The question, what is the public policy of a State, and what is contrary to it, if inquired into beyond these limits, will be found to be one of great vagueness and uncertainty, and to involve discussions which scarcely come within the range of judicial duty and functions, and upon which men may and will complexionally differ; above all, when that topic is connected with religious polity, in a country composed of such a variety of religious sects as our country, it is impossible not to feel that it would be attended with almost insuperable difficulties, and involve differences of opinion almost endless in their variety. We disclaim any right to enter upon such examinations, beyond what the State constitutions, and laws, and decisions necessarily bring before us.

It is also said, and truly, that the Christian religion is a part of the common law of Pennsylvania. But this proposition is to be received with its appropriate qualifications, and in connection with the bill of rights of that State, as found in its constitution of government. The constitution of 1790 (and the like provision will, in substance, be found in the constitution of 1776, and in the existing constitution of 1838) expressly declares, "That all men have a natural and indefeasible right to worship Almighty God according to the dictates of their own consciences; no man can of right be compelled to attend, erect, or support any place of worship, or to maintain any ministry against his consent; no human authority can, in any case whatever, control or interfere with the rights of conscience; and no preference shall ever be given by law to any religious establishments or modes of worship." Language more comprehensive for the complete protection of every variety of religious opinion could scarcely be used; and it must have been intended to extend equally to all sects, whether they were Jews or infidels. So that we are compelled to admit that although Christianity be a part of the common law of the State, yet it is so in this qualified sense, that its divine origin and truth are admitted, and therefore it is not to be maliciously and openly reviled and blasphemed against, to the annoyance of believers or the injury of the public. Such was the doctrine of the Supreme Court of Pennsylvania in Updegraff v. The Commonwealth.

It is unnecessary for us, however, to consider what would be the legal effect of a devise in Pennsylvania for the establishment of a school or college, for the propagation of Judaism, or Deism, or any other form of infidelity. Such a case is not to be presumed to exist in a Christian country; and therefore it must be made out by clear and indisputable proof. Remote inferences, or possible results, or speculative tendencies, are not to be drawn or adopted for such purposes. There must be plain, positive, and express provisions, demonstrating not only that Christianity is not to be taught; but that it is to be impugned or repudiated.

Now, in the present case, there is no pretense to say that any such positive or express provisions exist, or are even shadowed forth in the will. The testator does not say that Christianity shall not be taught in the college. But only that no ecclesiastic of any sect shall hold or exercise any station or duty in the college. Suppose, instead of this, he had said that no person but a layman shall be an instructor or officer or visitor in the college, what legal objection could have been made to such a restriction? And yet the actual prohibition is in effect the same in substance. But it is asked; why are ecclesiastics excluded, if it is not because they are the stated and appropriate preachers of Christianity? The answer may be given in the very words of the testator. "In making this restriction," says he, "I do not mean to cast any reflection upon any sect or person whatsoever. But as there is such a multitude of sects and such a diversity of opinion amongst them, I desire to keep the tender minds of the orphans, who are to derive advantage from this bequest, free from the excitement which clashing doctrines and sectarian controversy are so apt to produce." Here, then, we have the reason given; and the question is not, whether it is satisfactory to us or not; nor whether the history of religion does or does not justify such a sweeping statement; but the question is, whether the exclusion be not such as the testator had a right, consistently with the laws of Pennsylvania, to maintain, upon his own notions of religious instruction. Suppose the testator had excluded all religious instructors but Catholics, or Quakers, or Swedenborgians; or, to put a stronger case, he had excluded all religious instructors but Jews, would the bequest have been void on that account? Suppose he had excluded all lawyers, or all physicians, or all merchants from being instructors or visitors, would the prohibition have been fatal to the bequest? The truth is, that in cases of this sort, it is extremely difficult to draw any just and satisfactory line of distinction in a free country as to the qualifications or disqualifications which may be insisted upon by the donor of a charity as to those who shall administer or partake of his bounty.

But the objection itself assumes the proposition that Christianity is not to be taught, because ecclesiastics are not to be instructors or officers. But this is by no means a necessary or legitimate inference from the premises. Why may not a layman instruct in the general principles of Christianity as well as ecclesiastics. There is no restriction as to the religious opinions of the instructors and officers. They may be, and doubtless, under the auspices of the city government, they will always be, men, not only distinguished for learning and talents, but for piety and elevated virtue, and holy lives and characters. And we cannot overlook the blessings which such men by their conduct, as well as their instructions, may, nay must impart to their youthful pupils. Why may not the Bible, and especially the New Testament, without note or comment, be read and taught as a divine revelation in the college—its general precepts expounded, its evidences explained, and its glorious principles of morality inculcated? What is there to prevent a work, not sectarian, upon the general evidences of Christianity, from being read and taught in the college by lay teachers? Certainly there is nothing in the will that proscribes such studies. Above all, the testator positively enjoins, "that all the instructors and teachers in the college shall take pains to instil into the minds of the scholars the purest principles of morality, so that on their entrance into active life they may from inclination and habit evince benevolence towards their fellow-creatures, and a love of truth, sobriety, and industry, adopting at the same time such religious tenets as their matured reason may enable them to prefer." Now, it may well be asked, what is there in all this, which is positively enjoined, inconsistent with the spirit or truths of Christianity? Are not these truths all taught by Christianity, although it teaches much more? Where can the purest principles of morality be learned so clearly or so perfectly as from the New Testament? Where are benevolence, the love of truth, sobriety, and industry, so powerfully and irresistibly inculcated as in the sacred volume? The testator has not said how these great principals are to be taught, or by whom, except it be by laymen, nor what books are to be used to explain or enforce them. All that we can gather from his language is, that he desired to exclude sectarians and sectarianism from the college, leaving the instructors and officers free to teach the purest morality, the love of truth, sobriety, and industry, by all appropriate means; and of course including the best, the surest, and the most impressive. The objection, then, in this view, goes to this,—either that the testator has totally omitted to provide for religious instruction in his scheme of education (which, from what has been already said, is an inadmissible interpretation), or that it includes but partial and imperfect instruction in those truths. In either view can it be truly said that it contravenes the known law of Pennsylvania upon the subject of charities, or is not allowable under the article of the bill of rights already cited? Is an omission to provide for instruction in Christianity in any scheme of school or college education a fatal defect, which voids it according to the law of Pennsylvania? If the instruction provided for is incomplete and imperfect, is it equally fatal? These questions are propounded, because we are not aware that anything exists in the constitution or laws of Pennsylvania, or the judicial decisions of its tribunals, which would justify us in pronouncing that such defects would be so fatal. Let us take the case of a charitable donation to teach the poor orphans reading, writing, arithmetic, geography, and navigation, and excluding all other studies and instruction; would the donation be void, as a charity in Pennsylvania, as being deemed derogatory to Christianity? Hitherto it has been supposed that a charity for the instruction of the poor might be good and valid in England even if it did not go beyond the establishment of a grammar school. And in America, it has been thought, in the absence of any express legal prohibitions, that the donor might select the studies, as well as the classes of persons, who were to receive his bounty without being compellable to make religious instruction a necessary part of those studies. It has hitherto been thought sufficient, if he does not require anything to be taught inconsistent with Christianity.

Looking to the objection, therefore, in a mere juridicial view, which is the only one in which we are at liberty to consider it, we are satisfied that there is nothing in the devise establishing the college, or in the regulations and restrictions contained therein, which are inconsistent with the Christian religion, or are opposed to any known policy of the State of Pennsylvania.

This view of the whole matter renders it unnecessary for us to examine the other and remaining question, to whom, if the devise were void, the property would belong, whether it would fall into the residue of the estate devised to the city, or become a resulting trust for the heirs-at-law.

WATSON v. JONES 13 Wallace 679 (1872)

"The right to organize voluntary religious associations to assist in the expression and dissemination of any religious doctrine, and to create tribunals for the decision of controverted questions of faith within the association, is unquestioned. All who unite themselves to such a body do so with an implied consent to this government, and are bound to submit to it. But it would be a vain consent and would lead to the total subversion of such religious bodies, if any one aggrieved by one of their decisions could appeal to the secular courts and have them reversed."

Mr. Justice Miller

The congregation of the Walnut Street Church of Louisville found itself divided during and after the Civil War over the question of slavery. The General Assembly of The Presbyterian Church supported the Federal Government and expressed views favorable to emancipation and adverse to the institution of slavery. A large body of the churches in the insurrectionary states withdrew from the General Assembly and formed The Presbyterian Church of The Confederate States, endorsing the view that "the system of negro slavery in the South is a divine institution, and that it is the peculiar mission of the Southern Church to conserve that institution."

As the controversy ran its course the Walnut Street congregation split irreconcilably over the question of adherence to the General Assembly of the United States or to the Presbyterian Church of the Confederate States and brought their claims to the control of the Church property to the courts. (Part of the opinion is omitted.)

10

MR. JUSTICE MILLER DELIVERED THE OPINION OF THE COURT.

This case belongs to a class, happily rare in our courts, in which one of the parties to a controversy, essentially ecclesiastical, resorts to the judicial tribunals of the State for the maintenance of rights which the Church has refused to acknowledge, or found itself unable to protect. Much as such dissensions among the members of a religious society should be regretted, a regret which is increased when passing from the control of the judicial and legislative bodies of the entire organization to which the society belongs, an appeal is made to the secular authority; the courts when so called on must perform their functions as in other cases.

Religious organizations come before us in the same attitude as other voluntary associations for benevolent or charitable purposes, and their rights of property, or of contract, are equally under the protection of the law, and the actions of their members subject to its restraints. Conscious as we may be of the excited feeling engendered by this controversy, and of the extent to which it has agitated the intelligent and pious body of Christians in whose bosom it originated, we enter upon its consideration with the satisfaction of knowing that the principles on which we are to decide so much of it as is proper for our decision, are those applicable alike to all of its class, and that our duty is the simple one of applying those principles to the facts before us. . .

The questions which have come before the civil courts concerning the rights to property held by ecclesiastical bodies, may, so far as we have been able to examine them, be profitably classified under three general heads, which of course do not include cases governed by considerations applicable to a church established and supported by law as the religion of the State.

1. The first of these is when the property which is the subject of controversy has been, by the deed or will of the donor, or other instrument by which the property is held, by the express terms of the instrument devoted to the teaching, support or spread of some specific form of religious doctrine or belief.

2. The second is when the property is held by a religious congregation which, by the nature of its organization, is strictly independent of other ecclesiastical associations, and so far as church government is concerned, owes no fealty or obligation to any higher authority.

3. The third is where the religious congregation or ecclesiastical body holding the property is but a subordinate member of some general church organization in which there are superior ecclesiastical tribunals with a general and ultimate power of control more or less complete in some supreme judicatory over the whole membership of that general organization.

In regard to the first of these classes it seems hardly to admit a rational doubt that an individual or an association of individuals may dedicate property by way of trust to the purpose of sustaining, supporting and propagating definite religious doctrines or principles, providing that in doing so they violate no law of morality, and give to the instrument by which their purpose is evidenced, the formalities which the laws require. And it would seem also to be the obvious duty of the court, in a case properly made, to see that the property so dedicated is not diverted from the trust which is thus attached to its use. So long as there are persons qualified within the meaning of the original dedication, and who are also willing to teach the doctrines or principles prescribed in the act of dedication, and so long as there is any one so interested in the execution of the trust as to have a standing in court, it must be that they can prevent the diversion of the property or fund to other and different uses. This is the general doctrine of courts of equity as to charities, and it seems equally applicable to ecclesiastical matters.

In such case, if the trust is confided to a religious congregation of the independent or congregational form of church government, it is not in the power of the majority of that congregation, however preponderant, by reason of a change of views on religious subjects, to carry the property so confided to them to the support of new and conflicting doctrine. A pious man building and dedicating a house of worship to the sole and exclusive use of those who believe in the doctrine of the Holy Trinity, and placing it under the control of a congregation which at the time holds the same belief, has a right to expect that the law will prevent that property from being used as a means of support and dissemination of the Unitarian doctrine, and as a place of Unitarian worship. Nor is the principle varied when the organization to which the trust is confided is of the second or associated form of church government. The protection which the law throws around the trust is the same. And though the task may be a delicate one and a difficult one, it will be the duty of the court in such cases, when the doctrine to be taught or the the form of worship to be used is definitely and clearly laid down, to inquire whether the party accused of violating the trust is holding or teaching a different doctrine, or using a form of worship which is so far variant as to defeat the declared objects of the trust. In the leading case on this subject, in the English courts, Lord Eldon said: "I agree with the defendants that the religious belief of the parties is irrelevant to the matters in dispute, except so far as the King's Court is called upon to execute the trust." That was a case in which the trust deed declared the house which was erected under it, was for the worship and service of God. And though we may

12

not be satisfied with the very artificial and elaborate argument by which the Chancellor arrives at the conclusion, that because any other view of the nature of the Godhead than the Trinitarian view was heresy by the laws of England, and any one giving expression to the Unitarian view was liable to be severely punished for heresy by the secular courts, at the time the deed was made, that the trust was, therefore, for Trinitarian worship, we may still accept the statement that the court has the right to enforce a trust clearly defined on such a subject. . .

The second class of cases which we have described has reference to the case of a church of a strictly congregational or independent organization, governed solely within itself, either by a majority of its members or by such other local organism as it may have instituted for the purpose of ecclesiastical government; and to property held by such a church, either by way of purchase or donation, with no other specific trust attached to it in the hands of the church than that it is for the use of that congregation as a religious society.

In such cases, where there is a schism which leads to a separation into distinct and conflicting bodies, the rights of such bodies to the use of the property must be determined by the ordinary principles which govern voluntary associations. If the principle of government in such cases is that the majority rules, then the numerical majority of members must control the right to the use of the property. If there be within the congregation officers in whom are vested the powers of such control, then those who adhere to the acknowledged organism by which the body is governed are entitled to the use of the property. The minority in choosing to separate themselves into a distinct body, and refusing to recognize the authority of the governing body, can claim no rights in the property from the fact that they had once been members of the Church or congregation. This ruling admits of no inquiry into the existing religious opinions of those who comprise the legal or regular organization; for, if such was permitted, a very small minority, without any officers of the church among them, might be found to be the only faithful supporters of the religious dogmas of the founders of the Church. There being no such trust imposed upon the property when purchased or given, the court will not imply one for the purpose of expelling from its use those who by regular succession and order constitute the Church, because they may have changed in some respect their views of religious truth. . . .

The case of Smith v. Nelson asserts this doctrine in a case where a legacy was left to the Associate Congression of Ryegate, the interest whereof was to be annually paid to their minister forever. In that case, though the Ryegate congregation was one of a number of Presbyterian churches connected with the general Presbyterian body at large, the court held that the only inquiry was whether the society still exists, and whether they have a minister chosen and appointed by the majority and regularly ordained over the society, agreeably to the usage of that denomination. And though we may be of opinion that the doctrine of that case needs modification, so far as it discusses the relation of the Ryegate congregation to the other judicatories of the body to which it belongs, it certainly lays down the principle correctly if that congregation was to be treated as an independent one.

But the third of these classes of cases is the one which is oftenest found in the courts, and which, with reference to the number and difficulty of the questions involved, and to other considerations, is every way the most important.

It is the case of property acquired in any of the usual modes for the general use of a religious congregation which is itself part of a large and general organization of some religious denomination, with which it is more or less intimately connected by religious views and ecclesiastical government.

The case before us is one of this class, growing out of a schism which has divided the congregation and its officers, and the presbytery and synod, and which appeals to the courts to determine the right to the use of the property so acquired. Here is no case of property devoted forever by the instrument which conveyed it, or by any specific declaration of its owner, to the support of any special religious dogmas, or any peculiar form of worship, but of property purchased for the use of a religious congregation, and so long as any existing religious congregation can be ascertained to be that congregation, or its regular and legitimate successor, it is entitled to the use of the property. In the case of an independent congregation we have pointed out how this indentity, or succession, is to be ascertained, but in cases of this character we are bound to look at the fact that the local congregation is itself but a member of a much larger and more important religious organization, and is under its government and control, and is bound by its orders and judgments. There are in the Presbyterian system of ecclesiastical government, in regular succession, the Presbytery over the session or local church, the Synod over the Presbytery, and the General Assembly over all. These are called, in the language of the church organs "judicatories," and they entertain appeals from the decisions of those below, and prescribe corrective measures in other cases.

In this class of cases we think the rule of action which should govern the civil courts, founded in a broad and sound view of the relations of church and state under our system of laws, and supported by a preponderating weight of judicial authority is, that, whenever

14

the questions of discipline or of faith, or ecclesiastical rule, custom or law have been decided by the highest of these church judicatories to which the matter has been carried, the legal tribunals must accept such decisions as final, and as binding on them, in their application to the case before them.

We concede at the outset that the doctrine of the English courts is otherwise. In the case of The Attorney General v. Pearson, cited before, the proposition is laid down by Lord Eldon, and sustained by the peers, that it is the duty of the court in such cases to inquire and decide for itself, not only what was the nature and power of these church judicatories, but what is the true standard of faith in the church organization, and which of the contending parties before the court holds to this standard. And in the subsequent case of Craigdallie v. Aikman, the same learned judge expresses in strong terms his chagrin that the Court of Sessions of Scotland, from which the case had been appealed, had failed to find on this latter subject, so that he could rest the case on religious belief, but had declared that in this matter there was no difference between the parties. And we can very well understand how the Lord Chancellor of England, who is, in his office, in a large sense, the head and representative of the Established Church, who controls very largely the church patronage, and whose judicial decision may be, and not unfrequently is, invoked in cases of heresy and ecclesiastical contumacy, should feel, even in dealing with a dissenting church, but little delicacy in grappling with the most abstruse problems of theological controversy, or in construing the instruments which those churches have adopted as their rules of government, or inquiring into their customs and usages. The dissenting church in England is not a free church in the sense in which we apply the term in this country, and it was much less free in Lord Eldon's time than now. Laws then existed upon the statute book hampering the free exercise of religious belief and worship in many most oppressive forms, and although Protestant dissenters were less burdened than Catholics and Jews, there did not exist that full, entire and practical freedom for all forms of religious belief and practice which lies at the foundation of our political principles. . .

In this country the full and free right to entertain any religious belief, to practice any religious principle, and to teach any religious doctrine which does not violate the laws of morality and property, and which does not infringe personal rights, is conceded to all. The law knows no heresy, and is committed to the support of no dogma, the establishment of no sect. The right to organize voluntary religious associations to assist in the expression and dissemination of any religious doctrine, and to create tribunals for the decision of controverted questions of faith within the association, and for the ecclesiastical government of all the individual members, congregations and officers within the general association, is unquestioned. All who unite themselves to such a body do so with an implied consent to this government, and are bound to submit to it. But it would be a vain consent and would lead to the total subversion of such religious bodies, if any one aggrieved by one of their decisions could appeal to the secular courts and have them reversed. It is of the essence of these religious unions, and of their right to establish tribunals for the decision of questions arising among themselves, that those decisions should be binding in all cases of ecclesiastical cognizance, subject only to such appeals as the organism itself provides for.

Nor do we see that justice would be likely to be promoted by submitting those decisions to review in the ordinary judicial tribunals. Each of these large and influential bodies (to mention no others, let reference be had to the Protestant Episcopal, the Methodist Episcopal, and the Presbyterian churches) has a body of constitutional and ecclesiastical law of its own, to be found in their written organic laws, their books of discipline, in their collections of precedents, in their usage and customs, which as to each constitute a system of ecclesiastical law and religious faith that tasks the ablest minds to become familiar with. It is not to be supposed that the judges of the civil courts can be as competent in the ecclesiastical law and religious faith of all these bodies as the ablest men in each are in reference to their own. It would therefore be an appeal from the more learned tribunal in the law which should decide the case, to one which is less so.

We have said that these views are supported by the preponderant weight of authority in this country, and for the reasons which we have given, we do not think the doctrines of the English Chancery Court on this subject should have with us the influence which we would cheerfully accord to it on others. . .

One of the most careful and well considered judgments on the subject is that of the Court of Appeals of South Carolina, delivered by Chancellor Johnson in the case of Harmon v. Dreher. The case turned upon certain rights in the use of the church property claimed by the minister notwithstanding his expulsion from the synod as one of its members. "He stands," says the Chancellor, "convicted of the offenses alleged against him, by the sentence of the spiritual body of which he was a voluntary member, and whose proceedings he had bound himself to abide. It belongs not to the civil power to enter into or review the proceedings of a spiritual court. The structure of our government has, for the preservation of civil liberty, rescued the temporal institutions from religious interference. On the other hand, it has secured religious liberty from the invasion of the civil authority. The judgments, therefore, of religious associations, bearing on their own members, are not examinable here, and I am not to inquire whether the doctrines attributed to Mr. Dreher were held by him, or whether if held were anti-Lutheran; or whether his conduct was or was not in accordance with the duty he owed to the synod or to his denomination. . . . When a civil right depends upon an ecclesiastical matter, it is the civil court and not the ecclesiastical which is to decide. But the civil tribunal tries the civil right, and no more, taking the ecclesiastical decisions out of which the civil right arises, as it finds them." The principle is re-affirmed by the same court in the John's Island Church case. . .

The Supreme Court of Illinois, in the case of Ferraria v. Vasconcelles, refers to the case of Shannon v. Frost, with approval, and adopts the language of the court that "the judicial eye cannot penetrate the veil of the church for the forbidden purpose of vindicating the alleged wrongs of excised members; when they became members they did so upon the condition of continuing or not as they and their churches might determine, and they thereby submit to the ecclesiastical power and cannot now invoke the supervisory power of the civil tribunals."

In the very important case of Chase v. Cheny, recently decided in the same court, Judge Lawrence, who dissented, says: "We understand the opinion as implying that in the administration of ecclesiastical discipline, and where no other right of property is involved than loss of the clerical office or salary incident to such discipline, a spiritual court is the exclusive judge of its own jurisdiction, and that its decision of that question is binding on the secular courts." And he dissents with Judge Shelden from the opinion because it so holds.

In the case of Watson v. Farris, which was a case growing out of the schism in the Presbyterian Church in Missouri in regard to this same declaration and testimony and the action of the General Assembly, that court held that whether a case was regularly or irregularly before the Assembly was a question which the Assembly had the right to determine for itself, and no civil court could reverse, modify, or impair its action in a matter of merely ecclesiastical concern.

We cannot better close this review of the authorities than in the language of the Supreme Court of Pennsylvania, in the case of The German Ref. Ch. v. Seibert: "The decisions of ecclesiastical courts, like every other judicial tribunal, are final, as they are the best judges of what constitutes an offense against the word of God and the discipline of the Church. Any other than those courts must be incompetent judges of matters of faith, discipline and doctrine; and civil courts, if they should be so unwise as to attempt to supervise their judgments on matters which come within their jurisdiction, would only involve themselves in a sea of uncertainty and doubt which would do anything but improve either religion or good morals". . .

The Court of Appeals of Kentucky, in the case of Watson v. Avery, before referred to, while admitting the general principle here laid down, maintains that when a decision of an ecclesiastical tribunal is set up in the civil courts, it is always open to inquiry whether the tribunal acted within its jurisdiction, and if it did not, its decision could not be conclusive.

There is, perhaps, no word in legal terminology so frequently used as the word "jurisdiction," so capable of use in a general and vague sense, and which is used so often by men learned in the law without a due regard to precision in its application. As regards its use in the matters we have been discussing, it may very well be conceded that if the General Assembly of the Presbyterian Church should undertake to try one of its members for murder, and punish him with death or imprisonment, its sentence would be of no validity in a civil court or anywhere else. Or if it should at the instance of one of its members entertain jurisdiction as between him and another member as to their individual right to property, real or personal, the right in no sense depending on ecclesiastical questions, its decision would be utterly disregarded by any civil court where it might be set up. And it might be said in a certain general sense very justly, that it was because the General Assembly had no jurisdiction of the case. Illustrations of this character could be multiplied in which the proposition of the Kentucky court would be strictly applicable.

But it is a very different thing where a subject matter of dispute, strictly and purely ecclesiastical in its character—a matter over which the civil courts exercise no jurisdiction—a matter which concerns theological controversy, church discipline, ecclesiastical government, or the conformity of the members of the church to the standard of morals required of them—becomes the subject of its action. It may be said here, also, that no jurisdiction has been conferred on the tribunal to try the particular case before it, or that, in its judgment, it exceeds the powers conferred upon it, or that the laws of the church do not authorize the particular form of proceeding adopted; and, in a sense often used in the courts, all of those may be said to be questions of jurisdiction. But it is easy to see that if the civil courts are to inquire into all these matters, the whole subject of the doctrinal theology, the usages and customs, the written laws, and fundamental organization of every religious denomination may, and must, be examined into with minuteness and care, for they would become, in almost every case, the criteria by which the validity of the ecclesiastical decree would be determined in the civil court. This principle would deprive these bodies of the right of construing their own church laws, would open the way to all the evils which we have depicted as attendant upon the doctrine of Lord Eldon, and would in effect transfer to the civil courts where property rights were concerned the decision of all ecclesiastical questions.

And this is precisely what the Court of Appeals of Kentucky did in the case of Watson v. Avery. Under cover of inquiries into the jurisdiction of the synod and presbytery over the congregation, and of the General Assembly over all, it went into an elaborate examination of the principles of Presbyterian Church government, and ended by overruling the decision of the highest judicatory of that church in the United States, both on the jurisdiction and the merits; and, substituting its own judgment for that of the ecclesiastical court, decides that ruling elders, declared to be such by that tribunal, are not such, and must not be recognized by the congregation, though four fifths of its members believe in the judgment of the Assembly and desired to conform to its decree.

But we need pursue this subject no further. Whatever may have been the case before the Kentucky court, the appellants in the case presented to us have separated themselves wholly from the church organization to which they belonged when this controversy commenced. They now deny its authority, denounce its action and refuse to abide by its judgments. They have first erected themselves into a new organization, and have since joined themselves to another totally different, if not hostile, to the one to which they belonged when the difficulty first began. Under any of the decisions which we have examined, the appellants, in their present position, have no right to the property, or to the use of it, which is the subject of this suit.

The novelty of the questions presented to this court for the first time, their intrinsic importance and far reaching influence, and the knowledge that the schism in which the case originated has divided the Presbyterian churches throughout Kentucky and Missouri, have seemed to us to justify the careful and laborious examination and discussion which we have made of the principles which should govern the case. For the same reasons we have held it under advisement for a year; not uninfluenced by the hope that since the civil commotion, which evidently lay at the foundation of the trouble, has passed away, that charity, which is so large an element in the faith of both parties, and which, by one of the apostles of that religion is said to be the greatest of all the Christian virtues, would have brought about a reconciliation. But we have been disappointed. It is not for us to determine or apportion the moral responsibility which attaches to the parties for this result. We can only pronounce the judgment of the law as applicable to the case presented to us, and that requires us to affirm the decree of the Circuit Court as it stands.

The Chief Justice did not sit on the argument of this case, and took no part in its decision.

REYNOLDS v. UNITED STATES   98 US 145 (1879)

> "So here, as a law of the organization of society under the exclusive dominion of the United States, it is provided that plural marriages shall not be allowed. Can a man be excused his practices to the contrary because of his religious belief? To permit this would be to make the professed doctrines of religious belief superior to the law of the land, and in effect to permit every citizen to become a law unto himself. Government could exist only in name under such circumstances."
>
> Mr. Chief Justice Waite

This is the first of the Mormon cases. It is the Court's first discussion of the "free exercise" clause of the First Amendment and it is here that Jefferson's phrase, "a wall of separation between Church and State" makes its initial appearance in judicial literature. Congress, said the Court, was deprived of all legislative power over "mere opinion," but it was left free to deal with "actions" in violation of social duties or subversive of good order. The "wall" thus seems to separate the realms of belief and action. (Part of the opinion is omitted.)

MR. CHIEF JUSTICE WAITE DELIVERED THE OPINION OF THE COURT.

This is an indictment for bigamy under Section 5352, Revised Statutes, which, omitting its exceptions, is as follows:

"Every person having a husband or wife living, who marries another, whether married or single, in a Territory, or other place over which the United States have exclusive jurisdiction, is guilty of bigamy, and shall be punished by a fine of not more than $500, and by imprisonment for a term of not more than five years."

The assignments of error, when grouped, present the following questions:

1. Was the indictment bad because found by a grand jury of less than sixteen persons?

2. Were the challenges of certain petit jurors by the accused improperly overruled?

3. Were the challenges of certain other jurors by the Government improperly sustained?

4. Was the testimony of Amelia Jane Schofield, given at a former trial for the same offense, but under another indictment, improperly admitted in evidence?

5. Should the accused have been acquitted if he married the second time, because he believed it to be his religious duty?

6. Did the court err in that part of the charge which directed the attention of the jury to the consequences of polygamy?

These questions will be considered in their order. . . [We omit discussion of first four points.]

5. As to the defense of religious belief or duty.

On the trial, the plaintiff in error, the accused, proved that at the time of his alleged second marriage he was, and for many years before had been, a member of the Church of Jesus Christ of Latter-Day Saints, commonly called the Mormon Church, and a believer in its doctrines: that it was an accepted doctrine of that Church "That it was the duty of male members of said Church, circumstances permitting, to practice polygamy: . . . that this duty was enjoined by different books which the members of said Church believed to be of divine origin, and among others the Holy Bible, and also that the members of the Church believed that the practice of polygamy was directly enjoined upon the male members thereof by the Almighty God, in a revelation to Joseph Smith, the founder and prophet of said Church; that the failing or refusing to practice polygamy by such male members of said Church, when circumstances would admit, would be punished, and that the penalty for such failure and refusal would be damnation in the life to come." He also proved "That he had received permission from the recognized authorities in said Church to enter into polygamous marriage; . . . that Daniel H. Wells, one having authority in said Church to perform the marriage ceremony, married the said defendant on or about the time the crime is alleged to have been committed, to some woman by the name of Schofield, and that such marriage ceremony was performed under and pursuant to the doctrines of said Church."

Upon this proof he asked the court to instruct the jury that if they found from the evidence that he "was married as charged (if he was married) in pursuance of and in conformity with what he believed at the time to be a religious duty, that the verdict must be 'not guilty.'" This request was refused, and the court did charge "That there must have been a criminal intent, but that if the defendant, under the influence of a religious belief that it was right—under an inspiration, if you please, that it was right—deliberately married a second time, having a first wife living, the want of consciousness of evil intent, the want of understanding on his part that he was committing a crime, did not excuse him; but the law inexorably in such case implies the criminal intent."

Upon this charge and refusal to charge the question is raised, whether religious belief can be accepted as a justification of an overt act made criminal by the law of the land. The inquiry is not as to the power of Congress to prescribe criminal laws for the Territories, but as to the guilt of one who knowingly violates a law which has been properly enacted, if he entertains a belief that the law is wrong.

Congress cannot pass a law for the government of the Territories which shall prohibt the free exercise of religion. The first amendment to the Constitution expressly forbids such legislation. Religious freedom is guarantied everywhere throughout the United States. so far as congressional interference is concerned. The question to be determined is, whether the law now under consideration comes within the prohibition.

The word "religion" is not defined in the Constitution. We must go elsewhere, therefore, to ascertain its meaning, and nowhere more appropriately, we think, than to the history of the times in the midst of which the provision was adopted. The precise point of the inquiry is, what is the religious freedom which has been guarantied?

Before the adoption of the Constitution, attempts were made in some of the Colonies and States to legislate not only in respect to the establishment of religion, but in respect to its doctrines and precepts as well. The people were taxed, against their will, for the support of religion, and sometimes for the support of particular sects to whose tenets they could not and did not subscribe. Punishments were prescribed for a failure to attend upon public worship, and sometimes for entertaining heretical opinions. The controversy upon this general subject was animated in many of the States, but seemed at last to culminate in Virginia. In 1784, the House of Delegates of that State having under consideration "A bill establishing provision for teachers of the Christian religion," postponed it until the next session, and directed that the bill should be published and distributed, and that the People be requested "to signify their opinion respecting the adoption of such a bill at the next session of Assembly."

This brought out a determined opposition. Amongst others, Mr. Madison prepared a "Memorial and Remonstrance," which was widely circulated and signed, and in which he demonstrated "that religion, or the duty we owe the Creator," was not within the cognizance of civil government. At the next session the proposed bill was not only defeated, but another, "for establishing religious freedom," drafted by Mr. Jefferson was passed. In the preamble of this Act, religious freedom is defined; and after a recital "That to suffer the civil magis-

22

trate to intrude his powers into the field of opinion, and to restrain the profession or propagation of principles on supposition of their ill tendency, is a dangerous fallacy which at once destroys all religious liberty," it is declared "that it is time enough for the rightful purposes of civil government for its officers to interfere when principles break out into overt acts against peace and good order." In these two sentences is found the true distinction between what properly belongs to the Church and what to the State.

In a little more than a year after the passage of this statute the convention met which prepared the Constitution of the United States. Of this convention Mr. Jefferson was not a member, he being then absent as minister to France. As soon as he saw the draft of the Constitution proposed for adoption, he, in a letter to a friend, expressed his disappointment at the absence of an express declaration insuring the freedom of religion, but was willing to accept it as it was, trusting that the good sense and honest intentions of the people would bring about the necessary alterations. Five of the States, while adopting the Constitution, proposed amendments. Three, New Hampshire, New York and Virginia, included in one form or another a declaration of religious freedom in the changes they desired to have made, as did also North Carolina, where the convention at first declined to ratify the Constitution until the proposed amendments were acted upon. Accordingly, at the first session of the first Congress the amendment now under consideration was proposed with others by Mr. Madison. It met the views of the advocates of religious freedom, and was adopted. Mr. Jefferson afterwards, in reply to an address to him by a committee of the Danbury Baptist Association, took occasion to say: "Believing with you that religion is a matter which lies solely between man and his God; that he owes account to none other for his faith or his worship; that the legislative powers of the Government reach actions only, and not opinions, I contemplate with sovereign reverence that act of the whole American people which declared that their Legislature should 'make no law respecting an establishment of religion or prohibiting the free exercise thereof,' thus building a wall of separation between Church and State. Adhering to this expression of the Supreme will of the Nation in behalf of the rights of conscience, I shall see, with sincere satisfaction, the progress of those sentiments which tend to restore man to all his natural rights, convinced he has no natural right in opposition to his social duties." Coming as this does from an acknowledged leader of the advocates of the measure, it may be accepted almost as an authoritative declaration of the scope and effect of the amendment thus secured. Congress was deprived of all legislative power over mere opinion, but was left free to reach actions which were in violation of social duties or subversive of good order.

Polygamy has always been odious among the Northern and Western Nations of Europe and, until the establishment of the Mormon Church, was almost exclusively a feature of the life of Asiatic and African people. At common law, the second marriage was always void, and from the earliest history of England polygamy has been treated as an offense against society. After the establishment of the ecclesiastical courts, and until the time of James I., it was punished through the instrumentality of those tribunals, not merely because ecclesiastical rights had been violated, but because upon the separation of the ecclesiastical courts from the civil, the ecclesiastical were supposed to be the most appropriate for the trial of matrimonial causes and offenses against the rights of marriage; just as they were for testamentary causes and the settlement of the estates of deceased persons.

By the Statute of 1 James I., ch. 11, the offense, if committed in England or Wales, was made punishable in the civil courts, and the penalty was death. As this statute was limited in its operation to England and Wales, it was at a very early period re-enacted, generally with some modifications, in all the Colonies. In connection with the case we are now considering, it is a significant fact that on the 8th of December, 1788, after the passage of the Act establishing religious freedom, and after the convention of Virginia had recommended as an amendment to the Constitution of the United States the declaration in a Bill of Rights that "All men have an equal, natural and unalienable right to the free exercise of religion, according to the dictates of conscience," the Legislature of that State substantially enacted the Statute of James I., death penalty included, because as recited in the preamble, "It hath been doubted whether bigamy or polygamy be punishable by the laws of this Commonwealth." From that day to this we think it may safely be said there never has been a time in any State of the Union when polygamy has not been an offense against society, cognizable by the civil courts and punishable with more or less severity. In the face of all this evidence, it is impossible to believe that the constitutional guaranty of religious freedom was intended to prohibit legislation in respect to this most important feature of social life. Marriage, while from its very nature a sacred obligation, is, nevertheless, in most civilized nations, a civil contract, and usually regulated by law. Upon it society may be said to be built, and out of its fruits spring social relations and social obligations and duties, with which government is necessarily required to deal. In fact, according as monogamous or polygamous marriages are allowed, do we find the principles on which the Government of the People, to a

24

greater or less extent, rests. Professor Lieber says: polygamy leads to the patriarchal principle, and which, when applied to large communities, fetters the people in stationary despotism, while that principle cannot long exist in connection with monogamy. Chancellor Kent observes that this remark is equally striking and profound. An exceptional colony of polygamists under an exceptional leadership may sometimes exist for a time without appearing to disturb the social condition of the people who surround it; but there cannot be a doubt that, unless restricted by some form of constitution, it is within the legitimate scope of the power of every civil government to determine whether polygamy or monogamy shall be the law of social life under its dominion.

In our opinion the statute immediately under consideration is within the legislative power of Congress. It is constitutional and valid as prescribing a rule of action for all those residing in the Territories, and in places over which the United States have exclusively control. This being so, the only question which remains is, whether those who make polygamy a part of their religion are excepted from the operation of the statute. If they are, then those who do not make polygamy a part of their religious belief may be found guilty and punished, while those who do must be acquitted and go free. This would be introducing a new element into criminal law. Laws are made for the government of actions, and while they cannot interfere with mere religious belief and opinions, they may with practices. Suppose one believed that human sacrifices were a necessary part of religious worship, would it be seriously contended that the civil government under which he lived could not interfere to prevent a sacrifice? Or if a wife religiously believed it was her duty to burn herself upon the funeral pile of her dead husband, would it be beyond the power of the civil government to prevent her carrying her belief into practice?

So here, as a law of the organization of society under the exclusive dominion of the United States, it is provided that plural marriages shall not be allowed. Can a man excuse his practices to the contrary because of his religious belief? To permit this would be to make the professed doctrines of religious belief superior to the law of the land, and in effect to permit every citizen to become a law unto himself. Government could exist only in name under such circumstances.

A criminal intent is generally an element of crime, but every man is presumed to intend the necessary and legitimate consequences of what he knowingly does. Here the accused knew he had been once married, and that his first wife was living. He also knew that his second marriage was forbidden by law. When, therefore, he married the second time, he is presumed to have intended to break the law. And the breaking of the law is the crime. Every act necessary to constitute the crime was knowingly done, and the crime was, therefore, knowingly committed. Ignorance of a fact may sometimes be taken as evidence of a want of criminal intent, but not ignorance of the law. The only defense of the accused in this case is his belief that the law ought not to have been enacted. It matters not that his belief was a part of his professed religion; it was still belief, and belief only.

In Regina v. Wagstaffe, the parents of a sick child, who omitted to call in medical attendance because of their religious belief that what they did for its cure would be effective, were held not to be guilty of manslaughter, while it was said the contrary would have been the result if the child had actually been starved to death by the parents, under the notion that it was their religious duty to abstain from giving it food. But when the offense consists of a positive act which is knowingly done, it would be dangerous to hold that the offender might escape punishment because he religiously believed the law which he had broken ought never to have been made. No case, we believe, can be found that has gone so far.

6. As to that part of the charge which directed the attention of the jury to the consequences of polygamy.

The passage complained of is as follows: "I think it not improper, in the discharge of your duties in this case, that you should consider what are to be the consequences to the innocent victims of this delusion. As this contest goes on, they multiply, and there are pure-minded women and there are innocent children; innocent in a sense even beyond the degree of the innocence of childhood itself. These are to be the sufferers; and as jurors fail to do their duty, and as these cases come up in the Territory of Utah, just so do these victims multiply and spread themselves over the land."

While every appeal by the court to the passions or the prejudices of a jury should be promptly rebuked, and while it is the imperative duty of a reviewing court to take care that wrong is not done in this way, we see no just cause for complaint in this case. Congress, in 1862, saw fit to make bigamy a crime in the Territories. This was done because of the evil consequences that were supposed to flow from plural marriages. All the court did was to call the attention of the jury to the peculiar character of the crime for which the accused was on trial, and to remind them of the duty they had to perform. There was no appeal to the passions, no instigation of prejudice. Upon the showing made by the accused himself, he was guilty of a violation of the law under which he had been indicted: and the effort of the court seems to have been not to withdraw the minds of the jury from the issue to be tried, but to bring them to it; not to make them partial, but to keep them impartial.

Upon a careful consideration of the whole case, we are satisfied that no error was committed by the court below, and the judgment is consequently affirmed.

DAVIS v. BEASON   133 US 333 (1890)

"Bigamy and polygamy are crimes by the laws of all civilized and Christian countries . . . To call their advocacy a tenet of religion is to offend the common sense of mankind. If they are crimes, then to teach, advise and counsel their practice is to aid in their commission, and such teaching and counseling are themselves criminal and proper subjects of punishment, as aiding and abetting crime are in all other cases."

Mr. Justice Field

Mr. Samuel Davis wanted to vote. He appeared before the appropriate registrar in the Territory of Idaho and took the following prescribed oath:

"I do swear (or affirm) that I am a male citizen of the United States of the age of twenty-one years (or will be on the 6th day of November, 1888): and that I have (or will have) actually resided in this Territory four months and in this county for thirty days next preceding the day of the next ensuing election; that I have never been convicted of treason, felony or bribery; and that I am not registered or entitled to vote at any other place in this Territory; and I do further swear that I am not a bigamist or polygamist; that I am not a member of any order, organization or association which teaches, advises, counsels or encourages its members, devotees or any other person to commit the crime of bigamy or polygamy or any other crime defined by law, as a duty arising or resulting from membership in such order, organization or association, or which practices bigamy, polygamy or plural or celestial marriage as a doctrinal right of such organization; that I do not and will not, publicly or privately, or in any manner whatever, teach, advise, counsel or encourage any person to commit the crime of bigamy or polygamy, or any other crime defined by law, either as a religious duty or otherwise; that I do regard the Constitution of the United States and the laws thereof and the laws of this Territory, as interpreted by the courts, as the supreme laws of the land, the teachings of any order, organization or association to the contrary notwithstanding, so help me God."

But Mr. Davis was a Mormon and was indicted for conspiring to obstruct the due administration of the laws of the Territory by seeking to register as a voter in spite of the fact that he knew he belonged to such an organization as was described in the oath.

He argued, among other things, "that so much of the Statute of the Territory which provides that no person is entitled to register or vote at any election who is 'a member of any order, organization or association which teaches, advises, counsels or encourages its members, devotees or any other person to commit the crime of bigamy or polygamy, or any other crime defined by law, as a duty arising or resulting from membership in such order, organization or association, or which practices bigamy or polygamy or plural or celestial marriage as a doctrinal rite of such organization,' is a 'law respecting an establishment of religion,' in violation of the First Amendment of the Constitution, and void."

An earlier case, Murphy v. Ramsey (114 US 15, 1885) also upheld the denial of the right of Mormons to vote and is quoted in this opinion. (Part of the opinion is omitted.)

MR. JUSTICE FIELD DELIVERED THE OPINION OF THE COURT.

On this appeal our only inquiry is whether the District Court of the Territory had jurisdiction of the offense charged in the indictment of which the defendant was found guilty. If it had jurisdiction, we can go no farther. We cannot look into any alleged errors in its rulings on the trial of the defendant. The writ of habeas corpus cannot be turned into a writ of error to review the action of that court. Nor can we inquire whether the evidence established the fact alleged, that the defendant was a member of an order or organization known as the Mormon Church, called the Church of Jesus Christ of Latter Day Saints, or the fact that the order or organization taught and counseled its members and devotees to commit the crimes of bigamy and polygamy as duties arising from membership therein. On this hearing we can only consider whether, these allegations being taken as true, an offense was committed of which the territorial court had jurisdiction to try the defendant. And on this point there can be no serious discussion or difference of opinion. Bigamy and polygamy are crimes by the laws of all civilized and Christian countries. They are crimes by the laws of the United States, and they are crimes by the laws of Idaho. They tend to destroy the purity of the marriage relation, to disturb the peace of families, to degrade woman and to debase man. Few crimes are more pernicious to the best interests of society and receive more general or more deserved punishment. To extend exemption from punishment for such crimes would be to shock the moral judgment of the community. To call their advocacy a tenet of religion is to offend the common sense of mankind. If they are crimes, then to teach, advise and counsel their practice is to aid in their commission, and such teaching and counseling are themselves criminal and proper subjects of punishment, as aiding and abetting crime are in all other cases.

The term "religion" has reference to one's views of his relations to his Creator, and to the obligations they impose of reverence for his being and character, and of obedience to his will. It is often confounded with the cultus or form of worship of a particular sect, but is distinguishable from the latter. The First Amendment to the Constitution, in declaring that Congress shall make no law respecting the establishment of religion, or forbidding the free exercise thereof, was intended to allow everyone under the jurisdiction of the United States to entertain such notions respecting his relations to his Maker and the duties they impose as may be approved by his judgment and conscience, and to exhibit his sentiments in such form of worship as he may think proper, not injurious to the equal rights of others, and to prohibit legislation for the support of any religious tenets, or the modes or worship of any sect. The oppressive measures adopted, and the cruelties and punishments inflicted by the governments of Europe for many ages, to compel parties to conform in their religious beliefs and modes of worship to the views of the most numerous sect, and the folly of attempting in that way to control the mental operations of persons and enforce an outward conformity to a prescribed standard, led to the adoption of the Amendment in question. It was never intended or supposed that the Amendment could be invoked as a protection against legislation for the punishment of acts inimical to the peace, good order and morals of society. With man's relations to his Maker and the obligations he may think they impose, and the manner in which an expression shall be made by him of his belief on those subjects, no interference can be permitted, provided always the laws of society, designed to secure its peace and prosperity, and the morals of its people, are not interfered with. However free the exercise of religion may be, it must be subordinate to the criminal laws of the country, passed with reference to actions regarded by general consent as properly the subjects of punitive legislation. There have been sects which denied as part of their religious tenets that there should be any marriage tie, and advocated promiscuous intercourse of the sexes as prompted by the passions of their members. And history discloses the fact that the necessity of human sacrifices, on special occasions, has been a tenet of many sects. Should a sect of either of these kinds ever find its way into this country, swift punishment would follow the carrying into effect of its doctrines, and no heed would be given to the pretense that, as religious beliefs, their supporters could be protected in their

29

exercise by the Constitution of the United States. Probably never before in the history of this country has it been seriously contended that the whole punitive power of the government, for acts recognized by the general consent of the Christian world in modern times as proper matters for prohibitory legislation, must be suspended in order that the tenets of a religious sect encouraging crime may be carried out without hindrance.

On this subject the observations of this court through the late Chief Justice Waite, in Reynolds v. United States, are pertinent. . . . And in Murphy v. Ramsey, referring to the Act of Congress excluding polygamists and bigamists from voting or holding office, the court, speaking by Mr. Justice Matthews, said: "Certainly no legislation can be supposed more wholesome and necessary in the founding of a free, self-governing commonwealth, fit to take rank as one of the co-ordinate States of the Union, than that which seeks to establish it on the basis of the idea of the family, as consisting in and springing from the union for life of one man and one woman in the holy estate of matrimony—the sure foundation of all that is stable and noble in our civilization; the best guaranty of that reverent morality which is the source of all beneficent progress in social and political improvement. And to this end no means are more directly and immediately suitable than those provided by this Act, which endeavors to withdraw all political influence from those who are practically hostile to its attainment."

It is assumed by counsel of the petitioner that, because no mode of worship can be established or religious tenets enforced in this country, therefore any form of worship may be followed and any tenets, however destructive of society, may be held and advocated, if asserted to be a part of the religious doctrines of those advocating and practicing them. But nothing is further from the truth. Whilst legislation for the establishment of a religion is forbidden, and its free exercise permitted, it does not follow that everything which may be so called can be tolerated. Crime is not the less odious because sanctioned by what any particular sect may designate as religion.

It only remains to refer to the laws which authorized the Legislature of the Territory of Idaho to prescribe the qualifications of voters and the oath they were required to take. The Revised Statutes provide that "the legislative power of every Territory shall extend to all rightful subjects of legislation not inconsistent with the Constitution and laws of the United States. But no law shall be passed interfering with the primary disposal of the soil; no tax shall be imposed upon the property of the United States; nor shall the lands or other property

30

of nonresidents be taxed higher than the lands or other property of residents."

Under this general authority it would seem that the Territorial Legislature was authorized to prescribe any qualifications for voters calculated to secure obedience to its laws. But, in addition to the above law, section 1859 of the Revised Statutes provides that "every male citizen above the age of twenty-one, including persons who have legally declared their intention to become citizens in any Territory hereafter organized, and who are actual residents of such Territory at the time of the organization thereof, shall be entitled to vote at the first election in such Territory, and to hold any office therein; subject, nevertheless, to the limitations specified in the next section," namely, that at all elections in any Territory subsequently organized by Congress, as well as at all elections in Territories already organized, the qualifications of voters and for holding office shall be such as may be prescribed by the Legislative Assembly of each Territory, subject, nevertheless, to the following restrictions:

First. That the right of suffrage and of holding office shall be exercised only by citizens of the United States above the age of twenty-one or persons above that age who have declared their intention to become such citizens;

Second. That the elective franchise or the right of holding office shall not be denied to any citizen on account of race, color or previous condition of servitude;

Third. That no soldier or sailor or other person in the army or navy, or attached to troops in the service of the United States, shall be allowed to vote unless he has made his permanent domicile in the Territory for six months; and

Fourth. That no person belonging to the army or navy shall be elected to or hold a civil office or appointment in the Territory.

These limitations are the only ones placed upon the authority of Territorial Legislatures against granting the right of suffrage or of holding office. They have the power, therefore, to prescribe any reasonable qualifications of voters and for holding office not inconsistent with the above limitations. In our judgment, section 501 of the Revised Statutes of Idaho Territory, which provides that "no person under guardianship, non compos mentis or insane, nor any person convicted of treason, felony or bribery in this Territory, or in any other State or Territory in the Union, unless restored to civil rights; nor any person who is a bigamist or polygamist, or who teaches, advises, counsels or encourages any person or persons to become bigamists or polygamists, or to commit any other crime defined by law, or to enter into what is known as plural or celestial marriage, or who is a member of any order, organization or association which teaches, advises, counsels or encourages its members or devotees or any other persons to commit the crime of bigamy or polygamy, or any other crime defined by law, either as a rite or ceremony of such order, organization or association, or otherwise, is permitted to vote at any election, or to hold any position or office of honor, trust or profit within this Territory," is not open to any constitutional or legal objection. With the exception of persons under guardianship or of unsound mind, it simply excludes from the privilege of voting, or of holding any office of honor, trust or profit, those who have been convicted of certain offenses, and those who advocate a practical resistance to the laws of the Territory and justify and approve the commission of crimes forbidden by it. The second subdivision of section 504 of the Revised Statutes of Idaho, requiring every person desiring to have his name registered as a voter to take an oath that he does not belong to an order that advises a disregard of the criminal law of the Territory, is not open to any valid legal objection to which our attention has been called.

The position that Congress has, by its Statute, covered the whole subject of punitive legislation against bigamy and polygamy, leaving nothing for territorial action on the subject, does not impress us as entitled to much weight. The Statute of Congress of March 22, 1882, amending a previous section of the Revised Statutes in reference to bigamy, declares "that no polygamist, bigamist or any person cohabiting with more than one woman, and no woman cohabiting with any of the persons described as aforesaid in this section, in any Territory or other place over which the United States have exclusive jurisdiction, shall be entitled to vote at any election held in any such Territory or other place, or be eligible for election or appointment to or be entitled to hold any office or place of public trust, honor or emolument in, under or for any such Territory or place, or under the United States.

This is a general law applicable to all Territories and other places under the exclusive jurisdiction of the United States. It does not purport to restrict the legislation of the Territories over kindred offenses or over the means for their ascertainment and prevention. The cases in which the legislation of Congress will supersede the legislation of a State or Territory, without specific provisions to that effect, are those in which the same matter is the subject of legislation by both. There the action of Congress may well be considered as covering the entire ground. But here there is nothing of this kind. The Act of Congress does not touch upon teaching, advising and counseling the practice of bigamy and polygamy, that is, upon aiding and abetting in the commission of those crimes, nor upon the mode adopted, by means of the oath required for registration, to prevent persons from being enabled by their votes to defeat the criminal laws of the country.

The judgment of the court below is therefore affirmed.

THE LATE CORPORATION OF THE CHURCH OF JESUS CHRIST OF LATTER-DAY SAINTS v. UNITED STATES   136 US 1 (1890)

"... we have before us—Congress had before it—a contumacious organization, wielding by its resources an immense power in the Territory of Utah, and employing those resources and that power in constantly attempting to oppose, thwart and subvert the legislation of Congress and the will of the government of the United States. Under these circumstances we have no doubt of the power of Congress to do as it did."

Mr. Justice Bradley

Congress, in 1887, acted to annul the charter of the Corporation of the Church of Jesus Christ of Latter-Day Saints and to declare forfeited to the government all its real estate except a small portion used exclusively for public worship. (We reproduce here only a small part of a long opinion.)

MR. JUSTICE BRADLEY DELIVERED THE OPINION OF THE COURT.

Where a charitable corporation is dissolved, and no private donor or founder appears to be entitled to its real estate (its personal property not being subject to such reclamation), the government, or sovereign authority, as the chief and common guardian of the state, either through its judicial tribunals or otherwise, necessarily has the disposition of the funds of such corporation, to be exercised, however, with due regard to the objects and purposes of the charitable uses to which the property was originally devoted, so far as they are lawful and not repugnant to public policy. This is the general principle, which will be more fully discussed further on. In this direction, it will be pertinent, in the mean time, to examine into the character of the Corporation of the Church of Jesus Christ of Latter-Day Saints, and the objects which, by its constitution and principles, it promoted and had in view.

It is distinctly stated in the pleadings and findings of fact that the property of the said Corporation was held for the purpose of religious and charitable uses. But it is also stated in the findings of fact, and is a matter of public notoriety, that the religious and charitable uses intended to be subserved and promoted are the inculcation and spread of the doctrines and usages of the Mormon Church, or Church of Latter-Day Saints, one of the distinguishing features of which is the practice of polygamy—a crime against the laws, and abhorrent to the sentiments and feelings of the civilized world. Notwithstanding the stringent laws which have been passed by Congress—notwithstanding all the efforts made to suppress this barbarous practice—the sect or community composing the Church of Jesus Christ of Latter-Day Saints perseveres, in defiance of law, in preaching, upholding, promoting and defending it. It is a matter of public notoriety that its emissaries are engaged in many countries in propagating this nefarious doctrine, and urging its converts to join the community in Utah. The existence of such a propaganda is a blot on our civilization. The organization of a community for the spread and practice of polygamy is, in a measure, a return to barbarism. It is contrary to the spirit of Christianity and of the civilization which Christianity has produced in the Western World. The question therefore is whether the promotion of such a nefarious system and practice, so repugnant to our laws and to the principles of our civilization, is to be allowed to continue by the sanction of the government itself; and whether the funds accumulated for that purpose shall be restored to the same unlawful uses as heretofore to the detriment of the true interests of civil society.

It is unnecessary here to refer to the past history of the sect, to their defiance of the government authorities, to their attempt to establish an independent community, to their efforts to drive from the Territory all who were not connected with them in communion and sympathy. The tale is one of patience on the part of the American government and people, and of contempt of authority and resistance to law on the part of the Mormons. Whatever persecutions they may have suffered in the early part of their history, in Missouri and Illinois, they have no excuse for their persistent defiance of law under the government of the United States.

One pretense for this obstinate course is, that their belief in the practice of polygamy, or in the right to indulge in it, is a religious belief, and therefore under the protection of the constitutional guaranty of religious freedom. This is altogether a sophistical plea. No doubt the Thugs of India imagined that their belief in the right of assassination was a religious belief; but their thinking so did not make it so. The practice of suttee by the Hindu widows may have sprung from a supposed religious conviction. The offering of human sacrifices by our own ancestors in Britain was no doubt sanctioned by an equally conscientious impulse. But no one, on that account, would hesitate to brand these practices, now, as crimes against society, and obnoxious to condemnation and punishment by the civil authority.

The state has a perfect right to prohibit polygamy, and all other open offenses against the enlightened sentiment of mankind, notwithstanding the pretense of religious conviction by which they may be advocated and practised. And since polygamy has been forbidden by the laws of the United States, under severe penalties, and since the Church of Jesus Christ of Latter-Day Saints has persistently used, and claimed the right to use, and the unincorporated community still claims the same right to use, the funds with which the Late Corporation was endowed for the purpose of promoting and propagating the unlawful practice as an integral part of their religious usages, the question arises, whether the government, finding these funds without legal ownership, has or has not the right, through its courts, and in due course of administration, to cause them to be seized and devoted to objects of undoubted charity and usefulness—such for example as the maintenance of schools—for the benefit of the community whose leaders are now misusing them in the unlawful manner above described; setting apart, however, for the exclusive possession and use of the Church, sufficient and suitable portions of the property for the purposes of public worship, parsonage buildings and burying grounds, as provided in the Law.

CHURCH OF THE HOLY TRINITY v. UNITED STATES   143 US 226 (1892)

"There is no dissonance in these declarations. There is a universal language pervading them all, having one meaning; they affirm and reaffirm that this is a religious nation."

Mr. Justice Brewer

The Court holds that it could not have been the intention of Congress, in making it illegal to bring aliens into the country to work, to "make it a misdemeanor for a church of this country to contract for the services of a Christian minister residing in another nation." To impute such an intent to Congress would be to ignore the fact that "we are a religious people," and the Court marshals evidence of our religious character.

MR. JUSTICE BREWER DELIVERED THE OPINION OF THE COURT.

Plaintiff in error is a corporation, duly organized and incorporated as a religious society, under the laws of the State of New York. E. Walpole Warren was prior to September, 1887, an alien residing in England. In that month the plaintiff in error made a contract with him, by which he was to remove to the city of New York and enter into its service as rector and pastor; and, in pursuance of such contract,

Warren did so remove and enter upon such service. It is claimed by the United States that this contract on the part of the plaintiff in error was forbidden by chapter 164,23 Stat. at L. 332, and an action was commenced to recover the penalty prescribed by that Act. The Circuit Court held that the contract was within the prohibition of the statute, and rendered judgment accordingly; and the single question presented for our determination is whether it erred in that conclusion.

The first section describes the act forbidden, and is in these words:

"Be it enacted by the Senate and House of Representatives of the United States of America in Congress assembled, That from and after the passage of this Act it shall be unlawful for any person, company, partnership or corporation, in any manner whatsoever, to prepay the transportation, or in any way assist or encourage the importation or migration of any alien or aliens, any foreigner or foreigners, into the United States, its territories or the District of Columbia, under contract or agreement, parol or special, express or implied, made previous to the importation or migration of such alien or aliens, foreigner or foreigners, to perform labor or service of any kind in the United States, its territories or the District of Columbia."

It must be conceded that the act of the corporation is within the letter of this section, for the relation of rector to his church is one of service, and implies labor on the one side with compensation on the other. Not only are the general words "labor" and "service" both used, but also, as it were to guard against any narrow interpretation and emphasize a breadth of meaning, to them is added "of any kind"; and further, as noticed by the Circuit Judge in his opinion, the fifth section, which makes specific exceptions, among them professional actors, artists, lecturers, singers and domestic servants, strengthens the idea that every other kind of labor and service was intended to be reached by the first section. While there is great force in this reasoning, we cannot think Congress intended to denounce with penalties a transaction like that in the present case . . . [We omit some discussion of theory of judicial construction.]

We find, therefore, that the title of the Act, the evil which was intended to be remedied, the circumstances surrounding the appeal to Congress, the reports of the committee of each house, all concur in affirming that the intent of Congress was simply to stay the influx of this cheap unskilled labor.

But beyond all these matters no purpose of action against religion can be imputed to any legislation, State or Nation, because this is a religious people. This is historically true. From the discovery of this continent to the present hour there is a single voice making this affirmation. The commission to Christopher Columbus, prior to his sail westward, is from "Ferdinand and Isabella, by the grace of God, King and Queen of Castile," etc., and recites that "it is hoped that by God's assistance some of the continents and islands in the ocean will be discovered," etc. The first colonial grant, that made to Sir Walter Raleigh in 1584, was from "Elizabeth, by the grace of God, of England, France and Ireland, queene, defender of the faith," etc.; and the grant authorizing him to enact statutes for the government of the proposed colony provided that "they be not against the true Christian faith nowe professed in the Church of England." The first charter of Virginia, granted by King James I in 1606, after reciting the application of certain parties for a charter, commenced the grant in these words: "We, greatly commending, and graciously accepting of, their Desires for the Furtherance of so noble a Work, which may, by the Providence of Almighty God, hereafter tend to the Glory of his Divine Majesty, in propagating of Christian Religion to such People, as yet live in Darkness and miserable Ignorance of the true Knowledge and Worship of God, and may in time bring the Infidels and Savages, living in those parts, to human Civility, and to a settled and quiet Government; DO, by these our Letters Patents, graciously accept of, and agree to, their humble and well intended Desires."

Language of similar import may be found in the subsequent charters of that colony, from the same King, in 1609 and 1611, and the same is true of the various charters granted to the other colonies. In language more or less emphatic is the establishment of the Christian religion declared to be one of the purposes of the grant. The celebrated compact made by the Pilgrims in the Mayflower 1620, recites: "Having undertaken for the Glory of God, and Advancement of the Christian Faith, and the Honour of our King and Country, a Voyage to plant the first Colony in the northern Parts of Virginia; Do by these Present, solemnly and mutually, in the Presence of God and one another, covenant and combine ourselves together into a civil Body Politick, for our better Ordering and Preservation, and Furtherance of the Ends aforesaid."

The fundamental orders of Connecticut, under which a provisional government was instituted in 1638–1639, commence with this declaration: "Forasmuch as it hath pleased the Allmighty God by the wise desposition of his diuyne pruidence so to Order and dispose of things that we the Inhabitants and Residents of Windsor, Hartford and Wethersfield are now cohabiting and dwelling in and uppon the River of Conectecotte and the Lands there unto adioyneing; And well knowing where a people are gathered togather the word of God requires that to mayntayne the peace and union of such a people there should be an orderly and decent Gouerment established according to God, to order and dispose of the affayres of the people at all seasons as occasion shall require; doe therefore assotiate and conioyne our selues to be as one Publike State or Comonselth; and doe, for our selues and our Successors and such as shall be adioyned to vs att any tyme hereafter, enter into Combination and Confederation togather, to mayntayne and presearue the liberty and purity of the gospell of our Lord Jesus wch we now prfesse, as also the disciplyne of the Churches, wch according to the truth of the said gospell is now practised amongst vs."

In the charter of privileges granted by William Penn to the province of Pennsylvania, in 1701, it is recited: "Because no People can be truly happy, though under the greatest Enjoyment of Civil Liberties, if abridged of the Freedom of their Consciences, as to their Religious Profession and Worship; and Almighty God being the only Lord of Conscience, Father of Lights and Spirits; and the Author as well as Object of all divine Knowledge, Faith and Worship, who only doth enlighten the Minds, and persuade and convince the Understandings of People, I do hereby grant and declare," etc.

Coming nearer to the present time, the Declaration of Independence recognizes the presence of the Divine in human affairs in these words: "We hold these truths to be self-evident, that all men are created equal, that they are endowed by their Creator with certain unalienable Rights, that among these are Life, Liberty, and the pursuit of Happiness." "We, therefore, the Representatives of the United States of America, in General Congress, Assembled, appealing to the Supreme Judge of the world for the rectitude of our intentions, do, in the Name and by Authority of the good People of these Colonies, solemnly publish and declare," etc.; "And for the support of this Declaration, with a firm reliance on the Protection of Divine Providence, we mutually pledge to each other our Lives, our Fortunes, and our sacred Honor."

If we examine the constitutions of the various states we find in them a constant recognition of religious obligations. Every constitution of every one of the forty-four states contains language which either directly or by clear implication recognizes a profound reverence for religion and an assumption that its influence in all human affairs is essential to the well being of the community. This recognition may be in the preamble, such as is found in the constitution of Illinois, 1870: "We, the people of the State of Illinois, grateful to Almighty God for the civil, political, and religious liberty which He hath so long permitted us to enjoy, and looking to him for a blessing upon our endeavors to secure and transmit the same unimpaired to succeeding generations," etc.

It may be only in the familiar requisition that all officers shall take an oath closing with the declaration "so help me God." It may be in clauses like that of the Constitution of Indiana, 1816, article XI., section 4: "The manner of administering an oath or affirmation shall be such as is most consistent with the conscience of the deponent, and shall be esteemed the most solemn appeal to God." Or in provisions such as are found in Articles 36 and 37 of the Declaration of Rights of the Constitution of Maryland, 1867: "That as it is the duty of every man to worship God in such manner as he thinks most acceptable to Him, all persons are equally entitled to protection in their religious liberty; therefore, no person ought, by any law, to be molested in his person or estate on account of his religious persuasion or profession, or for his religious practice, unless, under the color of religion, he shall disturb the good order, peace, or safety of the State, or shall infringe the laws of morality, or injure others in their natural, civil or religious rights; nor ought any person to be compelled to frequent or maintain or contribute, unless on contract, to maintain any place of worship, or any ministry; nor shall any person, otherwise competent, be deemed incompetent as a witness, or juror, on account of his religious belief: Provided, He believes in the existence of God, and that, under His dispensation, such person will be held morally accountable for his acts, and be rewarded or punished therefor, either in this world or the world to come. That no religious test ought ever to be required as a qualification for any office of profit or trust in this State, other than a declaration of belief in the existence of God; nor shall the Legislature prescribe any other oath of office than the oath prescribed by this constitution." Or like that in articles 2 and 3, of Part 1st, of the Constitution of Massachusetts, 1780: "It is the right as well as the duty of all men in society publicly and at stated seasons, to worship the Supreme Being, the great Creator and Preserver of the universe: . . . As the happiness of a people and the good order and preservation of civil government essentially depend upon piety, religion, and morality, and as these cannot be generally diffused through a community but by the institution of the public worship of God and of public instructions in piety, religion and morality: Therefore, to promote their happiness and to secure the good order and preservation of their government, the people of this commonwealth have a right to invest their Legislature with power to authorize and require and the Legislature shall, from time to time, authorize and require, the several towns, parishes, precincts, and other bodies politic or religious societies to make suitable provision, at their own expense, for the institution of the public worship of God and for the support and maintenance of public Protestant teachers of piety, religion, and morality in all cases where such provision shall not be made voluntarily." Or as in sections 5 and 14 of article 7, of the Constitution of Mississippi, 1832: "No person who denied the being of a God or a future state of rewards and punishments, shall hold any office in the civil department of this State . . . . Religion, morality, and knowledge being necessary to good government, the preservation of liberty, and the happiness of mankind, schools, and the means of education, shall forever be encouraged in this State." Or by Article 22 of the Constitution of Delaware, 1776, which required all officers, besides an oath of allegiance, to make and subscribe the following declaration: "I, A. B., do profess faith in God the Father, and in Jesus Christ His only Son, and in the Holy Ghost, one God, blessed for evermore; and I do acknowledge the Holy Scriptures of the Old and New Testament to be given by divine inspiration."

Even the Constitution of the United States, which is supposed to have little touch upon the private life of the individual, contains in the 1st Amendment a declaration common to the constitutions of all the States, as follows: "Congress shall make no law respecting an establishment of religion, or prohibiting the free exercise thereof," etc. And also provides in article 1, section 7 (a provision common to many constitutions), that the Executive shall have ten days (Sundays excepted) within which to determine whether he will approve or veto a bill.

There is no dissonance in these declarations. There is a universal language pervading them all, having one meaning; they affirm and reaffirm that this is a religious nation. These are not individual sayings, declarations of private persons; they are organic utterances; they speak the voice of the entire people. While because of a general recognition of this truth the question has seldom been presented to the courts, yet we find that in Updegraph v. Com., it was decided that, "Christianity, general Christianity, is, and always has been, a part of the common law of Pennsylvania; . . . not Christianity with an established church, and tithes, and spiritual courts; but Christianity with liberty of conscience to all men." And in People v. Ruggles, Chancellor Kent, the great commentator on American law, speaking as Chief Justice of the Supreme Court of New York, said: "The people of this State, in common with the people of this country, profess the general doctrines of Christianity, as the rule of their faith and practice; and to scandalize the author of these doctrines is not only, in a religious point of view, extremely impious, but even in respect to the obligations due to society, is a gross violation of decency and good order. . . . The free, equal, and undisturbed enjoyment of religious opinion, whatever it may be, and free and decent discussions on any religious subject, is granted and secured; but to revile, with malicious and blasphemous contempt, the religion professed by almost the whole community, is an abuse of that right. Nor are we bound, by any expressions in the Constitution, as some have strangely supposed, either not to punish at all, or to punish indiscriminately, the like attacks upon the religion of Mahomet or of the Grand Lama; and for this plain reason, that the case assumes that we

40

are a Christian people, and the morality of the country is deeply ingrafted upon Christianity, and not upon the doctrines or worship of those impostors." And in the famous case of Vidal v. Girard, this court, while sustaining the will of Mr. Girard, with its provision for the creation of a college into which no minister should be permitted to enter, observed: "It is also said, and truly, that the Christian religion is a part of the common law of Pennsylvania."

If we pass beyond these matters to a view of American life as expressed by its laws, its business, its customs and its society, we find everywhere a clear recognition of the same truth. Among other matters note the following: The form of oath universally prevailing, concluding with an appeal to the Almighty; the custom of opening sessions of all deliberative bodies and most conventions with prayers; the prefatory words of all wills, "In the name of God, amen"; the laws respecting the observance of the Sabbath; with the general cessation of all secular business, and the closing of courts, Legislatures, and other similar public assemblies on that day; the churches and church organizations which abound in every city, town, and hamlet; the multitude of charitable organizations existing everywhere under Christian auspices; the gigantic missionary associations, with general support, and aiming to establish Christian missions in every quarter of the globe. These, and many other matters which might be noticed, add a volume of unofficial declarations to the mass of organic utterances that this is a Christian nation. In the face of all these, shall it be believed that a Congress of the United States intended to make it a misdemeanor for a church of this country to contract for the services of a Christian minister residing in another nation?

Suppose in the Congress that passed this Act some member had offered a bill which in terms declared that, if any Roman Catholic church in this country should contract with Cardinal Manning to come to this country and enter into its service as pastor and priest; or any Episcopal church should enter into a like contract with Canon Farrar; or any Baptist church should make similar arrangements with Rev. Mr. Spurgeon; or any Jewish synagogue with some eminent Rabbi, such contract should be adjudged unlawful and void, and the church making it be subject to prosecution and punishment, can it be believed that it would have received a minute of approving thought or a single vote? Yet it is contended that such was in effect the meaning of this statute. The construction invoked cannot be accepted as correct. It is a case where there was presented a definite evil, in view of which the Legislature used general terms with the purpose of reaching all phases of that evil, and thereafter, unexpectedly, it is developed that the general language thus employed is broad enough to reach cases and acts which the whole history and life of the country affirm could not have been intentionally legislated against. It is the duty of the courts, under those circumstances, to say that however broad the language of the statute may be, the act, although within the letter, is not within the intention of the Legislature, and therefore cannot be within the statute.

The judgment will be reversed, and the case remanded for further proceedings in accordance with this opinion.

BRADFIELD v. ROBERTS   175 US 291 (1899)

"Nor is it material that the hospital may be conducted under the auspices of the Roman Catholic Church . . . That the influence of any particular church may be powerful over the members of a nonsectarian and secular corporation, incorporated for a certain defined purpose with clearly stated powers, is surely not sufficient to convert such a corporation into a religious or sectarian body."

Mr. Justice Peckham

An agreement between the commissioners of the District of Columbia and the Providence Hospital, operated by a sisterhood of the Roman Catholic Church, was said, in the complaint, to "involve a principle and a precedent, for the appropriation of the funds of the United States for the use and support of religious societies, contrary to the article of the Constitution which declares that Congress shall make no law respecting a religious establishment, and also a precedent for giving to religious societies a legal agency in carrying into effect a public and civil duty which would, if once established, speedily obliterate the essential distinction between civil and religious functions."

MR. JUSTICE PECKHAM DELIVERED THE OPINION OF THE COURT.

Passing the various objections made to the maintenance of this suit on account of an alleged defect of parties, and also in regard to the character in which the complainant sues, merely that of a citizen and taxpayer of the United States and a resident of the District of Columbia, we come to the main question as to the validity of the agreement between the commissioners of the District and the directors of the hospital, founded upon the appropriation contained in the act of Congress, the contention being that the agreement if carried out would result in an appropriation by Congress of money to a religious society, thereby violating the constitutional provision which forbids Congress from passing any law respecting an establishment of religion. Art. 1 of the Amendments to Constitution.

The appropriation is to be found in the general appropriation act for the government of the District of Columbia, approved March 3, 1897.

It reads: "For two isolating buildings, to be constructed, in the discretion of the commissioners of the District of Columbia, on the grounds of two hospitals, and to be operated as a part of such hospitals, thirty thousand dollars." Acting under the authority of this appropriation the commissioners entered into the agreement in question.

As the bill alleges that Providence Hospital was incorporated by an act of Congress approved April 8, 1864, and assumes to give some of its provisions, the act thus referred to is substantially made a part of the bill . . .

The act shows that the individuals named therein and their successors in office were incorporated under the name of "The Directors of Providence Hospital," with power to receive, hold, and convey personal and real property, as provided in its 1st section. By the 2d section the corporation was granted "full power and all the rights of opening and keeping a hospital in the city of Washington for the care of such sick and invalid persons as may place themselves under the treatment and care of the said corporation." The 3d section gave it full power to make such by-laws, rules, and regulations that might be necessary for the general accomplishment of the objects of the hospital, not inconsistent with the laws in force in the District of Columbia. Nothing is said about religion or about the religious faith of the incorporators of this institution in the act of incorporation. It is simply the ordinary case of the incorporation of a hospital for the purposes for which such an institution is generally conducted. It is claimed that the allegation in the complainant's bill, that the said "Providence Hospital is a private eleemosynary corporation, and that to the best of complainant's knowledge and belief it is composed of members of a monastic order or sisterhood of the Roman Catholic Church, and is conducted under the auspices of said church; that the title to its property is vested in the Sisters of Charity of Emmitsburg, Maryland," renders the agreement void for the reason therein stated, which is that Congress has no power to make "a law respecting a religious establishment," a phrase which is not synonymous with that used in the Constitution, which prohibits the passage of a law "respecting an establishment of religion."

If we were to assume, for the purpose of this question only, that under this appropriation an agreement with a religious corporation of the tenor of this agreement would be invalid, as resulting indirectly in the passage of an act respecting an establishment of religion, we are unable to see that the complainant in his bill shows that the corporation is of the kind described, but on the contrary he has clearly shown that it is not.

The above-mentioned allegations in the complainant's bill do not change the legal character of the corporation or render it on that account a religious or sectarian body. Assuming that the hospital is a private eleemosynary corporation, the fact that its members, according to the belief of the complainant, are members of a monastic order or sisterhood of the Roman Catholic Church, and the further fact that the hospital is conducted under the auspices of said church, are wholly immaterial, as is also the allegation regarding the title to its property. The statute provides as to its property and makes no provision for its being held by anyone other than itself. The facts above stated do not in the least change the legal character of the hospital, or make a religious corporation out of a purely secular one as constituted by the law of its being. Whether the individuals who compose the corporation under its charter happen to be all Roman Catholics, or all Methodists, or Presbyterians, or Unitarians, or members of any other religious organization, or of no organization at all, is of not the slightest consequence with reference to the law of its incorporation, nor can the individual beliefs upon religious matters of the various incorporators be inquired into. Nor is it material that the hospital may be conducted under the auspices of the Roman Catholic Church. To be conducted under the auspices is to be conducted under the influence or patronage of that church. The meaning of the allegation is that the church exercises great and perhaps controlling influence over the management of the hospital. It must, however, be managed pursuant to the law of its being. That the influence of any particular church may be powerful over the members of a nonsectarian and secular corporation, incorporated for a certain defined purpose and with clearly stated powers, is surely not sufficient to convert such a corporation into a religious or sectarian body. That fact does not alter the legal character of the corporation, which is incorporated under an act of Congress, and its powers, duties, and character are to be solely measured by the charter under which it alone has any legal existence. There is no allegation that its hospital work is confined to members of that church or that in its management the hospital has been conducted as to violate its charter in the smallest degree. It is simply the case of a secular corporation being managed by people who hold to the doctrines of the Roman Catholic Church, but who nevertheless are managing the corporation according to the law under which it exists. The charter itself does not limit the exercise of its corporate powers to the members of any particular religious denomination, but, on the contrary, those powers are to be exercised in favor of anyone seeking the ministrations of that kind of an institution. All that can be said of the corporation itself is that it has been incorporated by an act of Congress, and for its legal powers and duties that act must be exclusively referred to. As stated in the opinion of the court of appeals, this corporation "is not declared the trustee of any church or

44

religious society. Its property is to be acquired in its own name and for its own purposes; that property and its business are to be managed in its own way, subject to no visitation, supervision, or control by any ecclesiastical authority whatever, but only to that of the government which created it. In respect then, of its creation, organization, management, and ownership of property it is an ordinary private corporation whose rights are determinable by the laws of the land, and the religious opinions of whose members are not subjects of inquiry."

It is not contended that Congress has no power in the District to appropriate money for the purpose expressed in the appropriation, and it is not doubted that it has power to authorize the commissioners of the District of Columbia to enter into a contract with the trustees of an incorporated hospital for the purposes mentioned in the agreement in this case, and the only objection set up is the alleged "sectarian character of the hospital and the specific and limited object of its creation."

The other allegations in complainant's bill are simply statements of his opinion in regard to the results necessarily flowing from the appropriation in question when connected with the agreement mentioned.

The act of Congress, however, shows there is nothing sectarian in the corporation, and "the specific and limited object of its creation" is the opening and keeping a hospital in the city of Washington for the care of such sick and invalid persons as may place themselves under the treatment and care of the corporation. To make the agreement was within the discretion of the commissioners, and was a fair exercise thereof.

The right reserved in the third section of the charter to amend, alter, or repeal the act leaves full power in Congress to remedy any abuse of the charter privileges.

Without adverting to any other objections to the maintenance of this suit, it is plain that complainant wholly fails to set forth a cause of action, and the bill was properly dismissed by the Court of Appeals, and its decree will therefore be affirmed.

PIERCE v. SOCIETY OF SISTERS   268 US 510 (1925)

"The fundamental theory of liberty upon which all governments in this Union repose excludes any general power of the state to standardize its children by forcing them to accept instruction from public teachers only. The child is not the mere creature of the state; those who nurture him and direct his destiny have the right, coupled with the high duty, to recognize and prepare him for additional obligations."

Mr. Justice McReynolds

This famous case, precipitated by an Oregon law requiring attendance at public schools, is often regarded as the parochial school Magna Carta.

MR. JUSTICE MC REYNOLDS DELIVERED THE OPINION OF THE COURT.

These appeals are from decrees, based upon undenied allegations, which granted preliminary orders restraining appellants from threatening or attempting to enforce the Compulsory Education Act adopted November 7, 1922, under the initiative provision of her Constitution by the voters of Oregon. They present the same points of law: there are no controverted questions of fact. Rights said to be guaranteed by the Federal Constitution were specially set up, and appropriate prayers asked for their protection.

The challenged act, effective September 1, 1926, requires every parent, guardian, or other person having control or charge or custody of a child between eight and sixteen years to send him "to a public school for the period of time a public school shall be held during the current year" in the district where the child resides; and failure so to do is declared a misdemeanor. There are exemptions—not specially important here— for children who are not normal, or who have completed the eighth grade, or whose parents or private teachers reside at considerable distances from any public school, or who hold special permits from the county superintendent. The manifest purpose is to compel general attendance at public schools by normal children, between eight and sixteen, who have not completed the eighth grade. And without doubt enforcement of the statute would seriously impair, perhaps destroy, the profitable features of appellees' business, and greatly diminish the value of their property.

Appellee the Society of Sisters is an Oregon corporation, organized in 1880, with power to care for orphans, educate and instruct the youth, establish and maintain academies or schools, and acquire necessary real and personal property. It has long devoted its property and effort to the secular and religious education and care of children, and has acquired the valuable good will of many parents and guardians. It conducts interdependent primary and high schools and junior colleges, and maintains orphanages for the custody and control of children between eight and sixteen. In its primary schools many children between those ages are taught the subjects usually pursued in Oregon public schools during the first eight years. Systematic religious instruction and moral training according to the tenets of the Roman Catholic Church are also regularly provided. All courses of study, both temporal and religious, contemplate continuity of training under appellee's charge; the primary schools are essential to the system and the most profitable.

It owns valuable buildings, especially constructed and equipped for school purposes. The business is remunerative—the annual income from primary schools exceeds $30,000—and the successful conduct of this requires long-time contracts with teachers and parents. The Compulsory Education Act of 1922 has already caused the withdrawal from its schools of children who would otherwise continue, and their income has steadily declined. The appellants, public officers, have proclaimed their purpose strictly to enforce the statute.

After setting out the above facts, the Society's bill alleges that the enactment conflicts with the right of parents to choose schools where their children will receive appropriate mental and religious training, the right of the child to influence the parents' choice of a school, the right of schools and teachers therein to engage in a useful business or profession, and is accordingly repugnant to the Constitution and void. And, further, that unless enforcement of the measure is enjoined, the corporation's business and property will suffer irreparable injury.

Appellee Hill Military Academy is a private corporation organized in 1908 under the laws of Oregon, engaged in owning, operating, and conducting for profit an elementary, college preparatory, and military training school for boys between the ages of five and twenty-one years. The average attendance is one hundred, and the annual fees received for each student amount to some $800. The elementary department is divided into eight grades, as in the public schools; the college preparatory department has four grades, similar to those of the public high schools; the courses of study conform to the requirements of the state board of education. Military instruction and training are also given, under the supervision of an Army officer. It owns considerable real and personal property, some useful only for school purposes. The business and incident good will are very valuable. In order to conduct its affairs long-time contracts must be made for supplies, equipment, teachers, and pupils. Appellants, law officers of the state and county, have publicly announced that the Act of November 7, 1922, is valid, and have declared their intention to enforce it. By reason of the statute and threat of enforcement, appellee's business is being destroyed and its property depreciated; parents and guardians are refusing to make contracts for the future instruction of their sons, and some are being withdrawn.

The Academy's bill states the foregoing facts and then alleges that the challenged act contravenes the corporation's rights guaranteed by the 14th Amendment, and that unless appellants are restrained from proclaiming its validity and threatening to enforce it, irreparable injury will result. The prayer is for an appropriate injunction.

No answer was interposed in either cause, and after proper notices they were heard by three judges on motions for preliminary injunctions upon the specifically alleged facts. The court ruled that the 14th Amendment guaranteed appellees against the deprivation of their property without due process of law consequent upon the unlawful interference by appellants with the free choice of patrons, present and prospective. It declared the right to conduct schools was property, and that parents and guardians, as a part of their liberty, might direct the education of children by selecting reputable teachers and places. Also, that appellees' schools were not unfit or harmful to the public, and that enforcement of the challenged statute would unlawfully deprive them of patronage, and thereby destroy appellee's business and property. Finally, that the threats to enforce the act would continue to cause irreparable injury; and the suits were not premature.

No question is raised concerning the power of the state reasonably to regulate all schools, to inspect, supervise, and examine them, their teachers and pupils; to require that all children of proper age attend some school, that teachers shall be of good moral character and patriotic disposition, that certain studies plainly essential to good citizenship must be taught, and that nothing be taught which is manifestly inimical to the public welfare.

The inevitable practical result of enforcing the act under consideration would be destruction of appellees' primary schools, and perhaps all other private primary schools for normal children within the state of Oregon. Appellees are engaged in a kind of undertaking not inherently harmful, but long regarded as useful and meritorious. Certainly there is nothing in the present records to indicate that they have failed to discharge their obligations to patrons, students, or the state. And there are no peculiar circumstances or present emergencies which demand extraordinary measures relative to primary education.

Under the doctrine of Meyer v. Nebraska, we think it entirely plain that the Act of 1922 unreasonably interferes with the liberty of parents and guardians to direct the upbringing and education of children under their control. As often heretofore pointed out, rights guaranteed by the Constitution may not be abridged by legislation which has no reasonable relation to some purpose within the competency of the state. The fundamental theory of liberty upon which all governments in this Union repose excludes any general power of the state to standardize its children by forcing them to accept instruction from public teachers only. The child is not the mere creature of the state; those who nurture him and direct his destiny have the right, coupled with the high duty, to recognize and prepare him for additional obligations.

Appellees are corporations, and therefore, it is said, they cannot claim for themselves the liberty which the 14th Amendment guarantees.

Accepted in the proper sense, this is true. But they have business and property for which they claim protection. These are threatened with destruction through the unwarranted compulsion which appellants are exercising over present and prospective patrons of their schools. And this court has gone very far to protect against loss threatened by such action.

The courts of the state have not construed the act, and we must determine its meaning for ourselves. Evidently it was expected to have general application, and cannot be construed as though merely intended to amend the charters of certain private corporations, as in Berea College v. Kentucky. No argument in favor of such view has been advanced.

Generally it is entirely true, as urged by counsel, that no person in any business has such an interest in possible customers as to enable him to restrain exercise of proper power of the state upon the ground that he will be deprived of patronage. But the injunctions here sought are not against the exercise of any proper power. Appellees asked protection against arbitrary, unreasonable, and unlawful interference with their patrons, and the consequent destruction of their business and property. Their interest is clear and immediate, within the rule approved in Truax v. Raich, Truax v. Corrigan, and Terrace v. Thompson, and many other cases where injunctions have issued to protect business enterprises against interference with the freedom of patrons or customers.

The suits were not premature. The injury to appellees was present and very real,—not a mere possibility in the remote future. If no relief had been possible prior to the effective date of the act, the injury would have become irreparable. Prevention of impending injury by unlawful action is a well-recognized function of courts of equity.

The decrees below are affirmed.

COCHRAN v. BOARD OF EDUCATION
281 US 370 (1930)

"The schools, however, are not the beneficiaries of these appropriations . . . The school children and the state alone are the beneficiaries."
Mr. Chief Justice Hughes

The Court here upholds a state law providing free textbooks for school children whether attending public or parochial schools. It expresses a "child-benefit" view which is to appear subsequently in the school bus case.

MR. CHIEF JUSTICE HUGHES DELIVERED THE OPINION OF THE COURT.

The appellants, as citizens and taxpayers of the State of Louisiana, brought this suit to restrain the State Board of Education and other state officials from expending any part of the severance tax fund in purchasing school books and in supplying them free of cost to the school children of the State, under Acts No. 100 and No. 143 of 1928, upon the ground that the legislation violated specified provisions of the constitution of the State and also section 4 of Article IV and the Fourteenth Amendment of the Federal Constitution. The Supreme Court of the State affirmed the judgment of the trial court, which refused to issue an injunction.

Act No. 100 of 1928 provided that the severance tax fund of the State, after allowing funds and appropriations as required by the state constitution, should be devoted "first, to supplying school books to the school children of the State." The Board of Education was directed to provide "school books for school children free of cost to such children." Act No. 143 of 1928 made appropriations in accordance with the above provisions.

The Supreme Court of the State, following its decision in Borden v. Louisiana State Board of Education, held that these acts were not repugnant to either the state or the Federal Constitution.

No substantial Federal question is presented under section 4 of Article IV of the Federal Constitution guaranteeing to every State a republican form of government, as questions arising under this provision are political, not judicial, in character.

The contention of the appellant under the Fourteenth Amendment is that taxation for the purchase of school books constituted a taking of private property for a private purpose. The purpose is said to be to aid private, religious, sectarian, and other schools not embraced in the public educational system of the State by furnishing text-books free to the children attending such private schools. The operation and effect of the legislation in question were described by the Supreme Court of the State as follows:

"One may scan the acts in vain to ascertain where any money is appropriated for the purchase of school books for the use of any church, private, sectarian or even public school. The appropriations were made for the specific purpose of purchasing school books for the use of the school children of the state, free of cost to them. It was for their benefit and the resulting benefit to the state that the appropriations were made. True, these children attend some school, public or private, the latter, sectarian or non-sectarian, and that the books are to be furnished them for their use, free of cost, whichever they attend. The schools, however, are not the beneficiaries of these appropriations. They obtain nothing from them, nor are they relieved of a single obligation, because of them. The school children and the state alone are the beneficiaries. It is also true that the sectarian schools, which some of the children attend, instruct their pupils in religion, and books are used for that purpose, but one may search diligently the acts, though without result, in an effort to find anything to the effect that it is the purpose of the state to furnish religious books for the use of such children. . . . What the statutes contemplate is that the same books that are furnished children attending public schools shall be furnished children attending private schools. This is the only practical way of interpreting and executing the statutes, and this is what the state board of education is doing. Among these books, naturally, none is to be expected, adapted to religious instruction."

The Court also stated, although the point is not of importance in relation to the Federal question, that it was "only the use of the books that is granted to the children, or, in other words, the books are lent to them."

Viewing the statute as having the effect thus attributed to it, we can not doubt that the taxing power of the State is exerted for a public purpose. The legislation does not segregate private schools, or their pupils, as its beneficiaries or attempt to interfere with any matters of exclusively private concern. Its interest is education, broadly; its method, comprehensive. Individual interests are aided only as the common interest is safeguarded.

Judgment affirmed.

UNITED STATES v. MACINTOSH 283 US 605 (1931)

"When he speaks of putting his allegiance to the will of God above his allegiance to the government, it is evident . . . that he means to make his own interpretation of the will of God the decisive test which shall conclude the government and stay its hand."

Mr. Justice Sutherland, for the Court

"There is abundant room for enforcing the requisite authority of law as it is enacted and requires obedience, and for maintaining the conception of the supremacy of law as essential to orderly government, without demanding that either citizens or applicants for citizenship shall assume by oath an obligation to regard allegiance to God as subordinate to allegiance to civil power."

Mr. Chief Justice Hughes, dissenting

Two years before this case was decided Rosika Schwimmer, a fifty-year-old woman, well known as a pacifist and suffragette, was denied naturalization because of her refusal to state her willingness to take up arms in the defense of the country. The problem is more fully canvassed in this case. (Part of opinion is omitted.)

MR. JUSTICE SUTHERLAND DELIVERED THE OPINION OF THE COURT. The respondent was born in the Dominion of Canada. He came to the United States in 1916, and in 1925 declared his intention to become a citizen. His petition for naturalization was presented to the federal district court for Connecticut, and that court, after hearing and consideration, denied the application upon the ground that, since petitioner would not promise in advance to bear arms in defense of the United States unless he believed the war to be morally justified, he was not attached to the principles of the Constitution. The circuit court of appeals reversed the decree and directed the district court to admit respondent to citizenship. . . .

The applicant had complied with all the formal requirements of the law, and his personal character and conduct were shown to be good in all respects. His right to naturalization turns altogether upon the effect to be given to certain answers and qualifying statements made in response to interrogatories propounded to him.

Upon the preliminary form for petition for naturalization, the following questions, among others, appear: "20. Have you read the following oath of allegiance? [which is then quoted]. Are you willing to take up arms in defense of this country?" In response to the questions designated 20, he answered "Yes." In response to the question designated 22, he answered, "Yes; but I should want to be free to judge of the necessity." By a written memorandum subsequently filed, he amplified these answers as follows:

"20 and 22. I am willing to do what I judge to be in the best interests of my country, but only in so far as I can believe that this is not going to be against the best interests of humanity in the long run. I do not undertake to support 'my country, right or wrong' in any dispute which may arise, and I am not willing to promise beforehand, and without knowing the cause for which my country may go to war, either that I will or that I will not 'take up arms in defense of this country,' however 'necessary' the war may seem to be to the government of the day.

"It is only in a sense consistent with these statements that I am willing to promise to 'support and defend' the government of the United States 'against all enemies, foreign and domestic.' But, just because I am not certain that the language of questions 20 and 22 will bear the construction I should have to put upon it in order to be able to answer them in the affirmative, I have to say that I do not know that I can say 'Yes' in answer to these two questions."

Upon the hearing before the district court on the petition, he explained his position more in detail. He said that he was not a pacifist; that if allowed to interpret the oath for himself he would interpret it as not inconsistent with his position and would take it. He then proceeded to say that he would answer question 22 in the affirmative only on the understanding that he would have to believe that the war was morally justified before he would take up arms in it or give it his moral support. He was ready to give to the United States all the allegiance he ever had given or ever could give to any country, but he could not put allegiance to the government of any country before allegiance to the will of God. He did not anticipate engaging in any propaganda against the prosecution of a war which the government had already declared and which it considered to be justified; but he preferred not to make any absolute promise at the time of the hearing, because of his ignorance of all the circumstances which might affect his judgment with reference to such a war. He did not question that the government under certain conditions could regulate and restrain the conduct of the individual citizen, even to the extent of imprisonment. He recognized the principle of the submission of the individual citizen to the opinion of the majority in a democratic country; but he did not believe in having his own moral problems solved for him by the majority. The position thus taken was the only one he could take consistently with his moral principles and with what he understood to be the moral principles of Christianity. He recognized, in short, the right of the government to restrain the freedom of the individual for the good of the social whole; but was convinced, on the other hand, that the individual citizen should have the right respectfully to withhold from the government military services (involving, as they probably would, the taking of human life), when his best moral judgment would compel him to do so. He was willing to support his country, even to the extent of bearing arms, if asked to do so by the government, in any war which he could regard as morally justified.

There is more to the same effect, but the foregoing is sufficient to make plain his position.

These statements of the applicant fairly disclose that he is unwilling to take the oath of allegiance, except with these important qualifications: That he will do what he judges to be in the best interests of the country only in so far as he believes it will not be against the best interests of humanity in the long run; that he will not assist in the defense of the country by force of arms or give any war his moral support unless he believes it to be morally justified, however necessary the war might seem to the government of the day; that he will hold himself free to judge of the morality and necessity of the war, and, while he does not anticipate engaging in propaganda against the prosecution of a war declared and considered justified by the government, he prefers to make no promise even as to that; and that he is convinced that the individual citizen should have the right to withhold his military services when his best moral judgment impels him to do so.

Thus stated, the case is ruled in principle by United States v. Schwimmer. In that case the applicant, a woman, testified that she would not take up arms in defense of the country. She was willing to be treated on the basis of a conscientious objector who refused to take up arms in the recent war, and seemed to regard herself as belonging in that class. She was an uncompromising pacifist, with no sense of nationalism, and only a cosmic sense of belonging to the human family. Her objection to military service, we concluded, rested upon reasons other than her inability to bear arms because of sex or age; and we held that her application for naturalization should be denied upon the ground, primarily, that she failed to sustain the burden of showing that she did not oppose the principle making it a duty of citizens, by force of arms when necessary, to defend their country against its enemies. At page 650 we said:

"That it is the duty of citizens by force of arms to defend our government against all enemies whenever necessity arises is a fundamental principle of the Constitution.

"The common defense was one of the purposes for which the people ordained and established the Constitution. . . . We need not refer to the numerous statutes that contemplate defense of the United States, its Constitution and laws by armed citizens. This Court, in the Selective Draft Law Cases, speaking through Chief Justice White, said that 'the very conception of a just government and its duty to the citizen includes the reciprocal obligation of the citizen to render military service in case of need. . . .'

"Whatever tends to lessen the willingness of citizens to discharge their duty to bear arms in the country's defense detracts from the strength and safety of the government. And their opinions and beliefs as well as their behavior indicating a disposition to hinder in the performance of that duty are subjects of inquiry under the statutory provisions governing naturalization and are of vital importance, for if all or a large number of citizens oppose such defense the 'good order and happiness' of the United States cannot long endure. And it is evident that the views of applicants for naturalization in respect of such matters may not be disregarded. The influence of conscientious objectors against the use of military force in defense of the principles of our government is apt to be more detrimental than their mere refusal to bear arms. The fact that, by reason of sex, age or other cause, they may be unfit to serve does not lessen their purpose or power to influence others. It is clear from her own statements that the declared opinions of respondent as to armed defense by citizens against enemies of the country were directly pertinent to the investigation of her application."

There are few finer or more exalted sentiments than that which finds expression in opposition to war. Peace is a sweet and holy thing, and war is a hateful and an abominable thing to be avoided by any sacrifice or concession that a free people can make. But thus far mankind has been unable to devise any method of indefinitely prolonging the one or of entirely abolishing the other; and, unfortunately, there is nothing which seems to afford positive ground for thinking that the near future will witness the beginning of the reign of perpetual peace for which good men and women everywhere never cease to pray. The Constitution, therefore, wisely contemplating the ever present possibility of war, declares that one of its purposes is to "provide for the common defense." In express terms Congress is empowered "to declare war," which necessarily connotes the plenary power to wage war with all the force necessary to make it effective; and "to raise . . . armies," which necessarily connotes the like power to say who shall serve in them and in what way.

From its very nature the war power, when necessity calls for its exercise, tolerates no qualifications or limitations, unless found in the Constitution or in applicable principles of international law. In the words of John Quincy Adams,—"This power is tremendous; it is strictly constitutional; but it breaks down every barrier so anxiously erected for the protection of liberty, property and of life." To the end that war may not result in defeat, freedom of speech may, by act of Congress, be curtailed or denied so that the morale of the people and the spirit of the army may not be broken by seditious utterances; freedom of the press curtailed to preserve our military plans and movements from the knowledge of the enemy; deserters and spies put to death without indictment or trial by jury; ships and supplies requisitioned; property of alien enemies, theretofore under the protection of the Constitution, seized without process and converted to the public use without compensation and without due process of law in the ordinary sense of that term; prices of food and other necessities of life fixed or regulated; railways taken over and operated by the government; and other drastic powers, wholly inadmissible in time of peace, exercised to meet the emergencies of war.

These are but illustrations of the breadth of the power; and it necessarily results from their consideration that whether any citizen shall be exempt from serving in the armed forces of the nation in time of war is dependent upon the will of Congress and not upon the scruples of the individual, except as Congress provides. That body, thus far, has seen fit, by express enactment, to relieve from the obligation of armed service those persons who belong to the class known as conscientious objectors; and this policy is of such long standing that it is thought by some to be beyond the possibility of alteration. Indeed, it seems to be assumed in this case that the privilege is one that Congress itself is powerless to take away. Thus it is said in the carefully prepared brief of respondent:

"To demand from an alien who desires to be naturalized an unqualified promise to bear arms in every war that may be declared, despite the fact that he may have conscientious religious scruples against doing so in some hypothetical future war, would mean that such an alien would come into our citizenry on an unequal footing with the native born, and that he would be forced, as the price of citizenship, to forego a privilege enjoyed by others. That is the manifest result of the fixed principle of our Constitution, zealously guarded by our laws, that a citizen cannot be forced and need not bear arms in a war if he has conscientious religious scruples against doing so."

This, if it means what it seems to say, is an astonishing statement. Of course, there is no such principle of the Constitution, fixed or otherwise. The conscientious objector is relieved from the obligation to bear arms in obedience to no constitutional provision, express or implied; but because, and only because, it has accorded with the policy of Congress thus to relieve him. The alien, when he becomes a naturalized citizen, acquires, with one exception, every right possessed under the Constitution by those citizens who are native born, but he acquires no more. The privilege of the native-born conscientious objector to avoid bearing arms comes not from the Constitution, but from the acts of Congress. That body may grant or withhold the exemption as in its wisdom it sees fit; and if it be withheld, the native-born conscientious objector cannot successfully assert the privilege. No other conclusion is compatible with the well-nigh limitless extent of the war powers as above illustrated, which include, by necessary implication, the power, in the last extremity, to compel the armed service of any citizen in the land, without regard to his objections or his views in respect of the justice or morality of the particular war or of war in general. In Jacobson v. Massachusetts, this court, speaking of the liberties guaranteed to the individual by the 14th Amendment, said:

". . . and yet he may be compelled, by force if need be, against his will and without regard to his personal wishes or his pecuniary interests, or even his religious or political convictions, to take his place in the

56

ranks of the army of his country and risk the chance of being shot down in its defense."

The applicant for naturalization here is unwilling to become a citizen with this understanding. He is unwilling to leave the question of his future military service to the wisdom of Congress where it belongs, and where every native-born or admitted citizen is obliged to leave it. In effect, he offers to take the oath of allegiance only with the qualification that the question whether the war is necessarily or morally justified must, so far as his support is concerned, be conclusively determined by reference to his opinion.

When he speaks of putting his allegiance to the will of God above his allegiance to the government, it is evident, in the light of his entire statement, that he means to make *his own interpretation* of the will of God the decisive test which shall conclude the government and stay its hand. We are a Christian people, according to one another the equal right of religious freedom, and acknowledging with reverence the duty of obedience to the will of God. But, also, we are a nation with the duty to survive; a nation whose Constitution contemplates war as well as peace; whose government must go forward upon the assumption, and safely can proceed upon no other, that unqualified allegiance to the nation and submission and obedience to the laws of the land, as well those made for war as those made for peace, are not inconsistent with the will of God.

The applicant here rejects that view. He is unwilling to rely, as every native-born citizen is obliged to do, upon the probable continuance by Congress of the long established and approved practice of exempting the honest conscientious objector, while at the same time asserting his willingness to conform to whatever the future law constitutionally shall require of him; but discloses a present and fixed purpose to refuse to give his moral or armed support to any future war in which the country may be actually engaged, if, in his opinion, the war is not morally justified, the opinion of the nation as expressed by Congress to the contrary notwithstanding.

If the attitude of this claimant, as shown by his statements and the inferences properly to be deduced from them, be held immaterial to the question of his fitness for admission to citizenship, where shall the line be drawn? Upon what ground of distinction may we hereafter reject another applicant who shall express his willingness to respect any particular principle of the Constitution or obey any future statute only upon the condition that he shall entertain the opinion that it is morally justified? The applicant's attitude, in effect, is a refusal to take the oath of allegiance except in an altered form. The qualifications upon which he insists, it is true, are made by parol and not by way of written amendment to the oath; but the substance is the same.

It is not within the province of the courts to make bargains with those who seek naturalization. They must accept the grant and take the oath in accordance with the terms fixed by the law, or forego the privilege of citizenship. There is no middle choice. If one qualification of the oath be allowed, the door is opened for others, with utter confusion as the probable final result. As this court said in United States v. Manzi:

"Citizenship is a high privilege, and when doubts exist concerning a grant of it, generally at least, they should be resolved in favor of the United States and against the claimant."

The Naturalization Act is to be construed "with definite purpose to favor and support the government," and the United States is entitled to the benefit of any doubt which remains in the mind of the court as to any essential matter of fact. The burden was upon the applicant to show that his views were not opposed to "the principle that it is a duty of citizenship, by force of arms when necessary, to defend the country against all enemies, and that [his] opinions and beliefs would not prevent or impair the true faith and allegiance required by the act." We are of opinion that he did not meet this requirement. The examiner and the court of first instance who heard and weighed the evidence and saw the applicant and witnesses so concluded. That conclusion, if we were in doubt, would not be rejected except for good and persuasive reasons, which we are unable to find.

The decree of the Circuit Court of Appeals is reversed and that of the District Court is affirmed.

MR. CHIEF JUSTICE HUGHES DISSENTING.

I am unable to agree with the judgment in this case. It is solely one of law, as there is no controversy as to the facts. The question is not whether naturalization is a privilege to be granted or withheld. That it is such a privilege is undisputed. Nor, whether the Congress has the power to fix the conditions upon which the privilege is granted. That power is assumed. Nor, whether the Congress may in its discretion compel service in the army in time of war or punish the refusal to serve. That power is not here in dispute. Nor is the question one of the authority of Congress to exact a promise to bear arms as a condition of its grant of naturalization. That authority, for the present purpose, may also be assumed.

The question before the court is the narrower one whether the Congress has exacted such a promise. That the Congress has not made such an express requirement is apparent. The question is whether that exaction is to be implied from certain general words which do not, as it seems to me, either literally or historically, demand the implication. I think that the requirement should not be implied, because such a construction is directly opposed to the spirit of our institutions and to the historic practice of the Congress. It must be conceded that departmental zeal may not be permitted to outrun the authority conferred by statute. If such a promise is to be demanded, contrary to principles which have been respected as fundamental, the Congress should exact it in unequivocal terms, and we should not, by judicial decision, attempt to perform what, as I see it, is a legislative function.

In examining the requirements for naturalization, we find that the Congress has expressly laid down certain rules which concern the opinions and conduct of the applicant. Thus it is provided that no person shall be naturalized "who disbelieves in or who is opposed to organized government, or who is a member of or affiliated with any organization entertaining and teaching such disbelief in or opposition to organized government, or who advocates or teaches the duty, necessity, or propriety of the unlawful assaulting or killing of any officer or officers, either of specific individuals or of officers generally, of the government of the United States, or of any other organized government, because of his or their official character, or who is a polygamist." The respondent, Douglas Clyde Macintosh, entertained none of these disqualifying opinions and had none of the associations or relations disapproved. Among the specific requirements, as to beliefs, we find none to the effect that one shall not be naturalized if by reason of his religious convictions he is opposed to war or is unwilling to promise to bear arms. In view of the questions which have repeatedly been brought to the attention of the Congress in relation to such beliefs, and having regard to the action of the Congress when its decision was of immediate importance in the raising of armies, the omission of such an express requirement from the naturalization statute is highly significant.

Putting aside these specific requirements as fully satisfied, we come to the general conditions imposed by the statute. We find one as to good behavior during the specified period of residence preceding application. No applicant could appear to be more exemplary than Macintosh. A Canadian by birth, he first came to the United States as a graduate student at the University of Chicago, and in 1907 he was ordained as a Baptist minister. In 1909 he began to teach in Yale University and is now a member of the faculty of the Divinity School, Chaplain of the Yale Graduate School, and Dwight Professor of Theology. After the outbreak of the Great War, he voluntarily sought appointment as a chaplain with the Canadian Army and as such saw service at the front. Returning to this country, he made public addresses in 1917 in support of the Allies. In 1918, he went again to France where he had charge of an American Y.M.C.A. hut at the front until the armistice, when he resumed his duties at Yale University. It seems to me that the applicant has shown himself in his behavior and character to be highly desirable as a citizen and, if such a man is to be excluded from naturalization, I think the disqualification should be found in unambiguous terms and not in an implication which shuts him out and gives admission to a host far less worthy.

The principal ground for exclusion appears to relate to the terms of the oath which the applicant must take. It should be observed that the respondent was willing to take the oath, and he so stated in his petition. But, in response to further inquiries, he explained that he was not willing "to promise beforehand" to take up arms, "without knowing the cause for which my country may go to war" and that "he would have to believe that the war was morally justified." He declared that "his first allegiance was to the will of God"; that he was ready to give to the United States "all the allegiance he ever had given or ever could give to any country, but that he could not put allegiance to the government of any country before allegiance to the will of God." The question then is whether the terms of the oath are to be taken as necessarily implying an assurance of willingness to bear arms, so that one whose conscientious convictions or belief of supreme allegiance to the will of God will not permit him to make such an absolute promise, cannot take the oath and hence is disqualified for admission to citizenship.

The statutory provision as to the oath which is said to require this promise is this: "That he will support and defend the Constitution and laws of the United States against all enemies, foreign and domestic, and bear true faith and allegiance to the same." That these general words have not been regarded as implying a promise to bear arms notwithstanding religious or conscientious scruples, or as requiring one to promise to put allegiance to temporal power above what is sincerely believed to be one's duty of obedience to God, is apparent, I think, from a consideration of their history. This oath does not stand alone. It is the same oath in substance that is required by act of Congress of civil officers generally (except the President, whose oath is prescribed by the Constitution). The Congress, in prescribing such an oath for civil officers, acts under Article 6, of the Constitution, which provides: "The Senators and Representatives before mentioned, and the Members of the several State Legislatures, and all executive and judicial Officers, both of the United States and of the several States, shall be bound by Oath or Affirmation, to support this Constitution; but no religious test shall ever be required as a Qualification to any Office or public Trust under the United States." The general oath of office, in the form which has been prescribed by the Congress for over sixty years, contains the provision "that I will support and defend the Constitution of the United States against all enemies, foreign and domestic; that I will bear true faith and allegiance to the same; that I take this obligation freely, without any mental reservation or purpose of evasion." It goes without saying that it was not the intention of the Congress in framing the oath to impose any religious test. When we consider the history of the struggle for religious liberty, the large number of citizens of our country from the very beginning, who have been unwilling to sacrifice their religious convictions, and in particular, those who have been conscientiously opposed to war and who would not yield what they sincerely believed to be their allegiance to the will of God, I find it impossible to conclude that such persons are to be deemed disqualified for public office in this country because of the requirement of the oath which must be taken before they enter upon their duties. The terms of the promise "to support and defend the Constitution of the United States against all enemies, foreign and domestic" are not, I think, to be read as demanding any such result. There are other and most important methods of defense, even in time of war, apart from the personal bearing of arms. We have but to consider the defense given to our country in the late war, both in industry and in the field, by workers of all sorts, by engineers, nurses, doctors and chaplains, to realize that there is opportunity even at such a time for essential service in the activities of defense which do not require the overriding of such religious scruples. I think that the requirement of the oath of office should be read in the light of our regard from the beginning for freedom of conscience. While it has always been recognized that the supreme power of government may be exerted and disobedience to its commands may be punished, we know that with many of our worthy citizens it would be a most heart-searching question if they were asked whether they would promise to obey a law believed to be in conflict with religious duty. Many of their most honored exemplars in the past have been willing to suffer imprisonment or even death rather than to make such a promise. And we also know, in particular, that a promise to engage in war by bearing arms, or thus to engage in a war believed to be unjust, would be contrary to the tenets of religious groups among our citizens who are of patriotic purpose and exemplary conduct. To conclude that the general oath of office is to be interpreted as disregarding the religious scruples of these citizens and as disqualifying them for office because they could not take the oath with such an interpretation would, I believe, be generally regarded as contrary not only to the specific intent of the Congress but as repugnant to the fundamental principle of representative government.

But the naturalization oath is in substantially the same terms as the oath of office to which I have referred. I find no ground for saying that these words are to be interpreted differently in the two cases. On the contrary, when the Congress reproduced the historic words of the oath of office in the naturalization oath, I should suppose that, according to familiar rules of interpretation, they should be deemed to carry the same significance.

The question of the proper interpretation of the oath is, as I have said, distinct from that of legislative policy in exacting military service. The latter is not dependent upon the former. But the long-established practice of excusing from military service those whose religious convictions oppose it confirms the view that the Congress in the terms of the oath did not intend to require a promise to give such service. The policy of granting exemptions in such cases has been followed from colonial times and is abundantly shown by the provisions of colonial and state statutes, of state constitutions, and of acts of Congress. The first constitution of New York, adopted in 1777, in providing for the state militia, while strongly emphasizing the duty of defense, added "That all such of the inhabitants of this state (being of the people called Quakers) as, from scruples of conscience may be averse to the bearing of arms, be therefrom excused by the legislature, and do pay to the state such sums of money, in lieu of their personal service, as the same may, in the judgment of the legislature, be worth." A large number of similar provisions are found in other States. The importance of giving immunity to those having conscientious scruples against bearing arms has been emphasized in debates in Congress repeatedly from the very beginning of our government, and religious scruples have been recognized in draft acts. I agree with the statement in the opinion of the circuit court of appeals in the present case that "this Federal legislation is indicative of the actual operation of the principles of the Constitution, that a person with conscientious or religious scruples need not bear arms, although as a member of society, he may be obliged to render services of a noncombatant nature."

Much has been said of the paramount duty to the state, a duty to be recognized, it is urged, even though it conflicts with convictions of duty to God. Undoubtedly that duty to the state exists within the domain of power, for government may enforce obedience to laws regardless of scruples. When one's belief collides with the power of the state, the latter is supreme within its sphere and submission or punishment follows. But, in the forum of conscience, duty to a moral power higher than the state has always been maintained. The reservation of that supreme obligation, as a matter of principle, would unquestionably be made by many of our conscientious and law-abiding citizens. The essence of religion is belief in a relation to God involving duties superior to those arising from any human relation. As was stated by Mr. Justice Field, in Davis v. Beason, "The term 'religion' has reference to one's views of his relations to his Creator, and to the obligations they impose of reverence for his being and character, and of obedience to his will." One cannot speak of religious liberty, with proper appreciation of its essential and historic significance, without assuming the existence of a belief in supreme allegiance to the will of God. Professor Macintosh, when pressed by the inquiries put to him, stated what is axiomatic in religious doctrine. And, putting aside dogmas with their particular conceptions of deity, freedom of conscience itself implies respect for an innate conviction of paramount duty. The battle for religious liberty has been fought and won with respect to religious beliefs and practices, which are not in conflict with good order, upon the very ground of the supremacy of conscience within its proper field. What that field is, under our system of government, presents in part a question of constitutional law and also, in part, one of legislative policy in avoiding unnecessary clashes with the dictates of conscience. There is abundant room for enforcing the requisite authority of law as it is enacted and requires obedience, and for maintaining the conception of the supremacy of law as essential to orderly government, without demanding that either citizens or applicants for citizenship shall assume by oath an obligation to regard allegiance to God as subordinate to allegiance to civil power. The attempt to exact such a promise, and thus to bind one's conscience by the taking of oaths or the submission to tests, has been the cause of many deplorable conflicts. The Congress has sought to avoid such conflicts in this country by respecting our happy tradition. In no sphere of legislation has the intention to prevent such clashes been more conspicuous than in relation to the bearing of arms. It would require strong evidence that the Congress intended a reversal of its policy in prescribing the general terms of the naturalization oath. I find no such evidence.

Nor is there ground, in my opinion, for the exclusion of Professor Macintosh because his conscientious scruples have particular reference to wars, believed to be unjust. There is nothing new in such an attitude. Among the most eminent statesmen here and abroad have been those who condemned the action of their country in entering into wars they thought to be unjustified. Agreements for the renunciation of war presuppose a preponderant public sentiment against wars of aggression. If, while recognizing the power of Congress, the mere holding of religious or conscientious scruples against all wars should not disqualify a citizen from holding office in this country, or an applicant otherwise qualified from being admitted to citizenship, there would seem to be no reason why a reservation of religious or conscientious objection to participation in wars believed to be unjust should constitute such a disqualification.

Apart from the terms of the oath, it is said that the respondent has failed to meet the requirement of "attachment to the principles of the Constitution." Here, again, is a general phrase which should be construed, not in opposition to, but in accord with, the theory and practice of our government in relation to freedom of conscience. What I have said as to the provisions of the oath I think applies equally to this phase of the case.

The judgment in United States v. Schwimmer, stands upon the special facts of that case, but I do not regard it as requiring a reversal of the judgment here. I think that the judgment below should be affirmed.

Mr. Justice Holmes, Mr. Justice Brandeis and Mr. Justice Stone concur in this opinion.

HAMILTON v. REGENTS OF UNIVERSITY OF CALIFORNIA   293 US 245 (1934)

"Manifestly a different doctrine would carry us to lengths that have never yet been dreamed of. The conscientious objector, if his liberties were to be thus extended, might refuse to contribute taxes in furtherance of a war, whether for attack or defense, or in furtherance of any other end condemned by his conscience as irreligious or immoral. The right of private judgment has never yet been so exalted above the powers and the compulsion of the agencies of government."

Mr. Justice Cardozo, concurring

The court, without a dissenting voice, here rejects the claim to exemption from R.O.T.C. based on conscientious objection to war. (Part of opinion is omitted.)

MR. JUSTICE BUTLER DELIVERED THE OPINION OF THE COURT.

This is an appeal . . . from a judgment of the highest court of California sustaining a state law that requires students at its University to take a course in military science and tactics, the validity of which was by the appellants challenged as repugnant to the Constitution and laws of the United States.

The appellants are the above-named minors and the fathers of each as his guardian ad litem and individually. They are taxpayers and citizens of the United States and of California. Appellees are the regents constituting a corporation created by the state to administer the University, its president, and its provost. Appellants applied to the state Supreme Court for a writ of mandate compelling appellees to admit the minors into the University as students. So far as they are material to the questions presented here, the allegations of the petition are:

In October, 1933, each of these minors registered, became a student in the University, and fully conformed to all its requirements other than that compelling him to take the course in military science and tactics in the Reserve Officers Training Corps which they assert to be an integral part of the military establishment of the state. The primary object of there establishing units of the training corps is to qualify students for appointment in the Officers Reserve Corps. The courses in military training are those prescribed by the War Department. The regents require enrollment and participation of ablebodied male students who are citizens of the United States. These courses include instruction in rifle marksmanship, scouting and patrolling, drill and command, musketry, combat principles, and use of automatic rifles. Arms, equipment, and uniforms for use of students in such courses are furnished by the War Department of the United States government.

These minors are members of the Methodist Episcopal Church and of the Epworth League and connected religious societies and organizations. For many years their fathers have been ordained ministers of that church. The Southern California Conference at its 1931 session adopted a resolution:

"With full appreciation of the heroic sacrifices of all those who have conscientiously and unselfishly served their country in times of war, but with the belief that the time has come in the unfolding light of the new day for the settlement of human conflicts by pacific means, and because we as Christians owe our first and supreme allegiance to Jesus Christ. Because the Methodist Episcopal Church in her General Conference of 1928 has declared: 'We renounce war as an instrument of national policy.' Because our nation led the nations of the world in signing the Paris Peace Pact, and the Constitution of the United States, Article 6, Section 2, provides that: 'This Constitution and the laws of the United States which shall be made in pursuance thereof and all treaties made under authority of the United States shall be the Supreme Law of the Land'. Thus making the Paris Pact the supreme law of the land which declares: 'The high contracting parties agree that the settlement of all disputes or conflict shall never be sought except by pacific means.'

"Therefore we, the Southern California Conference, memorialize the General Conference which convenes in Atlantic City in May, 1932: to petition the United States Government to grant exemption from military service to such citizens who are members of the Methodist Episcopal Church, as conscientiously believe that participation in war is a denial of their supreme allegiance to Jesus Christ."

And in 1932 the General Conference of that church adopted as a part of its tenets and discipline:

"We hold that our country is benefited by having as citizens those who unswervingly follow the dictates of their consciences . . . Furthermore, we believe it to be the duty of the churches to give moral support to those individuals who hold conscientious scruples against participation in military training or military service. We petition the government of the United States to grant to members of the Methodist Episcopal Church who may be conscientious objectors to war the same exemption from military service as has long been granted to members of the Society of Friends and other similar religious organizations. Similarly we petition all educational institutions which require military training to excuse from such training any student belonging to the Methodist Episcopal Church who has conscientious scruples against it. We earnestly petition the government of the United States to cease to support financially all military training in civil educational institutions."

And the Southern California Conference at its 1933 session adopted the following:

"Reserve Officers' Training Corps—Recalling the action of the General Conference asking for exemption from military service for those members of our church to whom war and preparation for war is a violation of conscience, we request the authorities of our State Universities at Berkeley, Los Angeles and Tucson, to exempt Methodist students from the R. O. T. C. on the grounds of conscientious objection, and we hereby pledge the moral and official backing of this Conference, seeking such exemption, provided that it be understood that no conscientious objector shall participate in the financial profits of war. The Secretary of the Conference is asked to send copies of this paragraph to the governing boards of these institutions."

Appellants as members of that church accept and feel themselves morally, religiously, and conscientiously bound by its tenets and discipline as expressed in the quoted conference resolutions: each is a follower of the teachings of Jesus Christ: each accepts as a guide His teachings and those of the Bible, and holds as a part of his religious and conscientious belief that war, training for war, and military training are immoral, wrong, and contrary to the letter and spirit of His teaching and the precepts of the Christian religion.

Therefore these students at the beginning of the fall term in 1933 petitioned the University for exemption from military training and participation in the activities of the training corps, upon the ground of their religious and conscientious objection to war and to military training. Their petition was denied. Thereupon, through that church's bishop in California, they and their fathers petitioned the regents that military training be made optional in order that conscientious and religious objectors to war, training for war, and military training might not be confronted with the necessity of violating and forswearing their beliefs or being denied the right of education in the State University to which these minors are entitled under the Constitution and laws of the state of California and of the United States.

The regents refused to make military training optional or to exempt these students. Then, because of their religious and conscientious objections, they declined to take the prescribed course, and solely upon that ground the regents by formal notification suspended them from the University, but with leave to apply for readmission at any time conditioned upon their ability and willingness to comply with all applicable regulations of the University governing the matriculation and attendance of students. The University affords opportunity for education such as may not be had at any other institution in California except at a greater cost which these minors are not able to pay. And they, as appellees at the time of their suspension well knew, are willing to take as a substitute for military training such other courses as may be prescribed by the University.

Other allegations of the petition need not be stated, as they merely go to show the grounds upon which appellants under the state practice sought the writ of mandate. . . .

The petition is not to be understood as showing that students required by the regents' order to take the prescribed course thereby serve in the Army or in any sense become a part of the military establishment of the United States. Nor is the allegation that the courses are prescribed by the War Department to be taken literally. We take judicial notice of the long-established voluntary co-operation between federal and state authorities in respect of the military instruction given in the land grant colleges. The War Department has not been empowered to determine, or in any manner to prescribe, the military instruction in these institutions. The furnishing of officers, men, and equipment conditioned upon the giving of courses and the imposing of discipline deemed appropriate, recommended, or approved by the Department does not support the suggestion that the training is not exclusively prescribed and given under the authority of the state. The states are interested in the safety of the United States, the strength of its military forces, and its readiness to defend them in war and against every attack of public enemies. Undoubtedly every state has authority to train its able-bodied male citizens of suitable age appropriately to develop fitness, should any such duty be laid upon them, to serve in the United States Army or in state militia, always liable to be called forth by federal authority to execute the laws of the Union, suppress insurrection, or repel invasion, or as members of local constabulary forces or as officers needed effectively to police the state. And, when made possible by the national government, the state, in order more effectively to teach and train its citizens for these and like purposes, may avail itself of the services of officers and equipment belonging to the military establishment of the United States. So long as its action is within retained powers and not inconsistent with any exertion of the authority of the national government and transgresses no right safeguarded to the citizen by the Federal Constitution, the state is the sole judge of the means to be employed and the amount of training to be exacted for the effective accomplishment of these ends.

The clauses of the Fourteenth Amendment invoked by appellants declare: "No State shall make or enforce any law which shall abridge the privileges or immunities of citizens of the United States: nor shall any State deprive any person of life, liberty, or property, without due process of law." Appellants' contentions are that the enforcement of the order prescribing instruction in military science and tactics abridges some privilege or immunity covered by the first clause and deprives of liberty safeguarded by the second. The "privileges and immunities" protected are only those that belong to citizens of the United States as distinguished from citizens of the states—those that arise from the Constitution and laws of the United States as contrasted with those that spring from other sources. Appellants assert—unquestionably in good faith—that all war, preparation for war, and the training required by the University are repugnant to the tenets and discipline of their church, to their religion, and to their consciences. The "privilege" of attending the University as a student comes not from federal sources but is given by the state. It is not within the asserted protection. The only "immunity" claimed by these students is freedom from obligation to comply with the rule prescribing military training. But that "immunity" cannot be regarded as not within, or as distinguishable from, the "liberty" of which they claim to have been deprived by the enforcement of the regents' order. If the regents' order is not repugnant to the due process clause, then it does not violate the privileges and immunities clause. Therefore we need only decide whether by state action the "liberty" of these students has been infringed.

There need be no attempt to enumerate or comprehensively to define what is included in the "liberty" protected by the due process clause. Undoubtedly it does include the right to entertain the beliefs, to adhere to the principles, and to teach the doctrines on which these students base their objections to the order prescribing military training. The fact that they are able to pay their way in this University but not in any other institution in California is without significance upon any constitutional or other question here involved. California has not drafted or called them to attend the University. They are seeking education offered by the state and at the same time insisting that they be excluded from the prescribed course solely upon grounds of their religious beliefs and conscientious objections to war, preparation for war, and military education. Taken on the basis of the facts alleged in the petition, appellants' contentions amount to no more than an assertion that the due process clause of the Fourteenth Amendment as a safeguard of "liberty" confers the right to be students in the State University free from obligation to take military training as one of the conditions of attendance.

Viewed in the light of our decisions, that proposition must at once be put aside as untenable.

Government, federal and state, each in its own sphere owes a duty to the people within its jurisdiction to preserve itself in adequate strength to maintain peace and order and to assure the just enforcement of law. And every citizen owes the reciprocal duty, according to his capacity, to support and defend government against all enemies.

United States v. Schwimmer, involved a petition for naturalization by one opposed to bearing arms in defense of country. Holding the applicant not entitled to citizenship we said: "That it is the duty of citizens by force of arms to defend our government against all enemies . . . whenever necessity arises is a fundamental principle of the Constitution. Whatever tends to lessen the willingness of citizens to discharge their duty to bear arms in the country's defense detracts from the strength and safety of the government."

In United States v. Macintosh, a later naturalization case, the applicant was unwilling, because of conscientious objections, to take unqualifiedly the statutory oath of allegiance which contains this statement: "That he will support and defend the Constitution and laws of the United States against all enemies, foreign and domestic, and bear true faith and allegiance to the same." His petition stated that he was willing, if necessary, to take up arms in defense of this country, "but I should want to be free to judge of the necessity." In amplification he said: "I do not undertake to support 'my country, right or wrong' in any dispute which may arise, and I am not willing to promise beforehand, and without knowing the cause for which my country may go to war, either that I will or that I will not 'take up arms in defense of this country,' however 'necessary' the war may seem to be to the Government of the day." The opinion of this court quotes from petitioner's brief a statement to the effect that it is a "fixed principle of our Constitution, zealously guarded by our laws, that a citizen cannot be forced and need not bear arms in a war if he has conscientious religious scruples against doing so." And, referring to that part of the argument in behalf of the applicant, this court said: "This, if it means what it seems to say, is an astonishing statement. Of course, there is no such principle of the Constitution, fixed or otherwise. The conscientious objector is relieved from the obligation to bear arms in obedience to no constitutional provision, express or implied; but because, and only because, it has accorded with the policy of Congress thus to relieve him. . . . The privilege of the native-born conscientious objector to avoid bearing arms comes, not from the Constitution, but from the acts of Congress. That body may grant or withhold the exemption as in its wisdom it sees fit; and, if it be withheld, the native-born conscientious objector cannot successfully assert the privilege. No other conclusion is compatible with the well-nigh limitless extent of the war powers as above illustrated, which include, by necessary implication, the power, in the last extremity, to compel the armed service of any citizen in the land, without regard to his objections or his views in respect of the justice or morality of the particular war or of war in general. In Jacobson v. Massachusetts, this court (upholding a state compulsory vaccination law), speaking of the liberties guaranteed to the individual by the Fourteenth Amendment, said: . . . And yet he may be compelled, by force if need be, against his will and without regard to his personal wishes or his pecuniary interests, or even his religious or political convictions, to take his place in the ranks of the army of his country, and risk the chance of being shot down in its defense.' "

And see Pearson v. Coale, a case, similar to that now before us, decided against the contention of a student in the University of Maryland who on conscientious grounds objected to military training there required. His appeal to this Court was dismissed for the want of a substantial federal question.

Plainly there is no ground for the contention that the regents' order, requiring able-bodied male students under the age of twenty-four as a condition of their enrollment to take the prescribed instruction in military science and tactics, transgresses any constitutional right asserted by these appellants.

The contention that the regents' order is repugnant to the Briand-Kellogg Peace Pact requires little consideration. In that instrument the United States and the other high contracting parties declare that they condemn recourse to war for the solution of international controversies and renounce it as an instrument of national policy in their relations with one another and agree that the settlement or solution of all disputes or conflicts which may arise among them shall never be sought except by pacific means. Clearly there is no conflict between the regents' order and the provisions of this treaty.

MR. JUSTICE CARDOZO.

Concurring in the opinion, I wish to say an extra word.

I assume for present purposes that the religious liberty protected by the First Amendment against invasion by the nation is protected by the Fourteenth Amendment against invasion by the states.

Accepting that premise, I cannot find in the respondents' ordinance an obstruction by the state to "the free exercise" of religion as the phrase was understood by the founders of the nation, and by the generations that have followed.

There is no occasion at this time to mark the limits of governmental power in the exaction of military service when the nation is at peace. The petitioners have not been required to bear arms for any hostile purpose, offensive or defensive, either now or in the future. They have not even been required in any absolute or peremptory way to join in courses of instruction that will fit them to bear arms. If they elect to resort to an institution for higher education maintained with the state's moneys, then and only then they are commanded to follow courses of instruction believed by the state to be vital to its welfare. This may be condemned by some as unwise or illiberal or unfair when there is violence to conscientious scruples, either religious or merely ethical. More must be shown to set the ordinance at naught. In controversies of this order, courts do not concern themselves with matters of legislative policy, unrelated to privileges or liberties secured by the organic law. The First Amendment, if it be read into the Fourteenth, makes invalid any state law "respecting an establishment of religion, or prohibiting the free exercise thereof." Instruction in military science is not instruction in the practice or tenets of a religion. Neither directly nor indirectly is government establishing a state religion when it insists upon such training. Instruction in military science, unaccompanied here by any pledge of military service, is not an interference by the state with the free exercise of religion when the liberties of the Constitution are read in the light of a century and a half of history during days of peace and war.

The meaning of those liberties has striking illustration in statutes that were enacted in colonial times and later. They will be found collected in the opinion of the lower court in MacIntosh v. U.S., and more fully in the briefs of counsel. From the beginnings of our history, Quakers and other conscientious objectors have been exempted as an act of grace from military service, but the exemption, when granted, has been coupled with a condition, at least in many instances, that they supply the Army with a substitute or with the money necessary to hire one. This was done in Virginia in 1738 and 1782; in North Carolina; and in New York Colonial Laws. A like practice has been continued in the Constitutions of many of the states. For one opposed to force, the affront to conscience must be greater in furnishing men and money wherewith to wage a pending contest than in studying military science without the duty or the pledge of service. Never in our history has the notion been accepted, or even, it is believed advanced, that acts thus indirectly related to service in the camp or field are so tied to the practice of religion as to be exempt, in law or in morals, from regulation by the state. On the contrary, the very lawmakers who are willing to give release from warlike acts had no thought that they were doing anything inconsistent with the moral claims of an objector, still less with his constitutional immunities, in coupling the exemption with these collateral conditions.

Manifestly a different doctrine would carry us to lengths that have never yet been dreamed of. The conscientious objector, if his liberties were to be thus extended, might refuse to contribute taxes in furtherance of a war, whether for attack or for defense, or in furtherance of any other end condemned by his conscience as irreligious or immoral. The right of private judgment has never yet been so exalted above the powers and the compulsion of the agencies of government. One who is a martyr to a principle—which may turn out in the end to be a delusion or an error—does not prove by his martyrdom that he has kept within the law.

I am authorized to state that Mr. Justice Brandeis and Mr. Justice Stone join in this opinion.

CANTWELL v. CONNECTICUT   310 US 296 (1940)

"In the realm of religious faith, and in that of political belief, sharp differences arise. In both fields the tenets of one man may seem the rankest error to his neighbor. To persuade others to his own point of view, the pleader, as we know, at times, resorts to exaggeration, to vilification of men who have been, or are, prominent in church or state, and even to false statement. But the people of this nation have ordained in the light of history, that, in spite of the probability of excesses and abuses, these liberties are, in the long view, essential to enlightened opinion and right conduct on the part of citizens of a democracy."

Mr. Justice Roberts, for the Court

This is the first of a series of cases involving Jehovah's Witnesses. It is also the first of a number of cases dealing with problems growing out of the attempts of communities to regulate or control proselytizing.

MR. JUSTICE ROBERTS DELIVERED THE OPINION OF THE COURT.

Newton Cantwell and his two sons, Jesse and Russell, members of a group known as Jehovah's Witnesses, and claiming to be ordained ministers were arrested in New Haven, Connecticut, and each was charged by information in five counts, with statutary and common law offenses. After trial in the Court of Common Pleas of New Haven County each of them was convicted on the third count, which charged a violation of 6294 of the General Statutes of Connecticut, and on the fifth count, which charged commission of the common law offenses of inciting a breach of the peace. On appeal to the Supreme Court the conviction of all three on the third count was affirmed. The conviction of Jesse Cantwell, on the fifth count, was also affirmed, but the conviction of Newton and Russell on that count was reversed and a new trial ordered as to them.

By demurrers to the information, by requests for rulings of law at the trial, and by their assignments of error in the State Supreme Court, the appellants pressed the contention that the statute under which the third count was drawn was offensive to the due process clause of the Fourteenth Amendment because, on its face and as construed and applied, it denied them freedom of speech and prohibited their free exercise of religion. In like manner they made the point that they could not be found guilty on the fifth count, without violation of the Amendment.

We have jurisdiction on appeal from the judgments on the third count, as there was drawn in question the validity of a state statute under the Federal Constitution, and the decision was in favor of validity. Since the conviction on the fifth count was not based upon a statute, but presents a substantial question under the Federal Constitution, we granted the writ of certiorari in respect of it.

The facts adduced to sustain the convictions on the third count follow. On the day of their arrest the appellants were engaged in going singly from house to house on Cassius Street in New Haven. They were individually equipped with a bag containing books and pamphlets on religious subjects, a portable phonograph and a set of records, each of which, when played, introduced, and was a description of, one of the books. Each appellant asked the person who responded to his call for permission to play one of the records. If permission was granted he asked the person to buy the book described and, upon refusal, he solicited such contribution towards the publication of the pamphlets as the listener was willing to make. If a contribution was received a pamphlet was delivered upon condition that it would be read.

Cassius Street is in a thickly populated neighborhood, where about ninety per cent of the residents are Roman Catholics. A phonograph record, describing a book entitled "Enemies," included an attack on the Catholic religion. None of the persons interviewed were members of Jehovah's Witnesses.

The statute under which the appellants were charged provides:

"No person shall solicit money, services, subscriptions or any valuable thing for any alleged religious, charitable or philanthropic cause, from other than a member of the organization for whose benefit such person is soliciting or within the county in which such person or organization is located unless such cause shall have been approved by the secretary of the public welfare council. Upon application of any person in behalf of such cause, the secretary shall determine whether such cause is a religious one or is a bona fide object of charity or philanthropy and conforms to reasonable standards of efficiency and integrity, and, if he shall so find, shall approve the same and issue to the authority in charge a certificate to that effect. Such certificate may be revoked at any time. Any person violating any provision of this section shall be fined not more than one hundred dollars or imprisoned not more than thirty days or both."

The appellants claimed that their activities were not within the statute but consisted only of distribution of books, pamphlets, and periodicals. The State Supreme Court construed the finding of the trial court to be that "in addition to the sale of the books and the distribution of the pamphlets the defendants were also soliciting contributions or donations of money for an alleged religious cause, and thereby came within the purview of the statute." It overruled the contention that the Act, as applied to the appellants, offends the due process clause of the Fourteenth Amendment, because it abridges or denies religious freedom and liberty of speech and press. The court stated that it was the solicitation that brought the appellants within the sweep of the Act and not their other activities in the dissemination of literature. It declared the legislation constitutional as an effort by the State to protect the public against fraud and imposition in the solicitation of funds for what purported to be religious, charitable, or philanthropic causes.

The facts which were held to support the conviction of Jesse Cantwell on the fifth count were that he stopped two men in the street, asked, and received, permission to play a phonograph record, and played the record "Enemies," which attacked the religion and church of the two men, who were Catholics. Both were incensed by the contents of the record and were tempted to strike Cantwell unless he went away. On being told to be on his way he left their presence. There was no evidence that he was personally offensive or entered into any argument with those he interviewed.

The court held that the charge was not assault or breach of the peace or threats on Cantwell's part, but invoking or inciting others to breach of the peace, and that the facts supported the conviction of that offense.

First. We hold that the statute, as construed and applied to the appellants, deprives them of their liberty without due process of law in contravention of the Fourteenth Amendment. The fundamental concept of liberty embodied in that Amendment embraces the liberties guaranteed by the First Amendment. The First Amendment declares that Congress shall make no law respecting an establishment of religion or prohibiting the free exercise thereof. The Fourteenth Amendment has rendered the legislatures of the states as incompetent as Congress to enact such laws. The constitutional inhibition of legislation on the subject of religion has a double aspect. On the one hand, it forestalls compulsion by law of the acceptance of any creed or the practice of any form of worship. Freedom of conscience and freedom to adhere to such religious organization or form of worship as the individual may choose cannot be restricted by law. On the other hand, it safeguards the free exercise of the chosen form of religion. Thus the Amendment embraces two concepts,—freedom to believe and freedom to act. The first is absolute but, in the nature of things, the second cannot be. Conduct remains subject to regulation for the protection of society. The freedom to act must have appropriate definition to preserve the enforcement of that protection. In every case the power to regulate must be so exercised as not, in attaining a permissible end, unduly to infringe the protected freedom. No one would contest the proposition that a State may not, by statute, wholly deny the right to preach or to disseminate religious views. Plainly such a previous and absolute restraint would violate the terms of the guarantee. It is equally clear that a State may by general and non-discriminatory legislation regulate the times, the places, and the manner of soliciting upon its streets, and of holding meetings thereon; and may in other respects safeguard the peace, good order and comfort of the community, without unconstitutionally invading the liberties protected by the Fourteenth Amendment. The appellants are right in their insistence that the Act in question is not such a regulation. If a certificate is procured, solicitation is permitted without restraint but, in the absence of a certificate, solicitation is altogether prohibited.

The appellants urge that to require them to obtain a certificate as a condition of soliciting support for their views amounts to a prior restraint on the exercise of their religion within the meaning of the Constitution. The State insists that the Act, as construed by the Supreme Court of Connecticut, imposes no previous restraint upon the dissemination of religious views or teaching but merely safeguards against the perpetration of frauds under the cloak of religion. Conceding that this is so, the question remains whether the method adopted by Connecticut to that end transgresses the liberty safeguarded by the Constitution.

The general regulation, in the public interest, of solicitation, which does not involve any religious test and does not unreasonably obstruct or delay the collection of funds, is not open to any constitutional objection, even though the collection be for a religious purpose. Such regulation would not constitute a prohibited previous restraint on the free exercise of religion or interpose an inadmissible obstacle to its exercise.

It will be noted, however, that the Act requires an application to the secretary of the public welfare council of the State; that he is empowered to determine whether the cause is a religious one, and that the issue of a certificate depends upon his affirmative action. If he finds that the cause is not that of religion, to solicit for it becomes a crime. He is not to issue a certificate as a matter of course. His decision to issue or refuse it involves appraisal of facts, the exercise of judgment, and the formation of an opinion. He is authorized to withhold his approval if he determines that the cause is not a religious one. Such a censorship of religion as the means of determining its right to survive is a denial of liberty protected by the First Amendment and included in the liberty which is within the protection of the Fourteenth.

The State asserts that if the licensing officer acts arbitrarily, capriciously, or corruptly, his action is subject to judicial correction. Counsel refer to the rule prevailing in Connecticut that the decision of a commission or an administrative official will be reviewed upon a claim that "it works material damage to individual or corporate rights, or invades or threatens such rights, or is so unreasonable as to justify judicial intervention, or is not consonant with justice, or that a legal duty has not been performed." It is suggested that the statute is to be read as requiring the officer to issue a certificate unless the cause in question is clearly not a religious one; and that if he violates his duty his action will be corrected by a court.

To this suggestion there are several sufficient answers. The line between a discretionary and a ministerial act is not always easy to mark and the statute has not been construed by the state court to impose a mere ministerial duty on the secretary of the welfare council. Upon his decision as to the nature of the cause, the right to solicit depends. Moreover, the availability of a judicial remedy for abuses in the system of licensing still leaves that system one of previous restraint which, in the field of free speech and press, we have held inadmissible. A statute authorizing previous restraint upon the exercise of the guaranteed freedom by judicial decision after trial is as obnoxious to the Constitution as one providing for like restraint by administrative action.

Nothing we have said is intended even remotely to imply that, under the cloak of religion, persons may, with impunity, commit frauds upon the public. Certainly penal laws are available to punish such conduct. Even the exercise of religion may be at some slight inconvenience in order that the state may protect its citizens from injury. Without doubt a State may protect its citizens from fraudulent solicitation by requiring a stranger in the community, before permitting him publicly to solicit funds for any purpose, to establish his identity and his authority to act for the cause which he purports to represent. The State is likewise free to regulate the time and manner of solicitation generally, in the interest of public safety, peace, comfort or convenience. But to condition the solicitation of aid for the perpetuation of religious views or systems upon a license, the grant of which rests in the exercise of a determination by state authority as to what is a religious cause, is to lay a forbidden burden upon the exercise of liberty protected by the Constitution.

Second. We hold that, in the circumstances disclosed, the conviction of Jesse Cantwell on the fifth count must be set aside. Decision as to the lawfulness of the conviction demands the weighing of two conflicting interests. The fundamental law declares the interest of the United States that the free exercise of religion be not prohibited and that freedom to communicate information and opinion be not abridged. The State of Connecticut has an obvious interest in the preservation and protection of peace and good order within her borders. We must determine whether the alleged protection of the State's interest, means to which end would, in the absence of limitation by the Federal Constitution, lie wholly within the State's discretion, has been pressed, in this instance, to a point where it has come into fatal collision with the overriding interest protected by the federal compact.

Conviction on the fifth count was not pursuant to a statute evincing a legislative judgment that street discussion of religious affairs, because of its tendency to provoke disorder, should be regulated, or a judgment that the playing of a phonograph on the streets should in the interest of comfort or privacy be limited or prevented. Violation of an Act exhibiting such a legislative judgment and narrowly drawn to prevent the supposed evil, would pose a question differing from that we must here answer. Such a declaration of the State's policy would weigh heavily in any challenge of the law as infringing constitutional limitations. Here, however, the judgment is based on a common law concept of the most general and undefined nature. The court below has held that the petitioner's conduct constituted the commission of an offense under the state law, and we accept its decision as binding upon us to that extent.

The offense known as breach of the peace embraces a great variety of conduct destroying or menacing public order and tranquility. It includes not only violent acts but acts and words likely to produce violence in others. No one would have the hardihood to suggest that the principle of freedom of speech sanctions incitement to riot or that religious liberty connotes the privilege to exhort others to physical attack upon those belonging to another sect. When clear and present danger of riot, disorder, interference with traffic upon the public streets, or other immediate threat to public safety, peace, or order, appears, the power of the State to prevent or punish is obvious. Equally obvious is it that a State may not unduly suppress free communication of views, religious or other, under the guise of conserving desirable conditions. Here we have a situation analogous to a conviction under a statute sweeping in a great variety of conduct under a general and indefinite characterization, and leaving to the executive and judicial branches too wide a discretion in its application.

Having these considerations in mind, we note that Jesse Cantwell, on April 25, 1938, was upon a public street, where he had a right to be, and where he had a right peacefully to impart his views to others. There is no showing that his deportment was noisy, truculent, over-bearing or offensive. He requested of two pedestrians permission to play to them a phonograph record. The permission was granted. It is not claimed that he intended to insult or affront the hearers by playing the record. It is plain that he wished only to interest them in his propaganda. The sound of the phonograph is not shown to have disturbed residents of the street, to have drawn a crowd, or to have impeded traffic. Thus far he had invaded no right or interest of the public or of the men accosted.

The record played by Cantwell embodies a general attack on all organized religious systems as instruments of Satan and injurious to man; it then singles out the Roman Catholic Church for strictures couched in terms which naturally would offend not only persons of that persuasion, but all others who respect the honestly held religious faith of their fellows. The hearers were in fact highly offended. One of them said he felt like hitting Cantwell and the other that he was tempted to throw Cantwell off the street. The one who testified he felt like hitting Cantwell said, in answer to the question "Did you do anything else or have any other reaction?" "no, sir, because he said he would take the victrola and he went." The other witness testified that he told Cantwell he had better get off the street before something happened to him and that was the end of the matter as Cantwell picked up his books and walked up the street.

Cantwell's conduct, in the view of the court below, considered apart from the effect of his communication upon his hearers, did not amount to a breach of the peace. One may, however, be guilty of the offense if he commit acts or make statements likely to provoke violence and disturbance of good order, even though no such eventuality be intended. Decisions to this effect are many, but examination discloses that, in practically all, the provocative language which was held to amount to a breach of the peace consisted of profane, indecent, or abusive remarks directed to the person of the hearer. Resort to epithets or personal abuse is not in any proper sense communication of information or opinion safeguarded by the Constitution, and its punishment as a criminal act would raise no question under that instrument.

We find in the instant case no assault or threatening of bodily harm, no truculent bearing, no intentional discourtesy, no personal abuse. On the contrary, we find only an effort to persuade a willing listener to buy a book or to contribute money in the interest of what Cantwell, however misguided others may think him, conceived to be true religion.

In the realm of religious faith, and in that of political belief, sharp differences arise. In both fields the tenets of one man may seem the rankest error to his neighbor. To persuade others to his own point of view, the pleader, as we know, at times, resorts to exaggeration, to vilification of men who have been, or are, prominent in church or state, and even to false statement. But the people of this nation have ordained in the light of history, that, in spite of the probability of excesses and abuses, these liberties are, in the long view, essential to enlightened opinion and right conduct on the part of the citizens of a democracy.

The essential characteristic of these liberties is, that under their shield many types of life, character, opinion and belief can develop unmolested and unobstructed. Nowhere is this shield more necessary than in our own country for a people composed of many races and of many creeds. There are limits to the exercise of these liberties. The danger in these times from the coercive activities of those who in the delusion of racial or religious conceit would incite violence and breaches of the peace in order to deprive others of their equal right to the exercise of their liberties, is emphasized by events familiar to all. These and other transgressions of those limits the States appropriately may punish.

Although the contents of the record not unnaturally aroused animosity, we think that, in the absence of a statute narrowly drawn to define and punish specific conduct as constituting a clear and present danger to a substantial interest of the State, the petitioner's communication, considered in the light of the constitutional guarantees, raised no such clear and present menace to public peace and order as to render him liable to conviction of the common law offense in question.

The judgment affirming the convictions on the third and fifth counts is reversed and the cause is remanded for further proceedings not inconsistent with this opinion. Reversed.

MINERSVILLE SCHOOL DISTRICT v. GOBITIS
310 US 586 (1940)

"That the flag salute is an allowable portion of a school program for those who do not invoke conscientious scruples is surely not debatable. But for us to insist that, though the ceremony may be required, exceptional immunity must be given to dissidents, is to maintain that there is no basis for a legislative judgment that such an exemption might introduce elements of difficulty into the school discipline, might cast doubts in the minds of other children which would themselves weaken the effect of the exercise."

Mr. Justice Frankfurter, for the Court

". . . I am not prepared to say that the right of this small and helpless minority, including children having a strong religious conviction, whether they understand its nature or not, to refrain from an expression obnoxious to their religion, is to be overborne by the interest of the state in maintaining discipline in the schools."

Mr. Justice Stone, dissenting

This case may well be regarded as the opening shot of a battle which raged through the decade of the 1940's and which found the Court deeply divided over the meaning of the religious clauses of the First Amendment. The decision given here was widely discussed and criticized and when the problem came to the Court again in 1943 the Court reversed its position.

MR. JUSTICE FRANKFURTER DELIVERED THE OPINION OF THE COURT.

A grave responsibility confronts this Court whenever in course of litigation it must reconcile the conflicting claims of liberty and authority. But when the liberty invoked is liberty of conscience, and the authority is authority to safeguard the nation's fellowship, judicial conscience is put to its severest test. Of such a nature is the present controversy.

Lillian Gobitis, aged twelve, and her brother William, aged ten, were expelled from the public schools of Minersville, Pennsylvania, for refusing to salute the national flag as part of a daily school exercise. The local Board of Education required both teachers and pupils to participate in this ceremony. The ceremony is a familiar one. The right hand is placed on the breast and the following pledge recited in unison: "I pledge allegiance to my flag, and to the Republic for which it stands; one nation indivisible, with liberty and justice for all." While the words are spoken, teachers and pupils extend their right hands in salute to the flag. The Gobitis family are affiliated with "Jehovah's Witnesses," for whom the Bible as the Word of God is the supreme authority. The children had been brought up conscientiously to believe that such a gesture of respect for the flag was forbidden by command of Scripture.

The Gobitis children were of an age for which Pennsylvania makes school attendance compulsory. Thus they were denied a free education, and their parents had to put them into private schools. To be relieved of the financial burden thereby entailed, their father, on behalf of the children and in his own behalf, brought this suit. He sought to enjoin the authorities from continuing to exact participation in the flag-salute ceremony as a condition of his children's attendance at the Minersville school. After trial of the issues, Judge Maris gave relief in the District Court, on the basis of a thoughtful opinion at a preliminary stage of the litigation, his decree was affirmed by the Circuit Court of Appeals. Since this decision ran counter to several per curiam dispositions of this Court, we granted certiorari to give the matter full reconsideration. By their able submissions, the Committee on the Bill of Rights of the American Bar Association and the American Civil Liberties Union, as friends of the Court, have helped us to our conclusion.

We must decide whether the requirement of participation in such a ceremony, exacted from a child who refuses upon sincere religious grounds, infringes without due process of law the liberty guaranteed by the Fourteenth Amendment.

Centuries of strife over the erection of particular dogmas as exclusive or all-comprehending faiths led to the inclusion of a guarantee for religious freedom in the Bill of Rights. The First Amendment, and the Fourteenth through its absorption of the First, sought to guard against repetition of those bitter religious struggles by prohibiting the establishment of a state religion and by securing to every sect the free exercise of its faith. So pervasive is the acceptance of this precious right that its scope is brought into question, as here, only when the conscience of individuals collides with the felt necessities of society.

Certainly the affirmative pursuit of one's convictions about the ultimate mystery of the universe and man's relation to it is placed beyond the reach of law. Government may not interfere with organized or individual expression of belief or disbelief. Propagation of belief—or even of disbelief—in the supernatural is protected, whether in church or chapel, mosque or synagogue, tabernacle or meeting-house. Likewise the Constitution assures generous immunity to the individual from imposition of penalties for offending, in the course of his own religious activities, the religious views of others, be they a minority or those who are dominant in government.

But the manifold character of man's relations may bring his conception of religious duty into conflict with the secular interests of his fellow-men. When does the constitutional guarantee compel exemption from doing what society thinks necessary for the promotion of some great common end, or from a penalty for conduct which appears dangerous to the general good? To state the problem is to recall the truth that no single principle can answer all of life's complexities. The right to freedom of religious belief, however dissident and however obnoxious to the cherished beliefs of others—even of a majority—is itself the denial of an absolute. But to affirm that the freedom to follow conscience has itself no limits in the life of a society would deny that very plurality of principles which, as a matter of history, underlies protection of religious toleration. Our present task, then, as so often the case with courts, is to reconcile two rights in order to prevent either from destroying the other. But, because in safe-guarding conscience we are dealing with interests so subtle and so dear, every possible leeway should be given to the claims of religious faith.

In the judicial enforcement of religious freedom we are concerned with a historic concept. The religious liberty which the Constitution protects has never excluded legislation of general scope not directed against doctrinal loyalties of particular sects. Judicial nullification of legislation cannot be justified by attributing to the framers of the Bill of Rights views for which there is no historic warrant. Conscientious scruples have not, in the course of the long struggle for religious toleration, relieved the individual from obedience to a general law not aimed at the promotion or restriction of religious beliefs. The mere possession of religious convictions which contradict the relevant concerns of a political society does not relieve the citizen from the discharge of political responsibilities. The necessity for this adjustment has again and again been recognized. In a number of situations the exertion of political authority has been sustained, while basic considerations of religious freedom have been left inviolate. Reynolds v. United States; Davis v. Beason; Selective Draft Law Cases; Hamilton v. Regents. In all these cases the general laws in question, upheld in their application to those who refused obedience from religious conviction, were manifestations of specific powers of government deemed by the legislature essential to secure and maintain the orderly, tranquil, and free society without which religious toleration itself is unattainable. Nor does the freedom of speech assured by Due Process move in a more absolute circle of immunity than that enjoyed by religious freedom. Even if it were assumed that freedom of speech goes beyond the historic concept of full opportunity to utter and to disseminate views, however heretical or offensive to dominant opinion, and includes freedom from conveying what may be deemed an implied but rejected affirmation, the question remains whether school children, like the Gobitis children, must be excused from conduct required of all the other children in the promotion of national cohesion. We are dealing with an interest inferior to none in the hierarchy of legal values. National unity is the basis of national security. To deny the legislature the right to select appropriate means for its attainment presents a totally different order of problem from that of the propriety of subordinating the possible ugliness of littered streets to the free expression of opinion through distribution of handbills.

Situations like the present are phases of the profoundest problem confronting a democracy—the problem which Lincoln cast in memorable dilemma. "Must a government of necessity be too strong for the liberties of its people, or too weak to maintain its own existence?" No mere textual reading or logical talisman can solve the dilemma. And when the issue demands judicial determination, it is not the personal notion of judges of what wise adjustment requires which must prevail.

Unlike the instances we have cited, the case before us is not concerned with an exertion of legislative power for the promotion of some specific need or interest of secular society—the protection of the family, the promotion of health, the common defense, the raising of public revenues to defray the cost of government. But all these specific activities of government presuppose the existence of an organized political society. The ultimate foundation of a free society is the binding tie of cohesive sentiment. Such a sentiment is fostered by all those agencies of the mind and spirit which may serve to gather up the traditions of a people, transmit them from generation to generation, and thereby create that continuity of a treasured common life which constitutes a civilization. "We live by symbols." The flag is the symbol of our national unity, transcending all internal differences, however large, within the framework of the Constitution. This Court has had occasion to say that ". . . the flag is the symbol of the Nation's power, the emblem of freedom in its truest, best sense . . . it signifies government resting on the consent of the governed; liberty regulated by law; the protection of the weak against the strong; security against the exercise of arbitrary power; and absolute safety for free institutions against foreign aggression." Halter v. Nebraska.

The case before us must be viewed as though the legislature of Pennsylvania had itself formally directed the flag-salute for the children of Minersville; had made no exemption for children whose parents were possessed of conscientious scruples like those of the Gobitis family; and had indicated its belief in the desirable ends to be secured by having its public school children share a common experience at those periods of development when their minds are supposedly receptive to its assimilation, by an exercise appropriate in time and place and setting and one designed to evoke in them appreciation of the nation's hopes and dreams, its sufferings and sacrifices. The precise issue, then, for us to decide is whether the legislatures of the various states and the authorities in a thousand counties and school districts of this country are barred from determining the appropriateness of various means to evoke that unifying sentiment without which there can ultimately be no liberties, civil or religious.

To stigmatize legislative judgment in providing for this universal gesture of respect for the symbol of our national life in the setting of the common school as a lawless inroad on that freedom of conscience which the Constitution protects, would amount to no less than the pronouncement of pedagogical and psychological dogma in a field where courts possess no marked and certainly no controlling competence. The influences which help toward a common feeling for the common country are manifold. Some may seem harsh and others no doubt are foolish. Surely, however, the end is legitimate. And the effective means for its attainment are still so uncertain and so unauthenticated by science as to preclude us from putting the widely prevalent belief in flag-saluting beyond the pale of legislative power. It mocks reason and denies our whole history to find in the allowance of a requirement to salute our flag on fitting occasions the seeds of sanction for obeisance to a leader.

The wisdom of training children in patriotic impulses by those compulsions which necessarily pervade so much of the educational process is not for our independent judgment. Even were we convinced of the folly of such a measure, such belief would be no proof of its unconstitutionality. For ourselves, we might be tempted to say that the deepest patriotism is best engendered by giving unfettered scope to the most crochety beliefs. Perhaps it is best, even from the standpoint of those interests which ordinances like the one under review seek to promote, to give to the least popular sect leave from conformities like those here in issue. But the courtroom is not the arena for debating issues of educational policy. It is not our province to choose among competing considerations in the subtle process of securing effective loyalty to the traditional ideals of democracy, while respecting at the same time individual idiosyncracies among a people so diversified in racial origins and religious allegiances. So to hold would in effect make us the school board for the country. That authority has not been given to this Court, nor should we assume it.

We are dealing here with the formative period in the development of citizenship. Great diversity of psychological and ethical opinion exists among us concerning the best way to train children for their place in society. Because of these differences and because of reluctance to permit a single, iron-cast system of education to be imposed upon a nation compounded of so many strains, we have held that, even though public education is one of our most cherished democratic institutions, the Bill of Rights bars a state from compelling all children to attend the public schools. Pierce v. Society of Sisters. But it is a very different thing for this Court to exercise censorship over the conviction of legislatures that a particular program or exercise will best promote in the minds of children who attend the common schools an attachment to the institutions of their country.

What the school authorities are really asserting is the right to awaken in the child's mind considerations as to the significance of the flag contrary to those implanted by the parent. In such an attempt the state is normally at a disadvantage in competing with the parent's authority, so long—and this is the vital aspect of religious toleration—as parents are unmolested in their right to counteract by their own persuasiveness the wisdom and rightness of those loyalties which the state's educational system is seeking to promote. Except where the transgression of constitutional liberty is too plain for argument, personal freedom is best maintained—so long as the remedial channels of the democratic process remain open and unobstructed—when it is ingrained in a people's habits and not enforced against popular policy by the coercion of adjudicated law. That the flag-salute is an allowable portion of a school program for those who do not invoke conscientious scruples is surely not debatable. But for us to insist that, though the ceremony may be required, exceptional immunity must be given to dissidents, is to maintain that there is no basis for a legislative judgment that such an exemption might introduce elements of difficulty into the school discipline, might cast doubts in the minds of the other children which would themselves weaken the effect of the exercise.

The preciousness of the family relation, the authority and independence which give dignity to parenthood, indeed the enjoyment of all freedom, presuppose the kind of ordered society which is summarized by our flag. A society which is dedicated to the preservation of these ultimate values of civilization may in self-protection utilize the educational process for inculcating those almost unconscious feelings which bind men together in a comprehending loyalty, whatever may be their lesser differences and difficulties. That is to say, the process may be utilized so long as men's right to believe as they please, to win others to their way of belief, and their right to assemble in their chosen places of worship for the devotional ceremonies of their faith, are fully respected.

Judicial review, itself a limitation on popular government, is a fundamental part of our constitutional scheme. But to the legislature no less than to courts is committed the guardianship of deeply-cherished liberties. Where all the effective means of inducing political changes are left free from interference, education in the abandonment of foolish legislation is itself a training in liberty. To fight out the wise use of legislative authority in the forum of public opinion and before legislative assemblies rather than to transfer such a contest to the judicial arena, serves to vindicate the self-confidence of a free people.

MR. JUSTICE STONE, DISSENTING.

I think the judgment below should be affirmed.

Two youths, now fifteen and sixteen years of age, are by the judgment of this Court held liable to expulsion from the public schools and to denial of all publicly supported educational privileges because of their refusal to yield to the compulsion of a law which commands their participation in a school ceremony contrary to their religious convictions. They and their father are citizens and have not exhibited by any action or statement of opinion, any disloyalty to the Government of the United States. They are ready and willing to obey all its laws which do not conflict with what they sincerely believe to be the higher commandments of God. It is not doubted that these convictions are religious, that they are genuine, or that the refusal to yield to the compulsion of the law is in good faith and with all sincerity. It would be a denial of their faith as well as the teachings of most religions to say that children of their age could not have religious convictions.

The law which is thus sustained is unique in the history of Anglo-American legislation. It does more than suppress freedom of speech and more than prohibit the free exercise of religion, which concededly are forbidden by the First Amendment and are violations of the liberty guaranteed by the Fourteenth. For by this law the state seeks to coerce these children to express a sentiment which violates their deepest religious convictions. It is not denied that such compulsion is a prohibited infringement of personal liberty, freedom of speech and religion, guaranteed by the Bill of Rights, except in so far as it may be justified and supported as a proper exercise of the state's power over public education. Since the state, in competition with parents, may through teaching in the public schools indoctrinate the minds of the young, it is said that in aid of its undertaking to inspire loyalty and devotion to constituted authority and the flag which symbolizes it, it may coerce the pupil to make affirmation contrary to his belief and in violation of his religious faith. And, finally, it is said that since the Minersville School Board and others are of the opinion that the country will be better served by conformity than by the observance of religious liberty which the Constitution prescribes, the courts are not free to pass judgment on the Board's choice.

Concededly the constitutional guaranties of personal liberty are not always absolutes. Government has a right to survive and powers conferred upon it are not necessarily set at naught by the express prohibitions of the Bill of Rights. It may make war and raise armies. To that end it may compel citizens to give military service, and subject them to military training despite their religious objections.

It may suppress religious practices dangerous to morals, and presumably those also which are inimical to public safety, health and good order. But it is a long step, and one which I am unable to take, to the position that government may, as a supposed educational measure and as a means of disciplining the young, compel public affirmations which violate their religious conscience.

The very fact that we have constitutional guaranties of civil liberties and the specificity of their command where freedom of speech and of religion are concerned require some accommodation of the powers which government normally exercises, when no question of civil liberty is involved, to the constitutional demand that those liberties be protected against the action of government itself. The state concededly has power to require and control the education of its citizens, but it cannot by a general law compelling attendance to public schools preclude attendance at a private school adequate in its instruction, where the parent seeks to secure for the child the benefits of religious instruction not provided by the public school. And only recently we have held that the state's authority to control its public streets by generally applicable regulations is not an absolute to which free speech must yield, and cannot be made the medium of its suppression, any more than can its authority to penalize littering of the streets by a general law be used to suppress the distribution of handbills as a means of communicating ideas to their recipients.

In these cases it was pointed out that where there are competing demands of the interests of government and of liberty under the Constitution, and where the performance of governmental functions is brought into conflict with specific constitutional restrictions, there must, when that is possible, be reasonable accommodation between them so as to preserve the essentials of both and that it is the function of courts to determine whether such accommodation is reasonably possible. In the cases just mentioned the Court was of opinion that there were ways enough to secure the legitimate state end without infringing the asserted immunity, or that the inconvenience caused by the inability to secure that end satisfactorily through other means, did not outweigh freedom of speech or religion. So here, even if we believe that such compulsions will contribute to national unity, there are other ways to teach loyalty and patriotism which are the sources of national unity, than by compelling the pupil to affirm that which he does not believe and by commanding a form of affirmance which violates his religious convictions. Without recourse to such compulsion the state is free to compel attendance at school and require teaching by instruction and study of all in our history and in the structure and organization of our government, including the guaranties of civil liberty which tend to inspire patriotism and love of country. I cannot say that government here is deprived of any interest or function which it is entitled to maintain at the expense of the protection of civil liberties by requiring it to resort to the alternatives which do not coerce an affirmation of belief.

The guaranties of civil liberty are but guaranties of freedom of the human mind and spirit and of reasonable freedom and opportunity to express them. They presuppose the right of the individual to hold such opinions as he will and to give them reasonably free expression, and his freedom, and that of the state as well, to teach and persuade others by the communication of ideas. The very essence of the liberty which they guaranty is the freedom of the individual from compulsion as to what he shall think and what he shall say, at least where the compulsion is to bear false witness to his religion. If these guaranties are to have any meaning they must, I think, be deemed to withhold from the state any authority to compel belief or the expression of it where that expression violates religious convictions, whatever may be the legislative view of the desirability of such compulsion.

History teaches us that there have been but few infringements of personal liberty by the state which have not been justified, as they are here, in the name of righteousness and the public good, and few which have not been directed, as they are now, at politically helpless minorities. The framers were not unaware that under the system which they created most governmental curtailments of personal liberty would have the support of a legislative judgment that the public interest would be better served by its curtailment than by its constitutional protection. I cannot conceive that in prescribing, as limitations upon the powers of government, the freedom of the mind and spirit secured by the explicit guaranties of freedom of speech and religion, they intended or rightly could have left any latitude for a legislative judgment that the compulsory expression of belief which violates religious convictions would better serve the public interest than their protection. The Constitution may well elicit expressions of loyalty to it and to the government which it created, but it does not command such expressions or otherwise give any indication that compulsory expressions of loyalty play any such part in our scheme of government as to override the constitutional protection of freedom of speech and religion. And while such expressions of loyalty, when voluntarily given, may promote national unity, it is quite another matter to say that their own and their parents' religious convictions can be regarded as playing so important a part in our national unity as to leave school boards free to exact it despite the constitutional guarantee of freedom of religion. The very terms of the Bill of Rights preclude, it seems to me, any reconciliation of such compulsions with the constitutional guaranties by a legislative declaration that they are more important to the public welfare than the Bill of Rights.

But even if this view be rejected and it is considered that there is some scope for the determination by legislatures whether the citizen shall be compelled to give public expression of such sentiments contrary to his religion, I am not persuaded that we should refrain from passing upon the legislative judgment "as long as the remedial channels of the democratic process remain open and unobstructed." This seems to me no less than the surrender of the constitutional protection of the liberty of small minorities to the popular will. We have previously pointed to the importance of a searching judicial inquiry into the legislative judgment in situations where prejudice against discrete and insular minorities may tend to curtail the operation of those political processes ordinarily to be relied on to protect minorities. And until now we have not hesitated similarly to scrutinize legislation restricting the civil liberty of racial and religious minorities although no political process was affected. Here we have such a small minority entertaining in good faith a religious belief, which is such a departure from the usual course of human conduct, that most persons are disposed to regard it with little toleration or concern. In such circumstances careful scrutiny of legislative efforts to secure conformity of belief and opinion by a compulsory affirmation of the desired belief, is especially needful if civil rights are to receive any protection. Tested by this standard, I am not prepared to say that the right of this small and helpless minority, including children having a strong religious conviction, whether they understand its nature or not, to refrain from an expression obnoxious to their religion, is to be overborne by the interest of the state in maintaining discipline in the schools.

The Constitution expresses more than the conviction of the people that democratic processes must be preserved at all costs. It is also an expression of faith and a command that freedom of mind and spirit must be preserved, which government must obey, if it is to adhere to that justice and moderation without which no free government can exist. For this reason it would seem that legislation which operates to repress the religious freedom of small minorities, which is admittedly within the scope of the protection of the Bill of Rights, must at least be subject to the same judicial scrutiny as legislation which we have recently held to infringe the constitutional liberty of religious and racial minorities.

With such scrutiny I cannot say that the inconveniences which may attend some sensible adjustment of school discipline in order that the religious convictions of these children may be spared, presents a problem so momentous or pressing as to outweigh the freedom from compulsory violation of religious faith which has been thought worthy of constitutional protection.

NOTE

The problems posed by the proselytizing activity of Jehovah's Witnesses were not finally disposed of by the Cantwell case. The court found itself involved in a large number of cases posed by community attempts to apply to Witnesses various ordinances which impinged upon their proselytizing. To some extent these cases involve freedom of speech, press, and assembly as well as the free exercise of religion, and it is unnecessary to include all such cases here merely because the challenge to regulation is made by a religious group. The closely related group of cases presented here, however, reveals the complexity of the problem and develops its religious aspect.

JONES v. CITY OF OPELIKA   316 US 584 (1942)

"When proponents of religious or social theories use the ordinary commercial methods of sales of articles to raise propaganda funds, it is a natural and proper exercise of the power of the state to charge reasonable fees for the privilege of canvassing."

Mr. Justice Reed, for the Court

"The constitutional protection of the Bill of Rights is not to be evaded by classifying with business callings an activity whose sole purpose is the dissemination of ideas, and taxing it as business callings are taxed."

Mr. Chief Justice Stone, dissenting

"While perhaps not so orthodox as the oral sermon, the use of religious books is an old recognized and effective method of worship and means of proselytizing. For this petitioners were taxed. The mind rebels at the thought that a minister of any of the old established churches could be made to pay fees to the community before entering the pulpit. These taxes on petitioners' efforts to preach the "news of the Kingdom" should be struck down because they burden petitioners' right to worship the Deity in their own fashion and spread the gospel as they understand it."

Mr. Justice Murphy, dissenting

This case, dealing with licensing ordinances in three different municipalities, finds the Court divided 5–4. The majority upholds the ordinances against the claim by Jehovah's Witnesses that they interfere with the free exercise of religion. In dissent, Justices Black, Douglas, and Murphy announce that they now regard the recent decision in the Gobitis case as mistaken.

MR. JUSTICE REED DELIVERED THE OPINION OF THE COURT.

By writ of certiorari in Nos. 280 and 314 and by appeal in No. 966 we have before us the question of the constitutionality of various city ordinances imposing the license taxes upon the sale of printed matter for nonpayment of which the appellant, Jobin, and the petitioners, Jones, Bowden and Sanders, all members of the organization known as Jehovah's Witnesses, were convicted.

NO. 280

The City of Opelika, Alabama, filed a complaint in the Circuit Court of Lee County charging petitioner Jones with violation of its licensing ordinance by selling books without a license, by operating as a Book Agent without a license, and by operating as a transient agent, dealer or distributor of books without a license. The license fee for Book Agents (Bibles excepted) was $10 per annum, that for transient agents, dealers or distributors of books $5. Under section 1 of the ordinance all licenses were subject to revocation in the discretion of the City Commission, with or without notice. There is a clause providing for severance in case of invalidity of any section, condition or provision. Petitioner demurred, alleging that the ordinance because of unlimited discretion in revocation and requirement of a license was an unconstitutional encroachment upon freedom of the press. During the trial without a jury these contentions, with the added claim of interference with freedom of religion, were renewed at the end of the city's case, and at the close of all the evidence. The court overruled these motions, and found petitioner guilty on evidence that without a license he had been displaying pamphlets in his upraised hand and walking on a city street selling them two for five cents. The court excluded as irrelevant testimony designed to show that the petitioner was an ordained minister, and that his activities were in furtherance of his beliefs and the teaching of Jehovah's Witnesses. Once again by an unsuccessful motion for new trial the constitutional issues were raised. The Court of Appeals of Alabama reversed the conviction on appeal because it thought the unlimited discretion of the City Commission to revoke the licenses invalidated the ordinance. Without discussion of this point the Supreme Court of Alabama decided that non-discriminatory licensing of the sale of books or tracts was constitutional, reversed the Court of Appeals, and stayed execution pending certiorari. This Court, having granted certiorari, dismissed the writ for lack of a final judgment. The Court of Appeals thereupon entered a judgment sustaining the conviction, which was affirmed by the Alabama Supreme Court and is final. We therefore grant the petition for rehearing the dismissal of the writ and proceed with the consideration of the case.

NO. 314

Petitioners Bowden and Sanders were arrested by police officers of Fort Smith, Arkansas, brought before the Municipal Court on charges of violation of City Ordinance No. 1172, and convicted. They appealed to the Sebastian Circuit Court, and there moved to dismiss on the ground that the ordinance was an unconstitutional restriction of freedom of religion and of the press, contrary to the Fourteenth Amendment. The circuit judge heard the case de novo without a jury on stipulated facts. The ordinance required a license "For each person peddling dry goods, notions, wearing apparel, household goods or other articles not herein or otherwise specifically mentioned $25 per month, $10 per week, $2.50 per day. The petitioners, in the exercise of their beliefs concerning their duty to preach the gospel, admitted going from house to house without a license, playing phonographic transcriptions of Bible lectures, and distributing books setting forth their views to the residents in return for a contribution of twenty-five cents per book. When persons desiring books were unable to contribute, the books were in some instances given away free. The Circuit judge concluded as a matter of law that the books were "other goods" and that petitioners were guilty of peddling without a license. A motion for a new trial was denied. On appeal the Supreme Court of Arkansas held the ordinance constitutional on the authority of its previous decision in Cook v. Harrison, and affirmed the convictions. This Court denied certiorari, but later, because of the similarity of the issues presented to those in the Jobin case, No. 966, vacated the denial of certiorari and issued a writ.

NO. 966

The City of Casa Grande, Arizona, by ordinance made it a misdemeanor for any person to carry on any occupation or business specified without first procuring a license. Transient merchants, peddlers and street vendors were listed as subject to a quarterly license fee of $25.00, payable in advance. In the Superior Court of Pinal County Jobin was tried and convicted by a jury on a complaint charging that not having "a permanent place of business in the City" he there carried on the "business of peddling, vending, selling, offering for sale and soliciting the sale of goods, wares and merchandise, to wit: pamphlets, books and publications without first having procured a license," contrary to the ordinance. The evidence for the state showed that without a license the appellant called at two homes and a laundry and offered for sale and sold books and pamphlets of a religious nature. At one home, accompanied by his wife, he was refused admission, but was allowed by the girl who came to the door to play a portable phonograph on the porch. The girl purchased one of his stock of books, "Religion," for a quarter, and received a pamphlet free. During the conversation he stated that he was an ordained minister preaching the gospel and quoted passages from the Bible. At the second home the lady of the house allowed him and his wife to enter and play the phonograph, but she refused to buy either books or pamphlets. When departing the appellant left some literature on the table although informed by the lady that it would not be read and had better be given to someone else. At the laundry the appellant introduced himself as one of the Jehovah's Witnesses and discussed with the proprietor their work and religion generally. The proprietor bought the book "Religion" for a quarter but declined to buy others at the same price. He was given a pamphlet free. When arrested the appellant stated that he was "selling religious books and preaching the gospel of the kingdom," and that because of his religious beliefs he would not take out a license. A motion at the close of the evidence for a directed verdict of acquittal on the ground that the ordinance violated the Fourteenth Amendment was denied. The jury was instructed to acquit unless it found the defendant was selling books or pamphlets. It returned a verdict of guilty. On appeal the Supreme Court of Arizona held that the ordinance, an "ordinary occupational license tax ordinance," did not deny freedom of religion and of the press and affirmed the conviction. An appeal to this Court was allowed under 237 of the Judicial Code.

The Opelika ordinance required book agents to pay $10.00 per annum, transient distributors of books (annual only) $5.00. The license fee in Casa Grande was $25 per quarter, that in Fort Smith ranged from $2.50 per day to $85 per month. All the fees were small, yet substantial. But the appellant and the petitioners, so far as the records disclose, advanced no claim and presented no proof in the courts below that these fees were invalid because so high as to make the cost of compliance a deterrent to the further distribution of their literature in those cities. Although petitioners in No. 314 contended that their enterprise was operated at a loss there was no suggestion that they could not obtain from the same sources which now supply the funds to meet whatever deficit there may be sums sufficient to defray license fees also. The amount of the fees was not considered in the opinions below except for a bare statement by the Alabama court that the exaction was "reasonable," and neither the briefs nor the assignments of error in this Court have directed their attack specifically to that issue. Consequently there is not before us the question of the power to lay fees, objectionable in their effect because of their size, upon the constitutionally protected rights of free speech, press or the exercise of religion. If the size of the fees were to be considered, to reach a conclusion one would desire to know the estimated volume, the margin of profit, the solicitor's commission, the expense of policing and other pertinent facts of income and expense. In the circumstances we venture no opinion concerning the validity of license taxes if it were proved, or at least distinctly claimed, that the burden of the tax was a substantial clog upon activities of the sort here involved. The sole constitutional question considered is whether a nondiscriminatory license fee, presumably appropriate in amount, may be imposed upon these activities.

We turn to the constitutional problem squarely presented by these ordinances. There are ethical principles of greater value to mankind than the guarantees of the Constitution, personal liberties which are beyond the power of government to impair. These principles and liberties belong to the mental and spiritual realm where the judgments and decrees of mundane courts are ineffective to direct the course of man. The rights of which our Constitution speaks have a more earthy quality. They are not absolutes to be exercised independently of other cherished privileges, protected by the same organic instrument. Conflicts in the exercise of rights arise and the conflicting forces seek adjustments in the courts, as do these parties, claiming on the one side the freedom of religion, speech and the press, guaranteed by the Fourteenth Amendment, and on the other the right to employ the sovereign power explicitly reserved to the State by the Tenth Amendment to ensure orderly living without which constitutional guarantees of civil liberties would be a mockery. Courts, no more than Constitutions, can intrude into the consciences of men or compel them to believe contrary to their faith or think contrary to their convictions, but courts are competent to adjudge the acts men do under color of a constitutional right, such as that of freedom of speech or of the press or the free exercise of religion and to determine whether the claimed right is limited by other recognized powers, equally precious to mankind. So the mind and spirit of man remain forever free, while his actions rest subject to necessary accommodation to the competing needs of his fellows.

If all expression of religion or opinion, however, were subject to the discretion of authority, our unfettered dynamic thoughts or moral impulses might be made only colorless and sterile ideas. To give them life and force, the Constitution protects their use. No difference of view as to the importance of the freedoms of press or religion exist. They are "fundamental personal rights and liberties." To proscribe the dissemination of doctrines or arguments which do not transgress military or moral limits is to destroy the principal bases of democracy—knowledge and discussion. One man, with views contrary to the rest of his compatriots, is entitled to the privilege of expressing his ideas by speech or broadside to anyone willing to listen or to read. Too many settled beliefs have in time been rejected to justify this generation in refusing a hearing to its own dissentients. But that hearing may be limited by action of the proper legislative body to times, places and methods for the enlightenment of the community which in view of existing social and economic conditions, are not at odds with the preservation of peace and good order.

This means that the proponents of ideas cannot determine entirely for themselves the time and place and manner for the diffusion of knowledge or for their evangelism, any more than the civil authorities may hamper or suppress the public dissemination of facts and principles by the people. The ordinary requirements of civilized life compel this adjustment of interests. The task of reconcilement is made harder by the tendency to accept as dominant any contention supported by a claim of interference with the practice of religion or the spread of ideas. Believing as this nation has from the first that the freedoms of worship and expression are closely akin to the illimitable privileges of thought itself, any legislation affecting those freedoms is scrutinized to see that the interferences allowed are only those appropriate to the maintenance of a civilized society. The determination of what limitations may be permitted under such an abstract test rests with the legislative bodies, the courts, the executive and the people themselves guided by the experience of the past, the needs of revenue for law enforcement, the requirements and capacities of police protection, the dangers of disorder and other pertinent factors.

Upon the courts falls the duty of determining the validity of such enactments as may be challenged as unconstitutional by litigants. In dealing with these delicate adjustments this Court denies any place to administrative censorship of ideas or capricious approval of distributors. In Lovell v. Griffin, the requirement of permission from the city manager invalidated the ordinance; in Schneider v. State, that of a police officer. In the Cantwell case, the secretary of the public welfare council was to determine whether the object of charitable solicitation was worthy. We held the requirement bad. Ordinances absolutely prohibiting the exercise of the right to disseminate information are, a fortiori, invalid.

The differences between censorship and complete prohibition, either of subject matter or the individuals participating, upon the one hand, and regulation of the conduct of individuals in the time, manner and place of their activities upon the other, are decisive. "One who is a martyr to a principle . . . does not prove by his martyrdom that he has kept within the law," said Mr. Justice Cardozo concurring in Hamilton v. Regents, which held that conscientious objection to military training would not excuse a student, during his enrollment, from attending required courses in that science. There is to be noted, too, a distinction between nondiscriminatory regulation of operations which are imposed upon the religious rite itself or the unmixed dissemination of information. Casual reflection verifies the suggestion that both teachers and preachers need to receive support for themselves as well as alms and benefactions for charity and the spread of knowledge. But when, as in these cases, the practitioners of these noble callings choose to ultilize the vending of their religious books and tracts as a source of funds, the financial aspects of their transactions need not be wholly disregarded. To subject any religious or didactic group to a reasonable fee for their money-making activities does not require a finding that the licensed acts are purely commercial. It is enough that money is earned by the sale of articles. A book agent cannot escape a license requirement by a plea that it is a tax on knowledge. It would hardly be contended that the publication of newspapers is not subject to the usual governmental fiscal exactions, or the obligations placed by statutes on other business. The Constitution draws no line between a payment from gross receipts or a net income tax and a suitably calculated occupational license. Commercial advertising cannot escape control by the simple expedient of printing matter of public interest on the same sheet or handbill. Nor does the fact that to the participants a formation in the streets is an "information march," and "one of their ways of worship," suffice to exempt such a procession from a city ordinance which, narrowly construed, required a license for such a parade.

When proponents of religious or social theories use the ordinary commercial methods of sales of articles to raise propaganda funds, it is a natural and proper exercise of the power of the state to charge reasonable fees for the privilege of canvassing. Careful as we may and should be to protect the freedoms safeguarded by the Bill of Rights, it is difficult to see in such enactments a shadow of prohibition of the exercise of religion or of abridgement of the freedom of speech or the press. It is prohibition and unjustifiable abridgement which is interdicted, not taxation. Nor do we believe it can be fairly said that because such proper charges may be expanded into unjustifiable abridgements they are therefore invalid on their face. The freedoms claimed by those seeking relief here are guaranteed against abridgement by the Fourteenth Amendment. Its commands protect their rights. The legislative power of municipalities must yield when abridgement is shown. If we were to assume, as is here argued, that the licensed activities involve religious rites, a different question would be presented. These are not taxes on free will offerings. But it is because we view these sales as partaking more of commercial than religious or educational transactions that we find the ordinances, as here presented, valid. A tax on religion or a tax on interstate commerce may alike be forbidden by the Constitution. It does not follow that licenses for selling Bibles or for manufacture of articles of general use, measured by extra-state sales, must fall. It may well be that the wisdom of American communities will persuade them to permit the poor and weak to draw support from the petty sales of religious books without contributing anything for the privilege of using the streets and conveniences of the municipality. Such an exemption, however, would be a voluntary, not a constitutionally enforced, contribution.

In the ordinances of Casa Grande and Fort Smith, we have no discretionary power in the public authorities to refuse a license to any one desirous of selling religious literature. No censorship of the material which enters into the books or papers is authorized. No religious symbolism is involved such as was urged against the flag salute in Minersville District v. Gobitis. For us there is no occasion to apply here the principles taught by that opinion. Nothing more is asked from one group than from another which uses similar methods of propagation. We see nothing in the collection of a nondiscriminatory license fee, uncontested in amount, from those selling books or papers, which abridges the freedoms of worship, speech or press. As to the claim that even small license charges, if valid, will impose upon the itinerant colporteur a crushing aggregate, it is plain that if each single fee is, as we assume, commensurate with the activities licensed, then though the accumulation of fees from city to city may in time bulk large, he will have enjoyed a correlatively enlarged field of distribution. The First Amendment does not require a subsidy in the form of fiscal exemption. Accordingly the challenge to the Fort Smith and Casa Grande ordinances fails.

There is an additional contention by petitioner as to the Opelika ordinance. It is urged that since the licenses were revocable, arbitrarily, by the local authorities, there can be no true freedom for petitioners in the dissemination of information because of the censorship upon their actions after the issuance of the license. But there has been neither application for nor revocation of a license. The complaint was bottomed on sales without a license. It was that charge against which petitioner claimed the protection of the Constitution. This issue he had standing to raise. From what has been said previously it follows that the objection to the unconstitutionality of requiring a license fails. There is no occasion, at this time, to pass on the validity of the revocation section, as is does not affect his present defense.

In Lovell v. Griffin, we held invalid a statute which placed the grant of a license within the discretion of the licensing authority. By this discretion, the right to obtain a license was made an empty right. Therefore the formality of going through an application was naturally not deemed a prerequisite to insistence on a constitutional right. Here we have a very different situation. A license is required that may properly be required. The fact that such a license, if it were granted, may subsequently be revoked does not necessarily destroy the licensing ordinance. The hazard of such revocation is much too contingent for us now to declare the licensing provisions to be invalid. Lovell v. Griffin has, in effect, held that discretionary control in the general area of free speech is unconstitutional. Therefore, the hazard that the license properly granted would be improperly revoked is far too slight to justify declaring the valid part of the ordinance, which is alone now at issue, also unconstitutional.

The judgments in Nos. 280, 314 and 966 are affirmed.

MR. CHIEF JUSTICE STONE, DISSENTING.

The First Amendment, which the Fourteenth makes applicable to the states, declares: "Congress shall make no law respecting an establishment of religion, or prohibiting the free exercise thereof; or abridging the freedom of speech, or of the press". I think that the ordinance in each of these cases is on its face a prohibited invasion of the freedoms thus guaranteed, and that the judgment in each should be reversed.

The ordinance in the Opelika case should be held invalid on two independent grounds. One is that the annual tax in addition to the 50 cent "issuance fee" which the ordinance imposes is an unconstitutional restriction on those freedoms, for reasons which will presently appear. The other is that the requirement of a license for dissemination of ideas, when as here the license is revocable at will without cause and in the unrestrained discretion of administrative officers, is likewise an unconstitutional restraint on those freedoms.

The sole condition which the Opelika ordinance prescribes for grant of the license is payment of the designated annual tax and issuance fee. The privilege thus purchased, for the period of a year, is forthwith revocable in the unrestrained and unreviewable discretion of the licensing commission without cause and without notice or opportunity for a hearing. The case presents in its baldest form the question whether the freedoms which the Constitution purports to safeguard can be completely subjected to uncontrolled administrative action. Only recently this Court was unanimous in holding void on its face the requirement of a license for the distribution of pamphlets which was to be issued in the sole discretion of a municipal officer. The precise ground of our decision was that the ordinance made enjoyment of the freedom which the Constitution guarantees contingent upon the uncontrolled will of administrative officers. We declared:

"We think that the ordinance is invalid on its face. Whatever the motive which induced its adoption, its character is such that it strikes at the very foundation of the freedom of the press by subjecting it to license and censorship. The struggle for the freedom of the press was primarily directed against the power that John Milton directed his assault by his 'Appeal for the Liberty of Unlicensed Printing.' And the liberty of the press became initially a right to publish 'without a license what formerly could be published only with one.' While this freedom from previous restraint upon publication cannot be regarded as exhausting the guaranty of liberty, the prevention of that restraint was a leading purpose in the adoption of the constitutional provision."

That purpose cannot rightly be defeated by so transparent a subterfuge as the pronouncement that, while a license may not be required if its award is contingent upon the whim of an administrative officer, it may be if its retention and the enjoyment of the privilege which it purports to give is wholly contingent upon his whim. In either case enjoyment of the freedom is dependent upon the same contingency and the censorship is as effective in one as in the other. Nor is any palliative afforded by the assertion that the defendant's failure to apply for a license deprives him of standing to challenge the ordinance because of its revocation provision, by the terms of which retention of the license and exercise of the privilege may be cut off at any time without cause.

Indeed, the present ordinance is a more callous disregard of the constitutional right than that exhibited in Lovell v. Griffin. There at least the defendant might have been given a license if he had applied for it. In any event he would not have been compelled to pay a money exaction for a license to exercise the privilege of free speech—a license which if granted in this case would have been wholly illusory. Here the defendant Jones was prohibited from distributing his pamphlets at all unless he paid in advance a year's tax for the exercise of the privilege and subjected himself to termination of the license without cause, notice or hearing, at the will of city officials. To say that he who is free to withhold at will the privilege of publication exercises power of censorship prohibited by the Constitution, but that he who has unrestricted power to withdraw the privilege does not, would be to ignore history and deny the teachings of experience, as well as to perpetuate the evils at which the First Amendment was aimed.

It is of no significance that the defendant did not apply for a license. As this Court has often pointed out, when a licensing statute is on its face a lawful exercise of regulatory power, it will not be assumed that it will be unlawfully administered in advance of an actual denial of application for the license. But here it is the prohibition of publication, save at the uncontrolled will of public officials, which transgresses constitutional limitations and makes the ordinance void on its face. The Constitution can hardly be thought to deny to one subjected to the restraints of such an ordinance the right to attack its constitutionality, because he has not yielded to its demands. The question of standing to raise the issue in this case is indistinguishable from that in the Lovell case, where it was resolved in the only manner consistent with the First Amendment.

The separability provision of the Opelika ordinance cannot serve, in advance of judicial decision by the state court, to separate those parts which are constitutionally applicable from those which are not. We have no means of knowing that the city would grant any license if the license could not be made revocable at will. The state court applied the ordinance as written. It did not rely or pass upon the effect to be given to the separability clause, or determine whether any effect to be given to it. Until it has done so this Court—as we decided only last Monday —must determine the constitutional validity of the ordinance as it stands and as it stood when obedience to it was demanded and punishment for its violation inflicted.

In all three cases the question presented by the record and fully argued here and below is whether the ordinances—which as applied penalize the defendants for not having paid the flat fee taxes levied— violate the freedom of speech, press, and religion guaranteed by the First and Fourteenth Amendments. Defendants' challenge to the ordinances, naming them, is a challenge to the substantial taxes which they impose, in specified amounts, and not to some tax of a different or lesser amount which some other ordinance might levy. In their briefs here they argue, as upon the records they are entitled to do, that the taxes are an unconstitutional burden on the right of free speech and free religion comparable to license taxes which this Court has often held to be an inadmissible burden on interstate commerce. They argue also that the cumulative effect of such taxes, in town after town throughout the country, would be destructive of freedom of the press for all persons except those financially able to distribute their literature without soliciting funds for the support of their cause.

While these are questions which have been studiously left unanswered by the opinion of the Court, it seems inescapable that an answer must be given before the convictions can be sustained. Decision of them cannot rightly be avoided now by asserting that the amount of the tax has not been put in issue; that the tax is "uncontested in amount" by the defendants, and can therefore be assumed by us to be "presumably appropriate," "reasonable," or "suitably calculated"; that it has not been proved that the burden of the tax is a substantial clog on the activities of the defendants, or that those who have defrayed the expense of their religious activities will not willingly defray the license taxes also. All these are considerations which would seem to be irrelevant to the question now before us—whether a flat tax, more than a nominal fee to defray the expenses of a regulatory license, can constitutionally be laid on a non-commercial, non-profit activity devoted exclusively to the dissemination of ideas, educational and religious in character, to those persons who consent to receive them.

Nor is the essential issue here disguised by the reiterated characterization of these exactions, not as taxes but as "fees"—a characterization to which the records lend no support. All these ordinances on their face purport to be an exercise of the municipality's taxing power. In none is there the slightest pretense by the taxing authority, or the slightest suggestion by the state court, that the "fee" is to defray expenses of the licensing system. The amounts of the "fees," without more, demonstrate that such a contention is groundless. In No. 280, Opelika itself contends that the issue relates solely to its power to raise money for general revenue purposes, and the Supreme Court of Alabama referred to the levy as a "reasonable" tax. The tax exacted by Opelika, on the face of the ordinance, is in addition to a 50 cent "issuance fee," which alone is presumably what the city deems adequate to defray the cost of administering the licensing system. Similarly in the Fort Smith and Casa Grande cases, the state courts sustained the ordinances as a tax, and nothing else. If this litigation has involved any controversy—and state courts all seemed to think that it did—the controversy has been one solely relating to the power to tax, and not the power to collect a "fee" to support a licensing system which, as has already been indicated, has no regulatory purpose other than that involved in the raising of revenue.

This Court has often had occasion to point out that where the state may, as a regulatory measure, license activities which it is without constitutional authority to tax, it may charge a small or nominal fee sufficient to defray the expense of licensing, and similarly it may charge a reasonable fee for the use of its highways by interstate motor traffic which it cannot tax. But we are not concerned in these cases with a nominal fee for a regulatory license, which may be assumed for argument's sake to be valid. Here the licenses are not regulatory, save as the licenses conditioned upon payment of the tax may serve to restrain or suppress publication. None of the ordinances, if complied with, purports to or could control the time, place or manner of the distribution of the books and pamphlets concerned. None has any discernible relationship to the police protection or the good order of the community. The only condition and purpose of the licenses under all three ordinances is suppression of the specified distributions of literature in default of the payment of a substantial tax fixed in amount and measured neither by the extent of the defendants' activities under the license nor the amounts which they receive for and devote to religious purposes in the exercise of the licensed privilege. Opelika exacts a license fee for book agents of $10 per annum and of $5 per annum for transient distributors of books, in addition to a 50 cent "issuance fee" on each license. The Supreme Court of Alabama found it unnecessary to determine whether both or only one of these taxes was payable by defendant Jones. The Fort Smith tax of $25 a month or $10 a week or $2.50 a day is substantial in amount for transient distributors of literature of the character here involved; the Opelika exaction is even more onerous when applied against one who may be in the city for only a day or two; and the tax of $25 per quarter exacted by the Casa Grande ordinance, adopted in a community having an adult population of less than 1,000 and applied to distributions of literature like the present, is prohibitive in effect.

In considering the effect of such a tax on the defendants' activities it is important to note that the state courts have applied levies obviously devised for the taxation of business employments—in the first case the "business or vocation" of "book agent"; in the second the business of peddling specified types of merchandise or "other articles"; in the third, the practice of the callings of "peddlers, transient merchants and venders"—to activities which concededly are not ordinary business or commercial transactions. As appears by stipulation or undisputed testimony, the defendants are Jehovah's Witnesses, engaged in spreading their religious doctrines in conformity to the teachings of St. Matthew, Matt. 10:11–14 and 24:14, by going from city to city, from village to village, and house to house, to proclaim them. After asking and receiving permission from the householder, they play to him phonograph records and tender to him books or pamphlets advocating their religious views. For the latter they ask payment of a nominal amount, two to five cents for the pamphlets and twenty-five cents for books, as a contribution to the religious cause which they seek to advance. But they distribute the pamphlets, and sometimes the books, gratis when the householder is unwilling or unable to pay for them. The literature is published for such distribution by non-profit charitable corporations organized by Jehovah's Witnesses. The funds collected are used for the support of the religious movement and no one derives a profit from the publication and distribution of the literature. In the Opelika case the defendant's activities were confined to distribution of literature and solicitation of funds in the public streets.

No one could doubt that taxation which may be freely laid upon activities not within the protection of the Bill of Rights could—when applied to the dissemination of ideas—be made the ready instrument for destruction of that right. Few would deny that a license tax laid specifically on the privilege of disseminating ideas would infringe the right of free speech. For one reason among others, if the state may tax the privilege it may fix the rate of tax and, through the tax, control or suppress the activity which it taxes. If the distribution of the literature had been carried on by the defendants without solicitation of funds, there plainly would have been no basis, either statutory or constitutional, for levying the tax. It is the collection of funds which has been seized upon to justify the extension, to the defendants' activities, of the tax laid upon business callings. But if we assume, despite our recent decision in Schneider v. State, that the essential character of these activities is in some measure altered by the collection for the support of a religious undertaking, still it seems plain that the operation of the present flat tax is such as to abridge the privileges which the defendants here invoke.

It lends no support to the present tax to insist that its restraint on free speech and religion is non-discriminatory because the same levy is made upon business callings carried on for profit, many of which involve no question of freedom of speech and religion and all of which involve commercial elements—lacking here—which for present purposes may be assumed to afford a basis for taxation apart from the exercise of freedom of speech and religion. The constitutional protection of the Bill of Rights is not to be evaded by classifying with business callings an activity whose sole purpose is the dissemination of ideas, and taxing it as business callings are taxed. The immunity which press and religion enjoy may sometimes be lost when they are united with other activities not immune. But here the only activities involved are the dissemination of ideas, educational and religious, and the collection of funds for the propagation of those ideas, which we have said is likewise the subject of constitutional protection.

The First Amendment is not confined to safeguarding freedom of speech and freedom of religion against discriminatory attempts to wipe them out. On the contrary the Constitution, by virtue of the First and the Fourteenth Amendments, has put those freedoms in a preferred position. Their commands are not restricted to cases where the protected privilege is sought out for attack. They extend at least to every form of taxation which, because it is a condition of the exercise of the privilege, is capable of being used to control or suppress it.

Even were we to assume—what I do not concede—that there could be a lawful non-discriminatory license tax of a percentage of the gross receipts collected by churches and other religious orders in support of their religious work, we have no such tax here. The tax imposed by the ordinances in these cases is more burdensome and destructive of the activity taxed than any gross receipts tax. The tax is for a fixed amount, unrelated to the extent of the defendants' activities or the receipts derived from them. It is thus the type of flat tax which, when applied to interstate commerce, has repeatedly been deemed by this Court to be prohibited by the commerce clause. When applied as it is here to activities involving the exercise of religious freedom, its vice is emphasized in that it is levied and paid in advance of the activities taxed, and applied at rates well calculated to suppress those activities save only as others may volunteer to pay the tax. It requires a sizable out-of-pocket expense by someone who may never succeed in raising a penny in his exercise of the privilege which is taxed.

The defendants' activities, if taxable at all, are taxable only because of the funds which they solicit. But that solicitation is for funds for religious purposes, and the present taxes are in no way gauged to the receipts. The taxes are insupportable either as a tax on the dissemination of ideas or as a tax on the collection of funds for religious purposes. For on its face a flat license tax restrains in advance the freedom taxed and tends inevitably to suppress its exercise. The First Amendment prohibits all laws abridging freedom of press and religion, not merely some laws or all except tax laws. It is true that the constitutional guarantees of freedom of press and religion, like the commerce clause, make no distinction between fixed-sum taxes and other kinds. But that fact affords no excuse to courts, whose duty it is to enforce those guarantees, to close their eyes to the characteristics of a tax which render it destructive of freedom of press and religion.

We may lay to one side the Court's suggestion that a tax otherwise unconstitutional is to be deemed valid unless it is shown that there are none who, for religion's sake, will come forward to pay the unlawful exaction. The defendants to whom the ordinances have been applied have not paid it and there is nothing in the Constitution to compel them to seek the charity of others to pay it before protesting the tax.

It seems fairly obvious that if the present taxes, laid in small communities upon peripatetic religious propagandists, are to be sustained, a way has been found for the effective suppression of speech and press and religion despite constitutional guarantees. The very taxes now before us are better adapted to that end than were the stamp taxes which so successfully curtailed the dissemination of ideas by eighteenth century newspapers and pamphleteers, and which were a moving cause of the American Revolution. Vivid recollections of the effect of those taxes on the freedom of press survived to inspire the adoption of the First Amendment.

Freedom of press and religion, explicitly guaranteed by the Constitution, must at least be entitled to the same freedom from burdensome taxation which it has been thought that the more general phraseology of the commerce clause has extended to interstate commerce. Whatever doubts may be entertained as to this Court's function to relieve, unaided by Congressional legislation, from burdensome taxation under the commerce clause, it cannot be thought that function is wanting under the explicit guaranties of freedom of speech, press and religion. In any case the flat license tax can hardly become any the less burdensome or more permissible, when levied on activities within the protection extended by the First and Fourteenth Amendments both to the orderly communication of ideas, educational and religious, to persons willing to receive them, and to the practice of religion and the solicitation of funds in its support.

In its potency as a prior restraint on publication the flat license tax falls short only of outright censorship or suppression. The more humble and needy the cause, the more effective is the suppression.

Mr. Justice Black, Mr. Justice Douglas and Mr. Justice Murphy join in this opinion.

MR. JUSTICE MURPHY, WITH WHOM THE CHIEF JUSTICE, MR. JUSTICE BLACK, AND MR. JUSTICE DOUGLAS CONCUR, DISSENTING.

When a statute is challenged as impinging on freedom of speech, freedom of the press, or freedom of worship, those historic privileges which are so essential to our political welfare and spiritual progress, it is the duty of this Court to subject such legislation to examination, in the light of the evidence adduced, to determine whether it is so drawn as not to impair the substance of those cherished freedoms in reaching its objective. Ordinances that may operate to restrict the circulation or dissemination of ideas on religious or other subjects should be framed with fastidious care and precise language to avoid undue encroachment on these fundamental liberties. And the protection of the Constitution must be extended to all, not only to those whose views accord with prevailing thought but also to dissident minorities who energetically spread their beliefs. Being satisfied by the evidence that the ordinances in the cases now before us, as construed and applied in the state courts, impose a burden on the circulation and discussion of opinion and information in matters of religion, and therefore violate the petitioners' rights to freedom of speech, freedom of the press, and freedom of worship in contravention of the Fourteenth Amendment, I am obliged to dissent from the opinion of the Court.

It is not disputed that petitioners, Jehovah's Witnesses, were ordained ministers preaching the gospel, as they understood it, through the streets and from house to house, orally and by playing religious records with the consent of the householder, and by distributing books and pamphlets setting forth the tenets of their faith. It does not appear that their motives were commercial, but only that they were evangelizing their faith as they saw it.

In No. 280 the trial court excluded as irrelevant petitioner's testimony that he was an ordained minister and that his activities on the streets of Opelika were in furtherance of his ministerial duties. The testimony of ten clergymen of Opelika that they distributed free religious literature in their churches, the cost of which was defrayed by voluntary contribution, and that they had never been forced to pay any license fee, was also excluded. It is admitted here that petitioner was a Jehovah's Witness and considered himself an ordained minister.

The Supreme Court of Arizona stated in No. 966 that appellant was "a regularly ordained minister of the denomination commonly known as Jehovah's Witnesses . . . going from house to house in the city of Casa Grande preaching the gospel, as he understood it, by means of his spoken word, by playing various religious records on a phonograph, with the approval of the householder, and by distributing printed books, pamphlets and tracts which set forth his views as to the meaning of the Bible. The method of distribution of these printed books, pamphlets and tracts was as follows: He first offered them for sale at various prices ranging from five to twenty-five cents each. If the householder did not desire to purchase any of them he then left a small leaflet summarizing some of the doctrines which he preached."

The facts were stipulated in No. 314. Each petitioner "claims to be an ordained minister of the gospel. . . . 'They do not engage in this work for any selfish reason, but because they feel called to publish the news and preach the gospel of the Kingdom to all the world as a witness before the end comes. . . . They believe that the only effective way to preach is to go from house to house and make personal contact with the people and distribute to them books and pamphlets setting forth their views on Christianity' ". Petitioners "were going from house to house in the residential section within the City of Fort Smith . . . presenting to the residents of these houses various booklets, leaflets and periodicals setting forth their views of Christianity held by Jehovah's Witnesses." They solicited a "contribution of twenty-five cents for each book," but "these books in some instances are distributed free when people wishing them are unable to contribute."

There is no suggestion in any of these three cases that petitioners were perpetrating a fraud, that they were demeaning themselves in an obnoxious manner, that their activities created any public disturbance or inconvenience, that private rights were contravened, or that the literature distributed was offensive to morals or created any "clear and present danger" to organized society.

The ordinance in each case is sought to be sustained as a system of non-discriminatory taxation of various businesses, professions, and vocations, including the distribution of books for which contributions are asked, for the sole purpose of raising revenue. Any inclination to take the position that petitioners, who were proselytizing by distributing informative literature setting forth their religious tenets, and whose activities were wholly unrelated to any commercial purposes, were not within the purview of these occupational tax ordinances, is foreclosed by the decisions of the state courts below to the contrary. As so construed the ordinances in effect impose direct taxes on the dissemination of ideas and the distribution of literature, relating to and dealing with religious matters, for which a contribution is asked in an attempt to gain converts, because those were petitioners' activities. Such taxes have been held to violate the Fourteenth Amendment; and that should be the holding here.

FREEDOM OF SPEECH AND FREEDOM OF THE PRESS

In view of the recent decisions of this Court striking down acts which impair freedom of speech and freedom of the press no elaboration on that subject is now necessary. We have "unequivocally held that the streets are proper places for the exercise of the freedom of communicating information and disseminating opinion and that, though the states and municipalities may appropriately regulate the privilege in the public interest, they may not unduly burden or proscribe its employment in these public thoroughfares." And as the distribution of pamphlets to spread information and opinion on the streets and from house to house for non-commercial purposes is protected from the prior restraint of censorship, so should it be protected from the burden of taxation.

The opinion of the Court holds that the amount of the tax is not before us and that a "nondiscriminatory license fee, presumably appropriate in amount, may be imposed upon these activities". Both of these holdings must be rejected.

Where regulation or infringement of the liberty of discussion and the dissemination of information and opinion are involved, there are special reasons for testing the challenged statute on its face. That should be done here.

Consideration of the taxes leads to but one conclusion—that they prohibit or seriously hinder the distribution of petitioners' religious literature. The opinion of the Court admits that all the taxes are "substantial." The $25 quarterly tax of Casa Grande approaches prohibition. The 1940 population of that town was 1,545. With so few potential purchasers it would take a gifted evangelist, indeed, in view of the antagonism generally encountered by Jehovah's Witnesses, to sell enough tracts at prices ranging from five to twenty-five cents to gross enough to pay the tax. While the amount is actually lower in Opelika and may be lower in Fort Smith in that it is possible to get a license for a short period, and while the circle of purchasers is wider in those towns, these exactions also place a heavy hand on petitioners' activities. The petitioners should not be subjected to such tribute.

But whatever the amount, the taxes are in reality taxes upon the dissemination of religious ideas, a dissemination carried on by the distribution of religious literature for religious reasons alone and not for personal profit. As such they place a burden on freedom of speech, freedom of the press, and the exercise of religion even if the question of amount is laid aside. Liberty of circulation is very life blood of a free press, and taxes on the circulation of ideas have a long history of misuse against freedom of thought. And taxes on circulation solely for the purpose of revenue were successfully resisted, prior to the adoption of the First Amendment, as interferences with freedom of the press. Surely all this was familiar knowledge to the framers of the Bill of Rights. We need not shut our eyes to the possibility that use may again be made of such taxes, either by discrimination in enforcement or otherwise, to suppress the unpalatable views of militant minorities such as Jehovah's Witnesses. As the evidence excluded in No. 280 tended to show, no attempt was there made to apply the ordinance to ministers functioning in a more orthodox manner than petitioner.

Other objectionable features in addition to the factor of historical misuse exist. There is the unfairness present in any system of flat fee taxation, bearing no relation to the ability to pay. And there is the cumulative burden of many such taxes throughout the municipalities of the land, as the number of recent cases involving such ordinances abundantly demonstrates. The activities of Jehovah's Witnesses are wide-spread, and the aggregate effect of numerous exactions, no matter how small, can conceivably force them to choose between refraining from attempting to recoup part of the cost of their literature, or else paying out large sums in taxes. Either choice hinders and may even possibly put an end to their activities. There is no basis, other than a refusal to consider the characteristics of taxes such as these, for any assumption that such taxes are "commensurate with the activities licensed". Nor is there any assurance that "a correlatively enlarged field of distribution" will insure sufficient proceeds even to meet such exactions, let alone leaving any residue for the continuation of petitioners' evangelization.

Freedom of speech, freedom of the press, and freedom of religion all have a double aspect—freedom of thought and freedom of action. Freedom to think is absolute of its own nature; the most tyrannical government is powerless to control the inward workings of the mind. But even an aggressive mind is of no missionary value unless there is freedom of action, freedom to communicate its message to others by speech and writing. Since in any form of action there is a possibility of collision with the rights of others, there can be no doubt that this freedom to act is not absolute but qualified, being subject to regulation in the public interest which does not unduly infringe the right. However, there is no assertion here that the ordinances were regulatory, but if there were such a claim, they still should not be sustained. No abuses justifying regulation are advanced and the ordinances are not narrowly and precisely drawn to deal with actual, or even hypothetical evils, while at the same time preserving the substance of the right. They impose a tax on the dissemination of information and opinion anywhere within the city limits, whether on the streets or from house to house. "As we have said, the streets are natural and proper places for the dissemination of information and opinion; and one is not to have the exercise of his liberty of expression in appropriate places abridged on the plea that it may be exercised elsewhere." These taxes abridge that liberty.

It matters not that petitioners asked contributions for their literature. Freedom of speech and freedom of the press cannot and must not mean freedom only for those who can distribute their broadsides without charge. There may be others with messages more vital but purses less full, who must seek some reimbursement for their outlay or else forego passing on their ideas. The pamphlet, an historic weapon against oppression is today the convenient vehicle of those with limited resources because newspaper space and radio time are expensive and the cost of establishing such enterprises great. If freedom of speech and freedom of the press are to have any concrete meaning, people seeking to distribute information and opinion, to the end only that others shall have the benefit thereof, should not be taxed for circulating such matter. It is unnecessary to consider now the validity of such taxes on commercial enterprises engaged in the dissemination of ideas. Petitioners were not engaged in a traffic for profit. While the courts below held their activities were covered by the ordinances, it is clear that they were seeking only to further their religious convictions by preaching the gospel to others.

The exercise, without commercial motives, of freedom of speech, freedom of the press, or freedom of worship are not proper sources of taxation for general revenue purposes. In dealing with a permissible regulation of these freedoms and the fee charged in connection therewith, we emphasized the fact that the fee was "not a revenue tax, but one to meet the expense incident to the administration of the act and to the maintenance of public order", and stated only that, "There is nothing contrary to the Constitution in the charge of a fee limited to the purpose stated." The taxes here involved are ostensibly for revenue purposes; they are not regulatory fees. Respondents do not show that the instant activities of Jehovah's Witnesses create special problems causing a drain on the municipal coffers, or that these taxes are commensurate with any expenses entailed by the presence of the Witnesses. In the absence of such a showing I think no tax whatever can be levied on petitioners' activities in distributing their literature or disseminating their ideas. If the guaranties of freedom of speech and freedom of the press are to be preserved, municipalities should not be free to raise general revenue by taxes on the circulation of information and opinion in non-commercial causes; other sources can be found, the taxation of which will not choke off ideas. Taxes such as the instant ones violate petitioners' right to freedom of speech and freedom of the press, protected against state invasion by the Fourteenth Amendment.

FREEDOM OF RELIGION

Under the foregoing discussion of freedom of speech and freedom of the press any person would be exempt from taxation upon the act of distributing information or opinion of any kind, whether political, scientific, or religious in character, when done solely in an effort to spread knowledge and ideas, with no thought of commercial gain. But there is another, and perhaps more precious reason why these ordinances cannot constitutionally apply to petitioners. Important as free speech and a free press are to a free government and a free citizenry, there is a right even more dear to many individuals—the right to worship their Maker according to their needs and the dictates of their souls and to carry their message or their gospel to every living creature. These ordinances infringe that right, which is also protected by the Fourteenth Amendment.

Petitioners were itinerant ministers going through the streets and from house to house in different communities, preaching the gospel by distributing booklets and pamphlets setting forth their views of the Bible and the tenets of their faith. While perhaps not so orthodox as the oral sermon, the use of religious books is an old, recognized and effective mode of worship and means of proselytizing. For this petitioners were taxed. The mind rebels at the thought that a minister of any of the old established churches could be made to pay fees to the community before entering the pulpit. These taxes on petitioners' efforts to preach the "news of the Kingdom" should be struck down because they burden petitioners' right to worship the Deity in their own fashion and to spread the gospel as they understand it. There is here no contention that their manner of worship gives rise to conduct which calls for regulation, and these ordinances are not aimed at any such practices.

One need only read the decisions of this and other courts in the past few years to see the unpopularity of Jehovah's Witnesses and the difficulties put in their path because of their religious beliefs. An arresting parallel exists between the troubles of Jehovah's Witnesses and the struggles of various dissentient groups in the American colonies for religious liberty which culminated in the Virginia Statute for Religious Freedom, the Northwest Ordinance of 1787, and the First Amendment. In most of the colonies there was an established church, and the way of the dissenter was hard. All sects, including Quaker, Methodist, Baptist, Episcopalian, Separatist, Rigerine, and Catholic suffered. Many of the nonconforming ministers were itinerants, and measures were adopted to curb their unwanted activities. The books of certain denominations were banned. Virginia and Connecticut had burdensome licensing requirements. Other states required oaths before one could preach which many ministers could not conscientiously take. Research reveals no attempt to control or persecute by the more subtle means of taxing the function of preaching, or even any attempt to tap it as a source of revenue.

By applying these occupational taxes to petitioners' non-commercial activities, respondents now tax sincere efforts to spread religious beliefs, and a heavy burden falls upon a new set of itinerant zealots, the Witnesses. That burden should not be allowed to stand, especially if, as the excluded testimony in No. 280 indicates, the accepted clergymen of the town can take to their pulpits and distribute their literature without the impact of taxation. Liberty of conscience is too full of meaning for the individuals in this nation to permit taxation to prohibit or substantially impair the spread of religious ideas, even though they are controversial and run counter to the established notions of a community. If this Court is to err in evaluating claims that freedom of speech, freedom of the press, and freedom of religion have been invaded, far better that it err in being overprotective in these precious rights.

MR. JUSTICE BLACK, MR. JUSTICE DOUGLAS, MR. JUSTICE MURPHY.

The opinion of the Court sanctions a device which in our opinion suppresses or tends to suppress the free exercise of a religion practiced by a minority group. This is but another step in the direction which Minersville School District v. Gobitis, took against the same religious minority and is a logical extension of the principles upon which that decision rested. Since we joined in the opinion in the Gobitis case, we think this is an appropriate occasion to state that we now believe that it was also wrongly decided. Certainly our democratic form of government functioning under the historic Bill of Rights has a high responsibility to accommodate itself to the religious views of minorities however unpopular and unorthodox those views may be. The First Amendment does not put the right freely to exercise religion in a subordinate position. We fear, however, that the opinions in these and in the Gobitis case do exactly that.

MURDOCK v. COMMONWEALTH OF PENNSYLVANIA 319 US 105 (1943)

"But the mere fact that the religious literature is 'sold' by itinerant preachers rather than 'donated' does not transform evangelism into a commercial enterprise. If it did, then the passing of a collection plate in Church would make the Church service a commercial project. The constitutional rights of those spreading their religious beliefs through the spoken and printed word are not to be gauged by standards governing retailers or wholesalers of books."

Mr. Justice Douglas, for the Court

A year after Jones v. Opelika the Court, with Justice Rutledge replacing Justice Byrnes upon the latter's retirement, was able to marshal a 5-4 majority for the position of the dissenters in the Opelika case. In a short per curiam opinion the Opelika case was reversed. The position of the majority is here given by Justice Douglas in a case involving an ordinance of a municipality in Pennsylvania.

MR. JUSTICE DOUGLAS DELIVERED THE OPINION OF THE COURT.

The City of Jeannette, Pennsylvania, has an ordinance, some forty years old, which provides in part:

112

"'That all persons canvassing for or soliciting within said Borough, orders for goods, paintings, pictures, wares, or merchandise of any kind, or persons delivering such articles under orders so obtained or solicited, shall be required to procure from the Burgess a license to transact said business and shall pay to the Treasurer of said Borough therefore the following sums according to the time for which said license shall be granted.

"For one day $1.50, for one week seven dollars ($7.00), for two weeks twelve dollars ($12.00), for three weeks twenty dollars ($20.00), provided that the provisions of this ordinance shall not apply to persons selling by sample to manufacturers or licensed merchants or dealers doing business in said Borough of Jeannette."

Petitioners are "Jehovah's Witnesses." They went about from door to door in the City of Jeannette distributing literature and soliciting people to "purchase" certain religious books and pamphlets, all published by the Watch Tower Bible & Tract Society. The "price" of the books was twenty-five cents each, the "price" of the pamphlets five cents each. In connection with these activities petitioners used a phonograph on which they played a record expounding certain of their views on religion. None of them obtained a license under the ordinance. Before they were arrested each had made "sales" of books. There was evidence that it was their practice in making these solicitations to request a "contribution" of twenty-five cents each for the books and five cents each for the pamphlets but to accept lesser sums or even to donate the volumes in case an interested person was without funds. In the present case some donations of pamphlets were made when books were purchased. Petitioners were convicted and fined for violation of the ordinance. Their judgments of conviction were sustained by the Superior Court of Pennsylvania, against their contention that the ordinance deprived them of the freedom of speech, press, and religion guaranteed by the First Amendment. Petitions for leave to appeal to the Supreme Court of Pennsylvania were denied. The cases are here on petitions for writs of certiorari which we granted along with the petitions for rehearing of Jones v. Opelika, and its companion cases.

The First Amendment, which the Fourteenth makes applicable to the states, declares that "Congress shall make no law respecting an establishment of religion, or prohibiting the free exercise thereof; or abridging the freedom of speech, or of the press . . ." It could hardly be denied that a tax laid specifically on the exercise of those freedoms would be unconstitutional. Yet the license tax imposed by this ordinance is in substance just that.

Petitioners spread their interpretations of the Bible and their religious beliefs largely through the hand distribution of literature by full or part time workers. They claim to follow the example of Paul, teaching "publicly, and from house to house." Acts 20:20. They take literally the mandate of the Scriptures, "Go ye into all the world, and preach the gospel to every creature." Mark 16:15. In doing so they believe that they are obeying a commandment of God.

The hand distribution of religious tracts is an age-old form of missionary evangelism—as old as the history of printing presses. It has been a potent force in various religious movements down through the years. This form of evangelism is utilized today on a large scale by various religious sects whose colporteurs carry the Gospel to thousands upon thousands of homes and seek through personal visitations to win adherents to their faith. It is more than preaching; it is more than distribution of religious literature. It is a combination of both. Its purpose is as evangelical as the revival meeting. This form of religious activity occupies the same high estate under the First Amendment as do worship in the churches and preaching from the pulpits. It has the same claim to protection as the more orthodox and conventional exercises of religion. It also has the same claim as the others to the guarantees of freedom of speech and freedom of the press.

The integrity of this conduct or behavior as a religious practice has not been challenged. Nor do we have presented any question as to the sincerity of petitioners in their religious beliefs and practices, however misguided they may be thought to be. Moreover, we do not intimate or suggest in respecting their sincerity that any conduct can be made a religious rite and by the zeal of the practitioners swept into the First Amendment. Reynolds v. United States, and Davis v. Beason, denied any such claim to the practice of polygamy and bigamy. Other claims may well arise which deserve the same fate. We only hold that spreading one's religious beliefs or preaching the Gospel through distribution of religious literature and through personal visitations is an age-old type of evangelism with as high a claim to constitutional protection as the more orthodox types. The manner in which it is practiced at times gives rise to special problems with which the police power of the states is competent to deal. But that merely illustrates that the rights with which we are dealing are not absolutes. We are concerned, however, in these cases merely with one narrow issue. There is presented for decision no question whatsoever concerning punishment for any alleged unlawful acts during the solicitation. Nor is there involved here any question as to the validity of a registration system for colporteurs and other solicitors. The cases present a single issue—the constitutionality of an ordinance which as construed and applied requires religious colporteurs to pay a license tax as a condition to the pursuit of their activities.

The alleged justification for the exaction of this license tax is the fact that the religious literature is distributed with a solicitation of funds. Thus it was stated in Jones v. Opelika, that when a religious sect uses "ordinary commercial methods of sales of articles to raise propaganda funds," it is proper for the state to charge "reasonable fees for the privilege of canvassing." Situations will arise where it will be difficult to determine whether a particular activity is religious or purely commercial. The distinction at times is vital. As we stated only the other day in Jamison v. Texas, "The state can prohibit the use of the street for the distribution of purely commercial leaflets, even though such leaflets may have 'a civil appeal, or a moral platitude' appended. They may not prohibit the distribution of handbills in the pursuit of a clearly religious activity merely because the handbills invite the purchase of books for the improved understanding of the religion or because the handbills seek in a lawful fashion to promote the raising of funds for religious purposes." But the mere fact that the religious literature is "sold" by itinerant preachers rather than "donated" does not transform evangelism into a commercial enterprise. If it did, then the passing of the collection plate in church would make the church service a commercial project. The constitutional rights of those spreading their religious beliefs through the spoken and printed word are not to be gauged by standards governing retailers or wholesalers of books. The right to use the press for expressing one's views is not to be measured by the protection afforded commercial handbills. It should be remembered that the pamphlets of Thomas Paine were not distributed free of charge. It is plain that a religious organization needs funds to remain a going concern. But an itinerant evangelist, however misguided or intolerant he may be, does not become a mere book agent by selling the Bible or religious tracts to help defray his expenses or to sustain him. Freedom of speech, freedom of the press, freedom of religion are available to all, not merely to those who can pay their own way. As we have said, the problem of drawing the line between a purely commercial activity and a religious one will at times be difficult. On this record it plainly cannot be said that petitioners were engaged in a commercial rather than a religious venture. It is a distortion of the facts of record to describe their activities as the occupation of selling books and pamphlets. And the Pennsylvania court did not rest the judgments of conviction on that basis, though it did find that petitioners "sold" the literature. The Supreme Court of Iowa in State v. Mean, described the selling activities of members of this same sect as "merely incidental and collateral" to their "main object which was to preach and publicize the doctrines of their order." That accurately summarizes the present record.

We do not mean to say that religious groups and the press are free from all financial burdens of government. We have here something quite different, for example, from a tax on the income of one who engages in religious activities or a tax on property used or employed in connection with those activities. It is one thing to impose a tax on the income or property of a preacher. It is quite another thing to exact a tax from him for the privilege of delivering a sermon. The tax imposed by the City of Jeannette is a flat license tax, the payment of which is a condition of the exercise of these constitutional privileges. The power to tax the exercise of a privilege is the power to control or suppress its enjoyment. Those who can tax the exercise of this religious practice can make its exercise so costly as to deprive it of the resources necessary for its maintenance. Those who can tax the privilege of engaging in this form of missionary evangelism can close its doors to all those who do not have a full purse. Spreading religious beliefs in this ancient and honorable manner would thus be denied the needy. Those who can deprive religious groups of their colporteurs can take from them a part of the vital power of the press which has survived from the Reformation.

It is contended, however, that the fact that the license tax can suppress or control this activity is unimportant if it does not do so. But that is to disregard the nature of this tax. It is a license tax—a flat tax imposed on the exercise of a privilege granted by the Bill of Rights. A state may not impose a charge for the enjoyment of a right granted by the federal constitution. Thus, it may not exact a license tax for the privilege of carrying on interstate commerce, although it may tax the property used in, or the income derived from that commerce, so long as those taxes are not discriminatory. A license tax applied to activities guaranteed by the First Amendment, like the commerce clause, draws no distinction between license taxes, fixed sum taxes, and other kinds of taxes. But that is no reason why we should shut our eyes to the nature of the tax and its destructive influence. The power to impose a license tax on the exercise of these freedoms is indeed as potent as the power of censorship which this Court has repeatedly struck down. It was for that reason that the dissenting opinions in Jones v. Opelika, stressed the nature of this type of tax. In that case, as in the present ones, we have something very different from a registration system under which those going from house to house are required to give their names, addresses and other marks of identification to the authorities. In all of these cases the issuance of the permit or license is dependent on the payment of a license tax. And the license tax is fixed in amount and unrelated to the scope of the activities of petitioners or to their realized revenues. It is not a nominal fee imposed as a regulatory measure to defray the expenses of policing the activities in question. It is in no way apportioned. It is a flat license tax levied and collected as a condition to the pursuit of activities whose enjoyment is guaranteed by the First Amendment. Accordingly, it restrains in advance those constitutional liberties of press and religion and inevitably tends to suppress their exercise. That is almost uniformly recognized as the inherent vice and evil of this flat license tax. As stated by the Supreme Court of Illinois in a case involving this same sect and an ordinance similar to the present one, a person cannot be compelled "to purchase, through a license fee or a license tax, the privilege freely granted by the constitution." So it may not be said that proof is lacking that these license taxes either separately or cumulatively have restricted or are likely to restrict petitioners' religious activities. On their face they are a restriction of the free exercise of those freedoms which are protected by the First Amendment.

The taxes imposed by this ordinance can hardly help but be as severe and telling in their impact on the freedom of the press and religion as the "taxes on knowledge" at which the First Amendment was partly aimed. They may indeed operate even more subtly. Itinerant evangelists moving throughout a state or from state to state would feel immediately the cumulative effect of such ordinances as they become fashionable. The way of the religious dissenter has long been hard. But if the formula of this type of ordinance is approved, a new device for the suppression of religious minorities will have been found. This method of disseminating religious beliefs can be crushed and closed out by the sheer weight of the toll or tribute which is exacted town by town, village by village. The spread of religious ideas through personal visitations by the literature ministry of numerous religious groups would be stopped.

The fact that the ordinance is "nondiscriminatory" is immaterial. The protection afforded by the First Amendment is not so restricted. A license tax certainly does not acquire constitutional validity because it classifies the privileges protected by the First Amendment along with the wares and merchandise of hucksters and peddlers and treats them all alike. Such equality in treatment does not save the ordinance. Freedom of press, freedom of speech, freedom of religion are in a preferred position.

It is claimed, however, that the ultimate question in determining the constitutionality of this license tax is whether the state has given something for which it can ask a return. That principle has wide applicability. But it is quite irrelevant here. This tax is not a charge for the enjoyment of a privilege or benefit bestowed by the state. The privilege in question exists apart from state authority. It is guaranteed the people by the federal constitution.

Considerable emphasis is placed on the kind of literature which petitioners were distributing—its provocative, abusive, and ill-mannered character and the assault which it makes on our established churches and the cherished faiths of many of us. But those considerations are no justification for the license tax which the ordinance imposes. Plainly a community may not suppress, or the state tax, the dissemination of views because they are unpopular, annoying or distasteful. If that device were ever sanctioned, there would have been forged a ready instrument for the suppression of the faith which any minority cherishes but which does not happen to be in favor. That would be a complete repudiation of the philosophy of the Bill of Rights.

Jehovah's Witnesses are not "above the law." But the present ordinance is not directed to the problems with which the police power of the state is free to deal. It does not cover, and petitioners are not charged with, breaches of the peace. They are pursuing their solicitations peacefully and quietly. Petitioners, moreover, are not charged with or prosecuted for the use of language which is obscene, abusive, or which incites retaliation. Nor do we have here, as we did in Cox v. New Hampshire, and Chaplinsky v. New Hampshire, state regulation of the streets to protect and insure the safety, comfort, or convenience of the public. Furthermore, the present ordinance is not narrowly drawn to safeguard the people of the community in their homes against the evils of solicitations. As we have said, it is not merely a registration ordinance calling for an identification of the solicitors so as to give the authorities some basis for investigating strangers coming into the community. And the fee is not a nominal one, imposed as a regulatory measure and calculated to defray the expense of protecting those on the streets and at home against the abuses of solicitors. Nor can the present ordinance be construed to apply only to solicitation from house to house. The ordinance is not narrowly drawn to prevent or control abuses or evils arising from that activity. Rather, it sets aside the residential areas as prohibited zone, entry of which is denied petitioners unless the tax is paid. That restraint and one which is city wide in scope (Jones v. Opelika) are different only in degree. Each is an abridgment of freedom of press and a restraint on the free exercise of religion. They stand or fall together.

The judgment in Jones v. Opelika has this day been vacated. Freed from that controlling precedent, we can restore to their high, constitutional position the liberties of itinerant evangelists who disseminate their religious beliefs and the tenets of their faith through distribution of literature. The judgments are reversed and the causes are remanded to the Pennsylvania Superior Court for proceedings not inconsistent with this opinion.

JONES v. CITY OF OPELIKA   319 US 105 (1943)

> "Does the exemption apply to booksellers or distributors of magazines or only to religious publications? And if the latter to what distributors? Or to what books? Or is this court saying that a religious practice of book distribution is free from taxation because a state cannot prohibit the "free exercise thereof" and a newspaper is subject to the same tax even though the same Constitutional Amendment says the state cannot abridge the freedom of the press? It has never been thought before that freedom from taxation was a perquisite attaching to the privileges of the First Amendment."
>
> Mr. Justice Reed, dissenting

> "Plainly, a tax measure is not invalid under the federal Constitution merely because it falls upon persons engaged in activities of a religious nature."
>
> Mr. Justice Frankfurter, dissenting

Given here are the dissenting opinions of Justice Reed and Justice Frankfurter to the action of the court in reversing the first Jones v. Opelika case.

MR. JUSTICE REED, DISSENTING.

These cases present for solution the problem of the constitutionality of certain municipal ordinances levying a tax for the production of revenue on the sale of books and pamphlets in the streets or from door to door. Decisions sustaining the particular ordinances were entered in the three cases first listed at the last term of this Court. In that opinion the ordinances were set out and the facts and issues stated. A rehearing has been granted. The present judgments vacate the old and invalidate the ordinances. The eight cases of this term involve canvassing from door to door only under similar ordinances, which are in the form stated in the Court's opinion. By a per curiam opinion of this day, the Court affirms its acceptance of the arguments presented by the dissent of last term in Jones v. Opelika. The Court states its position anew in the Jeannette cases.

This dissent does not deal with an objection which theoretically could be made in each case, to wit, that the licenses are so excessive in amount as to be prohibitory. This matter is not considered because that defense is not relied upon in the pleadings, the briefs or at the bar. No evidence is offered to show the amount is oppressive. An unequal tax, levied on the activities of distributors of informatory publications, would be a phase of discrimination against the freedom of speech, press or religion. Nor do we deal with discrimination against the petitioners, as individuals or as members of the group, calling themselves Jehovah's Witnesses. There is no contention in any of these cases that such discrimination is practiced in the application of the ordinances. Obviously an improper application by a city, which resulted in the arrest of witnesses and failure to enforce the ordinance against other groups, such as the Adventists, would raise entirely distinct issues.

A further and important disclaimer must be made in order to focus attention sharply upon the constitutional issue. This dissent does not express, directly or by inference, any conclusion as to the constitutional rights of state or federal governments to place a privilege tax upon the soliciting of a free-will contribution for religious purposes. Petitioners suggest that their books and pamphlets are not sold but are given either without price or in appreciation of the recipient's gift for the furtherance of the work of the witnesses. The pittance sought, as well as the practice of leaving books with poor people without cost, gives strength to this argument. In our judgment, however, the plan of national distribution by the Watch Tower Bible & Tract Society, with its wholesale prices of five or twenty cents per copy, justifies the characterization of the transaction as a sale by all the state courts. The evidence is conclusive that the witnesses normally approach a prospect with an offer of a book for twenty-five cents. Sometimes, apparently rarely, a book is left with a prospect without payment. The quid pro quo is demanded. If the profit was greater, twenty cents or even one dollar, no difference in principle would emerge. The witness sells books to raise money for propagandising his faith, just as other religious groups might sponsor bazaars or peddle tickets to church suppers or sell Bibles or prayer books for the same object. However high the purpose or noble the aims of the witness, the transaction has been found by the state courts to be a sale under their ordinances and, though our doubt was greater than it is, the state's conclusion would influence us to follow its determination.

In the opinion in Jones v. Opelika, on the former hearing, attention was called to the differentiation between these cases of taxation and those of forbidden censorship, prohibition or discrimination. There is no occasion to repeat what has been written so recently as to the constitutional right to tax the money raising activities of religious or didactic groups. There are, however, other reasons not fully developed in that opinion that add to our conviction that the Constitution does not prohibit these general occupational taxes.

The real contention of the witnesses is that there can be no taxation of the occupation of selling books and pamphlets because to do so would be contrary to the due process clause of the Fourteenth Amendment, which now is held to have drawn the contents of the First Amendment into the category of individual rights protected from state deprivation. Since the publications teach a religion which conforms to our standards of legality, it is urged that these ordinances prohibit the free exercise of religion and abridge the freedom of speech and of the press.

The First Amendment reads as follows: "Congress shall make no law respecting an establishment of religion, or prohibiting the free exercise thereof; or abridging the freedom of speech or of the press; or the right of the people peaceably to assemble, and to petition the Government for a redress of grievances."

It was one of twelve proposed on September 25, 1789, to the States by the First Congress after the adoption of the Constitution. Ten were ratified. They were intended to be and have become our Bill of Rights. By their terms our people have a guarantee that so long as law as we know it shall prevail, they shall live protected from the tyranny of the despot or the mob. None of the provisions of our Constitutions is more venerated by the people or respected by legislatures and the courts than those which proclaim for our country the freedom of religion and expression. While the interpreters of the Constitution find the purpose was to allow the widest practical scope for the exercise of religion and the dissemination of information, no jurist has ever conceived that the prohibition of interference is absolute. Is subjection to nondiscriminatory, nonexcessive taxation in the distribution of religious literature, a prohibition of the exercise of religion or an abridgment of the freedom of the press?

Nothing has been brought to our attention which would lead to the conclusion that the contemporary advocates of the adoption of a Bill of Rights intended such an exemption. The words of the Amendment do not support such a construction. "Free" cannot be held to be without cost but rather its meaning must accord with the freedom guaranteed. "Free" means a privilege to print or pray without permission and without accounting to authority for one's actions. In the Constitutional Convention the proposal for a Bill of Rights of any kind received scant attention. In the course of the ratification of the Constitution, however, the absence of a Bill of Rights was used vigorously by the opponents of the new government. A number of the states suggested amendments. Where these suggestions have any bearing at all upon religion or free speech, they indicate nothing as to any feeling concerning taxation either of religious bodies or their evangelism. This was not because freedom of religion or free speech was not understood. It was because the subjects were looked upon from standpoints entirely distinct from taxation.

The available evidence of Congressional action shows clearly that the draftsmen of the amendments had in mind the practice of religion and the right to be heard, rather than any abridgment or interference with either by taxation in any form. The amendments were proposed by Mr. Madison. He was careful to explain to the Congress the meaning of the amendment on religion. The draft was commented upon by

Mr. Madison when it read: "No religion shall be established by law, nor shall the equal rights of conscience be infringed."

He said that he apprehended the meaning of the words on religion to be that Congress should not establish a religion and enforce the legal observation of it by law, nor compel men to worship God in any manner contrary to their conscience. No such specific interpretation of the amendment on freedom of expression has been found in the debates. The clearest is probably from Mr. Benson who said that "The committee who framed this report proceeded on the principle that these rights belonged to the people; they conceived them to be inherent; and all that they meant to provide against was their being infringed by the Government." . . .

There have been suggestions that the English taxes on newspapers, springing from the tax act of 10 Anne, influenced the adoption of the First Amendment. These taxes were obnoxious but an examination of the sources of the suggestion is convincing that there is nothing to support it except the fact that the tax on newspapers was in existence in England and was disliked. The simple answer is that if there had been any purpose of Congress to prohibit any kind of taxes on the press its knowledge of the abominated English taxes would have led it to ban them unequivocally.

It is only in recent years that the freedoms of the First Amendment have been recognized as among the fundamental personal rights protected by the Fourteenth Amendment from impairment by the states. Until then these liberties were not deemed to be guarded from state action by the Federal Constitution. The states placed restraints upon themselves in their own constitutions in order to protect their people in the exercise of the freedoms of speech and of religion. Pennsylvania may be taken as a fair example. Its constitution reads: "All men have a natural and indefeasible right to worship Almighty God according to the dictates of their own consciences; no man can of right be compelled to attend, erect or support any place of worship, or to maintain any ministry against his consent; no human authority can, in any case whatever, control or interfere with the rights of conscience and no preference shall ever be given by law to any religious establishments or modes of worship."

"No person who acknowledges the being of a God, and a future state of rewards and punishments shall, on account of his religious sentiments, be disqualified to hold any office or place of trust or profit under this Commonwealth."

"The printing press shall be free to every person who may undertake to examine the proceedings of the Legislature or any branch of government, and no law shall ever be made to restrain the right thereof. The free communication of thoughts and opinions is one of the invaluable rights of man, and every citizen may freely speak, write and print on any subject, being responsible for the abuse of that liberty. . . ."

It will be observed that there is no suggestion of freedom from taxation, and this statement is equally true of the other state constitutional provisions. It may be concluded that neither in the state nor the federal constitutions was general taxation of church or press interdicted.

Is there anything in the decisions of this Court which indicates that church or press is free from the financial burdens of government? We find nothing. Religious societies depend for their exemptions from taxation upon state constitutions or general statutes, not upon the Federal Constitution. This Court has held that the chief purpose of the free press guarantee was to prevent previous restraints upon publication. In Grosjean v. American Press Co., it was said that the predominant purpose was to preserve "an untrammeled press as a vital source of public information." In that case, a gross receipt tax on advertisements in papers with a circulation of more than twenty thousand copies per week was held invalid because "a deliberate and calculated device in the guise of a tax to limit the circulation. . . ." There was this further comment: "It is not intended by anything we have said to suggest that the owners of newspapers are immune from any of the ordinary forms of taxation for support of the government. But this is not an ordinary form of tax, but one single in kind, with a long history of hostile misuse against the freedom of the press."

It may be said, however, that ours is a too narrow, technical and legalistic approach to the problem of state taxation of the activities of church and press; that we should look not to the expressed or historical meaning of the First Amendment but to the broad principles of free speech and free exercise of religion which pervade our national way of life. It may be that the Fourteenth Amendment guarantees these principles rather than the more definite concept expressed in the First Amendment. This would mean that as a court, we should determine what sort of liberty it is that the due process clause of the Fourteenth Amendment guarantees against state restrictions on speech and church.

But whether we give content to the literal words of the First Amendment or to principles of the liberty of the press and the church, we conclude that cities or states may levy reasonable, nondiscriminatory taxes on such activities as occurred in these cases. Whatever exemptions exist from taxation arise from the prevailing law of the various states. The constitutions of Alabama and Pennsylvania, with substantial similarity to the exemption provisions of other constitutions, forbid the taxation of lots and buildings used exclusively for religious worship. These are the only exemptions of the press or church from taxation.

We find nothing more applicable to our problem in the other constitutions. Surely this unanimity of specific state action on exemptions of religious bodies from taxes would not have occurred throughout our history, if it had been conceived that the genius of our institutions, as expressed in the First Amendment, was incompatible with the taxation of church or press.

Nor do we understand that the Court now maintains that the Federal Constitution frees press or religion of any tax except such occupational taxes as those here levied. Income taxes, ad valorem taxes, even occupational taxes are presumably valid, save only a license tax on sales of religious books. Can it be that the Constitution permits a tax on the printing presses and the gross income of a metropolitan newspaper but denies the right to lay an occupational tax on the distributors of the same papers? Does the exemption apply to booksellers or distributors of magazines or only to religious publications? And if the latter to what distributors? Or to what books? Or is this Court saying that a religious practice of book distribution is free from taxation because a state cannot prohibit the "free exercise thereof" and a newspaper is subject to the same tax even though the same Constitutional Amendment says the state cannot abridge the freedom of the press? It has never been thought before that freedom from taxation was a perquisite attaching to the privileges of the First Amendment. The national Government grants exemptions to ministers and churches because it wishes to do so, not because the Constitution compels. Where camp meetings or revivals charge admissions, a federal tax would apply if Congress had not granted freedom from the exaction.

It is urged that such a tax as this may be used readily to restrict the dissemination of ideas. This must be conceded but the possibility of misuse does not make a tax unconstitutional. No abuse is claimed here. The ordinances in some of these cases are the general occupation license type covering many businesses. In the Jeannette prosecutions, the ordinance involved lays the usual tax on canvassing or soliciting sales of goods, wares and merchandise. It was passed in 1898. Every power of taxation or regulation is capable of abuse. Each one to some extent prohibits the free exercise of religion and abridges the freedom of the press but that is hardly a reason for denying the power. If the tax is used oppressively the law will protect the victims of such action.

This decision forces a tax subsidy notwithstanding our accepted belief in the separation of church and state. Instead of all bearing equally the burdens of government, this Court now fastens upon the communities the entire cost of policing the sales of religious literature. That the burden may be heavy is shown by the record in the Jeannette cases. There are only eight prosecutions but one hundred and four witnesses solicited in Jeannette the day of the arrests. They had been requested by the authorities to await the outcome of a test case before continuing their canvassing. The distributors of religious literature, possibly of all informatory publications, become today privileged to carry on their occupations without contributing their share to the support of the government which provides the opportunity for the exercise of their liberties.

Nor do we think it can be said, properly, that these sales of religious books are religious exercises. The opinion of the Court in the Jeannette cases emphasizes for the first time the argument that the sale of books and pamphlets is in itself a religious practice. The Court says the witnesses "spread their interpretations of the Bible and their religious beliefs largely through the hand distribution of literature by full or part time workers," "The hand distribution of religious tracts is an age-old form of missionary evangelism—as old as the history of printing presses." "It is more than preaching; it is more than distribution of religious literature. It is a combination of both. Its purpose is as evangelical as the revival meeting. This form of religious activity occupies the same high estate under the First Amendment as do worship in the churches and preaching from the pulpits." "Those who can tax the exercise of this religious practice can make its exercise so costly as to deprive it of the resources necessary for its maintenance." "The judgment in Jones v. Opelika has this day been vacated. Freed from that controlling precedent, we can restore to their high, constitutional position the liberties of itinerant evangelists who disseminate their religious beliefs and the tenets of their faith through distribution of literature." The record shows that books entitled "Creation" and "Salvation," as well as Bibles, were offered for sale. We shall assume the first two publications, also, are religious books. Certainly there can be no dissent from the statement that selling religious books is an age-old practice or that it is evangelism in the sense that the distributors hope the readers will be spiritually benefited. That does not carry us to the conviction, however, that when distribution of religious books is made at a price, the itinerant colporteur is performing a religious rite, is worshipping his Creator in his way. Many sects practice healing the sick as an evidence of their religious faith or maintain orphanages or homes for the aged or teach the young. These are, of course, in a sense, religious practices but hardly such examples of religious rites as are encompassed by the prohibition against the free exercise of religion.

And even if the distribution of religious books was a religious practice protected from regulation by the First Amendment, certainly the affixation of a price for the articles would destroy the sacred character of the transaction. The evangelist becomes also a book agent.

The rites which are protected by the First Amendment are in essence spiritual—prayer, mass, sermons, sacrament—not sales of religious goods. The card furnished each witness to identify him as an ordained minister does not go so far as to say the sale is a rite. It states only that the witnesses worship by exhibiting to people "the message of said gospel in printed form, such as the Bible, books, booklets and magazines, and thus afford the people the opportunity of learning of God's gracious provision for them." On the back of the card appears: "You may contribute twenty-five cents to the Lord's work and receive a copy of this beautiful book." The sale of these religious books has, we think, relation to their religious exercises, similar to the "information march" said by the witnesses to be one of their "ways of worship" and by this Court to be subject to regulation by license in Cox v. New Hampshire.

The attempted analogy in the dissenting opinion in Jones v. Opelika, which now becomes the decision of this Court, between the forbidden burden of a state tax for the privilege of engaging in interstate commerce and a state tax on the privilege of engaging in the distribution of religious literature is wholly irrelevant. A state tax on the privilege of engaging in the interstate commerce is held invalid because the regulation of commerce between the states has been delegated to the Federal Government. This grant includes the necessary means to carry the grant into effect and forbids state burdens without Congressional consent. It is not the power to tax interstate commerce which is interdicted but the exercise of that power by an unauthorized sovereign, the individual state. Although the fostering of commerce was one of the chief purposes for organizing the present Government, that commerce may be burdened with a tax by the United States. Commerce must pay its way. It is not exempt from any type of taxation if imposed by an authorized authority. The Court now holds that the First Amendment wholly exempts the church and press from a privilege tax, presumably by the national as well as the state governments.

The limitations of the Constitution are not maxims of social wisdom but definite controls on the legislative process. We are dealing with power, not its abuse. This late withdrawal of the power of taxation over the distribution activities of those covered by the First Amendment fixes what seems to us an unfortunate principle of tax exemption, capable of indefinite extension: We had thought that such an exemption required a clear and certain grant. This we do not find in the language of the First and Fourteenth Amendments. We are therefore of the opinion the judgments below should be affirmed.

Mr. Justice Roberts, Mr. Justice Frankfurter, and Mr. Justice Jackson join in this dissent.

126

While I wholly agree with the views expressed by Mr. Justice Reed, the controversy is of such a nature as to lead me to add a few words.

A tax can be a means for raising revenue, or a device for regulating conduct, or both. Challenge to the constitutional validity of a tax measure requires that it be analyzed and judged in all its aspects. We must therefore distinguish between the questions that are before us in these cases and those that are not. It is altogether incorrect to say that the question here is whether a state can limit the free exercise of religion by imposing burdensome taxes. As the opinion of my Brother Reed demonstrates, we have not here the question whether the taxes imposed in these cases are in practical operation an unjustifiable curtailment upon the petitioners' undoubted right to communicate their views to others. No claim is made that the effect of these taxes, either separately or cumulatively, has been or is likely to be to restrict the petitioners' religious propaganda activities in any degree. Counsel expressly disclaim any such contention. They insist on absolute immunity from any kind of monetary exaction for their occupation. Their claim is that no tax, no matter how trifling, can constitutionally be laid upon the activity of distributing religious literature, regardless of the actual effect of the tax upon such activity. That is the only ground upon which these ordinances have been attacked, that is the only question raised in or decided by the state courts, and that is the only question presented to us. No complaint is made against the size of the taxes. If an appropriate claim, indicating that the taxes were oppressive in their effect upon the petitioners' activities, had been made, the issues here would be very different. No such claim has been made, and it would be gratuitous to consider its merits.

Nor have we occasion to consider whether these measures are invalid on the ground that they unjustly or unreasonably discriminate against the petitioners. Counsel do not claim, as indeed they could not, that these ordinances were intended to or have been applied to discriminate against religious groups generally or Jehovah's Witnesses particularly. No claim is made that the effect of the taxes is to hinder or restrict the activities of Jehovah's Witnesses while other religious groups, perhaps older or more prosperous, can carry on theirs. This question, too, is not before us.

It cannot be said that the petitioners are constitutionally exempt from taxation merely because they may be engaged in religious activities or because such activities may constitute an exercise of a constitutional right. It will hardly be contended, for example, that a tax upon the income of a clergyman would violate the Bill of Rights, even though the tax is ultimately borne by the members of his church. A clergyman, no less than a judge, is a citizen. And not only in time of war would neither willingly enjoy immunity from the obligations of citizenship. It is only fair that he also who preaches the word of God should share in the costs of the benefits provided by government to him as well as to the other members of the community. And so no one would suggest that a clergyman who uses an automobile or the telephone in connection with his work thereby gains a constitutional exemption from taxes levied upon the use of automobiles or upon telephone calls. Equally alien is it to our constitutional system to suggest that the Constitution of the United States exempts church-held lands from state taxation. Plainly, a tax measure is not invalid under the federal Constitution merely because it falls upon persons engaged in activities of a religious nature.

Nor can a tax be invalidated merely because it falls upon activities which constitute an exercise of a constitutional right. The First Amendment of course protects the right to publish a newspaper or a magazine or a book. But the crucial question is—how much protection does the Amendment give, and against what is the right protected? It is certainly true that the protection afforded the freedom of the press by the First Amendment does not include exemption from all taxation. A tax upon newspaper publishing is not invalid simply because it falls upon the exercise of a constitutional right. Such a tax might be invalid if it invidiously singled out newspaper publishing for bearing the burdens of taxation or imposed upon them in such ways as to encroach on the essential scope of a free press. If the Court could justifiably hold that the tax measures in these cases were vulnerable on that ground, I would unreservedly agree. But the Court has not done so, and indeed could not.

The vice of the ordinances before us, the Court holds, is that they impose a special kind of tax, a "flat license tax, the payment of which is a condition of the exercise of these constitutional privileges (to engage in religious activities)." But the fact that an occupation tax is a "flat" tax certainly is not enough to condemn it. A legislature undoubtedly can tax all those who engage in an activity upon an equal basis. The Constitution certainly does not require that differentiations must be made among taxpayers upon the basis of the size of their incomes or the scope of their activities. Occupation taxes normally are flat taxes, and the Court surely does not mean to hold that a tax is bad merely because all taxpayers pursuing the very same activities and thereby demanding the same governmental services are treated alike. Nor, as I have indicated, can a tax be invalidated because the exercise of a constitutional privilege is conditioned upon its payment. It depends upon the nature of the condition that is imposed, its justification, and the extent to which it hinders or restricts the exercise of the privilege.

As I read the Court's opinion, it does not hold that the taxes in the cases before us in fact do hinder or restrict the petitioners in exercising their constitutional rights. It holds that "The power to tax the exercise of a privilege is the power to control or suppress its enjoyment." This assumes that because the taxing power exerted in Magnano Co. v. Hamilton, the well-known oleomargarine tax case, may have had the effect of "controlling" or "suppressing" the enjoyment of a privilege and still was sustained by this Court, and because all exertions of the taxing power may have that effect, if perchance a particular exercise of the taxing power does have that effect, it would have to be sustained under our ruling in the Magnano case.

The power to tax, like all powers of government, legislative, executive and judicial alike, can be abused or perverted. The power to tax is the power to destroy only in the sense that those who have power can misuse it. Mr. Justice Holmes disposed of this smooth phrase as a constitutional basis for invalidating taxes when he wrote "The power to tax is not the power to destroy while this Court sits." The fact that a power can be perverted does not mean that every exercise of the power is a perversion of the power. Thus, if a tax indirectly suppresses or controls the enjoyment of a constitutional privilege which a legislature cannot directly suppress or control, of course it is bad. But it is irrelevant that a tax can suppress or control if it does not. The Court holds that "Those who can tax the exercise of this religious practice can make its exercise so costly as to deprive it of the resources necessary for its maintenance." But this is not the same as saying that "Those who do tax the exercise of this religious practice have made its exercise so costly as to deprive it of the resources necessary for its maintenance."

The Court could not plausibly make such an assertion because the petitioners themselves disavow any claim that the taxes imposed in these cases impair their ability to exercise their constitutional rights. We cannot invalidate the tax measures before us simply because there may be others, not now before us, which are oppressive in their effect. The Court's opinion does not deny that the ordinances involved in these cases have in no way disabled the petitioners to engage in their religious activities. It holds only that "Those who can tax the privilege of engaging in this form of missionary evangelism can close its doors to all those who do not have a full purse." I quite agree with this statement as an abstract proposition. Those who possess the power to tax might wield it in tyrannical fashion. It does not follow, however, that every exercise of the power is an act of tyranny, or that government should be impotent because it might become tyrannical. The question before us now is whether these ordinances have deprived the petitioners of their constitutional rights, not whether some other ordinances not now before us might be enacted which might deprive them of such rights. To deny constitutional power to secular authority merely because of the possibility of its abuse is as valid as to deny the basis of spiritual authority because those in whom it is temporarily vested may misuse it.

The petitioners say they are immune as much from a flat occupation tax as from a licensing fee purporting explicitly to cover only the costs of regulation. They rightly reject any distinction between this occupation tax and such a licensing fee. There is no constitutional difference between a so-called regulatory fee and an imposition for purposes of revenue. The state exacts revenue to maintain the costs of government as an entirety. For certain purposes and at certain times a legislature may earmark exactions to cover the costs of specific governmental services. In most instances the revenues of the state are tapped from multitudinous sources for a common fund out of which the costs of government are paid. As a matter of public finance, it is often impossible to determine with nicety the governmental expenditures attributable to particular activities. But, in any event, whether government collects revenue for the costs of its services through an earmarked fund, or whether an approximation of the cost of regulation goes into the general revenues of government out of which all expenses are borne, is a matter of legislative discretion and not of constitutional distinction. Just so long as an occupation tax is not used as a cover for discrimination against a constitutionally protected right or as an unjustifiable burden upon it, from the point of view of the Constitution of the United States it can make no difference whether such a money exaction for governmental benefits is labeled a regulatory fee or a revenue measure.

It is strenuously urged that the Constitution denies a city the right to control the expression of men's minds and the right of men to win others to their views. But the Court is not divided on this proposition. No one disputes it. All members of the Court are equally familiar with the history that led to the adoption of the Bill of Rights and are equally zealous to enforce the constitutional protection of the free play of the human spirit. Escape from the real issue before us cannot be found in such generalities. The real issue here is not whether a city may charge for the dissemination of ideas but whether the states have power to require those who need additional facilities to help bear the cost of furnishing such facilities. Street hawkers make demands upon municipalities that involve the expenditure of dollars and cents, whether they hawk printed matter or other things. As the facts in these cases show, the cost of maintaining the peace, the additional demands upon governmental facilities for assuring security, involve outlays which have to be met. To say that the Constitution forbids the states to obtain the necessary revenue from the whole of a class that enjoys these benefits and facilities, when in fact no discrimination is suggested as between purveyors of printed matter and purveyors of other things, and the exaction is not claimed to be actually burdensome, is to say that the Constitution requires, not that the dissemination of ideas in the interest of religion shall be free, but that it shall be subsidized by the state. Such a claim offends the most important of all aspects of religious freedom in this country, namely, that of the separation of church and state.

The ultimate question in determining the constitutionality of a tax measure is—has the state given something for which it can ask a return? There can be no doubt that these petitioners, like all who use the streets, have received the benefits of government. Peace is maintained, traffic is regulated, health is safeguarded—these are only some of the many incidents of municipal administration. To secure them costs money, and a state's source of money is its taxing power. There is nothing in the Constitution which exempts persons engaged in religious activities from sharing equally in the costs of benefits to all, including themselves, provided by government.

I cannot say, therefore, that in these cases the community has demanded a return for that which it did not give. Nor am I called upon to say that the state has demanded unjustifiably more than the value of what it gave, nor that its demand in fact cramps activities pursued to promote religious beliefs. No such claim was made at the bar, and there is no evidence in the records to substantiate any such claim if it had been made. Under these circumstances, therefore, I am of opinion that the ordinances in these cases must stand.

Mr. Justice Jackson joins in this dissent.

DOUGLAS v. CITY OF JEANNETTE
319 US 157 (1943)

"In my view the First Amendment assures the broadest tolerable exercise of free speech, free press, and free assembly, not merely for religious purposes, but for political, economic, scientific, news, or informational ends as well. When limits are reached which such communications must observe, can one go farther under the cloak of religious evangelism? Does what is obscene, or commercial, or abusive or inciting become less so if employed to promote a religious ideology? I had not supposed that the rights of secular and non-religious communications were more narrow or in any way inferior to those of avowed religious groups."

Mr. Justice Jackson, dissenting

131

Justice Jackson examines in some detail the operations of Jehovah's Witnesses and criticizes the Court's "vague but fervent transcendental-ism."

MR. JUSTICE JACKSON.

Except the case of Douglas et al. v. City of Jeannette (Pennsylvania), all of these cases are decided upon the record of isolated prosecutions in which information is confined to a particular act of offense and to the behavior of an individual offender. Only the Douglas record gives a comprehensive story of the broad plan of campaign employed by Jehovah's Witnesses and its full impact on a living community. But the facts of this case are passed over as irrelevant to the theory on which the Court would decide its particular issue. Unless we are to reach judgments as did Plato's men who were chained in a cave so that they saw nothing but shadows we should consider the facts of the Douglas case at least as an hypothesis to test the validity of the conclusions in the other cases. This record shows us something of the strings as well as the marionettes. It reveals the problem of those in local authority when the right to proselyte comes in contact with what many people have an idea is their right to be let alone. The Chief Justice says for the Court in Douglas that "in view of the decision rendered today in Murdock et al. v. Commonwealth of Pennsylvania supra, we find no ground for supposing that the intervention of a federal court, in order to secure petitioners' constitutional rights, will be either necessary or appropriate," which could hardly be said if the constitutional issues presented by the facts of this case are not settled by the Murdock case. The facts of record in the Douglas case and their relation to the facts of the other cases seem to me worth recital and consideration if we are realistically to weigh the conflicting claims of rights in the related cases today decided.

From the record in Douglas we learn:

In 1939, a "Watch Tower Campaign" was instituted by Jehovah's Witnesses in Jeannette, Pennsylvania, an industrial city of some 16,000 inhabitants. Each home was visited, a bell was rung or the door knocked upon, and the householder advised that the Witness had important information. If the householder would listen, a record was played on the phonograph. Its subject was "Snare and Racket." The following words are representative of its contents: "Religion is wrong and a snare because it deceives the people, but that does not mean that all who follow religion are willingly bad. Religion is a racket because it has long been used and is still used to extract money from the people upon the theory and promise that the paying over of money to a priest will serve to relieve the party paying from punishment after death and

132

further insure his salvation." This line of attack is taken by the Witnesses generally upon all denominations, especially the Roman Catholic. The householder was asked to buy a variety of literature for a price or contribution. The price would be twenty-five cents for the books and smaller sums for the pamphlets. Oftentimes, if he was unwilling to purchase, the book or pamphlet was given to him anyway.

When this campaign began, many complaints from offended householders were received, and three or four of the Witnesses were arrested. Thereafter, the "zone servant" in charge of the campaign conferred with the Mayor. He told the Mayor it was their right to carry on the campaign and showed him a decision of the United States Supreme Court, said to have that effect, as proof of it. The Mayor told him that they were at liberty to distribute their literature in the streets of the city and that he would have no objection if they distributed the literature free of charge at the houses, but that the people objected to their attempt to force these sales, and particularly on Sunday. The Mayor asked whether it would not be possible to come on some other day and to distribute the literature without selling it. The zone servant replied that that was contrary to their method of "doing business" and refused. He also told the Mayor that he would bring enough Witnesses into the City of Jeannette to get the job done whether the Mayor liked it or not. The Mayor urged them to await the outcome of an appeal which was then pending in the other cases and let the matter take its course through the courts. This, too, was refused, and the threat to bring more people than the Mayor's police force could cope with was repeated.

On Palm Sunday of 1939, the threat was made good. Over 100 of the Witnesses appeared. They were strangers to the city and arrived in upwards of twenty-five automobiles. The automobiles were parked outside the city limits, and the headquarters were set up in a gasoline station with telephone facilities through which the director of the campaign could be notified when trouble occurred. He furnished bonds for the Witnesses as they were arrested. As they began their work, around 9:00 o'clock in the morning, telephone calls began to come in to the Police Headquarters, and complaints in large volume were made all during the day. They exceeded the number that the police could handle, and the Fire Department was called out to assist. The Witnesses called at homes singly and in groups, and some of the homes complained that they were called upon several times. Twenty-one Witnesses were arrested. Only those were arrested where definite proof was obtainable that the literature had been offered for sale or a sale had been made for a price. Three were later discharged for inadequacies in this proof, and eighteen were convicted. The "zone servant" furnished appeal bonds.

The national structure of the Jehovah's Witness movement is also somewhat revealed in this testimony. At the head of the movement in this country is the Watch Tower Bible & Tract Society, a corporation organized under the laws of Pennsylvania, but having its principal place of business in Brooklyn, N. Y. It prints all pamphlets, manufactures all books, supplies all phonographs and records, and provides other materials for the Witnesses. It "ordains" these Witnesses by furnishing each, on a basis which does not clearly appear, a certificate that he is a minister of the Gospel. Its output is large and its revenues must be considerable. Little is revealed of its affairs. One of its "zone servants" testified that its correspondence is signed only with the name of the corporation and anonymity as to its personnel is its policy. The assumption that it is a "non-profit charitable" corporation may be true, but it is without support beyond mere assertion. In none of these cases has the assertion been supported by such usual evidence as a balance sheet or an income statement. What its manufacturing costs and revenues are, what salaries or bonuses it pays, what contracts it has for supplies or services we simply do not know. The effort of counsel for Jeannette to obtain information, books and records of the local "companies" of Witnesses engaged in the Jeannette campaign in the trial was met by contradictory statements as to the methods and meaning of such meager accounts as were produced.

The publishing output of the Watch Tower corporation is disposed of through converts, some of whom are full-time and some part-time ministers. These are organized into groups or companies under the direction of "zone servants." It is their purpose to carry on in a thorough manner so that every home in the communities in which they work may be regularly visited three or four times a year. The full-time Witnesses acquire their literature from the Watch Tower Bible & Tract Society at a figure which enables them to distribute it at the prices printed thereon with a substantial differential. Some of the books they acquire for 5¢ and dispose of for a contribution of 25¢. On others, the margin is less. Part-time ministers have a differential between the 20¢ which they remit to the Watch Tower Society and the 25¢ which is the contribution they ask for the books. We are told that many of the Witnesses give away a substantial quantity of the literature to people who make no contributions. Apart from the fact that this differential exists and that it enables the distributors to meet in whole or in part their living expenses, it has proven impossible in these cases to learn the exact results of the campaigns from a financial point of view. There is evidence that the group accumulated a substantial amount from the differentials, but the tracing of the money was not possible because of the failure to obtain records and the failure, apparently, to keep them.

The literature thus distributed is voluminous and repetitious. Characterization is risky, but a few quotations will indicate something of its temper.

Taking as representative the book "Enemies," of which J. F. Rutherford, the lawyer who long headed this group, is the author, we find the following: "The greatest racket ever invented and practiced is that of religion. The most cruel and seductive public enemy is that which employs religion to carry on the racket, and by which means the people are deceived and the name of Almighty God is reproached. There are numerous systems of religion, but the most subtle, fraudulent and injurious to humankind is that which is generally labeled the 'Christian religion,' because it has the appearance of a worshipful devotion to the Supreme Being, and thereby easily misleads many honest and sincere persons." It analyzes the income of the Roman Catholic hierarchy and announces that it is "the great racket, a racket that is greater than all other rackets combined." It also says under the chapter heading "Song of the Harlot," "Referring now to the foregoing Scriptural definition of harlot: What religious system exactly fits the prophecies recorded in God's Word? There is but one answer, and that is, The Roman Catholic Church organization." "Those close or nearby and dependent upon the main organization, being of the same stripe, picture the Jewish and Protestant clergy and other allies of the Hierarchy who tag along behind the Hierarchy at the present time to do the bidding of the old 'whore.' " "Says the prophet of Jehovah: 'It shall come to pass in that day, that Tyre (modern Tyre, the Roman Catholic Hierarchy organization) shall be forgotten.' Forgotten by whom? By her former illicit paramours who have committed fornication with her." Throughout the literature statements of this kind appear amidst scriptural comment and prophecy, denunciation of demonology, which is used to characterize the Roman Catholic religion, criticism of government and those in authority, advocacy of obedience to the law of God instead of the law of man, and an interpretation of the law of God as they see it.

The spirit and temper of this campaign is most fairly stated perhaps in the words, again of Rutherford, in his book "Religion," p. 196–198:

"God's faithful servants go from house to house to bring the message of the kingdom to those who reside there, omitting none, not even the houses of the Roman Catholic Hierarchy, and there they give witness to the kingdom because they are commanded by the Most High to do so. 'They shall enter in at the windows like a thief.' They do not loot nor break into the houses, but they set up their phonographs before the doors and windows and send the message of the kingdom right into the houses into the ears of those who might wish to hear; and while those desiring to hear are hearing, some of the 'sourpusses' are compelled to hear. Locusts invade the homes of the people and even eat the varnish off the wood and eat the wood to some extent. Likewise God's faithful witnesses, likened unto locusts, get the kingdom message right into the house and they take the veneer off the religious things that are in that house, including candles and 'holy water,' remove the superstition from the minds of the people, and show them that the doctrines that have been taught to them are wood, hay and stubble, destructible by fire, and they cannot withstand the heat. The people are enabled to learn that 'purgatory' is a bogeyman, set up by the agents of Satan to frighten the people into the religious organizations, where they may be fleeced of their hard-earned money. Thus the kingdom message plagues the religionists, and the clergy find that they are unable to prevent it. Therefore, as described by the prophet, the message comes to them like a thief that enters in at the windows, and this message is a warning to those who are on the inside that Jesus Christ has come, and they remember his warning words, to wit: 'Behold, I come as a thief.' (Revelation 16:15). The day of Armageddon is very close, and that day comes upon the world in general like a thief in the night."

The day of Armageddon, to which all of this is prelude, is to be a violent and bloody one, for then shall be slain all "demonologists," including most of those who reject the teachings of Jehovah's Witnesses.

In the Murdock case, on another Sunday morning of the following Lent, we again find the Witnesses in Jeannette, travelling by twos and threes and carrying the cases for the books and phonographs. This time eight were arrested, as against the 21 arrested on the preceding Palm Sunday involved in the Douglas case.

In the Struthers case, we find the Witness knocking on the door of a total stranger at 4:00 on Sunday afternoon, July 7th. The householder's fourteen-year-old son answered, and, at the Witness's request, called his mother from the kitchen. His mother had previously become "very much disgusted about going to the door" to receive leaflets, particularly since another person had on a previous occasion called her to the door and told her, as she testified, "that I was doomed to go to hell because I would not let this literature in my home for my children to read." She testified that the Witness "shoved in the door" the circular being distributed, and that she "couldn't do much more than take" it, and she promptly tore it up in the presence of the Witness, for while she believed "in the worship of God," she did not "believe that anyone needs to be sent from door to door to tell us how to worship."

The record in the Struthers case is even more sparse than that in the Murdock case, but the householder did testify that at the time she was given the circular the Witness "told me that a number of them were in jail and would I call the Chief of Police and ask that their workers might be released."

Such is the activity which it is claimed no public authority can either regulate or tax. This claim is substantially, if not quite, sustained today. I dissent—a disagreement induced in no small part by the facts recited.

As individuals many of us would not find this activity seriously objectionable. The subject of the disputes involved may be a matter of indifference to our personal creeds. Moreover, we work in offices affording ample shelter from such importunities and live in homes where we do not personally answer such calls and bear the burden of turning away the unwelcome. But these observations do not hold true for all. The stubborn persistence of the officials of smaller communities in their efforts to regulate this conduct indicates a strongly held conviction that the Court's many decisions in this field are at odds with the realities of life in those communities where the householder himself drops whatever he may be doing to answer the summons to the door and is apt to have positive religious convictions of his own.

Three subjects discussed in the opinions in Murdock v. Commonwealth of Pennsylvania and Martin v. Struthers tend to obscure the effect of the decisions. The first of these relates to the form of the ordinances in question. One cannot determine whether this is mere makeweight or whether it is an argument addressed to the constitutionality of the ordinances; and whatever it is, I cannot reconcile the treatment of the subject by the two opinions. In Murdock the Court says "the present ordinance is not narrowly drawn to safeguard the people of the community in their homes against the evils of solicitations," and again "the ordinance is not narrowly drawn to prevent or control abuses or evils arising from" solicitation from house to house. It follows the recent tendency to invalidate ordinances in this general field that are not "narrowly drawn."

But in Struthers the ordinance is certainly narrowly drawn. Yet the Court denies the householder the narrow protection it gives. The city points out that this ordinance was narrowly drawn to meet a particular evil in that community where many men must work nights and rest by day. I had supposed that our question, except in respect to ordinances invalid on their face, is always whether the ordinance as applied denies constitutional rights. Nothing in the Constitution says or implies that real rights are more vulnerable to a narrow ordinance than to a broad one. I think our function is to take municipal ordinances as they are construed by the state courts and applied by local authorities and to decide their constitutionality accordingly, rather than to undertake censoring their draftsmanship.

Secondly, in neither opinion does the Court give clear-cut consideration to the particular activities claimed to be entitled to constitutional immunity, but in one case blends with them conduct of others not in question, and in the other confuses with the rights in question here certain alleged rights of others which these petitioners are in no position to assert as their own.

In the Murdock case the Court decides to "restore to their high, constitutional position the liberties of itinerant evangelists." That it does without stating what those privileges are, beyond declaring that "This form of religious activity occupies the same high estate under the First Amendment as do worship in the churches and preaching from the pulpits." How can we dispose of the questions in this case merely by citing the unquestioned right to minister to congregations voluntarily attending services?

Similarly, in the Struthers case the Court fails to deal with the behavior of the Witnesses on its own merits. It reaches its decision by weighing against the ordinance there in question not only the rights of the Witness but also "the right of the individual householder to determine whether he is willing to receive her message;" concludes that the ordinance "substitutes the judgment of the community for the judgment of the individual householder;" and decides the case on the basis that "it submits the distributer to criminal punishment for annoying the person on whom he calls, even though the recipient of the literature distributed is in fact glad to receive it." But the hospitable householder thus thrown in the balance with the Witness to make weight against the city ordinance is wholly hypothetical and the assumption is contrary to the evidence we have recited. Doubtless there exists fellow spirits who welcome these callers, but the issue here is what are the rights of those who do not and what is the right of the community to protect them in the exercise of their own faith in peace. That issue—the real issue—seems not to be dealt with.

Third, both opinions suggest that there are evils in this conduct that a municipality may do something about. But neither identifies it, nor lays down any workable guide in so doing. In Murdock the Court says that "the ordinance is not narrowly drawn to prevent or control abuses or evils arising" from house-to-house solicitation. What evils or abuses? It is also said in Murdock that we "have something very different from a registration system under which those going from house to house are required to give their names, addresses and other marks of identification to the authorities." What more? The fee of course. But we are told the fee is not "a nominal fee imposed as a regulatory measure to defray the expenses of policing the activities in question." Is it implied that such a registration for such a fee would be valid? Wherein does the suggestion differ from the ordinance we are striking down? This ordinance did nothing more, it did not give discretion to refuse the license nor to censor the literature. The fee ranged from $1.50 a day for one day to less than a dollar a day for two weeks. There is not a syllable of evidence that this amount exceeds the cost to the community of policing this activity. If this suggestion of new devices is not illusory, why is the present ordinance invalid? The City of Struthers decided merely that one with no more business at a home than the delivery of advertising matter should not obtrude himself farther by announcing the fact of delivery. He was free to make the distribution if he left the householder undisturbed, to take it in in his own time. The Court says the City has not even this much leeway in ordering its affairs, however complicated they may be as the result of round-the-clock industrial activity. If the local authorities must draw closer aim at evils than they did in these cases I doubt that they ever can hit them. What narrow area of regulation exists under these decisions? The Struthers opinion says, "the dangers of distribution can so easily be controlled by traditional legal methods." It suggests that the city may "by identification devices control the abuse of the privilege by criminals posing as canvassers." Of course to require registration and license is one of the few practical "identification devices." Merely giving one's name and his address to the authorities would afford them basis for investigating who the strange callers are and what their record has been. And that is what Murdock prohibits the city from asking. If the entire course of concerted conduct revealed to us is immune, I should think it neither fair nor wise to throw out to the cities encouragement to try new restraints. If some part of it passes the boundary of immunity, I think we should say what part and why in these cases we are denying the right to regulate it. The suggestion in Struthers that "the problem must be worked out by each community for itself" is somewhat ironical in view of the fate of the ordinances here involved.

Our difference of opinion cannot fairly be given the color of a disagreement as to whether the constitutional rights of Jehovah's Witnesses should be protected in so far as they are rights. These Witnesses, in common with all others, have extensive rights to proselyte and propagandize. These of course include the right to oppose and criticize the Roman Catholic Church or any other denomination. These rights are, and should be held to be, as extensive as any orderly society can tolerate in religious disputation. The real question is where their rights end and

139

the rights of others begin. The real task of determining the extent of their rights on balance with the rights of others is not met by pronouncement of general propositions with which there is no disagreement.

If we should strip these cases to the underlying questions, I find them too difficult as constitutional problems to be disposed of by a vague but fervent transcendentalism.

In my view the First Amendment assures the broadest tolerable exercise of free speech, free press, and free assembly, not merely for religious purposes, but for political, economic, scientific, news, or informational ends as well. When limits are reached which such communications must observe, can one go farther under the cloak of religious evangelism? Does what is obscene, or commercial, or abusive or inciting become less so if employed to promote a religious ideology? I had not supposed that the rights of secular and non-religious communications were more narrow or in any way inferior to those of avowed religious groups.

It may be asked why then does the First Amendment separately mention free exercise of religion? The history of religious persecution gives the answer. Religion needed specific protection because it was subject to attack from a separate quarter. It was often claimed that one was an heretic and guilty of blasphemy, because he failed to conform in mere belief, or in support of prevailing institutions and theology. It was to assure religious teaching as much freedom as secular discussion, rather than to assure it greater license, that led to its separate statement.

The First Amendment grew out of an experience which taught that society cannot trust the conscience of a majority to keep its religious zeal within the limits that a free society can tolerate. I do not think it any more intended to leave the conscience of a minority to fix its limits. Civil government can not let any group ride rough-shod over others simply because their "consciences" tell them to do so.

A common-sense test as to whether the Court has struck a proper balance of these rights is to ask what the effect would be if the right given to these Witnesses should be exercised by all sects and denominations. If each competing sect in the United States went after the householder by the same methods, I should think it intolerable. If a minority can put on this kind of drive in a community, what can a majority resorting to the same tactics do to individuals and minorities? Can we give to one sect a privilege that we could not give to all, merely in the hope that most of them will not resort to it? Religious freedom in the long run does not come from this kind of license to each sect to fix its own limits, but comes of hard-headed fixing of those limits by neutral authority with an eye to the widest freedom to proselyte compatible with the freedom of those subject to proselyting pressures.

140

I cannot accept the holding in the Murdock case that the behavior revealed here "occupies the same high estate under the First Amendment as do worship in the churches and preaching from the pulpits." To put them on the same constitutional plane seems to me to have a dangerous tendency towards discrediting religious freedom.

Neither can I think it an essential part of freedom that religious differences be aired in language that is obscene, abusive, or inciting to retaliation. We have held that a Jehovah's Witness may not call a public officer a "God damned racketeer" and a "damned Fascist," because that is to use "fighting words," and such are not privileged. How then can the Court today hold it a "high constitutional privilege" to go to homes, including those of devout Catholics on Palm Sunday morning and thrust upon them literature calling their church a "whore" and their faith a "racket"?

Nor am I convinced that we can have freedom of religion only by denying the American's deep-seated conviction that his home is a refuge from the pulling and hauling of the market place and the street. For a stranger to corner a man in his home, summon him to the door and put him in the position either of arguing his religion or of ordering one of unknown disposition to leave is a questionable use of religious freedom.

I find it impossible to believe that the Struthers case can be solved by reference to the statement that "The authors of the First Amendment knew that novel and unconventional ideas might disturb the complacent, but they chose to encourage a freedom which they believed essential if vigorous enlightenment was ever to triumph over slothful ignorance." I doubt if only the slothfully ignorant wish repose in their homes, or that the forefathers intended to open the door to such forced "enlightenment" as we have here.

In these cases local authorities caught between the offended householders and the drive of the Witnesses have been hard put to keep the peace of their communities. They have invoked old ordinances that are crude and clumsy for the purpose. I should think that the singular persistence of the turmoil about Jehovah's Witnesses, one which seems to result from the work of no other sect, would suggest to this Court a thorough examination of their methods to see if they impinge unduly on the rights of others. Instead of that the Court has, in one way after another, tied the hands of all local authority and made the aggressive methods of this group the law of the land.

This Court is forever adding new stories to the temples of constitutional law, and the temples have a way of collapsing when one story too many is added. So it was with liberty of contract, which was discredited by being overdone. The Court is adding a new privilege to override the rights of others to what has before been regarded as religious liberty. In so doing it needlessly creates a risk of discrediting a wise provision of our Constitution which protects all—those in homes as well as those out of them—in the peaceful, orderly practice of the religion of their choice but which gives no right to force it upon others.

Civil liberties had their origin and must find their ultimate guaranty in the faith of the people. If that faith should be lost, five or nine men in Washington could not long supply its want. Therefore we must do our utmost to make clear and easily understandable the reasons for deciding these cases as we do. Forthright observance of rights presupposes their forthright definition.

I think that the majority has failed in this duty. I therefore dissent in Murdock and Struthers and concur in the result in Douglas.

I join in the opinions of Mr. Justice Reed in Murdock and Struthers, and in that of Mr. Justice Frankfurter in Murdock.

Mr. Justice Frankfurter joins in these views.

WEST VIRGINIA STATE BOARD OF EDUCATION v. BARNETTE   319 US 624 (1943)

"If there is any fixed star in our constitutional constellation, it is that no official, high or petty, can prescribe what shall be orthodox in politics, nationalism, religion, or other matters of opinion or force citizens to confess by word or act their faith therein."

Mr. Justice Jackson, for the Court

"Words uttered under coercion are proof of loyalty to nothing but self-interest."

Mr. Justice Black, concurring

"So far as the state was concerned, there was to be neither orthodoxy nor heterodoxy. And so Jefferson and those who followed him wrote guaranties of religious freedom into our constitutions. Religious minorities as well as religious majorities were to be equal in the eyes of the political state. But Jefferson and the others also knew that minorities may disrupt society. It never would have occurred to them to write into the Constitution the subordination of general civil authority of the state to sectarian scruples."

Mr. Justice Frankfurter, dissenting

The Court here reconsiders the problem it dealt with in the Gobitis case and reverses its position. Justice Frankfurter, defending the Gobitis position, writes a noteworthy dissent:

MR. JUSTICE JACKSON DELIVERED THE OPINION OF THE COURT.

Following the decision by this Court on June 3, 1940, in Minersville School District v. Gobitis, the West Virginia legislature amended its statutes to require all schools therein to conduct courses of instruction in history, civics, and in the Constitutions of the United States and of the State "for the purpose of teaching, fostering and perpetuating the ideals, principles and spirit of Americanism, and increasing the knowledge of the organization and machinery of the government."

Appellant Board of Education was directed, with advice of the State Superintendent of Schools, to "prescribe the courses of study covering these subjects" for public schools. The Act made it the duty of private, parochial and denominational schools to prescribe courses of study "similar to those required for the public schools."

The Board of Education on January 9, 1942, adopted a resolution containing recitals taken largely from the Court's Gobitis opinion and ordering that the salute to the Flag become "a regular part of the program of activities in the public schools," that all teachers and pupils "shall be required to participate in the salute honoring the Nation represented by the Flag; provided, however, that refusal to salute the Flag be regarded as an Act of insubordination, and shall be dealt with accordingly."

The resolution originally required the "commonly accepted salute to the Flag" which it defined. Objections to the salute as "being too much like Hitler's" were raised by the Parent and Teacher's Association, the Boy and Girl Scouts, the Red Cross, and the Federation of Women's Clubs. Some modification appears to have been made in deference to these objections, but no concession was made to Jehovah's Witnesses. What is now required is the "stiff-arm" salute, the saluter to keep the right hand raised with palm turned up while the following is repeated: "I pledge allegiance to the Flag of the United States of America and to the Republic for which it stands; one Nation, indivisible, with liberty and justice for all."

Failure to conform is "insubordination" dealt with by expulsion. Readmission is denied by statute until compliance. Meanwhile the expelled child is "unlawfully absent" and may be proceeded against as a delinquent. His parents or guardians are liable to prosecution, and if convicted are subject to fine not exceeding $50 and jail term not exceeding thirty days.

Appellees, citizens of the United States and of West Virginia, brought suit in the United States District Court for themselves and others similarly situated asking its injunction to restrain enforcement of these laws and regulations against Jehovah's Witnesses. The Witnesses are an unincorporated body teaching that the obligation imposed by law of God is superior to that of laws enacted by temporal government. Their religious beliefs include a literal version of Exodus, Chapter 20, verses 4 and 5, which says: "Thou shalt not make unto thee any graven image, or any likeness of anything that is in heaven above, or that is in the earth beneath, or that is in the water under the earth; thou shalt not bow down thyself to them nor serve them." They consider that the flag is an "image" within this command. For this reason they refuse to salute it.

Children of this faith have been expelled from school and are threatened with exclusion for no other cause. Officials threaten to send them to reformatories maintained for criminally inclined juveniles. Parents of such children have been prosecuted and are threatened with prosecutions for causing delinquency.

The Board of Education moved to dismiss the complaint setting forth these facts and alleging that the law and regulations are an unconstitutional denial of religious freedom, and of freedom of speech, and are invalid under the "due process" and "equal protection" clauses of the Fourteenth Amendment to the Federal Constitution. The cause was submitted on the pleadings to a District Court of three judges. It restrained enforcement as to the plaintiffs and those of that class. The Board of Education brought the case here by direct appeal.

This case calls upon us to reconsider a precedent decision, as the Court throughout its history often has been required to do. Before turning to the Gobitis case, however, it is desirable to notice certain characteristics by which this controversy is distinguished.

The freedom asserted by these appellees does not bring them into collision with rights asserted by any other individual. It is such conflicts which most frequently require intervention of the State to determine where the rights of one end and those of another begin. But the refusal of these persons to participate in the ceremony does not interfere with or deny rights of others to do so. Nor is there any question in this case that their behavior is peaceable and orderly. The sole conflict is between authority and rights of the individual. The State asserts power to condition access to public education on making a prescribed sign and profession and at the same time to coerce attendance by punishing both parent and child. The latter stand on a right of self-determination in matters that touch individual opinion and personal attitude.

As the present Chief Justice said in dissent in the Gobitis case, the State may "require teaching by instruction and study of all in our history and in the structure and organization of our government, including the guaranties of civil liberty which tend to inspire patriotism and love of country." Here, however, we are dealing with a compulsion of students to declare a belief. They are not merely made acquainted with the flag salute so that they may be informed as to what it is or even what it means. The issue here is whether this slow and easily

144

neglected route to aroused loyalties constitutionally may be short-cut by substituting a compulsory salute and slogan. This issue is not prejudiced by the Court's previous holding that where a State, without compelling attendance, extends college facilities to pupils who voluntarily enroll, it may prescribe military training as part of the course without offense to the Constitution. It was held that those who take advantage of its opportunities may not on ground of conscience refuse compliance with such conditions. In the present case attendance is not optional. That case is also to be distinguished from the present one because, independently of college privileges or requirements, the State has power to raise militia and impose the duties of service therein upon its citizens.

There is no doubt that, in connection with the pledges, the flag salute is a form of utterance. Symbolism is a primitive but effective way of communicating ideas. The use of an emblem or flag to symbolize some system, idea, institution, or personality, is a short cut from mind to mind. Causes and nations, political parties, lodges and ecclesiastical groups seek to knit the loyalty of their followings to a flag or banner, a color or design. The State announces rank, function, and authority through crowns and maces, uniforms and black robes; the church speaks through the Cross, the Crucifix, the altar and shrine, and clerical raiment. Symbols of State often convey political ideas just as religious symbols come to convey theological ones. Associated with many of these symbols are appropriate gestures of acceptance or respect: a salute, a bowed or bared head, a bended knee. A person gets from a symbol the meaning he puts into it, and what is one man's comfort and inspiration is another's jest and scorn.

Over a decade ago Chief Justice Hughes led this Court in holding that the display of a red flag as a symbol of opposition by peaceful and legal means to organized government was protected by the free speech guaranties of the Constitution. Here it is the State that employs a flag as a symbol of adherence to government as presently organized. It requires the individual to communicate by word and sign his acceptance of the political ideas it thus bespeaks. Objection to this form of communication when coerced is an old one, well known to the framers of the Bill of Rights.

It is also to be noted that the compulsory flag salute and pledge requires affirmation of a belief and an attitude of mind. It is not clear whether the regulation contemplates that pupils forego any contrary convictions of their own and become unwilling converts to the prescribed ceremony or whether it will be acceptable if they simulate assent by words without belief and by a gesture barren of meaning. It is now a commonplace that censorship or suppression of expression of opinion is tolerated by our Constitution only when the expression presents a clear and present danger of action of a kind the State is empowered to prevent and punish. It would seem that involuntary affirmation could be commanded only on even more immediate and urgent grounds than silence. But here the power of compulsion is invoked without any allegation that remaining passive during a flag salute ritual creates a clear and present danger that would justify an effort even to muffle expression. To sustain the compulsory flag salute we are required to say that a Bill of Rights which guard the individual's right to speak his own mind, left it open to public authorities to compel him to utter what is not in his mind.

Whether the First Amendment to the Constitution will permit officials to order observance of ritual of this nature does not depend upon whether as a voluntary exercise we would think it to be good, bad or merely innocuous. Any credo of nationalism is likely to include what some disapprove or to omit what others think essential, and to give off different overtones as it takes on different accents or interpretations. If official power exists to coerce acceptance of any patriotic creed, what it shall contain cannot be decided by courts, but must be largely discretionary with the ordaining authority, whose power to prescribe would no doubt include power to amend. Hence validity of the asserted power to force an American citizen publicly to profess any statement of belief or to engage in any ceremony of assent to one presents questions of power that must be considered independently of any idea we may have as to the utility of the ceremony in question.

Nor does the issue as we see it turn on one's possession of particular religious views or the sincerity with which they are held. While religion supplies appellees' motive for enduring the discomforts of making the issue in this case, many citizens who do not share these religious views hold such a compulsory rite to infringe constitutional liberty of the individual. It is not necessary to inquire whether non-conformist beliefs will exempt from the duty to salute unless we first find power to make the salute a legal duty.

The Gobitis decision, however, assumed, as did the argument in that case and in this, that power exists in the State to impose the flag salute discipline upon school children in general. The Court only examined and rejected a claim based on religious beliefs of immunity from an unquestioned general rule. The question which underlies the flag salute controversy is whether such a ceremony so touching matters of opinion and political attitude may be imposed upon the individual by official authority under powers committed to any political organization under our Constitution. We examine rather than assume existence of this power and, against this broader definition of issues in this case, re-examine specific grounds assigned for the Gobitis decision.

1. It was said that the flag-salute controversy confronted the Court with "the problem which Lincoln cast in memorable dilemma: 'Must a government of necessity be too strong for the liberties of its people, or too weak to maintain its own existence?' " and that the answer must be in favor of strength.

We think these issues may be examined free of pressure or restraint growing out of such considerations.

It may be doubted whether Mr. Lincoln would have thought that the strength of government to maintain itself would be impressively vindicated by our confirming power of the state to expel a handful of children from school. Such oversimplification, so handy in political debate, often lacks the precision necessary to postulates of judicial reasoning. If validly applied to this problem, the utterance cited would resolve every issue of power in favor of those in authority and would require us to override every liberty thought to weaken or delay execution of their policies.

Government of limited power need not be anemic government. Assurance that rights are secure tends to diminish fear and jealousy of strong government, and by making us feel safe to live under it makes for its better support. Without promise of a limiting Bill of Rights it is doubtful if our Constitution could have mustered enough strength to enable its ratification. To enforce those rights today is not to choose weak government over strong government. It is only to adhere as a means of strength to individual freedom of mind in preference to officially disciplined uniformity for which history indicates a disappointing and disastrous end.

The subject now before us exemplifies this principle. Free public education, if faithful to the ideal of secular instruction and political neutrality, will not be partisan or enemy of any class, creed, party, or faction. If it is to impose any ideological discipline, however, each party or denomination must seek to control, or failing that, to weaken the influence of the educational system. Observance of the limitations of the Constitution will not weaken government in the field appropriate for its exercise.

2. It was also considered in the Gobitis case that functions of educational officers in states, counties and school districts were such that to interfere with their authority "would in effect make us the school board for the country."

The Fourteenth Amendment, as now applied to the States, protects the citizen against the State itself and all of its creatures—Boards of

Education not excepted. These have, of course, important, delicate, and highly discretionary functions, but none that they may not perform within the limits of the Bill of Rights. That they are educating the young for citizenship is reason for scrupulous protection of Constitutional Freedoms of the individual, if we are not to strangle the free mind at its source and teach youth to discount important principles of our government as mere platitudes.

Such Boards are numerous and their territorial jurisdiction often small. But small and local authority may feel less sense of responsibility to the Constitution, and agencies of publicity may be less vigilant in calling it to account. The action of Congress in making flag observance voluntary and respecting the conscience of the objector in a matter so vital as raising the Army contrasts sharply with these local regulations in matters relatively trivial to the welfare of the nation. There are village tyrants as well as village Hampdens, but none who acts under color of law is beyond reach of the Constitution.

3. The Gobitis opinion reasoned that this is a field "where courts possess no marked and certainly no controlling competence," that it is committed to the legislatures as well as the courts to guard cherished liberties and that it is constitutionally appropriate to "fight out the wise use of legislative authority in the form of public opinion and before legislative assemblies rather than to transfer such a contest to the judicial arena," since all the "effective means of inducing political changes are left free."

The very purpose of a Bill of Rights was to withdraw certain subjects from the vicissitudes of political controversy, to place them beyond the reach of majorities and officials and to establish them as legal principles to be applied by the courts. One's right to life, liberty, and property, to free speech, a free press, freedom of worship and assembly, and other fundamental rights may not be submitted to vote; they depend on the outcome of no elections.

In weighing arguments of the parties it is important to distinguish between the due process clause of the Fourteenth Amendment as an instrument for transmitting the principles of the First Amendment and those cases in which it is applied for its own sake. The test of legislation which collides with the Fourteenth Amendment, because it also collides with the principles of the First, is much more definite than the test when only the Fourteenth is involved. Much of the vagueness of the due process clause disappears when the specific prohibitions of the First become its standard. The right of a State to regulate, for example, a public utility may well include, so far as the due process test is concerned, power to impose all of the restrictions which a legislature may have a "rational basis" for adopting. But freedoms of speech and of press, of assembly, and of worship may not be infringed on such slender grounds. They are susceptible of restriction only to prevent grave and immediate danger to interests which the state may lawfully protect. It is important to note that while it is the Fourteenth Amendment which bears directly upon the State it is the more specific limiting principles of the First Amendment that finally govern this case.

Nor does our duty to apply the Bill of Rights to assertions of official authority depend upon our possession of marked competence in the field where the invasion of rights occurs. True, the task of translating the majestic generalities of the Bill of Rights, conceived as part of the pattern of liberal government in the eighteenth century, into concrete restraints on officials dealing with the problems of the twentieth century, is one to disturb self-confidence. These principles grew in soil which also produced a philosophy that the individual was the center of society, that his liberty was attainable through mere absence of governmental restraints, and that government should be entrusted with few controls and only the mildest supervision over men's affairs. We must transplant these rights to a soil in which the laissez-faire concept or principle of non-interference has withered at least as to economic affairs, and social advancements are increasingly sought through closer integration of society and through expanded and strengthened governmental controls. These changed conditions often deprive precedents of reliability and cast us more than we would choose upon our own judgment. But we act in these matters not by authority of our competence but by force of our commissions. We cannot, because of modest estimates of our competence in such specialties as public education, withhold the judgment that history authenticates as the function of this Court when liberty is infringed.

4. Lastly, and this is the very heart of the Gobitis opinion, it reasons that "National unity is the basis of national security," that the authorities have "the right to select appropriate means for its attainment," and hence reaches the conclusion that such compulsory measures toward "national unity" are constitutional. Upon the verity of this assumption depends our answer in this case.

National unity as an end which officials may foster by persuasion and example is not in question. The problem is whether under our Constitution compulsion as here employed is a permissible means for its achievement.

Struggle to coerce uniformity of sentiment in support of some end thought essential to their time and country have been waged by many good as well as by evil men. Nationalism is a relatively recent phenomenon but at other times and places the ends have been racial or territorial security, support of a dynasty or regime, and particular plans for saving souls. As first and moderate methods to attain unity have failed, those bent on its accomplishment must resort to an ever increasing severity. As governmental pressure toward unity becomes greater, so strife becomes more bitter as to whose unity it shall be. Probably no deeper division of our people could proceed from any provocation than from finding it necessary to choose what doctrine and whose program public educational officials shall compel youth to unite in embracing. Ultimate futility of such attempts to compel coherence is the lesson of every such effort from the Roman drive to stamp out Christianity as a disturber of its pagan unity, the Inquisition, as a means to religious and dynastic unity, the Siberian exiles as a means to Russian unity, down the fast failing efforts of our present totalitarian enemies. Those who begin coercive elimination of dissent soon find themselves exterminating dissenters. Compulsory unification of opinion achieves only the unanimity of the graveyard.

It seems trite but necessary to say that the First Amendment to our Constitution was designed to avoid these ends by avoiding these beginnings. There is no mysticism in the American concept of the State or of the nature or origin of its authority. We set up government by consent of the governed, and the Bill of Rights denies those in power any legal opportunity to coerce that consent. Authority here is to be controlled by public opinion, not public opinion by authority.

The case is made difficult not because the principles of its decision are obscure but because the flag involved is our own. Nevertheless, we apply the limitations of the Constitution with no fear that freedom to be intellectually and spiritually diverse or even contrary will disintegrate the social organization. To believe that patriotism will not flourish if patriotic ceremonies are voluntary and spontaneous instead of a compulsory routine is to make an unflattering estimate of the appeal of our institutions to free minds. We can have intellectual individualism and the rich cultural diversities that we owe to exceptional minds only at the price of occasional eccentricity and abnormal attitudes. When they are so harmless to others or to the State as those we deal with here, the price is not too great. But freedom to differ is not limited to things that do not matter much. That would be a mere shadow of freedom. The test of its substance is the right to differ as to things that touch the heart of the existing order.

If there is any fixed star in our constitutional constellation, it is that no official, high or petty, can prescribe what shall be orthodox in politics, nationalism, religion, or other matters of opinion or force citizens to confess by word or act their faith therein. If there are any circumstances which permit an exception, they do not now occur to us.

We think the action of the local authorities in compelling the flag salute and pledge transcends constitutional limitations on their power and invades the sphere of intellect and spirit which it is the purpose of the First Amendment to our Constitution to reserve from all official control.

The decision of this Court in Minersville School District v. Gobitis and the holdings of those few per curiam decisions which preceded and foreshadowed it are over-ruled, and the judgment enjoining enforcement of the West Virginia Regulation is affirmed.

Mr Justice Roberts and Mr. Justice Reed adhere to the views expressed by the Court in Minersville School District v. Gobitis and are of the opinion that the judgment below should be reversed.

MR. JUSTICE BLACK AND MR. JUSTICE DOUGLAS, CONCURRING.

We are substantially in agreement with the opinion read, but since we originally joined with the Court in the Gobitis case, it is appropriate that we make a brief statement of reasons for our change of view.

Reluctance to make the Federal Constitution a rigid bar against state regulation of conduct thought inimical to the public welfare was the controlling influence which moved us to consent to the Gobitis decision. Long reflection convinced us that although the principle is sound, its application in the particular case was wrong. We believe that the statute before us fails to accord full scope to the freedom of religion secured to the appellees by the First and Fourteenth Amendments.

The statute requires the appellees to participate in a ceremony aimed at inculcating respect for the flag and for this country. The Jehovah's Witnesses, without any desire to show disrespect for either the flag or the country, interpret the Bible as commanding, at the risk of God's displeasure, that they not go through the form of a pledge of allegiance to any flag. The devoutness of their belief is evidenced by their willingness to suffer persecution and punishment, rather than make the pledge.

No well-ordered society can leave to the individuals an absolute right to make final decisions, unassailable to the State, as to everything they will or will not do. The First Amendment does not go so far. Religious faiths, honestly held, do not free individuals from responsibility to conduct themselves obediently to laws which are either imperatively necessary to protect society as a whole from grave and pressingly imminent dangers or which, without any general prohibition, merely regulate time, place or manner of religious activity. Decision as to the constitutionality of particular laws which strike at the substance of religious tenets and practices must be made by this Court. The duty is a solemn one, and in meeting it we cannot say that failure, because of religious scruples, to assume a particular physical position and to repeat the

151

words of a patriotic formula creates a grave danger to the nation. Such a statutory exaction is a form of test oath, and the test oath has always been abhorrent in the United States.

Words uttered under coercion are proof of loyalty to nothing but self-interest. Love of country must spring from willing hearts and free minds, inspired by a fair administration of wise laws enacted by the people's elected representatives within the bounds of express constitutional prohibitions. These laws must, to be consistent with the First Amendment, permit the widest toleration of conflicting viewpoints consistent with a society of free men.

Neither our domestic tranquillity in peace nor our martial effort in war depend on compelling little children to participate in a ceremony which ends in nothing for them but a fear of spiritual condemnation. If, as we think, their fears are groundless, time and reason are the proper antidotes for their errors. The ceremonial, when enforced against conscientious objectors, more likely to defeat than to serve its high purpose, is a handy implement for disguised religious persecution. As such, it is inconsistent with our Constitution's plan and purpose.

MR. JUSTICE MURPHY, CONCURRING.

I agree with the opinion of the Court and join in it.

The complaint challenges an order of the State Board of Education which requires teachers and pupils to participate in the prescribed salute to the flag. For refusal to conform with the requirement the State law prescribes expulsion. The offender is required by law to be treated as unlawfully absent from school and the parent or guardian is made liable to prosecution and punishment for such absence. Thus not only is the privilege of public education conditioned on compliance with the requirement, but non-compliance is virtually made unlawful. In effect compliance is compulsory and not optional. It is the claim of appellees that the regulation is invalid as a restriction on religious freedom and freedom of speech, secured to them against State infringement by the First and Fourteenth Amendment to the Constitution of the United States.

A reluctance to interfere with considered state action, the fact that the end sought is a desirable one, the emotion aroused by the flag as a symbol for which we have fought and are now fighting again,—all of these are understandable. But there is before us the right of freedom to believe, freedom to worship one's Maker according to the dictates of one's conscience, a right which the Constitution specifically shelters. Reflection has convinced me that as a judge I have no loftier duty or responsibility than to uphold that spiritual freedom to its farthest reaches.

The right of freedom of thought and of religion as guaranteed by the Constitution against State action includes both the right to speak freely and the right to refrain from speaking at all, except in so far as essential operations of government may require it for the preservation of an orderly society,—as in the case of compulsion to give evidence in court. Without wishing to disparage the purposes and intentions of those who hope to inculcate sentiments of loyalty and patriotism by requiring a declaration of allegiance as a feature of public education, or unduly belittle the benefits that may accrue therefrom, I am impelled to conclude that such a requirement is not essential to the maintenance of effective government and orderly society. To many it is deeply distasteful to join in a public chorus of affirmation of private belief. By some, including the members of this sect, it is apparently regarded as incompatible with a primary religious obligation, therefore a restriction on religious freedom. Official compulsion to affirm what is contrary to one's religious beliefs is the antithesis of freedom of worship which, it is well to recall, was achieved in this country only after what Jefferson characterized as the "severest contests in which I have ever been engaged."

I am unable to agree that the benefits that may accrue to society from the compulsory flag salute are sufficiently definite and tangible to justify the invasion of freedom and privacy that is entailed or to compensate for a restraint on the freedom of the individual to be vocal or silent according to his conscience or personal inclination. The trenchant words in the preamble to the Virginia Statute for Religious Freedom remain unanswerable: ". . . all attempts to influence (the mind) by temporal punishment, or burthens, or by civil incapacitations, tend only to beget habits of hypocrisy and meanness, . . .". Any spark of love for country which may be generated in a child or his associates by forcing him to make what is to him an empty gesture and recite words wrung from him contrary to his religious beliefs is overshadowed by the desirability of preserving freedom of conscience to the full. It is in that freedom and the example of persuasion, not in force and compulsion, that the real unity of America lies.

MR. JUSTICE FRANKFURTER, DISSENTING.

One who belongs to the most vilified and persecuted minority in history is not likely to be insensible to the freedoms guaranteed by our Constitution. Were my purely personal attitude relevant I should whole-heartedly associate myself with the general libertarian views in the Court's opinion, representing as they do the thought and action of a lifetime. But as judges we are neither Jew nor Gentile, neither Catholic nor agnostic. We owe equal attachment to the Constitution and are equally bound by our judicial obligations whether we derive our citizenship from the earliest or the latest immigrants to these shores. As a member of this Court I am not justified in writing my private notions of policy into the Constitution, no matter how deeply I may cherish them or how mischievous I may deem their disregard. The duty of a judge who must decide which of two claims before the Court shall prevail, that of a State to enact and enforce laws within its general competence or that of an individual to refuse obedience because of the demands of his conscience, is not that of the ordinary person. It can never be emphasized too much that one's own opinion about the wisdom or evil of a law should be excluded altogether when one is doing one's duty on the bench. The only opinion of our own even looking in that direction that is material is our opinion whether legislators could in reason have enacted such a law. In the light of all the circumstances, including the history of this question in this Court, it would require more daring than I possess to deny that reasonable legislators could have taken the action which is before us for review. Most unwillingly, therefore, I must differ from my brethren with regard to legislation like this. I cannot bring my mind to believe that the "liberty" secured by the Due Process Clause gives this Court authority to deny to the State of West Virginia the attainment of that which we all recognize as a legitimate legislative end, namely, the promotion of good citizenship, by employment of the means here chosen.

Not long ago we were admonished that "the only check upon our own exercise of power is our own sense of self-restraint. For the removal of unwise laws from the statute books appeal lies, not to the courts, but to the ballot and to the processes of democratic government." We have been told that generalities do not decide concrete cases. But the intensity with which a general principle is held may determine a particular issue, and whether we put first things first may decide a specific controversy.

The admonition that judicial self-restraint alone limits arbitrary exercise of our authority is relevant every time we are asked to nullify legislation. The Constitution does not give us greater veto power when dealing with one phase of "liberty" than with another, or when dealing with grade school regulations than with college regulations that offend conscience, as was the case in Hamilton v. Regents. In neither situation is our function comparable to that of a legislature or are we free to act as though we were a super-legislature. Judicial self-restraint is equally necessary whenever an exercise of political or legislative power is challenged. There is no warrant in the constitutional basis of this Court's authority for attributing different roles to it depending upon the nature of the challenge to the legislation. Our power does not vary according to the particular provision of the Bill of Rights which is invoked. The right not to have property taken without just compensation has, so far as the scope of judicial power is concerned, the same constitutional dignity as the right to be protected against unreasonable searches and seizures, and the latter has no less claim than freedom of the press or freedom of speech or religious freedom. In no instance is this Court the primary protector of the particular liberty that is invoked. This Court has recognized, what hardly could be denied, that all the provisions of the first ten Amendments are "specific" prohibitions. But each specific Amendment, in so far as embraced within the Fourteenth Amendment, must be equally respected, and the function of this Court does not differ in passing on the constitutionality of legislation challenged under different Amendments.

When Mr. Justice Holmes, speaking for this Court, wrote that "it must be remembered that legislatures are ultimate guardians of the liberties and welfare of the people in quite as great a degree as the courts," he went to the very essence of our constitutional system and the democratic conception of our society. He did not mean that for only some phases of civil government this Court was not to supplant legislatures and sit in judgment upon the right or wrong of a challenged measure. He was stating the comprehensive judicial duty and role of this Court in our constitutional scheme whenever legislation is sought to be nullified on any ground, namely, that responsibility for legislation lies with legislatures, answerable as they are directly to the people, and this Court's only and very narrow function is to determine whether within the broad grant of authority vested in legislatures they have exercised a judgment for which reasonable justification can be offered.

The framers of the federal Constitution might have chosen to assign an active share in the process of legislation to this Court. They had before them the well known example of New York's Council of Revision, which had been functioning since 1777. After stating that "laws inconsistent with the spirit of this constitution, or with the public good, may be hastily and unadvisedly passed," the state constitution made the judges of New York part of the legislative process by providing that "all bills which have passed the senate and assembly shall, before they become law," be presented to a Council of which the judges constituted a majority, "for their revisal and consideration." But the framers of the Constitution denied such legislative powers to the federal judiciary. They chose instead to insulate the judiciary from the legislative function. They did not grant to this Court supervision over legislation.

The reason why from the beginning even the narrow judicial authority to nullify legislation has been viewed with a jealous eye is that it serves to prevent the full play of the democratic process. The fact that it may be an undemocratic aspect of our scheme of government does not call for its rejection or its disuse. But it is the best of reasons, as this Court has frequently recognized, for the greatest caution in its use.

The precise scope of the question before us defines the limits of the constitutional power that is in issue. The State of West Virginia requires all pupils to share in the salute to the flag as part of school training in citizenship. The present action is one to enjoin the enforcement of this requirement by those in school attendance. We have not before us any attempt by the State to punish disobedient children or visit penal consequences on their parents. All that is in question is the right of the state to compel participation in this exercise by those who choose to attend the public schools.

We are not reviewing merely the action of a local school board. The flag salute requirement in this case comes before us with the full authority of the State of West Virginia. We are in fact passing judgment on the power of the State as a whole." Practically we are passing upon the political power of each of the forty-eight states. Moreover, since the First Amendment has been read into the Fourteenth, our problem is precisely the same as it would be if we had before us an Act of Congress for the District of Columbia. To suggest that we are here concerned with the heedless action of some village tyrants is to distort the augustness of the Constitutional issue and the reach of the consequences of our decision.

Under our constitutional system the legislature is charged solely with civil concerns of society. If the avowed or intrinsic legislative purpose is either to promote or to discourage some religious community or creed, it is clearly within the constitutional restrictions imposed on legislatures and cannot stand. But it by no means follows that legislative power is wanting whenever a general nondiscriminatory civil regulation in fact touches conscientious scruples or religious beliefs of an individual or a group. Regard for such scruples or beliefs undoubtedly presents one of the most reasonable claims for the exertion of legislative accommodation. It is, of course, beyond our power to rewrite the state's requirement, by providing exemptions for those who do not wish to participate in the flag salute or by making some other accommodations to meet their scruples. That wisdom might suggest the making of such accommodations and that the school administration would not find it too difficult to make them and yet maintain the ceremony for those not refusing to conform, is outside our province to suggest. Tact, respect, and generosity toward variant views will always commend themselves to those charged with the duties of legislation so as to achieve a maximum of good will and to require a minimum of unwilling submission to a general law. But the real question is who is to make such accommodations, the courts or the legislature?

This is no dry, technical matter. It cuts deep into one's conception of the democratic process—it concerns no less the practical differences between the means for making these accommodations that are open to courts and to legislatures. A court can only strike down. It can only say "This or that law is void." It cannot modify or qualify, it cannot make exceptions to a general requirement. And it strikes down not merely for a day. At least the finding of unconstitutionality ought not to have ephemeral significance unless the Constitution is to be reduced to the fugitive importance of mere legislation. When we are dealing with the Constitution of the United States, and more particularly with the great safeguards of the Bill of Rights, we are dealing with principles of liberty and justice "so rooted in the traditions and conscience of our people as to be ranked as fundamental"—something without which "a fair and enlightened system of justice would be impossible." If the function of this Court is to be essentially no different from that of a legislature, if the considerations governing constitutional construction are to be substantially those that underlie legislation, then indeed judges should not have life tenure and they should be made directly responsible to the electorate. There have been many but unsuccessful proposals in the last sixty years to amend the Constitution to that end.

Conscientious scruples, all would admit, cannot stand against every legislative compulsion to do positive acts in conflict with such scruples. We have been told that such compulsions override religious scruples only as to major concerns of the state. But the determination of what is major and what is minor itself raises questions of policy. For the way in which men equally guided by reason appraise importance goes to the very heart of policy. Judges should be very diffident in setting their judgment against that of a state in determining what is and what is not a major concern, what means are appropriate to proper ends, and what is the total social cost in striking the balance of imponderables.

What one can say with assurance is that the history out of which grew constitutional provisions for religious equality, and the writings of the great exponents of religious freedom—Jefferson, Madison, John Adams, Benjamin Franklin—are totally wanting in justification for a claim by dissidents of exceptional immunity from civic measures of general applicability, measures not in fact disguised assaults upon such dissident views. The great leaders of the American Revolution were determined to remove political support from every religious establishment. They put on an equality the different religious sects—Episcopalians, Presbyterians, Catholics, Baptists, Methodists, Quakers,

Huguenots,—which as dissenters, had been under the heel of the various orthodoxies that prevailed in different colonies. So far as the state was concerned, there was to be neither orthodoxy nor heterodoxy. And so Jefferson and those who followed him wrote guaranties of religious freedom into our constitutions. Religious minorities as well as religious majorities were to be equal in the eyes of the political state. But Jefferson and the others also knew that minorities may disrupt society. It never would have occurred to them to write into the Constitution the subordination of the general civil authority of the state to sectarian scruples.

The constitutional protection of religious freedom terminated disabilities, it did not create new privileges. It gave religious equality, not civil immunity. Its essence is freedom from conformity to religious dogma, not freedom from conformity to law because of religious dogma. Religious loyalties may be exercised without hindrance from the state, not the state may not exercise that which except by leave of religious loyalties is within the domain of temporal power. Otherwise each individual could set up his own censor against obedience to laws conscientiously deemed for the public good by those whose business it is to make laws.

The prohibition against any religious establishment by the government placed denominations on an equal footing—it assured freedom from support by the government to any mode of worship and the freedom of individuals to support any mode of worship. Any person may therefore believe or disbelieve what he pleases. He may practice what he will in his own house of worship or publicly within the limits of public order. But the lawmaking authority is not circumscribed by the variety of religious beliefs, otherwise the constitutional guaranty would be not a protection of the free exercise of religion but a denial of the exercise of legislation.

The essence of the religious freedom guaranteed by our Constitution if therefore this: no religion shall either receive the state's support or incur its hostility. Religion is outside the sphere of political government. This does not mean that all matters on which religious organizations or beliefs may pronounce are outside the sphere of government. Were this so, instead of the separation of church and state, there would be the subordination of the state on any matter deemed within the sovereignty of the religious conscience. Much that is the concern of temporal authority affects the spiritual interests of men. But it is not enough to strike down a non-discriminatory law that it may hurt or offend some dissident view. It would be too easy to cite numerous prohibitions and injunctions to which laws run counter if the variant interpretations of the Bible were made the tests of the obedience to law. The validity of secular laws cannot be measured by their conformity to religious doctrines. It is only in a theocratic state that ecclesiastical doctrines measure legal right or wrong.

An act compelling profession of allegiance to a religion, no matter how subtly or tenuously promoted, is bad. But an act promoting good citizenship and national allegiance is within the domain of governmental authority and is therefore to be judged by the same considerations of power and of constitutionality as those involved in the many claims of immunity from civil obedience because of religious scruples.

That claims are pressed on behalf of sincere religious convictions does not of itself establish their constitutional validity. Nor does waving the banner of religious freedom relieve us from examining the power we are asked to deny the states. Otherwise the doctrine of separation of church and state, so cardinal in the history of this nation and for the liberty of our people, would mean not the disestablishment of a state church but the establishment of all churches and of all religious groups.

The subjection of dissidents to the general requirement of saluting the flag, as a measure conducive to the training of children in good citizenship, is very far from being the first instance of exacting obedience to general laws that have offended deep religious scruples. Compulsory vaccination, compulsory medical treatment, these are but illustrations of conduct that has often been compelled in the enforcement of legislation of general applicability even though the religious consciences of particular individuals rebelled at the exaction.

Law is concerned with external behavior and not with the inner life of man. It rests in large measure upon compulsion. Socrates lives in history partly because he gave his life for the conviction that duty of obedience to secular law does not pre-suppose consent to its enactment or belief in its virtue. The consent upon which free government rests is the consent that comes from sharing in the process of making and unmaking laws. The state is not shut out from a domain because the individual conscience may deny the state's claim. The individual conscience may profess what faith it chooses. It may affirm and promote that faith—in the language of the Constitution, it may "exercise" it freely—but it cannot thereby restrict community action through political organs in matters of community concern, so long as the action is not asserted in a discriminatory way either openly or by stealth. One may have the right to practice one's religion and at the same time owe the duty of formal obedience to laws that run counter to one's beliefs. Compelling belief implies denial of opportunity to combat it and to assert dissident views. Such compulsion is one thing. Quite another matter is submission to conformity of action while denying its wisdom

159

or virtue and with ample opportunity for seeking its change or abrogation.

In Hamilton v. Regents, this Court unanimously held that one attending a state-maintained university cannot refuse attendance on courses that offend his religious scruples. That decision is not overruled today, but is distinguished on the ground that attendance at the institution for higher education was voluntary and therefore a student could not refuse compliance with its conditions and yet take advantage of its opportunities. But West Virginia does not compel the attendance at its public schools. As to its public schools, West Virginia imposes conditions which it deems necessary in the development of future citizens precisely as California deemed necessary the requirements that offended the student's conscience in the Hamilton case. The need for higher education and the duty of the state to provide it as part of a public educational system, are part of the democratic faith of most of our states. The right to secure such education in institutions not maintained by public funds is unquestioned. But the practical opportunities for obtaining what is becoming in increasing measure the conventional equipment of American youth may be no less burdensome than that which parents are increasingly called upon to bear in sending their children to parochial schools because the education provided by public schools though supported by their taxes, does not satisfy their ethical and educational necessities. I find it impossible, so far as constitutional power is concerned, to differentiate what was sanctioned in the Hamilton case from what is nullified in this case. And for me it still remains to be explained why the grounds of Mr. Justice Cardozo's opinion in Hamilton v. Regents are not sufficient to sustain the flag salute requirement. Such a requirement, like the requirement in the Hamilton case, "is not an interference by the state with the free exercise of religion when the liberties of the Constitution are read in the light of a century and a half of history during days of peace and war." The religious worshiper, "if his liberties were to be thus extended, might refuse to contribute taxes . . . in furtherance of any other end condemned by his conscience as irreligious or immoral. The right of private judgment has never yet been so exalted above the powers and the compulsion of the agencies of government."

Parents have the privilege of choosing which schools they wish their children to attend. And the question here is whether the state may make certain requirements that seem to it desirable or important for the proper education of those future citizens who go to schools maintained by the states, or whether the pupils in those schools may be relieved from those requirements if they run counter to the consciences of their parents. Not only have parents the right to send children to schools of their own choosing but the state has no right to bring such schools "under a strict governmental control" or give "affirmative direction concerning the intimate and essential details of such schools, intrust their control to public officers, and deny both owners and patrons reasonable choice and discretion in respect of teachers, curriculum and textbooks." Why should not the state likewise have constitutional power to make reasonable provisions for the proper instruction of children in schools maintained by it?

When dealing with religious scruples we are dealing with an almost numberless variety of doctrines and beliefs, entertained with equal sincerity by the particular groups for which they satisfy man's needs in his relation to the mysteries of the universe. There are in the United States more than 250 distinctive established religious denominations. In the State of Pennsylvania there are 120 of these, and in West Virginia as many as 65. But if religious scruples afford immunity from civic obedience to laws, they may be invoked by the religious beliefs of any individual even though he holds no membership in any sect or organized denomination. Certainly this Court cannot be called upon to determine what claims of conscience should be recognized and what should be rejected as satisfying the "religion" which the Constitution protects. That would indeed resurrect the very discriminatory treatment of religion which the Constitution sought forever to forbid. And so, when confronted with the task of considering the claims of immunity from obedience to a law dealing with civil affairs because of religious scruples, we cannot conceive religion more narrowly than in the terms in which Judge Augustus N. Hand recently characterized it: "It is unnecessary to attempt a definition of religion; the content of the term is found in the history of the human race and is incapable of compression into a few words. Religious belief arises from a sense of the inadequacy of reason as a means of relating the individual to his fellow-men and to his universe. . . . [It] may justly be regarded as a response of the individual to an inward mentor, call it conscience or God, that is for many persons at the present time the equivalent of what has always been thought a religious impulse."

Consider the controversial issue of compulsory Bible-reading in public schools. The educational policies of the states are in great conflict over this, and the state courts are divided in their decisions on the issue whether the requirement of Bible-reading offends constitutional provisions dealing with religious freedom. The requirement of Bible-reading has been justified by various state courts as an appropriate means of inculcating ethical precepts and familiarizing pupils with the most lasting expression of great English literature. Is this Court to overthrow such variant state educational policies by denying states the right to entertain such convictions in regard to their school systems because of a belief that the King James version is in fact a sectarian text which parents of the Catholic and Jewish faiths and of some Protestant persuasions may rightly object to having their children exposed? On the other hand the religious consciences of some parents may rebel at the absence of any Bible-reading in the schools. Or is this Court to enter the old controversy between science and religion by unduly defining the limits within which a state may experiment with its school curricula? The religious consciences of some parents may be offended by subjecting their children to the Biblical account of creation, while another state may offend parents by prohibiting a teaching of biology that contradicts such Biblical account. What of conscientious objections to what is devoutly felt by parents to be the poisoning of impressionable minds of children by chauvinistic teaching of history? This is very far from a fanciful suggestion for in the belief of many thoughtful people nationalism is the seed-bed of war.

There are other issues in the offing which admonish us of the difficulties and complexities that confront states in the duty of administering their local school systems. All citizens are taxed for the support of public schools although this Court has denied the right of a state to compel all children to go to such schools and has recognized the right of parents to send children to privately maintained schools. Parents who are dissatisfied with the public schools thus carry a double educational burden. Children who go to public school enjoy in many states derivative advantages such as free textbooks, free lunch, and free transportation in going to and from school. What of the claims for equality of treatment of those parents who, because of religious scruples, cannot send their children to public schools? What of the claim that if the right to send children to privately maintained schools is partly an exercise of religious conviction, to render effective this right it should be accompanied by equality of treatment by the state in supplying free textbooks, free lunch, and free transportation to children who go to private schools? What of the claim that such grants are offensive to the cardinal constitutional doctrine of separation of church and state?

These questions assume increasing importance in view of the steady growth of parochial schools both in number and in population. I am not borrowing trouble by adumbrating these issues nor am I parading horrible examples of the consequences of today's decision. I am aware that we must decide the case before us and not some other case. But that does not mean that a case is dissociated from the past and unrelated to the future. We must decide this case with due regard for what went before and no less regard for what may come after. Is it really a fair construction of such a fundamental concept as the right freely to exercise one's religion that a state cannot choose to require all children who attend public school to make the same gesture of allegiance to the symbol of our national life because it may offend the conscience of some children, but that it may compel all children to attend public school to listen to the King James version although it may offend the consciences of their parents? And what of the larger issue of claiming immunity from obedience to a general civil regulation that has a reasonable relation to a public purpose within the general competence of the state? Another member of the sect now before us insisted that in forbidding her two little girls, aged nine and twelve, to distribute pamphlets Oregon infringed her and their freedom of religion in that the children were engaged in "preaching the gospel of God's Kingdom." A procedural technicality led to the dismissal of the case, but the problem remains.

These questions are not lightly stirred. They touch the most delicate issue and their solution challenges the best wisdom of political and religious statesmen. But it presents awful possibilities to try to encase the solution of these problems within the rigid prohibitions of unconstitutionality.

We are told that a flag salute is a doubtful substitute for adequate understanding of our institutions. The states that require such a school exercise do not have to justify it as the only means for promoting good citizenship in children, but merely as one of diverse means for accomplishing a worthy end. We may deem it a foolish measure, but the point is that this Court is not the organ of government to resolve doubts as to whether it will fulfill its purpose. Only if there be no doubt that any reasonable mind could entertain can we deny to the states the right to resolve doubts their way and not ours.

That which to the majority may seem essential for the welfare of the state may offend the conscience of a minority. But, so long as no inroads are made upon the actual exercise of religion by the minority, to deny the political power of the majority to enact laws concerned with civil matter, simply because they may offend the consciences of a minority, really means that the consciences of a minority are more sacred and more enshrined in the Constitution than the consciences of a majority.

We are told that symbolism is a dramatic but primitive way of communicating ideas. Symbolism is inescapable. Even the most sophisticated live by symbols. But it is not for this Court to make psychological judgments as to the effectiveness of a particular symbol in inculcating concededly indispensable feeling, particularly if the state happens to see fit to utilize the symbol that represents our heritage and our hopes.

163

And surely only flippancy could be responsible for the suggestion that constitutional validity of a requirement to salute our flag implies equal validity of a requirement to salute a dictator. The significance of a symbol lies in what it represents. To reject the swastika does not imply rejection of the Cross. And so it bears repetition to say that it mocks reason and denies our whole history to find in the allowance of a requirement to salute our flag on fitting occasions the seeds of sanction for obeisance to a leader. To deny the power to employ educational symbols is to say that the state's educational system may not stimulate the imagination because this may lead to unwise stimulation.

The right of West Virginia to utilize the flag salute as part of its educational process is denied because, so it is argued, it cannot be justified as a means of meeting a "clear and present danger" to national unity. In passing it deserves to be noted that the four cases which unanimously sustained the power of states to utilize such an educational measure arose and were all decided before the present World War. But to measure the state's power to make such regulations as are here resisted by the imminence of national danger is wholly to misconceive the origin and purpose of the concept of "clear and present danger." To apply such a test is for the Court to assume, however unwittingly, a legislative responsibility that does not belong to it. To talk about "clear and present danger" as the touchstone of allowable educational policy by the states whenever school curricula may impinge upon the boundaries of individual conscience, is to take a felicitous phrase out of the context of the particular situation where it arose and for which it was adapted. Mr. Justice Holmes used the phrase "clear and present danger" in a case involving mere speech as a means by which alone to accomplish sedition in time of war. By that phrase he meant merely to indicate that, in view of the protection given to utterance by the First Amendment, in order that mere utterance may not be prescribed, "the words used are used in such circumstances and are of such a nature as to create a clear and present danger that they will bring about the substantive evils that Congress has a right to prevent." The "substantive evils" about which he was speaking were inducement of insubordination in the military and naval forces of the United States and obstruction of enlistment while the country was at war. He was not enunciating a formal rule that there can be no restriction upon speech and, still less, no compulsion where conscience balks, unless imminent danger would thereby be wrought "to our institutions or our government."

The flag salute exercise has no kinship whatever to the oath tests so odious in history For the oath test was one of the instruments for suppressing heretical beliefs. Saluting the flag suppresses no belief nor curbs it. Children and their parents may believe what they please, avow their belief and practice it. It is not even remotely suggested that the requirement for saluting the flag involves the slightest restriction against the fullest opportunity on the part both of the children and of their parents to disavow as publicly as they choose to do so the meaning that others attach to the gesture of salute. All channels of affirmative free expression are open to both children and parents. Had we before us any act of the state putting the slightest curbs upon such free expression, I should not lag behind any member of this Court in striking down such an invasion of the right to freedom of thought and freedom of speech protected by the Constitution.

I am fortified in my view of this case by the history of the flag salute controversy in this Court. Five times has the precise question now before us been adjudicated. Four times the Court unanimously found that the requirement of such a school exercise was not beyond the powers of the states. Indeed in the first three cases to come before the Court the constitutional claim now sustained was deemed so clearly unmeritorious that this Court dismissed the appeals for want of a substantial federal question. In the fourth case the judgment of the district court upholding the state law was summarily affirmed on the authority of the earlier cases. The fifth case, Minersville District v. Gobitis, was brought here because the decision of the Circuit Court of Appeals for the Third Circuit ran counter to our rulings. They were reaffirmed after full consideration, with one Justice dissenting.

What may be even more significant than this uniform recognition of state authority is the fact that every Justice—thirteen in all—who has hitherto participated in judging this matter has at one or more times found no constitutional infirmity in what is now condemned. Only the two Justices sitting for the first time on this matter have not heretofore found this legislation inoffensive to the "liberty" guaranteed by the Constitution. And among the Justices who sustained this measure were outstanding judicial leaders in the zealous enforcement of constitutional safeguards of civil liberties—men like Chief Justice Hughes, Mr. Justice Brandeis, and Mr. Justice Cardozo, to mention only those no longer on the Court.

One's conception of the Constitution cannot be severed from one's conception of a judge's function in applying it. The Court has no reason for existence if it merely reflects the pressures of the day. Our system is built on the faith that men set apart for this special function, freed from the influences of immediacy and from the deflections of worldly ambition, will become able to take a view of longer range than the period of responsibility entrusted to Congress and legislatures. We are dealing with matters as to which legislators and voters have conflicting views. Are we as judges to impose our strong convictions on where wisdom lies? That which three years ago had seemed to five successive Courts to lie within permissible areas of legislation is now outlawed by the deciding shift of opinion of two Justices. What reason is there to believe that they or their successors may not have another view a few years hence? Is that which was deemed to be of so fundamental a nature as to be written into the Constitution to endure for all times to be the sport of shifting winds of doctrine? Of course, judicial opinions, even as to questions of constitutionality, are not immutable. As has been true in the past, the Court will from time to time reverse its position. But I believe that never before these Jehovah's Witnesses Cases (except for minor deviations subsequently retraced) has this Court overruled decisions so as to restrict the powers of democratic government. Always heretofore, it has withdrawn narrow views of legislative authority so as to authorize what formerly it had denied.

In view of this history it must be plain that what thirteen Justices found to be within the constitutional authority of a state, legislators can not be deemed unreasonable in enacting. Therefore, in denying the states what heretofore has received such impressive judicial sanction, some other tests of unconstitutionality must surely be guiding the Court than the absence of a rational justification for the legislation. But I know of no other test which this Court is authorized to apply in nullifying legislation.

In the past this Court has from time to time set its views of policy against that embodied in legislation by finding laws in conflict with what was called the "spirit of the Constitution." Such undefined destructive power was not conferred on this Court by the Constitution. Before a duly enacted law can be judicially nullified, it must be forbidden by some explicit restriction upon political authority in the Constitution. Equally inadmissible is the claim to strike down legislation because to us as individuals it seems opposed to the "plan and purpose" of the Constitution. That is too tempting a basis for finding in one's personal views the purposes of the Founders.

The uncontrollable power wielded by this Court brings it very close to the most sensitive areas of public affairs. As appeal from legislation to adjudication becomes more frequent, and its consequences more far-reaching, judicial self-restraint becomes more and not less important, lest we unwarrantably enter social and political domains wholly outside our concern. I think I appreciate fully the objections to the law before us. But to deny that it presents a question upon which men might reasonably differ appears to me to be intolerance. And since men may so reasonably differ, I deem it beyond my constitutional power to assert my view of the wisdom of this law against the view of the State of West Virginia.

Jefferson's opposition to judicial review has not been accepted by history, but it still serves as an admonition against confusion between judicial and political functions. As a rule of judicial self-restraint, it is still as valid as Lincoln's admonition. For those who pass laws not only are under duty to pass laws. They are also under duty to observe the Constitution. And even though legislation relates to civil liberties, our duty of deference to those who have the responsibility for making the laws is no less relevant or less exacting. And this is so especially when we consider the accidental contingencies by which one man may determine constitutionality and thereby confine the political power of the Congress of the United States and the legislatures of forty-eight states. The attitude of judicial humility which these considerations enjoin is not an abdication of the judicial function. It is a due observance of its limits. Moreover, it is to be borne in mind that in a question like this we are not passing on the proper distribution of political power as between the states and the central government. We are not discharging the basic function of this Court as the mediator of powers within the federal system. To strike down a law like this is to deny a power to all government.

The whole Court is conscious that this case reaches ultimate questions of judicial power and its relation to our scheme of government. It is appropriate, therefore, to recall an utterance as wise as any that I know in analyzing what is really involved when the theory of this Court's function is put to the test of practice. The analysis is that of James Bradley Thayer: ". . . there has developed a vast and growing increase of judicial interference with legislation. This is a very different state of things from what our fathers contemplated, a century and more ago, in framing the new system. Seldom, indeed, as they imagined, under our system, would this great, novel, tremendous power of the courts be exerted,—would this sacred ark of the covenant be taken from within the veil. Marshall himself expressed truly one aspect of the matter, when he said in one of the later years of his life: 'No questions can be brought before a judicial tribunal of greater delicacy than those which involve the constitutionality of legislative acts. If they become indispensably necessary to the case, the court must meet and decide them; but if the case may be determined on other grounds, a just respect for the legislature requires that the obligation of its laws should not be unnecessarily and wantonly assailed.' And again, a little earlier than this, he laid down the one true rule of duty for the courts. When he went to Philadelphia at the end of September, in 1831, on that painful errand of which I have spoken, in answering a cordial tribute from the bar of that city he remarked that if he might be permitted to claim for himself and his associates any part of the kind things they had said, it would be this, that they had 'never sought to enlarge the judicial power beyond its proper bounds, nor feared to carry it to the fullest extent that duty required.'

"That is the safe twofold rule; nor is the first part of it any whit less important than the second; nay, more; to-day it is the part which most requires to be emphasized. For just here comes in a consideration of very great weight. Great and, indeed, inestimable as are the advantages in a popular government of this conservative influence,—the power of the judiciary to disregard unconstitutional legislation,—it should be remembered that the exercise of it, even when unavoidable, is always attended with a serious evil, namely, that the correction of legislative mistakes comes from the outside, and the people thus lose the political experience, and the moral education and stimulus that come from fighting the question out in the ordinary way, and correcting their own errors. If the decision in Munn v. Illinois and the 'Granger Cases,' twenty-five years ago, and in the 'Legal Tender Cases,' nearly thirty years ago, had been different; and the legislation there in question, thought by many to be unconstitutional and by many more to be ill-advised, had been set aside, we should have been saved some trouble and some harm. But I venture to think that the good which came to the country and its people from the vigorous thinking that had to be done in the political debates that followed, from the infiltration through every part of the population of sound ideas and sentiments, from the rousing into activity of opposite elements, the enlargement of ideas, the strengthening of moral fibre, and the growth of political experience that came out of it all,—that all this far more than outweighed any evil which ever flowed from the refusal of the court to interfere with the work of the legislature.

"The tendency of a common and easy resort to this great function, now lamentably too common, is to dwarf the political capacity of the people, and to deaden its sense of moral responsibility. It is no light thing to do that.

"What can be done? It is the courts that can do most to cure the evil; and the opportunity is a very great one. Let them resolutely adhere to first principles. Let them consider how narrow is the function which the constitutions have conferred on them,—the office merely of deciding litigated cases; how large, therefore, is the duty intrusted to others, and above all to the legislature. It is that body which is charged, primarily, with the duty of judging of the constitutionality of its work. The constitutions generally give them no authority to call upon a court for advice; they must decide for themselves, and the courts may never be able to say a word. Such a body, charged in every State, with almost all the legislative power of the people, is entitled to the most entire and real respect; is entitled, as among all rationally permissible opinions as to what the constitution allows, to its own choice. Courts, as has often been said, are not to think of the legislators, but of the legislature,—the great, continuous body itself, abstracted from all the transitory individuals who may happen to hold its power. It is this majestic representative of the people whose action is in question, a coordinate department of the government charged with the greatest functions, and invested, in contemplation of law, with whatsoever wisdom, virtue, and knowledge the exercise of such functions requires.

"To set aside the acts of such a body, representing in its own field, which is the very highest of all, the ultimate sovereign, should be a solemn, unusual, and painful act. Something is wrong when it can ever be other than that. And if it be true that the holders of legislative power are careless or evil, yet the constitutional duty of the court remains untouched; it cannot rightly attempt to protect the people, by undertaking a function not its own. On the other hand, by adhering rigidly to its own duty, the court will help, as nothing else can, to fix the spot where responsibility lies, and to bring down on that precise locality the thunderbolt of popular condemnation. The judiciary, to-day, in dealing with the acts of their coordinate legislators, owe to the country no greater or clearer duty than that of keeping their hands off these acts wherever it is possible to do it. For that course—the true course of judicial duty always—will powerfully help to bring the people and their representatives to a sense of their own responsibility. There will still remain to the judiciary an ample field for the determinations of this remarkable jurisdiction, of which our American law has so much reason to be proud; a jurisdiction which has had some of its chief illustrations and its greatest triumphs as in Marshall's time, so in ours, while the courts were refusing to exercise it."

Of course patriotism cannot be enforced by the flag salute. But neither can the liberal spirit be enforced by judicial invalidation of illiberal legislation. Our constant preoccupation with the constitutionality of legislation rather than with its wisdom tends to preoccupation of the American mind with a false value. The tendency of focusing attention on constitutionality is to make constitutionality synonymous with wisdom, to regard a law as all right if it is constitutional. Such an attitude is a great enemy of liberalism. Particularly in legislation affecting freedom of thought and freedom of speech much which should offend a free-spirited society is constitutional. Reliance for the most precious interests of civilization, therefore, must be found outside of their vindication in courts of law. Only a persistent positive translation of the faith of a free society into the convictions and habits and actions of a community is the ultimate reliance against unabated temptations to fetter the human spirit.

PRINCE v. COMMONWEALTH OF MASSACHUSETTS
321 US 158 (1944)

"The parents' conflict with the state over control of the child and his training is serious enough when only secular matters are concerned. It becomes more so when an element of religious conviction enters . . . Parents may be free to become martyrs themselves. But it does not follow they are free, in identical circumstances, to make martyrs of their children before they have reached the age of full and legal discretion when they can make that choice for themselves."

Mr. Justice Rutledge, for the Court

"From ancient times to the present day, the ingenuity of man has known no limits in its ability to forge weapons of oppression for use against those who dare to express or practice unorthodox religious beliefs. And the Jehovah's Witnesses are living proof of the fact that even in this nation, conceived as it was in the ideals of freedom, the right to practice religion in unconventional ways is still far from secure."

Mr. Justice Murphy, dissenting

The court having, in the previous year, supported the claims of Jehovah's Witnesses in the flag-salute and licensing cases here upholds a child-labor regulation against the claim that it prevents a child from performing her religious duty.

MR. JUSTICE RUTLEDGE DELIVERED THE OPINION OF THE COURT.

The case brings for review another episode in the conflict between Jehovah's Witnesses and state authority. This time Sarah Prince appeals from convictions for violating Massachusetts' child labor laws, by acts said to be a rightful exercise of her religious convictions.

When the offenses were committed she was the aunt and custodian of Betty M. Simmons, a girl nine years of age. Originally there were three separate complaints. They were, shortly, for (1) refusal to disclose Betty's identity and age to a public officer whose duty was to enforce the statutes; (2) furnishing her with magazines, knowing she was to sell them unlawfully, that is, on the street; and (3) as Betty's custodian, permitting her to work contrary to law. The complaints were made, respectively, pursuant to Sections 79, 80 and 81 of Chapter 149, Gen. Laws of Mass. The Supreme Judicial Court reversed the conviction under the first complaint on the state grounds; but sustained the judgments founded on the other two. They present the only questions for our decision. These are whether Sections 80 and 81, as applied, contravene the Fourteenth Amendment by denying or abridging appellant's freedom of religion and by denying to her the equal protection of the laws.

Sections 80 and 81 form parts of Massachusetts' comprehensive child labor law. They provide methods for enforcing the prohibitions of Section 69, which is as follows:

"No boy under twelve and no girl under eighteen shall sell, expose or offer for sale any newspapers, magazines, periodicals or any other articles of merchandise of any description, or exercise the trade of bootblack or scavenger, or any other trade, in any street or public place."

Sections 80 and 81, so far as pertinent, read:

"Whoever furnishes or sells to any minor any article of any description with the knowledge that the minor intends to sell such article in violation of any provision of sections sixty-nine to seventy-three, inclusive, or after having received written notice to this effect from any officer charged with the enforcement thereof, or knowingly procures or encourages any minor to violate any provisions of said sections, shall be punished by a fine of not less than ten nor more than two hundred dollars or by imprisonment for not more than two months, or both." (Section 80)

"Any parent, guardian or custodian having a minor under his control who compels or permits such minor to work in violation of any provision of sections sixty to seventy-four inclusive, . . ." (Section 81)

The story told by the evidence has become familiar. It hardly needs repeating, except to give setting to the variations introduced through the part played by a child of tender years. Mrs. Prince, living in Brockton, is the mother of two young sons. She also has legal custody of Betty Simmons who lives with them. The children too are Jehovah's Witnesses and both Mrs. Prince and Betty testified they were ordained ministers. The former was accustomed to go each week on the streets of Brockton to distribute "Watchtower" and "Consolation," according to the usual plan. She had permitted the children to engage in this activity previously, and had been warned against doing so by the school attendance officer, Mr. Perkins. But, until December 18, 1941, she generally did not take them with her at night.

That evening, as Mrs. Prince was preparing to leave her home, the children asked to go. She at first refused. Childlike, they resorted to tears and, motherlike, she yielded. Arriving downtown, Mrs. Prince permitted the children "to engage in the preaching work with her upon the sidewalks." That is, with specific reference to Betty, she and Mrs. Prince took positions about twenty feet apart near a street intersection.

171

Betty held up in her hand, for passersby to see, copies of "Watchtower" and "Consolation." From her shoulder hung the usual canvas magazine bag, on which was printed "Watchtower and Consolation 5¢ per copy." No one accepted a copy from Betty that evening and she received no money. Nor did her aunt. But on other occasions, Betty had received funds and given out copies.

Mrs. Prince and Betty remained until 8:45 P.M. A few minutes before this Mr. Perkins approached Mrs. Prince. A discussion ensued. He inquired and she refused to give Betty's name. However, she stated the child attended the Shaw School. Mr. Perkins referred to his previous warnings and said he would allow five minutes for them to get off the street. Mrs. Prince admitted she supplied Betty with the magazines and said, "Neither you nor anybody else can stop me . . . . This child is exercising her God-given right and her constitutional right to preach the gospel, and no creature has a right to interfere with God's commands." However, Mrs. Prince and Betty departed. She remarked as she went, "I'm not going through this any more. We've been through it time and time again. I'm going home and put the little girl to bed." It may be added that testimony, by Betty, her aunt and others, was offered at the trials, and was excluded, to show that Betty believed it was her religious duty to perform this work and failure would bring condemnation "to everlasting destruction at Armageddon."

As the case reaches us, the questions are no longer open whether what the child did was a "sale" or an "offer to sell" within Section 69 or was "work" within Section 81. The state court's decision has foreclosed them adversely to appellant as a matter of state law. The only question remaining therefore is whether, as construed and applied, the statute is valid. Upon this the court said: "We think that freedom of the press and of religion is subject to incidental regulation to the slight degree involved in the prohibition of the selling of religious literature in streets and public places by boys under twelve and girls under eighteen and in the further statutory provisions herein considered, which have been adopted as a means of enforcing that prohibition."

Appellant does not stand on freedom of the press. Regarding it as secular, she concedes it may be restricted as Massachusetts has done. Hence, she rests squarely on freedom of religion under the First Amendment, applied by the Fourteenth to the states. She buttresses this foundation, however, with a claim of parental right as secured by the due process clause of the latter Amendment. These guaranties, she thinks, guard alike herself and the child in what they have done. Thus, two claimed liberties are at stake. One is the parent's, to bring up the child in the way he should go, which for appellant means to teach him the tenets and the practices of their faith. The other freedom is the child's, to observe these; and among them is "to preach the gospel . . . by public distribution" of "Watchtower" and "Consolation" in conformity with the scripture: "A little child shall lead them."

If by this position appellant seeks for freedom of conscience a broader protection than for freedom of the mind, it may be doubted that any of the great liberties insured by the First Article can be given higher place than the others. All have preferred position in our basic scheme. All are interwoven there together. Differences there are, in them and in the modes appropriate for their exercise. But they have unity in the charter's prime place because they have unity in their human sources and functionings. Heart and mind are not identical. Intuitive faith and reasoned judgment are not the same. Spirit is not always thought. But in the everyday business of living, secular or otherwise, these variant aspects of personality find inseparable expression in a thousand ways. They cannot be altogether parted in law more than in life.

To make accommodation between these freedoms and an exercise of state authority always is delicate. It hardly could be more so than in such a clash as this case presents. On one side is the obviously earnest claim for freedom of conscience and religious practice. With it is allied the parent's claim to authority in her own household and in the rearing of her children. The parent's conflict with the state over control of the child and his training is serious enough when only secular matters are concerned. It becomes the more so when an element of religious conviction enters. Against these sacred private interests, basic in a democracy, stand the interests of society to protect the welfare of children, and the state's assertion of authority to that end, made here in a manner conceded valid if only secular things were involved. The last is no mere corporate concern of official authority. It is the interest of youth itself, and of the whole community, that children be both safeguarded from abuses and given opportunities for growth into free and independent well-developed men and citizens. Between contrary pulls of such weight, the safest and most objective recourse is to the lines already marked out, not precisely but for guides, in narrowing the no man's land where this battle has gone on.

The rights of children to exercise their religion, and of parents to give them religious training and to encourage them in the practice of religious belief, as against preponderant sentiment and assertion of state power voicing it, have had recognition here, most recently in West Virginia State Board of Education v. Barnette. Previously in Pierce v. Society of Sisters, this Court had sustained the parent's authority to provide religious with secular schooling, and the child's right to receive it, as against the state's requirement of attendance at public schools. And in Meyer v. Nebraska, children's rights to receive teaching in languages other than the nation's common tongue were guarded against the state's encroachment. It is cardinal with us that the custody, care and nurture of the child reside first in the parents, whose primary function and freedom include preparation for obligations the state can neither supply nor hinder. And it is in recognition of this that these decisions have respected the private realm of family life which the state cannot enter.

But the family itself is not beyond regulation in the public interest, as against a claim of religious liberty. And neither rights of religion nor rights of parenthood are beyond limitation. Acting to guard the general interest in youth's well being, the state as parens patriae may restrict the parent's control by requiring school attendance, regulating or prohibiting the child's labor, and in many other ways. Its authority is not nullified merely because the parent grounds his claim to control the child's course of conduct on religion or conscience. Thus, he cannot claim freedom from compulsory vaccination for the child more than for himself on religious grounds. The right to practice religion freely does not include liberty to expose the community or the child to communicable disease or the latter to ill health or death. The catalogue need not be lengthened. It is sufficient to show what indeed appellant hardly disputes, that the state has a wide range of power for limiting parental freedom and authority in things affecting the child's welfare; and that this includes, to some extent, matters of conscience and religious conviction.

But it is said the state cannot do so here. This, first, because when state action impinges upon a claimed religious freedom, it must fall unless shown to be necessary for or conducive to the child's protection against some clear and present danger; and, it is added, there was no such showing here. The child's presence on the street, with her guardian, distributing or offering to distribute the magazines, it is urged, was in no way harmful to her, nor in any event more so than the presence of many other children at the same time and place, engaged in shopping and other activities not prohibited. Accordingly, in view of the preferred position the freedoms of the First Article occupy, the statute in its present application must fall. It cannot be sustained by any presumption of validity. And, finally, it is said, the statute is, as to children, an absolute prohibition, not merely a reasonable regulation, of the denounced activity.

Concededly a statute or ordinance identical in terms with Section 69, except that it is applicable to adults or all persons generally, would be invalid. But the mere fact a state could not wholly prohibit this form of adult activity, whether characterized locally as a "sale" or otherwise, does not mean it cannot do so for children. Such a conclusion granted would mean that a state could impose no greater limitation upon child labor than upon adult labor. Or, if an adult were free to enter dance halls, saloons, and disreputable places generally, in order to discharge his conceived religious duty to admonish or dissuade persons from frequenting such places, so would be a child with similar convictions and objectives, if not alone then in the parent's company, against the state's command.

The state's authority over children's activities is broader than over like actions of adults. This is peculiarly true of public activities and in matters of employment. A democratic society rests, for its continuance, upon the healthy, well rounded growth of young people into full maturity as citizens, with all that implies. It may secure this against impeding restraints and dangers, within a broad range of selection. Among evils most appropriate for such action are the crippling effects of child employment, more especially in public places, and the possible harms arising from other activities subject to all the diverse influences of the street. It is too late now to doubt that legislation appropriately designed to reach such evils is within the state's police power, whether against the parent's claim to control of the child or one that religious scruples dictate contrary action.

It is true children have rights, in common with older people, in the primary use of highways. But even in such use streets afford dangers for them not affecting adults. And in other uses, whether in work or in other things, this difference may be magnified. This is so not only when children are unaccompanied but certainly to some extent when they are with their parents. What may be wholly permissible for adults therefore may not be so for children, either with or without their parents' presence.

Street preaching, whether oral or by handing out literature, is not the primary use of the highway, even for adults. While for them it cannot be wholly prohibited, it can be regulated within reasonable limits in accommodation to the primary and other incidental uses. But, for obvious reasons, notwithstanding appellant's contrary view, the validity of such a prohibition applied to children not accompanied by an older person hardly would seem open to question. The case reduces itself therefore to the question whether the presence of the child's guardian puts a limit to the state's power. That fact may lessen the likelihood that some evils the legislation seeks to avert will occur. But it cannot forestall all of them. The zealous though lawful exercise of the right to engage in propagandizing the community, whether in religious, political or other matters, may and at times does create situations difficult enough for adults to cope with and wholly inappropriate for children, especially of tender years, to face. Other harmful possibilities could be stated, of emotional excitement and psychological or physical injury. Parents may be free to become martyrs themselves. But it does not follow they are free, in identical circumstances, to make martyrs of their children before they have reached the age of full and legal discretion when they can make that choice for themselves. Massachusetts has determined that an absolute prohibition, though one limited to streets and public places and to the incidental uses proscribed, is necessary to accomplish its legitimate objectives. Its power to attain them is broad enough to reach these peripheral instances in which the parent's supervision may reduce but cannot eliminate entirely the ill effects of the prohibited conduct. We think that with reference to the public proclaiming of religion, upon the streets and in other similar public places, the power of the state to control the conduct of children reaches beyond the scope of its authority over adults, as is true in the case of other freedoms, and the rightful boundary of its power has not been crossed in this case.

In so ruling we dispose also of appellant's argument founded upon denial of equal protection. It falls with that based on denial of religious freedom, since in this instance the one is but another phrasing of the other. Shortly, the contention is that the street, for Jehovah's Witnesses and their children, is their church, since their conviction makes it so; and to deny them access to it for religious purposes as was done here has the same effect as excluding altar boys, youthful choristers, and other children from the edifices in which they practice their religious beliefs and worship. The argument hardly needs more than statement, after what has been said, to refute it. However Jehovah's Witnesses may conceive them, the public highways have not become their religious property merely by their assertion. And there is no denial of equal protection in excluding their children from doing there what no other children may do.

Our ruling does not extend beyond the facts the case presents. We neither lay the foundation "for any (that is, every) state intervention in the indoctrination and participation of children in religion" which may be done "in the name of their health and welfare" nor give warrant for "every limitation on their religious training and activities." The religious training and indoctrination of children may be accomplished in many ways, some of which, as we have noted, have received constitutional protection through decisions of this Court. These and all others except the public proclaiming of religion on the streets, if this may be taken as either training or indoctrination of the proclaimer, remain unaffected by the decision.

The judgment is affirmed.

MR. JUSTICE JACKSON.

The novel feature of this decision is this: the Court holds that a state may apply child labor laws to restrict or prohibit an activity of which, as recently as last term, it held: "This form of religious activity occupies the same high estate under the First Amendment as do worship in the churches and preaching from the pulpits. It has the same claim to protection as the more orthodox and conventional exercises of religion." ". . . the mere fact that the religious literature is 'sold' by itinerant preachers rather than 'donated' does not transform evangelism into a commercial enterprise. If it did, then the passing of the collection plate in church would make the church service a commercial project. The constitutional rights of those spreading their religious beliefs through the spoken and printed word are not to be gauged by standards governing retailers or wholesalers of books." Murdock v. Pennsylvania.

It is difficult for me to believe that going upon the streets to accost the public is the same thing for application of public law as withdrawing to a private structure for religious worship. But if worship in the churches and the activity of Jehovah's Witnesses on the streets "occupy the same high estate" and have the "same claim to protection" it would seem that child labor laws may be applied to both if to either. If the Murdock doctrine stands along with today's decision, a foundation is laid for any state intervention in the indoctrination and participation of children in religion, provided it is done in the name of their health or welfare.

This case brings to the surface the real basis of disagreement among members of this Court in previous Jehovah's Witness cases. Our basic difference seems to be as to the method of establishing limitations which of necessity bound religious freedom.

My own view may be shortly put: I think the limits begin to operate whenever activities begin to affect or collide with liberties of others or of the public. Religious activities which concern only members of the faith are and ought to be free—as nearly absolutely free as anything can be. But beyond these, many religious denominations or sects engage in collateral and secular activities intended to obtain means from unbelievers to sustain the worshippers and their leaders. They raise money, not merely by passing the plate to those who voluntarily attend services or by contributions by their own people, but by solicitations and drives addressed to the public by holding public dinners and entertainments, by various kinds of sales and Bingo games and lotteries. All such money-raising activities on a public scale are, I think, Caesar's affairs and may be regulated by the state so long as it does not discriminate against one because he is doing them for a religious purpose, and the regulation is not arbitrary and capricious, in violation of other provisions of the Constitution.

The Court in the Murdock case rejected this principle of separating immune religious activities from secular ones in declaring the disabilities which the Constitution imposed on local authorities. Instead, the Court now draws a line based on age that cuts across both true exercise of religion and auxiliary secular activities. I think this is not a correct principle for defining the activities immune from regulation on grounds of religion, and Murdock overrules the grounds on which I think affirmance should rest. I have no alternative but to dissent from the grounds of affirmance of a judgment which I think was rightly decided, and upon right grounds, by the Supreme Judicial Court of Massachusetts.

Mr. Justice Roberts and Mr. Justice Frankfurter join in this opinion.

MR. JUSTICE MURPHY, DISSENTING.

This attempt by the state of Massachusetts to prohibit a child from exercising her constitutional right to practice her religion on the public streets cannot, in my opinion, be sustained.

The record makes clear the basic fact that Betty Simmons, the nine-year-old child in question, was engaged in a genuine religious, rather than commercial, activity. She was a member of Jehovah's Witnesses and had been taught the tenets of that sect by her guardian, the appellant. Such tenets included the duty of publicly distributing religious tracts on the street and from door to door. Pursuant to this religious duty and in the company of the appellant, Betty Simmons on the night of December 18, 1941, was standing on a public street corner and offering to distribute Jehovah's Witness literature to passersby. There was no expectation of pecuniary profit to herself or to appellant. It is undisputed, furthermore, that she did this of her own desire and with appellant's consent. She testified that she was motivated by her love of the Lord and that He commanded her to distribute this literature; this was, she declared, her way of worshipping God. She was occupied, in other words, in "an age-old form of missionary evangelism" with a purpose "as evangelical as the revival meeting."

Religious training and activity, whether performed by adult or child, are protected by the Fourteenth Amendment against interference by state action, except insofar as they violate reasonable regulations adopted for the protection of the public health, morals and welfare. Our problem here is whether a state, under the guise of enforcing its child labor laws, can lawfully prohibit girls under the age of eighteen and boys under the age of twelve from practicing their religious faith insofar as it involves the distribution or sale of religious tracts on the public streets. No question of freedom of speech or freedom of press is present and we are not called upon to determine the permissible restraints on those rights. Nor are any truancy or curfew restrictions in issue. The statutes in question prohibit all children within the specified age limits from selling or offering to sell "any newspapers, magazines, periodicals or any other articles of merchandise of any description . . . in any street or public place." Criminal sanctions are imposed on the parents and guardians who compel or permit minors in their control to engage in the prohibited transactions. The state court has construed these statutes to cover the activities here involved, thereby imposing an indirect restraint through the parents and guardians on the free exercise by minors of their religious beliefs. This indirect restraint is no less effective than a direct one. A square conflict between the constitutional guarantee of religious freedom and the state's legitimate interest in protecting the welfare of its children is thus presented.

As the opinion of the Court demonstrates, the power of the state lawfully to control the religious and other activities of children is greater than its power over similar activities of adults. But that fact is no more decisive of the issue posed by this case than is the obvious fact that the family itself is subject to reasonable regulation in the public interest. We are concerned solely with the reasonableness of this particular prohibition of religious activity by children.

In dealing with the validity of statutes which directly or indirectly infringe religious freedom and the right of parents to encourage their children in the practice of a religious belief, we are not aided by any strong presumption of the constitutionality of such legislation. On the contrary, the human freedoms enumerated in the First Amendment and carried over into the Fourteenth Amendment are to be presumed to be invulnerable and any attempt to sweep away those freedoms is prima facie invalid. It follows that any restriction or prohibition must be justified by those who deny that the freedoms have been unlawfully invaded. The burden was therefore on the state of Massachusetts to prove the reasonableness and necessity of prohibiting children from engaging in religious activity of the type involved in this case.

The burden in this instance, however, is not met by vague references to the reasonableness underlying child labor legislation in general. The great interest of the state in shielding minors from the evil vicissitudes of early life does not warrant every limitation on their religious training and activities. The reasonableness that justifies the prohibition of the ordinary distribution of literature in the public streets by children is not necessarily the reasonableness that justifies such a drastic restriction when the distribution is part of their religious faith. If the right of a child to practice its religion in that manner is to be forbidden by constitutional means, there must be convincing proof that such a practice constitutes a grave and immediate danger to the state or to the health, morals or welfare of the child. The vital freedom of religion, which is "of the very essence of a scheme of ordered liberty," cannot be erased by slender references to the state's power to restrict the more secular activities of children.

The state, in my opinion, has completely failed to sustain its burden of proving the existence of any grave or immediate danger to any interest which it may lawfully protect. There is no proof that Betty Simmons' mode of worship constituted a serious menace to the public. It was carried on in an orderly, lawful manner at a public street corner. And "one who is rightfully on a street which the state has left open to the public carries with him there as elsewhere the constitutional right to express his views in an orderly fashion. This right extends to the communication of ideas by handbills and literature as well as by the spoken word." The sidewalk, no less than the cathedral or the evangelist's tent, is a proper place, under the Constitution, for the orderly worship of God. Such use of the streets is as necessary to the Jehovah's Witnesses, the Salvation Army and others who practice religion without benefit of conventional shelters as is the use of the streets for purposes of passage.

It is claimed, however, that such activity was likely to affect adversely the health, morals and welfare of the child. Reference is made in the majority opinion to "the crippling effects of child employment, more especially in public places, and the possible harms arising from other activities subject to all the diverse influences of the streets." To the extent that they flow from participation in ordinary commercial activities, these harms are irrelevant to this case. And the bare possibility that such harms might emanate from distribution of religious literature is not, standing alone, sufficient justification for restricting freedom of conscience and religion. Nor can parents or guardians be subjected to criminal liability because of vague possibilities that their religious teachings might cause injury to the child. The evils must be grave, immediate, substantial. Yet there is not the slightest indication in this record, or in sources subject to judicial notice, that children engaged in distributing literature pursuant to their religious beliefs have been or are likely to be subject to any of the harmful "diverse influences of the street." Indeed, if probabilities are to be indulged in, the likelihood is that children engaged in serious religious endeavor are immune from such influences. Gambling, truancy, irregular eating and sleeping habits, and the more serious vices are not consistent with the high moral character ordinarily displayed by children fulfilling religious obligations. Moreover, Jehovah's Witness children invariably make their distributions in groups subject at all times to adult or parental control, as was done in this case. The dangers are thus exceedingly remote, to say the least.

And the fact that the zealous exercise of the right to propagandize the community may result in violent or disorderly situations difficult for children to face is no excuse for prohibiting the exercise of that right.

No chapter in human history has been so largely written in terms of persecution and intolerance as the one dealing with religious freedom. From ancient times to the present day, the ingenuity of man has known no limits in its ability to forge weapons of oppression for use against those who dare to express or practice unorthodox religious beliefs. And the Jehovah's Witnesses are living proof of the fact that even in this nation, conceived as it was in the ideals of freedom, the right to practice religion in unconventional ways is still far from secure. Theirs is a militant and unpopular faith, pursued with a fanatical zeal. They have suffered brutal beatings; their property has been destroyed; they have been harassed at every turn by the resurrection and enforcement of little used ordinances and statutes. To them, along with other present-day religious minorities, befalls the burden of testing our devotion to the ideals and constitutional guarantees of religious freedom. We should therefore hesitate before approving the application of a statute that might be used as another instrument of oppression. Religious freedom is too sacred a right to be restricted or prohibited in any degree without convincing proof that a legitimate interest of the state is in grave danger.

UNITED STATES v. BALLARD   322 US 78 (1944)

"The religious views expressed by the respondent might seem incredible, if not preposterous, to most people. But if those doctrines are subject to trial before a jury charged with finding their truth or falsity, then the same can be done with the religious beliefs of any sect. When the triers of fact undertake that task, they enter a forbidden domain."

Mr. Justice Douglas, for the Court

"I cannot say that freedom of thought and worship includes freedom to procure money by making knowingly false statements about one's religious experiences."

Mr. Chief Justice Stone, dissenting

"When does less than full belief in a professional credo become actionable fraud if one is soliciting gifts or legacies? Such inquiries may discomfort orthodox as well as unconventional religious teachers, for even the most regular of them are sometimes accused of taking their orthodoxy with a grain of salt."

Mr. Justice Jackson, dissenting

The Court upholds the view that the truth of religious claims is not for secular authority to determine.

Respondents were indicted and convicted for using, and conspiring to use, the mails to defraud. The indictment was in twelve counts. It charged a scheme to defraud by organizing and promoting the "I Am" movement through the use of the mails. The charge was that certain designated corporations were formed, literature distributed and sold, funds solicited, and memberships in the "I Am" movement sought "by means of false and fraudulent representations, pretenses and promises." The false representations charged were eighteen in number. It is sufficient at this point to say that they covered respondents' alleged religious doctrines or beliefs. They were all set forth in the first count. The following are representative: "that Guy W. Ballard, now deceased, alias Saint Germain, Jesus, George Washington, and Godfre Ray King, had been selected and thereby designated by the alleged 'ascertained master,' Saint Germain, as a divine messenger; and that the words of 'ascended masters' and the words of the alleged divine entity, Saint Germain, would be transmitted to mankind through the medium of the said Guy W. Ballard; that Guy W. Ballard, during his lifetime, and Edna W. Ballard, and Donald Ballard, by reason of their alleged high spiritual attainments and righteous conduct, had been elected as divine messengers through which the words of the alleged 'ascended master,' including the alleged Saint Germain, would be communicated to mankind under the teachings commonly known as the 'I Am' movement; "that Guy W. Ballard, during his lifetime, and Edna W. Ballard and Donald Ballard had, by reason of supernatural attainments, the power to heal persons of ailments and diseases and to make well persons afflicted with any diseases, injuries, or ailments, and did falsely represent to persons intended to be defrauded that the three designated persons had the ability and power to cure persons of those diseases normally classified as curable and also of diseases which are ordinarily classified by the medical profession as being incurable diseases; and did further represent that the three designated persons had in fact cured either by the activity of one, either, or all of said persons hundreds of persons afflicted with diseases and ailments."

Each of the representations enumerated in the indictment was followed by the charge that respondents "well knew" it was false. After enumerating the eighteen misrepresentations the indictment also alleged:

"At the time of making, all of the afore-alleged representations were false and untrue and were made with the intention on the part of the defendants, and each of them, to cheat, wrong, and defraud persons intended to be defrauded, and to obtain from persons intended to be defrauded by the defendants, money, property, and other things of value and to convert the same to the use and the benefit of the defendants, and each of them."

The indictment contained twelve counts, one of which charged a conspiracy to defraud. The first count set forth all of the eighteen representations, as we have said. Each of the other counts incorporated and realleged all of them and added no additional ones. There was a demurrer and a motion to quash each of which asserted among other things that the indictment attacked the religious beliefs of respondents and sought to restrict the free exercise of their religion in violation of the Constitution of the United States. These motions were denied by the District Court. Early in the trial, however, objections were raised to the admission of certain evidence concerning respondents' religious beliefs. The court conferred with counsel in absence of the jury and with the acquiescence of counsel for the United States and for respondents confined the issues on this phase of the case to the question of the good faith of respondents. At the request of counsel for both sides the court advised the jury of that action in the following language:

"Now, gentlemen, here is the issue in this case:

"First, the defendants in this case made certain representations of belief in a divinity and in a supernatural power. Some of the teachings of the defendants, representations, might seem extremely improbable to a great many people. For instance, the appearance of Jesus to dictate some of the works that we have had introduced in evidence, as testified to here at the opening transcription, or shaking hands with Jesus, to some people that might seem highly improbable. I point that out as one of the many statements.

"Whether that is true or not is not the concern of this Court and is not the concern of the jury—and they are going to be told so in their instructions. As far as this Court sees the issue, it is immaterial what these defendants preached or wrote or taught in their classes. They are not going to be permitted to speculate on the actuality of the happening of those incidents. Now, I think I have made that as clear as I can. Therefore, the religious beliefs of these defendants cannot be an issue in this court.

"The issue is: Did these defendants honestly and in good faith believe those things? If they did, they should be acquitted. I cannot make it any clearer than that.

"If these defendants did not believe those things, they did not believe that Jesus came down and dictated, or that Saint Germain came down and dictated, did not believe the things that they wrote, the things that they preached, but used the mail for the purpose of getting money, the jury should find them guilty. Therefore, gentlemen, religion cannot come into this case."

The District Court reiterated that admonition in the charge to the jury and made it abundantly clear. The following portion of the charge is typical:

"The question of the defendants' good faith is the cardinal question in this case. You are not to be concerned with the religious belief of the defendants, or any of them. The jury will be called upon to pass on the question of whether or not the defendants honestly and in good faith believed the representations which are set forth in the indictment, and honestly and in good faith believed that the benefits which they represented would flow from their belief to those who embraced and followed their teachings, or whether these representations were mere pretenses without honest belief on the part of the defendants or any of them, and, were the representations made for the purpose of procuring money, and were the mails used for this purpose."

As we have said, counsel for the defense acquiesced in this treatment of the matter, made no objection to it during the trial, and indeed treated it without protest as the law of the case throughout the proceedings prior to the verdict. Respondents did not change their position before the District Court after verdict and contend that the truth or verity of their religious doctrines or beliefs should have been submitted to the jury. In their motion for new trial they did contend, however, that the withdrawal of these issues from the jury was error because it was in effect an amendment of the indictment. That was also one of their specifications of errors on appeal. And other errors urged on appeal included the overruling of the demurrer to the indictment and the motion to quash, and the disallowance of proof of the truth of respondents' religious doctrines or beliefs.

The Circuit Court of Appeals reversed the judgment of conviction and granted a new trial, one judge dissenting. In its view the restriction of the issue in question to that of good faith was error. Its reason was that the scheme to defraud alleged in the indictment was that respondents made the eighteen alleged false representations; and that to prove that defendants devised the scheme described in the indictment "it was necessary to prove that they schemed to make some, at least, of the (eighteen) representations . . . and that some, at least, of the representations which they schemed to make were false." One judge thought that the ruling of the District Court was also error because it was "as prejudicial to the issue of honest belief as to the issue of purposeful misrepresentation."

The case is here on a petition for a writ of certiorari which we granted because of the importance of the question presented.

The United States contends that the District Court withdrew from the jury's consideration only the truth or falsity of those representations which related to religious concepts or beliefs and that there were representations charged in the indictment which fell within a different category. The argument is that this latter group of representations was submitted to the jury, that they were adequate to constitute an offense under the Act, and that they were supported by the requisite evidence. It is thus sought to bring the case within the rule of Hall v. United States, which held that where an indictment contained "all the necessary averments to constitute an offense created by the statute," a conviction would not be set aside because a "totally immaterial fact" was averred but not proved. We do not stop to ascertain the relevance of that rule to this case, for we are of the view that all of the representations charged in the indictment which related at least in part to the religious doctrines or beliefs of respondents were withheld from the jury. The trial judge did not differentiate them. He referred in the charge to the "religious beliefs" and "doctrines taught by the defendants" as matters withheld from the jury. And in stating that the issue of good faith was the "cardinal question" in the case he charged, as already noted, that "The jury will be called upon to pass on the question of whether or not the defendants honestly and in good faith believed the representations which are set forth in the indictment." Nowhere in the charge were any of the separate representations submitted to the jury. A careful reading of the whole charge leads us to agree with the Circuit Court of Appeals on this phase of the case that the only issue submitted to the jury was the question as stated by the District Court, of respondents' "belief in their representations and promises."

The United States contends that respondents acquiesced in the withdrawal from the jury of the truth of their religious doctrines or beliefs and that their consent bars them from insisting on a different course once that one turned out to be unsuccessful. Reliance for that position is sought in Johnson v. United States. That case stands for the proposition that, apart from situations involving an unfair trial, an appellate court will not grant a new trial to a defendant on the ground of improper introduction of evidence or improper comment by the prosecutor, where the defendant acquiesced in that course and made no objection to it. In fairness to respondents that principle cannot be applied here. The real objection of respondents is not that the truth of their religious doctrines or beliefs should have been submitted to the jury. Their demurrer and motion to quash made clear their position that the issue should be withheld from the jury on the basis of the First Amendment. Moreover, their position at all times was and still is that the court should have gone the whole way and withheld from the jury both that issue and the issue of their good faith. Their demurrer and motion to quash asked for dismissal of the entire indictment. Their argument that the truth of their religious doctrines or beliefs should have gone to the jury when the question of their good faith was submitted was and is merely an alternative argument. They never forsook their position that the indictment should have been dismissed and that none of it was good. Moreover, respondents' motion for new trial challenged the propriety of the action of the District Court in withdrawing from the jury the issue of the truth of their religious doctrines or beliefs without also withdrawing the question of their good faith. So we conclude that the rule of Johnson v. United States, does not prevent respondents from reasserting now that no part of the indictment should have been submitted to the Jury.

As we have noted, the Circuit Court of Appeals held that the question of the truth of the representations concerning respondents' religious doctrines or beliefs should have been submitted to the jury. And it remanded the case for a new trial. It may be that the Circuit Court of Appeals took that action because it did not think that the indictment could be properly construed as charging a scheme to defraud by means other than misrepresentations of respondents' religious doctrines or beliefs. Or that court may have concluded that the withdrawal of the issue of the truth of those religious doctrines or beliefs was unwarranted because it resulted in a substantial change in the character of the crime charged. But on whichever basis that court rested its action, we do not agree that the truth or verity of respondents' religious doctrines or beliefs should have been submitted to the jury. Whatever this particular indictment might require, the First Amendment precludes such a course, as the United States seems to concede. "The law knows no heresy, and is committed to the support of no dogma, the establishment of no sect." Watson v. Jones. The First Amendment has a dual aspect. It not only "forestalls compulsion by law of the acceptance of any creed or the practice of any form of worship" but also "safeguards the free exercise of the chosen form of religion." "Thus the Amendment embraces two concepts—freedom to believe and freedom to act. The first is absolute but, in the nature of things, the second cannot be." Freedom of thought, which includes freedom of religious belief, is basic in a society of free men. It embraces the right to maintain theories of life and of death and of the hereafter which are rank heresy to followers of the orthodox faiths. Heresy trials are foreign to our Constitution. Men may believe what they cannot prove. They may not be put to the proof of their religious doctrines or beliefs. Religious experiences which are as real as life to some may be incomprehensible to others. Yet the fact that they may be beyond the ken of mortals does not mean that they can be made suspect before the law. Many take their gospel from the New

Testament. But it would hardly be supposed that they could be tried before a jury charged with the duty of determining whether those teachings contained false representations. The miracles of the New Testament, the Divinity of Christ, life after death, the power of prayer are deep in the religious convictions of many. If one could be sent to jail because a jury in a hostile environment found those teachings false, little indeed would be left of religious freedom. The Fathers of the Constitution were not unaware of the varied and extreme views of religious sects, of the violence of disagreement among them, and of the lack of any one religious creed on which all men would agree. They fashioned a charter of government which envisaged the widest possible toleration of conflicting views. Man's relation to his God was made no concern of the state. He was granted the right to worship as he pleased and to answer to no man for the verity of his religious views. The religious views espoused by respondents might seem incredible, if not preposterous, to most people. But if those doctrines are subject to trial before a jury charged with finding their truth or falsity, then the same can be done with the religious beliefs of any sect. When the triers of fact undertake that task, they enter forbidden domain. The First Amendment does not select any one group or any one type of religion for preferred treatment It puts them all in that position. "With man's relations to his Maker and the obligations he may think they impose, and the manner in which an expression shall be made by him of his belief on those subjects, no interference can be permitted, provided always the laws of society, designed to secure its peace and prosperity, and the morals of its people, are not interfered with." So we conclude that the District Court ruled properly when it withheld from the jury all questions concerning the truth or falsity of the religious beliefs or doctrines of respondents.

Respondents maintain that the reversal of the judgment of conviction was justified on other distinct grounds. The Circuit Court of Appeals did not reach those questions. Respondents may, of course, urge them here in support of the judgment of the Circuit Court of Appeals. But since attention was centered on the issues which we have discussed, the remaining questions were not fully presented to this Court either in the briefs or oral argument. In view of these circumstances we deem it more appropriate to remand the cause to the Circuit Court of Appeals so that it may pass on the questions reserved. If any questions of importance survive and are presented here, we will then have the benefit of the views of the Circuit Court of Appeals. Until that additional consideration is had, we cannot be sure that it will be necessary to pass on any of the other constitutional issues which respondents claim to have reserved.

The judgment is reversed and the cause is remanded to the Circuit Court of Appeals for further proceedings in conformity to this opinion. Reversed.

MR. CHIEF JUSTICE STONE, DISSENTING.

I am not prepared to say that the constitutional guaranty of freedom of religion affords immunity from criminal prosecution for the fraudulent procurement of money by false statements as to one's religious experiences, more than it renders polygamy or libel immune from criminal prosecution. I cannot say that freedom of thought and worship includes freedom to procure money by making knowingly false statements about one's religious experiences. To go no further, if it were shown that a defendant in this case had asserted as a part of the alleged fraudulent scheme, that he had physically shaken hands with St. Germain in San Francisco on a day named, or that, as the indictment here alleges, by the exertion of his spiritual power he "had in fact cured . . . hundreds of persons afflicted with diseases and ailments," I should not doubt that it would be open to the Government to submit to the jury proof that he had never been in San Francisco and that no such cures had ever been effected. In any event I see no occasion for making any pronouncement on this subject in the present case.

The indictment charges respondents' use of the mails to defraud and a conspiracy to commit that offense by false statements of their religious experiences which had not in fact occurred. But it also charged that the representations were "falsely and fraudulently" made, that respondents "well knew" that these representations were untrue, and that they were made by respondents with the intent to cheat and defraud those to whom they were made. With the assent of the prosecution and the defense the trial judge withdrew from the consideration of the jury the question whether the alleged religious experiences had in fact occurred, but submitted to the jury the single issue whether petitioners honestly believed that they had occurred, with the instruction that if the jury did not so find, then it should return a verdict of guilty. On this issue the jury, on ample evidence that respondents were without belief in the statements which they had made to their victims, found a verdict of guilty. The state of one's mind is a fact as capable of fraudulent misrepresentation as is one's physical condition or the state of his bodily health. There are no exceptions to the charge and no contention that the trial court rejected any relevant evidence which petitioners sought to offer. Since the indictment and the evidence support the conviction, it is irrelevant whether the religious experiences alleged did or did not in fact occur or whether that issue could or could not, for constitutional reasons, have been rightly submitted to the jury. Certainly none of respondents' constitutional rights are violated if they are prosecuted for the fraudulent procurement of money by false representations as to their beliefs, religious or otherwise.

Obviously if the question whether the religious experiences in fact occurred could not constitutionally have been submitted to the jury the court rightly withdrew it. If it could have been submitted I know of no reason why the parties could not, with the advice of counsel, assent to its withdrawal from the jury. And where, as here, the indictment charges two sets of false statements, each independently sufficient to sustain the conviction, I cannot accept respondents' contention that the withdrawal of one set and the submission of the other to the jury amounted to an amendment of the indictment.

An indictment is amended when it is so altered as to charge a different offense from that found by the grand jury. But here there was no alteration of the indictment, nor did the court's action, in effect, add anything to it by submitting to the jury matters which it did not charge. In Salinger v. United States, we explicitly held that where an indictment charges several offenses, or the commission of one offense in several ways the withdrawal from the jury's consideration of one offense or one alleged method of committing it does not constitute a forbidden amendment of the indictment. Were the rule otherwise the common practice of withdrawing from the jury's consideration one count of an indictment while submitting others for its verdict, sustained in Dealy v. United States, would be a fatal error.

We may assume that under some circumstances the submission to the jury of part only of the matters alleged in the indictment might result in such surprise to the defendant as to amount to the denial of a fair trial. But, as in the analogous case of a variance between pleading and proof, a conviction can be reversed only upon a showing of injury to the "substantial rights" of the accused. Here no claim of surprise had been or could be made. The indictment plainly charged both falsity of, and lack of good faith belief in the representations made, and it was agreed at the outset of the trial, without objection from the defendants, that only the issue of respondents' good faith belief in the representations of religious experiences would be submitted to the jury. Respondents, who were represented by counsel, at no time in the course of the trial offered any objection to this limitation of the issues, or any contention that it would result in a prohibited amendment of the indictment. So far as appears from the record before us the point was raised for the first time in the specifications of errors in the Circuit Court of Appeals. It is asserted that it was argued to the District Court on motions for new trial and in arrest of judgment. If so, there was still no surprise by a ruling to which, as we have said, respondents' counsel assented when it was made.

On the issue submitted to the jury in this case it properly rendered a verdict of guilty. As no legally sufficient reason for disturbing it appears, I think the judgment below should be reversed and that of the District Court reinstated.

Mr. Justice Roberts and Mr. Justice Frankfurter join in this opinion.

MR. JUSTICE JACKSON, DISSENTING.

I should say the defendants have done just that for which they are indicted. If I might agree to their conviction without creating a precedent, I cheerfully would do so. I can see in their teachings nothing but humbug, untainted by any trace of truth. But that does not dispose of the constitutional question whether misrepresentation of religious experience or belief is prosecutable; it rather emphasizes the danger of such prosecutions.

The Ballard family claimed miraculous communication with the spirit world and supernatural power to heal the sick. They are brought to trial for mail fraud on an indictment which charged that their representations were false and that they "well knew" they were false. The trial judge, obviously troubled, ruled that the court could not try whether the statements were untrue, but could inquire whether the defendants knew them to be untrue; and, if so, they could be convicted.

I find it difficult to reconcile this conclusion with our traditional religious freedoms.

In the first place, as a matter of either practice or philosophy I do not see how we can separate an issue as to what is believed from consideration as to what is believable. The most convincing proof that one believes his statements is to show that they have been true in his experience. Likewise, that one knowingly falsified is best proved by showing that what he said happened never did happen. How can the Government prove these persons knew something to be false which it cannot prove to be false? If we try religious sincerity severed from religious verity, we isolate the dispute from the very considerations which in common experience provide its most reliable answer.

In the second place, any inquiry into intellectual honesty in religion raises profound psychological problems. William James, who wrote on these matters as a scientist, reminds us that it is not theology and ceremonies which keep religion going. Its vitality is in the religious experiences of many people. "If you ask what these experiences are, they are conversations with the unseen, voices and visions, responses to prayer, changes of heart, deliverances from fear, inflowings of help, assurances of support, whenever certain persons set their own internal attitude in certain appropriate ways." If religious liberty includes, as it must, the right to communicate such experiences to others, it seems to me an impossible task for juries to separate fancied ones from real ones, dreams from happenings, and hallucinations from true clairvoyance. Such experiences, like some tones and colors, have existence for one, but none at all for another. They cannot be verified to the minds of those whose field of consciousness does not include religious insight. When one comes to trial which turns on any aspect of religious belief or representation, unbelievers among his judges are likely not to understand and are almost certain not to believe him.

And then I do not know what degree of skepticism or disbelief in a religious representation amounts to actionable fraud. James points out that "Faith means belief in something concerning which doubt is theoretically possible." Belief in what one may demonstrate to the senses is not faith. All schools of religious thought make enormous assumptions, generally on the basis of revelations authenticated by some sign or miracle. The appeal in such matters is to a very different plane of credulity than is invoked by representations of secular fact in commerce. Some who profess belief in the Bible read literally what others read as allegory or metaphor, as they read Aesop's fables. Religious symbolism is even used by some with the same mental reservations one has in teaching of Santa Claus or Uncle Sam or Easter bunnies or dispassionate judges. It is hard in matters so mystical to say how far it is reliance upon a teacher's literal belief which induces followers to give him money.

There appear to be persons—let us hope not many—who find refreshment and courage in the teachings of the "I Am" cult. If the members of the sect get comfort from the celestial guidance of their "Saint Germain," however doubtful it seems to me, it is hard to say that they do not get what they pay for. Scores of sects flourish in this country by teaching what to me are queer notions. It is plain that there is wide variety in American religious taste. The Ballards are not alone in catering to it with a pretty dubious product.

The chief wrong which false prophets do to their following is not financial. The collections aggregate a tempting total, but individual payments are not ruinous. I doubt if the vigilance of the law is equal to making money stick by over-credulous people. But the real harm is on the mental and spiritual plane. There are those who hunger and thirst after higher values which they feel wanting in their humdrum lives. They live in mental confusion or moral anarchy and seek vaguely for truth and beauty and moral support. When they are deluded and then disillusioned, cynicism and confusion follow. The wrong of these

191

things, as I see it, is not in the money the victims part with half so much as in the mental and spiritual poison they get. But that is precisely the thing the Constitution put beyond the reach of the prosecutor, for the price of freedom of religion or of speech or of the press is that we must put up with, and even pay for, a good deal of rubbish.

Prosecutions of this character easily could degenerate into religious persecution. I do not doubt that religious leaders may be convicted of fraud for making false representations on matters other than faith or experience, as for example if one represents that funds are being used to construct a church when in fact they are being used for personal purposes. But that is not this case, which reaches into wholly dangerous ground. When does less than full belief in a professed credo become actionable fraud if one is soliciting gifts or legacies? Such inquiries may discomfort orthodox as well as unconventional religious teachers, for even the most regular of them are sometimes accused of taking their orthodoxy with a grain of salt.

I would dismiss the indictment and have done with this business of judicially examining other people's faiths.

IN RE SUMMERS   325 US 561 (1945)

"Thus a court . . . charged particularly with the protection of justice in the courts of Illinois through supervision of admissions to the bar found itself faced with the dilemma of excluding an applicant whom it deemed disqualified for the responsibilities of the profession of law or of admitting the applicant because of its deeply rooted tradition in freedom of belief."

Mr. Justice Reed, for the Court

"It may be, as many people think, that Christ's Gospel of love and submission is not suited to a world in which men still fight and kill one another. But I am not ready to say that a mere profession of belief in that Gospel is a sufficient reason to keep otherwise qualified men out of the legal profession, or to drive law-abiding lawyers of that belief out of the profession, which would be the next logical development."

Mr. Justice Black, dissenting

The Court upholds, 5-4, the denial, to an otherwise qualified applicant, of admission to the bar based on the applicant's religiously motivated "conscientious scruples against participation in war."

MR. JUSTICE REED DELIVERED THE OPINION OF THE COURT.

Petitioner sought a writ of certiorari from this Court under Section 247 (b) of the Judicial Code, to review the action of the Supreme Court of Illinois in denying petitioner's prayer for admission to the practice of law in that state. It was alleged that the denial was "on the sole ground that he is a conscientious objector to war" or to phrase petitioner's contention slightly differently "because of his conscientious scruples against participation in war." Petitioner challenges here the right of the Supreme Court to exclude him from the bar under the due process clause of the Fourteenth Amendment to the Constitution of the United States which secured to him protection against state action in violation of the principles of the First Amendment. Because of the importance of the tendered issue in the domain of civil right, we granted certiorari.

Since the proceedings were not treated as judicial by the Supreme Court of Illinois, the record is not in the customary form. It shows accurately, however, the steps by which the issue was developed and the action of the Supreme Court on the prayer for admission to the practice of law in the State of Illinois. From the record it appears that Clyde Wilson Summers has complied with all prerequisites for admission to the bar of Illinois except that he has not obtained the certificate of the Committee on Character and Fitness. No report appears in the record from the Committee. An unofficial letter from the Secretary gives his personal views. A petition was filed in the Supreme Court on August 2, 1943, which alleged that petitioner was informed in January, 1943, that the Committee declined to sign a favorable certificate. The petition set out that the sole reason for the Committee's refusal was that petitioner was a conscientious objector to war, and averred that such reason did not justify his exclusion because of the due process clause of the Fourteenth Amendment. The denial of the petition for admission is informal. It consists of a letter of September 20, 1943, to the Secretary of the Committee . . ., a letter of the same date to Mr. Summers and a third letter of March 22, 1944, to Mr. Summers' attorney on petition for rehearing . . .

The answer of the Justices to these allegations does not appear in the record which was transmitted from the Supreme Court of Illinois to this Court but in their return to the rule to show cause why certiorari should not be granted. The answer is two-fold: First, that the proceedings were not a matter of judicial cognizance in Illinois and that no case or controversy exists in this Court under Article III of the Federal Constitution; second, that assuming the sole ground for refusing to petitioner admission to practice was his profession of conscientious objection to military service, such refusal did not violate the Fourteenth Amendment because the requirement for applicants for admission to the bar to take an oath to support the Constitution of Illinois could not be met. In view of his religious affirmations, petitioner could not agree, freely, to serve in the Illinois militia. Therefore petitioner was not barred because of his religion but because he could not in good faith take the prescribed oath, even though he might be willing to do so. We turn to consideration of the Justices' contentions.

[part of opinion omitted]

The Justices justify their refusal to admit petitioner to practice before the courts of Illinois on the ground of petitioner's inability to take in good faith the required oath to support the Constitution of Illinois. His inability to take such an oath, the Justices submit, shows that the Committee on Character and Fitness properly refused to certify to his moral character and moral fitness to be an officer of the Court, charged with the administration of justice under the Illinois law. His good citizenship, they think, judged by the standards required for practicing law in Illinois, is not satisfactorily shown. A conscientious belief in non-violence to the extent that the believer will not use force to prevent wrong, no matter how aggravated, and so cannot swear in good faith to support the Illinois Constitution, the Justices contend, must disqualify such a believer for admission.

Petitioner appraises the denial of admission from the viewpoint of a religionist; he said in his petition:

"The so-called 'misconduct' for which petitioner could be reproached for is his taking the New Testament too seriously. Instead of merely reading or preaching the Sermon on the Mount, he tries to practice it. The only fault of the petitioner consists in his attempt to act as a good Christian in accordance with his interpretation of the Bible, and according to the dictates of his conscience. We respectfully submit that the profession of law does not shut its gates to persons who have qualified in all other respects, even when they follow in the footsteps of that Great Teacher of mankind who delivered the Sermon on the Mount. We respectfully submit that under our Constitutional guarantees even good Christians who have met all the requirements for the admission to the bar may be admitted to practice law."

Thus a court created to administer the laws of Illinois, as it understands them and charged particularly with the protection of justice in the courts of Illinois through supervision of admissions to the bar found itself faced with the dilemma of excluding an applicant whom it deemed disqualified for the responsibilities of the profession of law or of admitting the applicant because of its deeply rooted tradition in freedom of belief. The responsibility for choice as to the personnel of its bar rests with Illinois. Only a decision which violated a federal right secured by the Fourteenth Amendment would authorize our intervention. It is said that the action of the Supreme Court of Illinois is contrary to the principles of that portion of the First Amendment which guarantees the free exercise of religion. Of course, under our Constitutional system, men could not be excluded from the practice of law, or indeed from following any other calling, simply because they belong to any of our religious groups, whether Protestant, Catholic, Quaker or Jewish, assuming it conceivable that any state of the Union would draw such a religious line. We cannot say that any such purpose to discriminate motivated the action of the Illinois Supreme Court.

The sincerity of petitioner's beliefs are not questioned. He has been classified as a conscientious objector under the Selective Training and Service Act of 1940. Without detailing petitioner's testimony before the Committee or his subsequent statements in the record, his position may be compendiously stated as one of non-violence. Petitioner will not serve in the armed forces. While he recognizes a difference between the military and police forces, he would not act in the latter to coerce threatened violations. Petitioner would not use force to meet aggressions against himself or his family, no matter how aggravated or whether or not carrying a danger of bodily harm to himself or others. He is a believer in passive resistance. We need to consider only his attitude toward service in the armed forces.

Illinois has constitutional provisions which require service in the militia in time of war of men of petitioner's age group. The return of the Justices alleges that petitioner has not made any showing that he would serve notwithstanding his conscientious objections. This allegation is undenied in the record and unchallenged by brief. We accept the allegation as to unwillingness to serve in the militia as established. While under Section 5 (g) of the Selective Training and Service Act, conscientious objectors to participation in war in any form now are permitted to do non-war work of national importance, this is by grace of Congressional recognition of their beliefs. The Act may be repealed. No similar exemption during war exists under Illinois law. The Hamilton decision was made in 1934, in time of peace. This decision as to the powers of the state government over military training is applicable to the power of Illinois to require military service from her citizens.

The United States does not admit to citizenship the alien who refuses to pledge military service. Even the powerful dissents which emphasized the deep cleavage in this Court on the issue of admission to citizenship did not challenge the right of Congress to require military service from every able-bodied man. It is impossible for us to conclude that the insistence of Illinois that an officer who is charged with the administration of justice must take an oath to support the Constitution of Illinois and Illinois' interpretation of that oath to require a willingness to perform military service violates the principles of religious freedom which the Fourteenth Amendment secures against state action,

195

when a like interpretation of a similar oath as to the Federal Constitution bars an alien from national citizenship.

Affirmed.

MR. JUSTICE BLACK, DISSENTING.

The State of Illinois has denied the petitioner the right to practice his profession and to earn his living as a lawyer. It has denied him a license on the ground that his present religious beliefs disqualify him for membership in the legal profession. The question is, therefore, whether a state which requires a license as a prerequisite to practicing law can deny an applicant a license solely because of his deeply-rooted religious convictions. The fact that petitioner measures up to every other requirement for admission to the Bar set by the State demonstrates beyond doubt that the only reason for his rejection was his religious beliefs.

The state does not deny that petitioner possesses the following qualifications:

He is honest, moral, and intelligent, has had a college and a law school education. He has been a law professor and fully measures up to the high standards of legal knowledge Illinois has set as a prerequisite to admission to practice law in that State. He has never been convicted for, or charged with, a violation of law. That he would serve his clients faithfully and efficiently if admitted to practice is not denied. His ideals of what a lawyer should be indicate that his activities would not reflect discredit upon the bar, that he would strive to make the legal system a more effective instrument of justice. Because he thinks that "Lawsuits do not bring love and brotherliness, they just create antagonisms," he would, as a lawyer, exert himself to adjust controversies out of court, but would vigorously press his client's cause in court if efforts to adjust failed. Explaining to his examiners some of the reasons why he wanted to be a lawyer, he told them: "I think there is a lot of work to be done in the law. . . . I think the law has a place to see to it that every man has a chance to eat and a chance to live equally. I think the law has a place where people can go and get justice done for themselves without paying too much, for the bulk of people that are too poor." No one contends that such a vision of the law in action is either illegal or reprehensible.

The petitioner's disqualifying religious beliefs stem chiefly from a study of the New Testament and a literal acceptance of the teachings of Christ as he understands them. Those beliefs are these:

He is opposed to the use of force for either offensive or defensive purposes. The taking of human life under any circumstances he believes to be against the Law of God and contrary to the best interests of man. He would if he could, he told his examiners, obey to the letter these precepts of Christ: "Love your Enemies; Do good to those that hate you; Even though your enemy strike you on your right cheek, turn to him your left cheek also." The record of his evidence before us bears convincing marks of the deep sincerity of his convictions, and counsel for Illinois with commendable candor does not question the genuineness of his professions.

I cannot believe that a state statute would be consistent with our constitutional guarantee of freedom of religion if it specifically denied the right to practice law to all members of one of our great religious groups, Protestant, Catholic, or Jewish. Yet the Quakers have had a long and honorable part in the growth of our nation, and an amicus curiae brief filed in their behalf informs us that under the test applied to this petitioner, not one of them could qualify for the bar in Illinois. And it is obvious that the same disqualification would exist as to every conscientious objector to the use of force, even though the Congress of the United States should continue its practice of absolving them from military service. The conclusion seems to me inescapable that if Illinois can bar this petitioner from the practice of law it can bar every person from every public occupation solely because he believes in non-resistance rather than in force. For a lawyer is no more subject to call for military duty than a plumber, a highway worker, a Secretary of State, or a prison chaplain.

It may be, as many people think, that Christ's Gospel of love and submission is not suited to a world in which men still fight and kill one another. But I am not ready to say that a mere profession of belief in that Gospel is a sufficient reason to keep otherwise well qualified men out of the legal profession, or to drive law-abiding lawyers of that belief out of the profession, which would be the next logical development.

Nor am I willing to say that such a belief can be penalized through the circuitous method of prescribing an oath, and then barring an applicant on the ground that his present belief might later prompt him to do or refrain from doing something that might violate that oath. Test oaths, designed to impose civil disabilities upon men for their beliefs rather than for unlawful conduct, were an abomination to the founders of this nation. This feeling was made manifest in Article VI of the Constitution which provides that "no religious Test shall ever be required as a Qualification to any Office or public Trust under the United States."

The state's denial of petitioner's application to practice law resolves itself into a holding that it is lawfully required that all lawyers take an oath to support the state constitution and that petitioner's religious convictions against the use of force make it impossible for him to observe that oath. The petitioner denies this and is willing to take the oath. The particular constitutional provision involved authorizes the legislature to draft Illinois citizens from 18 to 45 years of age for militia service. It can be assumed that the State of Illinois has the constitutional power to draft conscientious objectors for war duty and to punish them for a refusal to serve as soldiers,—powers which this Court held the United States possesses in United States v. Schwimmer, and United States v. Macintosh. But that is not to say that Illinois could constitutionally use the test oath it did in this case. In the Schwimmer and Macintosh cases aliens were barred from naturalization because their then religious beliefs would bar them from bearing arms to defend the country. Dissents in both cases rested in part on the premise that religious tests are incompatible with our constitutional guarantee of freedom of thought and religion. In the Schwimmer case dissent, Mr. Justice Holmes said that "if there is any principle of the Constitution that more imperatively calls for attachment than any other it is the principle of free thought—not free thought for those who agree with us but freedom for the thought that we hate. I think that we should adhere to that principle with regard to admission into, as well as to life within this country." In the Macintosh case dissent, Mr. Chief Justice Hughes said, "To conclude that the general oath of office is to be interpreted as disregarding the religious scruples of these citizens and as disqualifying them for office because they could not take the oath with such an interpretation would, I believe, be generally regarded as contrary not only to the specific intent of the Congress but as repugnant to the fundamental principle of representative government." I agree with the constitutional philosophy underlying the dissents of Mr. Justice Holmes and Mr. Chief Justice Hughes.

The Illinois Constitution itself prohibits the draft of conscientious objectors except in time of war and also excepts from militia duty persons who are "exempted by the laws of the United States." It has not drafted men into the militia since 1864, and if it ever should again, no one can say that it will not, as has the Congress of the United States, exempt men who honestly entertain the views that this petitioner does. Thus the probability that Illinois would ever call the petitioner to serve in a war has little more reality than an imaginary quantity in mathematics.

I cannot agree that a state can lawfully bar from a semi-public position, a well-qualified man of good character solely because he entertains a religious belief which might prompt him at some time in the future to violate a law which has not yet been and may never be enacted. Under our Constitution men are punished for what they do or fail to do and not for what they think and believe. Freedom to think, to believe, and to worship, has too exalted a position in our country to be penalized on such an illusory basis.

I would reverse the decision of the State Supreme Court.

Mr. Justice Douglas, Mr. Justice Murphy, and Mr. Justice Rutledge concur in this opinion.

GIROUARD v. UNITED STATES   328 US 61 (1946)

"The struggle for religious liberty has through the centuries been an effort to accommodate the demands of the State to the conscience of the individual. The victory for freedom of thought recorded in our Bill of Rights recognizes that in the domain of conscience there is a moral power higher than the State."

Mr. Justice Douglas, for the Court

In this case the Court reverses the position it had taken earlier on the naturalization of conscientious objectors and adopts the position stated by Holmes and Hughes in their dissents in the Schwimmer and Macintosh cases. (The dissenting opinion of Chief Justice Stone is omitted since it is directed largely at the question of the intent of Congress as evidenced by its failure to modify the naturalization statutes after the Schwimmer and Macintosh cases.)

MR. JUSTICE DOUGLAS DELIVERED THE OPINION OF THE COURT.

In 1943 petitioner, a native of Canada, filed his petition for naturalization in the District Court of Massachusetts. He stated in his application that he understood the principles of the government of the United States, believed in its form of government, and was willing to take the oath of allegiance which reads as follows:

"I hereby declare, on oath, that I absolutely and entirely renounce and abjure all allegiance and fidelity to any foreign prince, potentate, state, or sovereignty of whom or which I have heretofore been a subject or citizen; that I will support and defend the Constitution and laws of the United States of America against all enemies, foreign and domestic; that I will bear true faith and allegiance to the same; and that I take this obligation freely without any mental reservation or purpose of evasion: So help me God."

To the question in the application "If necessary, are you willing to take up arms in defense of this country?" he replied, "No (Non-combatant) Seventh Day Adventist." He explained that answer before the examiner by saying "it is a purely religious matter with me, I have no political or personal reasons other than that." He did not claim before his Selective Service board exemption from all military service, but only from combatant military duty. At the hearing in the District Court petitioner testified that he was a member of the Seventh Day Adventist denomination, of whom approximately 10,000 were then serving in the armed forces of the United States as non-combatants, especially in the medical corps; and that he was willing to serve in the army but would not bear arms. The District Court admitted him to citizenship. The Circuit Court of Appeals reversed, one judge dissenting. It took that action on the authority of United States v. Schwimmer; United States v. Macintosh, and United States v. Bland, saying that the facts of the present case brought it squarely within the principles of those cases. The case is here on a petition for a writ of certiorari which we granted so that those authorities might be re-examined.

The Schwimmer, Macintosh and Bland cases involved, as does the present one, a question of statutory construction. At the time of those cases, Congress required an alien, before admission to citizenship, to declare on oath in open court that "he will support and defend the Constitution and laws of the United States against all enemies, foreign and domestic, and bear true faith and allegiance to the same." It also required the court to be satisfied that the alien had during the five year period immediately preceding the date of his application "behaved as a man of good moral character, attached to the principles of the Constitution of the United States, and well disposed to the good order and happiness of the same." Those provisions were reenacted into the present law in substantially the same form.

While there are some factual distinctions between this case and the Schwimmer and Macintosh cases, the Bland case on its facts is indistinguishable. But the principle emerging from the three cases obliterates any factual distinction among them. As we recognized in In Re Summers, they stand for the same general rule—that an alien who refuses to bear arms will not be admitted to citizenship. As an original proposition, we could not agree with that rule. The fallacies underlying it were, we think, demonstrated in the dissents of Mr. Justice Holmes in the Schwimmer case and of Mr. Chief Justice Hughes in the Macintosh case.

The oath required of aliens does not in terms require that they promise to bear arms. Nor has Congress expressly made any such finding a prerequisite to citizenship. To hold that it is required is to read it into the Act by implication. But we could not assume that Congress intended to make such an abrupt and radical departure from our traditions unless it spoke in unequivocal terms.

The bearing of arms, important as it is, is not the only way in which our institutions may be supported and defended, even in times of great peril. Total war in its modern form dramatizes as never before the great cooperative effort necessary for victory. The nuclear physicists who developed the atomic bomb, the worker at his lathe, the seaman on cargo vessels, construction battalions, nurses, engineers, litter bearers, doctors, chaplains—these, too, made essential contributions. And many of them made the supreme sacrifice. Mr. Justice Holmes stated in the Schwimmer case, that "the Quakers have done their share to make the country what it is." And the annals of the recent war show that many whose religious scruples prevented them from bearing arms, nevertheless were unselfish participants in the war effort. Refusal to bear arms is not necessarily a sign of disloyalty or a lack of attachment to our institutions. One may serve his country faithfully and devotedly, though his religious scruples make it impossible for him to shoulder a rifle. Devotion to one's country can be as real and as enduring among noncombatants as among combatants. One may adhere to what he deems to be his obligation to God and yet assume all military risks to secure victory. The effort of war is indivisible; and those whose religious scruples prevent them from killing are no less patriots than those whose special traits or handicaps result in their assignment to duties far behind the fighting front. Each is making the utmost contribution according to his capacity. The fact that his role may be limited by religious convictions rather than by physical characteristics has no necessary bearing on his attachment to his country or on his willingness to support and defend it to his utmost.

Petitioner's religious scruples would not disqualitfy him from becoming a member of Congress or holding other public offices. While Article VI, Clause 3 of the Constitution provides that such officials, both of the United States and the several States, "shall be bound by Oath or Affirmation, to support this Constitution," it significantly adds that "no religious Test shall ever be required as a Qualification to any Office or public Trust under the United States." The oath required is in no material respect different from that prescribed for aliens under the Naturalization Act. It has long contained the provision "that I will support and defend the Constitution of the United States against all enemies, foreign and domestic; that I will bear true faith and allegiance to the same; that I take this obligation freely, without any mental reservation or purpose of evasion." As Mr. Chief Justice Hughes pointed out in his dissent in the Macintosh case, "the history of the struggle for religious liberty, the large number of citizens of our country from the very beginning who have been unwilling to sacrifice their religious convictions, and, in particular, those who have been conscientiously opposed to war and who would not yield what they sincerely believed to be their allegiance to the will of God"—these considerations make it impossible to conclude "that such persons are to be deemed disqualified for public office in this country because of the requirement of the oath which must be taken before they enter upon their duties."

There is not the slightest suggestion that Congress set a stricter standard for aliens seeking admission to citizenship than it did for officials who make and enforce the laws of the nation and administer its affairs. It is hard to believe that one need forsake his religious scruples to become a citizen but not to sit in the high councils of state.

As Mr. Chief Justice Hughes pointed out, religious scruples against bearing arms have been recognized by Congress in the various draft laws. This is true of the Selective Training and Service Act of 1940, as it was of earlier acts. He who is inducted into the armed services takes an oath which includes the provision "that I will bear true faith and allegiance to the United States of America; that I will serve them honestly and faithfully against all their enemies whomsoever." Congress has thus recognized that one may adequately discharge his obligations as a citizen by rendering non-combatant as well as combatant services. This respect by Congress over the years for the conscience of those having religious scruples against bearing arms is cogent evidence of the meaning of the oath. It is recognition by Congress that even in time of war one may truly support and defend our institutions though he stops short of using weapons of war.

That construction of the naturalization oath received new support in 1942. In the Second War Powers Act, Congress relaxed certain of the requirements for aliens who served honorably in the armed forces of the United States during World War II and provided machinery to expedite their naturalization. Residence requirements were relaxed, educational tests were eliminated, and no fees were required. But no change in the oath was made; nor was any change made in the requirement that the alien be attached to the principles of the Constitution. Yet it is clear that these new provisions cover non-combatants as well as combatants. If petitioner had served as a non-combatant (as he was willing to do), he could have been admitted to citizenship by taking the identical oath which he is willing to take. Can it be that the oath means one thing to one who has served to the extent permitted by his religious scruples and another thing to one equally willing to serve but who has not had the opportunity? It is not enough to say that petitioner is not entitled to the benefits of the new Act since he did not serve in the armed forces. He is not seeking the benefits of the expedited procedure and the relaxed requirements. The oath which he must take is identical with the oath which both non-combatants and combatants must take. It would, indeed, be a strange construction to say that "support and defend the Constitution and laws of the United States of

America against all enemies, foreign and domestic" demands something more from some than it does from others. That oath can hardly be adequate for one who is unwilling to bear arms because of religious scruples and yet exact from another a promise to bear arms despite religious scruples.

Mr. Justice Holmes stated in the Schwimmer case, "if there is any principle of the Constitution that more imperatively calls for attachment than any other it is the principle of free thought—not free thought for those who agree with us but freedom for the thought that we hate. I think that we should adhere to that principle with regard to admission into, as well as to life within this country." The struggle for religious liberty has through the centuries been an effort to accommodate the demands of the State to the conscience of the individual. The victory for freedom of thought recorded in our Bill of Rights recognizes that in the domain of conscience there is a moral power higher than the State. Throughout the ages men have suffered death rather than subordinate their allegiance to God to the authority of the State. Freedom of religion guaranteed by the First Amendment is the product of that struggle. As we recently stated in United States v. Ballard, "Freedom of thought, which includes freedom of religious belief, is basic in a society of free men." The test oath is abhorrent to our tradition. Over the years Congress has meticulously respected that tradition and even in time of war has sought to accommodate the military requirements to the religious scruples of the individual. We do not believe that Congress intended to reverse that policy when it came to draft the naturalization oath. Such an abrupt and radical departure from our traditions should not be implied. Cogent evidence would be necessary to convince us that Congress took that course.

We conclude that the Schwimmer, Macintosh and Bland cases do not state the correct rule of law.

We are met, however, with the argument that even though those cases were wrongly decided, Congress has adopted the rule which they announced. The argument runs as follows: Many efforts were made to amend the law so as to change the rule announced by those cases; but in every instance the bill died in committee. Moreover, in 1940 when the new Naturalization Act was passed, Congress reenacted the oath in its pre-existing form, though at the same time it made extensive changes in the requirements and procedure for naturalization. From this it is argued that Congress adopted and reenacted the rule of the Schwimmer, Macintosh, and Bland cases.

We stated in Helvering v. Hallock, that "It would require very persuasive circumstances enveloping Congressional silence to debar this Court from re-examining its own doctrines." It is at best treacherous to find in Congressional silence alone the adoption of a controlling rule of law. We do not think under the circumstances of this legislative history that we can properly place on the shoulders of Congress the burden of the Court's own error. The history of the 1940 Act is at most equivocal. It contains no affirmative recognition of the rule of the Schwimmer, Macintosh and Bland cases. The silence of Congress and its inaction are as consistent with a desire to leave the problem fluid as they are with an adoption by silence of the rule of those cases. But for us, it is enough to say that since the date of those cases Congress never acted affirmatively on this question but once and that was in 1942. At that time as we have noted, Congress specifically granted naturalization privileges to non-combatants who like petitioner were prevented from bearing arms by their religious scruples. That was affirmative recognition that one could be attached to the principles of our government and could support and defend it even though his religious convictions prevented him from bearing arms. And, as we have said, we cannot believe that the oath was designed to exact something more from one person than from another. Thus the affirmative action taken by Congress in 1942 negatives any inference that otherwise might be drawn from its silence when it reenacted the oath in 1940.

Reversed.

EVERSON v. BOARD OF EDUCATION
330 US 1 (1947)

"In the words of Jefferson, the clause against establishment of religion by law was intended to erect 'a wall of separation between church and state.'

". . . we must be careful, in protecting the citizens of New Jersey against state-established churches, to be sure that we do not inadvertently prohibit New Jersey from extending its general State law benefits to all its citizens without regard to their religious belief."

Mr. Justice Black, for the Court

"Of course, the state may pay out tax-raised funds to relieve pauperism, but it may not spend funds to secure religion against skepticism. It may compensate individuals for loss of employment, but it cannot compensate them for adherence to a creed."

Mr. Justice Jackson, dissenting

"Two great drives are constantly in motion to abridge, in the name of education, the complete division of religion and civil authority which our forefathers made. One is to introduce religious education and observances into the public schools, the other is to obtain public funds for the aid and support of various private religious schools. In my opinion both avenues were closed by the Constitution."

Mr. Justice Rutledge, dissenting

Attention turns, in this, the famous bus-fare case, from the "free exercise" clause which has been chiefly involved in the problems of "fringe" groups like Mormons, Jehovah's Witnesses, and various conscientious objectors to the "establishment" clause and the meaning of "separation" of church and state. Its implications for the future of parochial schools and the extent to which they may enjoy, directly or indirectly, the support of public funds have made it one of the crucial modern Supreme Court cases. It is a 5-4 opinion.

MR. JUSTICE BLACK DELIVERED THE OPINION OF THE COURT.

A New Jersey statute authorizes its local school districts to make rules and contracts for the transportation of children to and from schools. The appellee, a township board of education, acting pursuant to this statute authorized reimbursement to parents of money expended by them for the bus transportation of their children on regular busses operated by the public transportation system. Part of this money was for the payment of transportation of some children in the community to Catholic parochial schools. These church schools give their students, in addition to secular education, regular religious instruction conforming to the religious tenets and modes of worship of the Catholic Faith. The superintendent of these schools is a Catholic priest.

The appellant, in his capacity as a district taxpayer, filed suit in a State court challenging the right of the Board to reimburse parents of parochial school students. He contended that the statute and the resolution passed pursuant to it violated both the State and the Federal Constitutions. That court held that the legislature was without power to authorize such payment under the State constitution. The New Jersey Court of Errors and Appeals reversed, holding that neither the statute nor the resolution passed pursuant to it was in conflict with the State constitution or the provisions of the Federal Constitution in issue.

Since there has been no attack on the statute on the ground that a part of its language excludes children attending private schools operated for profit from enjoying state payment for their transportation, we need not consider this exclusionary language; it has no relevancy to any constitutional question here presented. Furthermore, if the exclusion clause had been properly challenged, we do not know whether New Jersey's highest court would construe its statutes as precluding payment of the school transportation of any group of pupils, even those of a private school run for profit. Consequently, we put to one side the question as to the validity of the statute against the claim that it does not authorize payment for the transportation generally of school children in New Jersey.

The only contention here is that the State statute and the resolution, in so far as they authorized reimbursement to parents of children attending parochial schools, violate the Federal Constitution in these two respects, which to some extent, overlap. First. They authorize the State to take by taxation the private property of some and bestow it upon others, to be used for their own private purposes. This, it is alleged, violates the due process clause of the Fourteenth Amendment. Second. The statute and the resolution forced inhabitants to pay taxes to help support and maintain schools which are dedicated to, and which regularly teach, the Catholic Faith. This is alleged to be a use of State power to support church schools contrary to the prohibition of the First Amendment which the Fourteenth Amendment made applicable to the states.

First. The due process argument that the State law taxes some people to help others carry out their private purposes is framed in two phases. The first phase is that a state cannot tax A to reimburse B for the cost of transporting his children to church schools. This is said to violate the due process clause because the children are sent to these church schools to satisfy the personal desires of their parents, rather than the public's interest in the general education of all children. This argument, if valid, would apply equally to prohibit state payment for the transportation of children to any non-public school, whether operated by a church, or any other non-government individual or group. But, the New Jersey legislature has decided that a public purpose will be served by using tax-raised funds to pay the bus fares of all school children, including those who attend parochial schools. The New Jersey Court of Errors and Appeals has reached the same conclusion. The fact that a state law, passed to satisfy a public need, coincides with the personal desires of the individuals most directly affected is certainly an inadequate reason for us to say that a legislature has erroneously appraised the public need.

It is true that this Court has, in rare instances, struck down state statutes on the ground that the purpose for which tax-raised funds were to be expended was not a public one. But the Court has also pointed out that this far-reaching authority must be exercised with the most extreme caution. Otherwise, a state's power to legislate for the public welfare might be seriously curtailed, a power which is a primary reason for the existence of states. Changing local conditions create new local problems which may lead a state's people and its local authorities to believe that laws authorizing new types of public services are necessary to promote the general well-being of the people. The Fourteenth Amendment did not strip the states of their power to meet problems previously left for individual solution.

It is much too late to argue that legislation intended to facilitate the opportunity of children to get a secular education serves no public purpose. The same thing is no less true of legislation to reimburse needy parents, or all parents, for payment of the fares of their children so that they can ride in public busses to and from schools rather than run the risk of traffic and other hazards incident to walking or "hitchhiking." Nor does it follow that a law has a private rather than a public purpose because it provides that tax-raised funds will be paid to reimburse individuals on account of money spent by them in a way which furthers a public program. Subsidies and loans to individuals such as farmers and home owners, and to privately owned transportation systems, as well as many other kinds of businesses, have been commonplace practices in our state and national history.

Insofar as the second phase of the due process argument may differ from the first, it is by suggesting that taxation for transportation of children to church schools constitutes support of a religion by the State. But if the law is invalid for this reason, it is because it violates the First Amendment's prohibition against the establishment of religion by law. This is the exact question raised by appellant's second contention, to consideration of which we now turn.

Second. The New Jersey statute is challenged as a "law respecting an establishment of religion." The First Amendment, as made applicable to the states by the Fourteenth, commands that a state "shall make no law respecting an establishment of religion, or prohibiting the free exercise thereof." These words of the First Amendment reflected in the minds of early Americans a vivid mental picture of conditions and practices which they fervently wished to stamp out in order to preserve liberty for themselves and for their posterity. Doubtless their goal has not been entirely reached; but so far has the Nation moved toward it that the expression "law respecting an establishment of religion," probably does not so vividly remind present-day Americans of the evils, fears, and political problems that caused that expression to be written into our Bill of Rights. Whether this New Jersey law is one respecting the "establishment of religion" requires an understanding of the meaning of that language, particularly with respect to the imposition of taxes. Once again, therefore, it is not inappropriate briefly to review the background and environment of the period in which that constitutional language was fashioned and adopted.

A large proportion of the early settlers of this country came here from Europe to escape the bondage of laws which compelled them to support and attend government favored churches. The centuries immediately before and contemporaneous with the colonization of America had been filled with turmoil, civil strife, and persecution, generated in large part by established sects determined to maintain their absolute political and religious supremacy. With the power of government supporting them, at various times and places, Catholics had persecuted Protestants, Protestants had persecuted Catholics, Protestant sects had persecuted other Protestant sects, Catholics of one shade of belief had persecuted Catholics of another shade of belief, and all of these had from time to time persecuted Jews. In efforts to force loyalty to whatever religious group happened to be on top and in league with the government of a particular time and place, men and women had been fined, cast in jail, cruelly tortured, and killed. Among the offenses for which these punishments had been inflicted were such things as speaking disrespectfully of the views of ministers of government-established churches, non-attendance at those churches, expressions of non-belief in their doctrines, and failure to pay taxes and tithes to support them.

These practices of the old world were transplanted to and began to thrive in the soil of the new America. The very charters granted by the English Crown to the individuals and companies designated to make the laws which would control the destinies of the colonials authorized these individuals and companies to erect religious establishments which all, whether believers or non-believers, would be required to support and attend. An exercise of this authority was accompanied by a repetition of many of the old-world practices and persecutions. Catholics found themselves hounded and proscribed because of their faith; Quakers who followed their conscience went to jail; Baptists were peculiarly obnoxious to certain dominant Protestant sects; men and women of varied faiths who happened to be in a minority in a particular locality were persecuted because they steadfastly persisted in worshipping God only as their own consciences dictated. And all of these dissenters were compelled to pay tithes and taxes to support government-sponsored churches whose ministers preached inflammatory sermons designed to strengthen and consolidate the established faith by generating a burning hatred against dissenters.

These practices became so commonplace as to shock the freedom-loving colonials into a feeling of abhorrence. The imposition of taxes to pay ministers' salaries and to build and maintain churches and church property aroused their indignation. It was these feelings which found expression in the First Amendment. No one locality and no one group throughout the Colonies can rightly be given entire credit for having aroused the sentiment that culminated in adoption of the Bill of Rights' provisions embracing religious liberty. But Virginia, where the established church had achieved a dominant influence in political affairs and where many excesses attracted wide public attention, provided a great stimulus and able leadership for the movement. The people there, as elsewhere, reached the conviction that individual religious liberty could be achieved best under a government which was stripped of all power to tax, to support, or otherwise to assist any or all religions, or to interfere with the beliefs of any religious individual or group.

The movement toward this end reached its dramatic climax in Virginia's tax levy for the support of the established church. Thomas Jefferson and James Madison led the fight against this tax. Madison wrote his great Memorial and Remonstrance against the law. In it, he eloquently argued that a true religion did not need the support of law; that no person, either believer or non-believer, should be taxed to support a religious institution of any kind; that the best interest of a society required that the minds of men always be wholly free; and that cruel persecutions were the inevitable result of government-established religions. Madison's Remonstrance received strong support throughout Virginia, and the Assembly postponed consideration of the proposed tax measure until its next session. When the proposal came up for consideration at that session, it not only died in committee, but the Assembly enacted the famous "Virginia Bill for Religious Liberty" originally written by Thomas Jefferson. The preamble to that Bill stated among other things that

"Almighty God hath created the mind free; that all attempts to influence it by temporal punishment, or burthens, or by civil incapacitations, tend only to beget habits of hypocrisy and meanness, and are a departure from the plan of the Holy author of our religion who being Lord both of body and mind, yet chose not to propagate it by coercions on either . . .; that to compel a man to furnish contributions of money for the propagation of opinions which he disbelieves, is sinful and tyrannical; that even the forcing him to support this or that teacher of his own religious persuasion, is depriving him of the comfortable liberty of giving his contributions to the particular pastor, whose morals he would make his pattern. . . ."

And the statute itself enacted

"That no man shall be compelled to frequent or support any religious worship, place, or ministry whatsoever, nor shall be enforced, restrained, molested, or burthened, in his body or goods, nor shall otherwise suffer on account of his religious opinions or belief . . ."

This Court has previously recognized that the provisions of the First Amendment, in the drafting and adoption of which Madison and Jefferson played such leading roles, had the same objective and were intended to provide the same protection against governmental intrusion on religious liberty as the Virginia statute. Prior to the adoption of the Fourteenth Amendment, the First Amendment did not apply as a restraint against the states. Most of them did soon provide similar constitutional protections for religious liberty. But some states persisted for about half a century in imposing restraints upon the free exercise of religion and in discriminating against particular religious groups. In recent years, so far as the provision against the establishment of a religion is concerned, the question has most frequently arisen in connection with proposed state aid to church schools and efforts to carry on religious teachings in the public schools in accordance with the tenets of a particular sect. Some churches have either sought or accepted state financial support for their schools. Here again the efforts to obtain state aid or acceptance of it have not been limited to any one particular faith. The state courts, in the main, have remained faithful to the language of their own constitutional provisions designated to protect religious freedom and to separate religions and governments. Their decisions, however, show the difficulty in drawing the line between tax legislation which provides funds for the welfare of the general public and that which is designed to support institutions which teach religion.

The meaning and scope of the First Amendment, preventing establishment of religion or prohibiting the free exercise thereof, in the light of its history and the evils it was designed forever to suppress, have been several times elaborated by the decisions of this Court prior to the application of the First Amendment to the states by the Fourteenth. The broad meaning given the Amendment by these earlier cases has been accepted by this Court in its decisions concerning an individual's religious freedom rendered since the Fourteenth Amendment was interpreted to make the prohibitions of the First applicable to state action abridging religious freedom. There is every reason to give the same application and broad interpretation to the "establishment of religion" clause. The interrelation of these complementary clauses was well summarized in a statement of the Court of Appeals of South Carolina, quoted with approval by this Court, in Watson v. Jones, "The structure of our government has, for the preservation of civil liberty, rescued the temporal institutions from religious interference. On the other hand, it has secured religious liberty from the invasions of the civil authority."

The "establishment of religion" clause of the First Amendment means at least this: Neither a state nor the Federal Government can set up a church. Neither can pass laws which aid one religion, aid all religions, or prefer one religion over another. Neither can force nor influence a person to go to or to remain away from church against his will or force him to profess a belief or disbelief in any religion. No person can be punished for entertaining or professing religious beliefs or disbeliefs, for church attendance or non-attendance. No tax in any amount, large or small, can be levied to support any religious activities or institutions, whatever they may be called, or whatever form they may adopt to teach or practice religion. Neither a state nor the Federal Government can, openly or secretly, participate in the affairs of any religious organizations or groups and vice versa. In the words of Jefferson, the clause against establishment of religion by law was intended to erect "a wall of separation between Church and State.".

We must consider the New Jersey statute in accordance with the foregoing limitations imposed by the First Amendment. But we must not strike that state statute down if it is within the state's constitutional power even though it approaches the verge of that power. New Jersey cannot consistently with the "establishment of religion" clause of the First Amendment contribute tax-raised funds to the support of an institution which teaches the tenets and faith of any church. On the other hand, other language of the amendment commands that New Jersey cannot exclude individual Catholics, Lutherans, Mohammedans, Baptists, Jews, Methodists, Non-believers, Presbyterians, or the members of any other faith, because of their faith, or lack of it, from receiving the benefits of public welfare legislation. While we do not mean to intimate that a state could not provide transportation only to children attending public schools, we must be careful, in protecting the citizens of New Jersey against state-established churches, to be sure that we do not inadvertently prohibit New Jersey from extending its general State law benefits to all its citizens without regard to their religious belief.

Measured by these standards, we cannot say that the First Amendment prohibits New Jersey from spending tax-raised funds to pay the bus fares of parochial school pupils as a part of a general program under which it pays the fares of pupils attending public and other schools. It is undoubtedly true that children are helped to get to church schools. There is even a possibility that some of the children might not be sent to the church schools if the parents were compelled to pay their children's bus fares out of their own pockets when transportation to a public school would have been paid for by the State. The same possibility exists where the state requires a local transit company to provide reduced fares to school children including those attending parochial schools, or where a municipally owned transportation system undertakes to carry all school children free of charge. Moreover, state-paid policemen, detailed to protect children going to and from church schools from the very real hazards of traffic, would serve much the same purpose and accomplish much the same result as state provisions intended to guarantee free transportation of a kind which the state deems to be best for the school children's welfare. And parents might refuse to risk their children to the serious danger of traffic accidents going to and from parochial schools, the approaches to which were not protected by policemen. Similarly, parents might be reluctant to permit their children to attend schools which the state had cut off from such general government services as ordinary police and fire protection, connections for sewage disposal, public highways and sidewalks. Of course, cutting off church schools from these services, so separate and so indisputably marked off from the religious function, would make it far more difficut for the schools to operate. But such is obviously not the purpose of the First Amendment. That Amendment requires the state to be a neutral in its relations with groups of religious believers and nonbelievers; it does not require the state to be their adversary. State power is no more to be used so as to handicap religions, than it is to favor them.

This Court has said that parents may, in the discharge of their duty under state compulsory education laws, send their children to a religious rather than a public school if the school meets the secular educational requirements which the state has power to impose. It appears that these parochial schools meet New Jersey's requirements. The State contributes no money to the schools. It does not support them. Its legislation, as applied, does no more than provide a general program to help parents get their children, regardless of their religion, safely and expeditiously to and from accredited schools.

The First Amendment has erected a wall between church and state. That wall must be kept high and impregnable. We could not approve the slightest breach. New Jersey has not breached it here.

Affirmed.

MR. JUSTICE JACKSON, DISSENTING.

I find myself, contrary to first impressions, unable to join in this decision. I have a sympathy, though it is not ideological, with Catholic citizens who are compelled by law to pay taxes for public schools, and also feel constrained by conscience and discipline to support other schools for their own children. Such relief to them as this case involves is not in itself a serious burden to taxpayers and I had assumed it to be as little serious in principle. Study of this case convinces me otherwise. The Court's opinion marshals every argument in favor of state aid and puts the case in its most favorable light, but much of its reasoning confirms my conclusions that there are no good grounds upon which to support the present legislation. In fact, the undertones of the opinion, advocating complete and uncompromising separation of Church from State, seem utterly discordant with its conclusion yielding support to their commingling in educational matters. The case which irresistibly comes to mind as the most fitting precedent is that of Julia who according to Byron's reports, "whispering 'I will ne'er consent,'—consented."

The Court sustains this legislation by assuming two deviations from the facts of this particular case; first, it assumes a state of facts the record does not support, and secondly, it refuses to consider facts which are inescapable on the record.

The Court concludes that this "legislation, as applied, does no more than provide a general program to help parents get their children, regardless of their religion, safely and expeditiously to and from accredited schools," and it draws a comparison between "state provisions intended to guarantee free transportation" for school children with services such as police and fire protection, and implies that we are here dealing with "laws authorizing new types of public services . . ." This hypothesis permeates the opinion. The facts will not bear that construction.

The Township of Ewing is not furnishing transportation to the children in any form; it is not operating school busses itself or contracting for their operation; and it is not performing any public service of any kind with this taxpayer's money. All school children are left to ride as ordinary paying passengers on the regular busses operated by the public transportation system. What the Township does, and what the taxpayer complains of, is at stated intervals to reimburse parents for the fares paid, provided the children attend either public schools or Catholic Church schools. This expenditure of tax funds has no possible effect on the child's safety or expedition in transit. As passengers on the public busses they travel as fast and no faster, and are safe and no safer, since their parents are reimbursed as before.

In addition to thus assuming a type of service that does not exist, the Court also insists that we must close our eyes to a discrimination which does exist. The resolution which authorizes disbursement of this taxpayer's money limits reimbursement to those who attend public schools and Catholic schools. That is the way the Act is applied to this taxpayer.

The New Jersey Act in question makes the character of the school, not the needs of the children determine the eligibility of parents to reimbursement. The Act permits payment for transportation to parochial schools or public schools but prohibits it to private schools operated in whole or in part for profit. Children often are sent to private schools because their parents feel that they require more individual instruction than public schools can provide, or because they are backward or defective and need special attention. If all children of the state were objects of impartial solicitude, no reason is obvious for denying transportation reimbursement to students of this class, for these often are as needy and as worthy as those who go to public or parochial schools. Refusal to reimburse those who attend such schools is understandable only in the light of a purpose to aid the schools, because the state might well abstain from aiding a profit-making private enterprise. Thus, under the Act and resolution brought to us by this case children are classified according to the schools they attend and are to be aided if they attend the public schools or private Catholic schools, and they are not allowed to be aided if they attend private secular schools or private religious schools of other faiths.

Of couse, this case is not one of a Baptist or a Jew or an Episcopalian or a pupil of a private school complaining of discrimination. It is one of a taxpayer urging that he is being taxed for an unconstitutional purpose. I think he is entitled to have us consider the Act just as it is written. The statement by the New Jersey court that it holds the Legislature may authorize use of local funds "for the transportation of pupils to any school," in view of the other constitutional views expressed, is not a holding that this Act authorizes transportation for all pupils to all schools. As applied to this taxpayer by the action he complains of, certainly the Act does not authorize reimbursement to those who choose any alternative to the public school except Catholic Church schools.

If we are to decide this case on the facts before us, our question is simply this: Is it constitutional to tax this complainant to pay the cost of carrying pupils to Church schools of one specified denomination?

II

Whether the taxpayer constitutionally can be made to contribute aid to parents of students because of their attendance at parochial schools depends upon the nature of those schools and their relation to the Church. The Constitution says nothing of education. It lays no obligation on the states to provide schools and does not undertake to regulate state systems of education if they see fit to maintain them. But they cannot, through school policy any more than through other means, invade rights secured to citizens by the Constitution of the United States. One of our basic rights is to be free of taxation to support a transgression of the constitutional command that the authorities "shall make no law respecting an establishment of religion, or prohibiting the free exercise thereof."

The function of the Church school is a subject on which this record is meager. It shows only that the schools are under superintendence of a priest and that "religion is taught as part of the curriculum." But we know that such schools are parochial only in name—they, in fact, represent a world-wide and age-old policy of the Roman Catholic Church. Under the rubric "Catholic Schools," the Canon Law of the Church by which all Catholics are bound, provides:

"1216. In every elementary school the children must, according to their age, be instructed in Christian doctrine.

"The young people who attend the higher schools are to receive a deeper religious knowledge, and the bishops shall appoint priests qualified for such work by their learning and piety. (Canon 1373.)"

"1217. Catholic children shall not attend non-Catholic, indifferent, schools that are mixed, that is to say schools open to Catholic and non-Catholics alike. The bishop of the diocese only has the right, in harmony with the instructions of the Holy See, to decide under what circumstances, and with what safeguards to prevent loss of faith, it may be tolerated that Catholic children go to such schools. (Canon 1374.)"

"1224. The religious teaching of youth in any schools is subject to the authority and inspection of the Church.

"The local Ordinaries have the right and duty to watch that nothing is taught contrary to faith or good morals, in any of the schools of their territory.

"They, moreover, have the right to approve the books of Christian doctrine and the teachers of religion, and to demand, for the sake of safeguarding religion and morals, the removal of teachers and books. (Canon 1381.)" (Woywod, Rev. Stanislaus, The New Canon Law, under imprimatur of Most Rev. Francis J. Spellman, Archbishop of New York and others, 1940.)

It is no exaggeration to say that the whole historic conflict in temporal policy between the Catholic Church and non-Catholics comes to a focus in their respective school policies. The Roman Catholic Church, counseled by experience in many ages and many lands and with all sorts and conditions of men, takes what, from the viewpoint of its own progress and the success of its mission, is a wise estimate of the importance of education to religion. It does not leave the individual to pick up religion by chance. It relies on early and indelible indoctrination in the faith and order of the Church by the word and example of persons consecrated to the task.

Our public school, if not a product of Protestantism, at least is more consistent with it than with the Catholic culture and scheme of values. It is a relatively recent development dating from about 1840. It is organized on the premise that secular education can be isolated from all religious teaching so that the school can inculcate all needed temporal knowledge and also maintain a strict and lofty neutrality as to religion. The assumption is that after the individual has been instructed in worldly wisdom he will be better fitted to choose his religion. Whether such a disjunction is possible, and if possible whether it is wise, are questions I need not to try to answer.

I should be surprised if any Catholic would deny that the parochial

215

school is a vital, if not the most vital, part of the Roman Catholic Church. If put to the choice, that venerable institution, I should expect, would forego its whole service for mature persons before it would give up education of the young, and it would be a wise choice. Its growth and cohesion, discipline and loyalty, spring from its schools. Catholic education is the rock on which the whole structure rests, and to render tax aid to its Church school is indistinguishable to me from rendering the same aid to the Church itself.

III

It is of no importance in this situation whether the beneficiary of this expenditure of tax-raised funds is primarily the parochial school and incidentally the pupil, or whether the aid is directly bestowed on the pupil with indirect benefits to the school. The state cannot maintain a Church and it can no more tax its citizens to furnish free carriage to those who attend a Church. The prohibition against establishment of religion cannot be circumvented by a subsidy, bonus or reimbursement of expense to individuals for receiving religious instruction and indoctrination.

The Court, however, compares this to other subsidies and loans to individuals and says, "Nor does it follow that a law has a private rather than a public purpose because it provides that tax-raised funds will be paid to reimburse individuals on account of money spent by them in a way which furthers a public program." Of course, the state may pay out tax-raised funds to relieve pauperism, but it may not spend funds to secure religion against skepticism. It may compensate individuals for loss of employment, but it cannot compensate them for adherence to a creed.

It seems to me that the basic fallacy in the Court's reasoning, which accounts for its failure to apply the principles it avows, is in ignoring the essentially religious test by which beneficiaries of this expenditure are selected. A policeman protects a Catholic, of course—but not because he is a Catholic, it is because he is a man and a member of our society. The fireman protects the Church school—but not because it is a Church school; it is because it is property, part of the assets of our society. Neither the fireman nor the policeman has to ask before he renders aid "Is this man or building identified with the Catholic Church?" But before these school authorities draw a check to reimburse for a student's fare they must ask just that question, and if the school is a Catholic one they may render aid because it is such, while if it is of any other faith or is run for profit, the help must be withheld. To consider the converse of the Court's reasoning will best disclose its fallacy. That there is no parallel between police and fire protection and this plan of reimbursement is apparent from the incongruity of the limitation of this Act if applied to police and fire service. Could we sustain an Act that said police shall protect pupils on the way to or from public schools and Catholic schools but not while going to and coming from other schools, and firemen shall extinguish a blaze in public or Catholic school buildings but shall not put out a blaze in Protestant Church schools or private schools operated for profit? That is the true analogy to the case we have before us and I should think it pretty plain that such a scheme would not be valid.

The Court's holding is that this taxpayer has no grievance because the state has decided to make the reimbursement a public purpose and therefore we are bound to regard it as such. I agree that this Court has left, and always should leave to each state, great latitude in deciding for itself, in the light of its own conditions, what shall be public purposes in its scheme of things. It may socialize utilities and economic enterprises and make taxpayers' business out of what conventionally had been private business. It may make public business of individual welfare, health, education, entertainment or security. But it cannot make public business of religious worship or instruction, or of attendance at religious institutions of any character. There is no answer to the proposition more fully expounded by Mr. Justice Rutledge that the effect of the religious freedom Amendment to our Constitution was to take every form of propagation of religion out of the realm of things which could directly or indirectly be made public business and thereby be supported in whole or in part at taxpayers' expense. That is a difference which the Constitution sets up between religion and almost every other subject matter of legislation, a difference which goes to the very root of religious freedom and which the Court is overlooking today. This freedom was first in the Bill of Rights because it was first in the forefathers' minds; it was set forth in absolute terms, and its strength is its rigidity. It was intended not only to keep the states' hands out of religion, but to keep religions' hands off the state, and above all, to keep bitter religious controversy out of public life by denying to every denomination any advantage from getting control of public policy or the public purse. Those great ends I cannot but think are immeasurably compromised by today's decision.

This policy of our Federal Constitution has never been wholly pleasing to most religious groups. They all are quick to invoke its protections; they all are irked when they feel its restraints. This Court has gone a long way, if not an unreasonable way, to hold that public business of such paramount importance as maintenance of public order, protection of the privacy of the home, and taxation may not be pursued by a state in a way that even indirectly will interfere with religious proselyting.

But we cannot have it both ways. Religious teaching cannot be a private affair when the state seeks to impose regulations which infringe on it indirectly, and a public affair when it comes to taxing citizens of one faith to aid another, or those of no faith to aid all. If these principles seem harsh in prohibiting aid to Catholic education, it must not be forgotten that it is the same Constitution that alone assures Catholics the right to maintain these schools at all when predominant local sentiment would forbid them. Nor should I think that those who have done so well without this aid would want to see this separation between Church and State broken down. If the state may aid these religious schools, it may therefore regulate them. Many groups have sought aid from tax funds only to find that it carried political controls with it. Indeed this Court has declared that "It is hardly lack of due process for the Government to regulate that which it subsidizes."

But in any event, the great purposes of the Constitution do not depend on the approval or convenience of those they restrain. I cannot read the history of the struggle to separate political from ecclesiastical affairs, well summarized in the opinion of Mr. Justice Rutledge in which I generally concur, without a conviction that the Court today is unconsciously giving the clock's hands a backward turn.

Mr. Justice Frankfurter joins in this opinion.

MR. JUSTICE RUTLEDGE, WITH WHOM MR. JUSTICE FRANKFURTER, MR. JUSTICE JACKSON AND MR. JUSTICE BURTON AGREE, DISSENTING.

"Congress shall make no law respecting an establishment of religion, or prohibiting the free exercise thereof. . . ." U. S. Const. Am. Art. I. . . .

"Well aware that Almighty God hath created the mind free; . . . that to compel a man to furnish contributions of money for the propagation of opinions which he disbelieves, is sinful and tyrannical; . . .

"We, the General Assembly, do enact, that no man shall be compelled to frequent or support any religious worship, place, or ministry whatsoever, nor shall be enforced, restrained, molested, or burthened in his body or goods, nor shall otherwise suffer on account of his religious opinions or belief. . . ."

I cannot believe that the great author of those words, or the men who made them law, could have joined in this decision. Neither so high nor so impregnable today as yesterday is the wall raised between church and state by Virginia's great statute of religious freedom and the First Amendment, now made applicable to all the states by the Fourteenth. New Jersey's statute sustained is the first, if indeed it is not the second breach to be made by this Court's action. That a third, and a fourth, and still others will be attempted, we may be sure. For just as Cochran v.

Louisiana State Board of Education, has opened the way by oblique ruling for this decision, so will the two make wider the breach for a third. Thus with time the most solid freedom steadily gives way before continuing corrosive decision.

This case forces us to determine squarely for the first time what was "an establishment of religion" in the First Amendment's conception; and by that measure to decide whether New Jersey's action violates its command. The facts may be stated shortly, to give setting and color to the constitutional problem.

By statute New Jersey has authorized local boards of education to provide for the transportation of children "to and from school other than a public school" except one operated for profit wholly or in part over established public school routes, or by other means when the child lives "remote from any school." The school board of Ewing Township has provided by resolution for "the transportation of pupils of Ewing to the Trenton and Pennington High Schools and Catholic Schools by way of public carrier. . . ."

Named parents have paid the cost of public conveyance of their children from their homes in Ewing to three public high schools and four parochial schools outside the district. Semiannually the Board has reimbursed the parents from public school funds raised by general taxation. Religion is taught as part of the curriculum in each of the four private schools, as appears affirmatively by the testimony of the superintendent of parochial schools in the Diocese of Trenton.

The Court of Errors and Appeals of New Jersey, reversing the Supreme Court's decision, has held the Ewing board's action not in contravention of the state constitution or statutes or of the Federal Constitution. We have to consider only whether this ruling accord with the prohibition of the First Amendment implied in the due process clause of the Fourteenth.

I

Not simply an established church, but any law respecting an establishment of religion is forbidden. The Amendment was broadly but not loosely phrased. It is the compact and exact summation of its author's views formed during his long struggle for religious freedom. In Madison's own words characterizing Jefferson's Bill for Establishing Religious Freedom, the guaranty he put in our national charter, like the bill he piloted through the Virginia Assembly, was "a Model of technical precision, and perspicuous brevity." Madison could not have confused "church" and "an establishment of religion."

The Amendment's purpose was not to strike merely at the official establishment of a single sect, creed or religion, outlawing only a formal relation such as had prevailed in England and some of the colonies. Necessarily it was to uproot all such relationships. But the object was broader than separating church and state in this narrow sense. It was to create a complete and permanent separation of the spheres of religious activity and civil authority by comprehensively forbidding every form of public aid or support for religion. In proof the Amendment's wording and history unite with this Court's consistent utterances whenever attention has been fixed directly upon the question.

"Religion" appears only once in the Amendment. But the word governs two prohibitions and governs them alike. It does not have two meanings, one narrow to forbid "an establishment" and another, much broader, for securing "the free exercise thereof." "Thereof" brings down "religion" with its entire and exact content, no more and no less, from the first into the second guaranty, so that Congress and now the states are as broadly restricted concerning the one as they are regarding the other.

No one would claim today that the Amendment is constricted, in "prohibiting the free exercise" of religion, to securing the free exercise of some formal or creedal observance of one sect or of many. It secures all forms of religious expression, creedal, sectarian or nonsectarian wherever and however taking place, except conduct which trenches upon the like freedoms of others or clearly and presently endangers the community's good order and security. For the protective purposes of this phase of the basic freedom street preaching, oral or by distribution of literature, has been given "the same high estate under the First Amendment as . . . worship in the churches and preaching from the pulpits." And on this basis parents have been held entitled to send their children to private, religious schools. Accordingly, daily religious education commingled with secular is "religion" within the guaranty's comprehensive scope. So are religious training and teaching in whatever form. The word connotes the broadest content, determined not by the form or formality of the teaching, or where it occurs, but by its essential nature regardless of those details.

"Religion" has the same broad significance in the twin prohibition concerning "an establishment." The Amendment was not duplicitous. "Religion" and "establishment" were not used in any formal or technical sense. The prohibition broadly forbids state support, financial or other, of religion in any guise, form or degree. It outlaws all use of public funds for religious purposes.

II

No provision of the Constitution is more closely tied to or given content by its generating history than the religious clause of the First

Amendment. It is at once the refined product and the terse summation of that history. The history includes not only Madison's authorship and the proceedings before the First Congress, but also the long and intensive struggle for religious freedom in America, more especially in Virginia, of which the Amendment was the direct culmination. In the documents of the times, particularly of Madison, who was leader in the Virginia struggle before he became the Amendment's sponsor, but also in the writings of Jefferson and others and in the issues which engendered them is to be found irrefutable confirmation of the Amendment's sweeping content.

For Madison, as also for Jefferson, religious freedom was the crux of the struggle for freedom in general. Madison was coauthor with George Mason of the religious clause in Virginia's great Declaration of Rights of 1776. He is credited with changing it from a mere statement of the principle of tolerence to the first official legislative pronouncement that freedom of conscience and religion are inherent rights of the individual. He sought also to have the Declaration expressly condemn the existing Virginia establishment. But the forces supporting it were then too strong.

Accordingly Madison yielded on this phase but not for long. At once he resumed the fight, continuing it before succeeding legislative sessions. As a member of the General Assembly in 1779 he threw his full weight behind Jefferson's historic Bill for Establishing Religious Freedom. That bill was a prime phase of Jefferson's broad program of democratic reform undertaken on his return from the Continental Congress in 1776 and submitted for the General Assembly's consideration in 1779 as his proposed revised Virginia code. With Jefferson's departure for Europe in 1784, Madison became the Bill's prime sponsor. Enactment failed in successive legislatures from its introduction in June 1779, until its adoption in January, 1786. But during all this time the fight for religious freedom moved forward in Virginia on various fronts with growing intensity. Madison led throughout, against Patrick Henry's powerful opposing leadership until Henry was elected governor in November, 1784.

The climax came in the legislative struggle of 1784–1785 over the Assessment Bill. See supplemental Appendix hereto. This was nothing more nor less than a taxing measure for the support of religion, designed to revive the payment of tithes suspended since 1777. So long as it singled out a particular sect for preference it incurred the active and general hostility of dissentient groups. It was broadened to include them, with the result that some subsided temporarily in their opposition. As altered, the bill gave to each taxpayer the privilege of designating which church should receive his share of the tax. In default of designation the legislature applied it to pious uses. But what is of the utmost significance here, "in its final form the bill left the taxpayer the option of giving his tax to education."

Madison was unyielding at all times, opposing with all his vigor the general and nondiscriminatory assessments proposed. The modified Assessment Bill passed second reading in December, 1784, and was all but enacted. Madison and his followers, however, maneuvered deferment of final consideration until November, 1785. And before the Assembly reconvened in the fall he issued his historic Memorial and Remonstrance.

This is Madison's complete, though not his only, interpretation of religious liberty. It is a broadside attack upon all forms of "establishment" of religion, both general and particular, nondiscriminatory or selective. Reflecting not only the many legislative conflicts over the Assessment Bill and the Bill for Establishing Religious Freedom but also, for example, the struggles for religious incorporations and the continued maintenance of the glebes, the Remonstrance is at once the most concise and the most accurate statement of the views of the First Amendment's author concerning what is "an establishment of religion." Because it behooves us in the dimming distance of time not to lose sight of what he and his coworkers had in mind when, by a single sweeping stroke of the pen, they forbade an establishment of religion and secured its free exercise, the text of the Remonstrance is appended at the end of this opinion for its wider current reference, together with a copy of the bill against which it was directed.

The Remonstrance, stirring up a storm of popular protest, killed the Assessment Bill. It collapsed in committee shortly before Christmas, 1785. With this, the way was cleared at last for enactment of Jefferson's Bill for Establishing Religious Freedom. Madison promptly drove it through in January of 1786, seven years from the time it was first introduced. This dual victory substantially ended the fight over establishments, settling the issue against them.

The next year Madison became a member of the Constitutional Convention. Its work done, he fought valiantly to secure the ratification of its great product in Virginia as elsewhere, and nowhere else more effectively. Madison was certain in his own mind that under the Constitution "there is not a shadow of right in the general government to intermeddle with religion" and that "this subject is, for the honor of America, perfectly free and unshackled. The Government has no jurisdiction over it. . . ." Nevertheless he pledged that he would work for a Bill of Rights, including a specific guaranty of religious freedom, and Virginia, with other states, ratified the Constitution on this assurance.

Ratification thus accomplished, Madison was sent to the first Congress. There he went at once about performing his pledge to establish freedom for the nation as he had done in Virginia. Within a little more than three years from his legislative victory at home he had proposed and secured the submission and ratification of the First Amendment as the first article of our Bill of Rights.

All the great instruments of the Virginia struggle for religious liberty thus became warp and woof of our constitutional tradition, not simply by the course of history, but by the common unifying force of Madison's life, thought and sponsorship. He epitomized the whole of that tradition in the Amendment's compact, but nonetheless comprehensive, phrasing.

As the Remonstrance discloses throughout, Madison opposed every form and degree of official relation between religion and civil authority. For him religion was a wholly private matter beyond the scope of civil power either to restrain or to support. Denial or abridgment of religious freedom was a violation of rights both of conscience and of natural equality. State aid was no less obnoxious or destructive to freedom and to religion itself than other forms of state interference. "Establishment" and "free exercise" were correlative and coextensive ideas, representing only different facets of the single great and fundamental freedom. The Remonstrance, following the Virginia statute's example, referred to the history of religious conflicts and the effects of all sorts of establishment, current and historical, to suppress religion's free exercise. With Jefferson, Madison believed that to tolerate any fragment of establishment would be by so much to perpetuate restraint upon that freedom. Hence he sought to tear out the institution not partially but root and branch, and to bar its return forever.

In no phase was he more unrelentingly absolute than in opposing state support or aid by taxation. Not even "three pence" contribution was thus to be exacted from any citizen for such a purpose. Tithes had been the life blood of establishment before and after other compulsions disappeared. Madison and his coworkers made no exceptions or abridgments to the complete separation they created. Their objection was not to small tithes. It was to any tithes whatsoever. "If it were lawful to impose a small tax for religion the admission would pave the way for oppressive levies." Not the amount but "the principle of assessment was wrong." And the principle was as much to prevent "the interference of law in religion" as to restrain religious intervention in political matters. In this field the authors of our freedom would not tolerate "the first experiment on our liberties" or "wait till usurped power had strengthened itself by exercise, and entangled the question in precedents." Nor should we.

In view of this history no further proof is needed that the Amendment forbids any appropriation, large or small, from public funds to aid or support any and all religious exercises. But if more were called for, the debates in the First Congress and this Court's consistent expressions, whenever it has touched on the matter directly, supply it.

By contrast with the Virginia history, the congressional debates on consideration of the Amendment reveal only sparse discussion, reflecting the fact that the essential issues had been settled. Indeed the matter had become so well understood as to have been taken for granted in all but formal phrasing. Hence, the only enlightening reference shows concern, not to preserve any power to use public funds in aid of religion, but to prevent the Amendment from outlawing private gifts inadvertently by virtue of the breadth of its wording.

III

Compulsory attendance upon religious exercise went out early in the process of separating church and state, together with forced observance of religious forms and ceremonies. Test oaths and religious qualification for office followed later. These things none devoted to our great tradition of religious liberty would think of bringing back. Hence today, apart from efforts to inject religious training or exercises and sectarian issues into the public schools, the only serious surviving threat to maintaining the complete and permanent separation of religion and civil power which the First Amendment commands is through use of the taxing power to support religion, religious establishment, or establishments having a religious foundation whatever their form or special religious function.

Does New Jersey's action furnish support for religion by use of the taxing power? Certainly it does, if the test remains undiluted as Jefferson and Madison made it, that money taken by taxation from one is not to be used or given to support another's religious training or belief, or indeed one's own. Today as then the furnishing of "contributions of money for the propagation of opinions which he disbelieves" is the forbidden exaction; and the prohibition is absolute for whatever measure brings that consequence and whatever amount may be sought or given to that end.

The funds used here were raised by taxation. The Court does not dispute nor could it that their use does in fact give aid and encouragement to religious instruction. It only concludes that this aid is not "support" in law. But Madison and Jefferson were concerned with aid and support in fact not as a legal conclusion "entangled in precedents." Here parents pay money to send their children to parochial schools and funds raised by taxation are used to reimburse them. This not only helps the children to get to school and the parents to send them. It aids them in a substantial way to get the very thing which they are sent to the particular school to secure, namely, religious training and teaching.

Believers of all faiths, and others who do not express their feeling toward ultimate issues of existence in any creedal form, pay the New Jersey tax. When the money so raised is used to pay for transportation to religious schools, the Catholic taxpayer to the extent of his proportionate share pays for the transportation of Lutheran, Jewish and otherwise religiously affiliated children to receive their non-Catholic religious instruction. Their parents likewise pay proportionately for the transportation of Catholic children to receive Catholic instruction. Each thus contributes to "the propagation of opinions which he disbelieves" in so far as their religions differ, as do others who accept no creed without regard to those differences. Each thus pays taxes also to support the teaching of his own religion, an exaction equally forbidden since it denies "the comfortable liberty" of giving one's contribution to the particular agency of instruction he approves.

New Jersey's action therefore exactly fits the type of exaction and the kind of evil at which Madison and Jefferson struck. Under the test they framed it cannot be said that the cost of transportation is no part of the cost of education or of the religious instruction given. That it is a substantial and a necessary element is shown most plainly by the continuing and increasing demand for the state to assume it. Nor is there pretense that it relates only to the secular instruction given in religious schools or that any attempt is or could be made toward allocating proportional shares as between the secular and the religious instruction. It is precisely because the instruction is religious and relates to a particular faith, whether one or another, that parents send their children to religious schools under the Pierce doctrine. And the very purpose of the state's contribution is to defray the cost of conveying the pupil to the place where he will receive not simply secular, but also and primarily religious, teaching and guidance.

Indeed the view is sincerely avowed by many of various faiths, that the basic purpose of all education is or should be religious, that the secular cannot be and should not be separated from the religious phase and emphasis. Hence, the inadequacy of public or secular education and the necessity for sending the child to a school where religion is taught. But whatever may be the philosophy or its justification, there is undeniably an admixture of religious with secular teaching in all such institutions. That is the very reason for their being. Certainly for purposes of constitutionality we cannot contradict the whole basis of the ethical and educational convictions of people who believe in religious schooling.

Yet this very admixture is what was disestablished when the First

225

Amendment forbade "an establishment of religion." Commingling the religious with the secular teaching does not divest the whole of its religious permeation and emphasis or make them of minor part, if proportion were material. Indeed, on any other view, the Constitutional prohibition always could be brought to naught by adding a modicum of the secular.

An appropriation from the public treasury to pay the cost of transportation to Sunday school, to weekday special classes at the church or parish house, or to the meeting of various young people's religious societies, such as the Y.M.C.A., the Y.W.C.A., the Y.M.H.A., the Epworth League, could not withstand the constitutional attack. This would be true, whether or not secular activities were mixed with the religious. If such an appropriation could not stand, then it is hard to see how one becomes valid for the same thing upon the more extended scale of daily instruction. Surely constitutionality does not turn on where or how often the mixed teaching occurs.

Finally transportation, where it is needed, is as essential to education as any other element. Its cost is as much a part of the total expense, except at times in amount, as the cost of textbooks, of school lunches, of athletic equipment, of writing and other materials; indeed of all other items composing the total burden. Now as always the core of the educational process is the teacher-pupil relationship. Without this the richest equipment and facilities would go for naught. But the proverbial Mark Hopkins conception no longer suffices for the country's requirements. Without buildings, without equipment, without library, textbooks and other materials, and without transportation to bring teacher and pupil together in such an effective teaching environment, there can be not even the skeleton of what our times require. Hardly can it be maintained that transportation is the least essential of these items, or that it does not in fact aid, encourage, sustain and support, just as they do, the very process which is its purpose to accomplish. No less essential is it or the payment of its cost, than the very teaching in the classroom, or the payment of the teacher's substenance. Many types of equipment, now considered essential, better could be done without.

For me, therefore, the feat is impossible to select so indispensable an item from the composite of total costs, and characterize it as not aiding, contributing to, promoting or sustaining the propagation of beliefs which it is the very end of all to bring about. Unless this can be maintained, and the Court does not maintain it, the aid thus given is outlawed. Payment of transportation is no more, nor is it any the less essential to education, whether religious or secular, than payment for tuitions, for teachers' salaries, for buildings, equipment and necessary materials. Nor is it any the less directly related, in a school giving religious instruction, to the primary religious objective all those essential items of cost are intended to achieve. No rational line can be drawn between payment for such larger, but not more necessary, items and payment for transportation. The only line that can be so drawn is one between more dollars and less. Certainly in this realm such a line can be no valid constitutional measure.

Now as in Madison's time, not the amount but the principle of assessment is wrong.

IV

But we are told that the New Jersey statute is valid in its present application because the appropriation is for a public, not a private purpose, namely, the promotion of education, and the majority accept this idea in the conclusion that all we have here is "public welfare legislation." If that is true and the Amendment's force can be thus destroyed, what has been said becomes all the more pertinent. For then there could be no possible objection to more extensive support of religious education by New Jersey.

If the fact alone be determinative that religious schools are engaged in education, thus promoting the general and individual welfare, together with the legislature's decision that the payment of public moneys for their aid makes their work a public function, then I can see no possible basis, except one of dubious legislative policy, for the state's refusal to make full appropriation for support of private, religious schools, just as is done for public instruction. There could not be, on that basis, valid constitutional objection.

Of course paying the cost of transportation promotes the general cause of education and the welfare of the individual. So does paying all other items of educational expense. And obviously, as the majority say, it is much too late to urge that legislation designed to facilitate the opportunities of children to secure a secular education serves no public purpose. Our nation-wide system of public education rests on the contrary view, as do all grants-in-aid of education, public or private, which is not religious in character.

These things are beside the real question. They have no possible materiality except to obscure the all-pervading inescapable issue. Stripped of its religious phase, the case presents no substantial federal question. The public function argument, by casting the issue in terms of promoting the general cause of education and the welfare of the individual, ignores the religious factor and its essential connection with the transportation, thereby leaving out the only vital element in the case. So of course do the "public welfare" and "social legislation" ideas, for they come to the same thing.

227

We have here then one substantial issue, not two. To say that New Jersey's appropriation and her use of the power of taxation for raising the funds appropriated are not for public purposes but are for private ends, is to say that they are for the support of religion and religious teaching. Conversely, to say that they are for public purposes is to say that they are not for religious ones.

This is precisely for the reason that education which includes religious training and teaching, and its support, have been made matters of private right and function not public, by the very terms of the First Amendment. That is the effect not only in its guaranty of religion's free exercise, but also in the prohibition of establishments. It was on this basis of the private character of the function of religious education that this Court held parents entitled to send their children to private, religious schools. Now it declares in effect that the appropriation of public funds to defray part of the cost of attending those schools is for a public purpose. If so, I do not understand why the state cannot go farther or why this case approaches the verge of its power.

In truth this view contradicts the whole purpose and effect of the First Amendment as heretofore conceived. The "public function"–"public welfare"–"social legislation" argument seeks in Madison's words, to "employ Religion (that is, here, religious education) as an engine of Civil policy." It is of one piece with the Assessment Bill's preamble, although with the vital difference that it wholly ignores what that preamble explicitly states.

Our constitutional policy is exactly the opposite. It does not deny the value or the necessity for religious training, teaching or observance. Rather it secures their free exercise. But to that end it does deny that the state can undertake or sustain them in any form or degree. For this reason the sphere of religious activity, as distinguished from the secular intellectual liberties, has been given the twofold protection and, as the state cannot forbid, neither can it perform or aid in performing the religious function. The dual prohibition makes that function altogether private. It cannot be made a public one by legislative act. This was the very heart of Madison's Remonstrance, as it is of the Amendment iself.

It is not because religious teaching does not promote the public or the individual's welfare, but because neither is furthered when the state promotes religious education, that the Constitution forbids it to do so. Both legislatures and courts are bound by that distinction. In failure to observe it lies the fallacy of the "public function"–"social legislation" argument, a fallacy facilitated by easy transference of the argument's basing from due process unrelated to any religious aspect to the First Amendment.

By no declaration that a gift of public money to religious uses will promote the general or individual welfare, or the cause of education generally, can legislative bodies overcome the Amendment's bar. Nor may the courts sustain their attempts to do so by finding such consequences for appropriations which in fact give aid to or promote religious uses. Legislatures are free to make, and courts to sustain, appropriations only when it can be found that in fact they do not aid, promote, encourage or sustain religious teaching or observances, be the amount large or small. No such finding has been or could be made in this case. The Amendment has removed this form of promoting the public welfare from legislative and judicial competence to make a public function. It is exclusively a private affair.

The reasons underlying the Amendment's policy have not vanished with time or diminished in force. Now as when it was adopted the price of religious freedom is double. It is that the church and religion shall live both within and upon that freedom. There cannot be freedom of religion, safeguarded by the state, and intervention by the church or its agencies in the state's domain or dependency on its largesse. The great condition of religious liberty is that it be free from sustenance, as also from other interferences, by the state. For when it comes to rest upon that secular foundation it vanished with the resting. Public money devoted to payment of religious costs, educational or other, brings the quest for more. It brings too the struggle of sect against sect for the larger share or for any. Here one by numbers alone will benefit most, there another. That is precisely the history of societies which have had an established religion and dissident groups. It is the very thing Jefferson and Madison experienced and sought to guard against, whether in its blunt or in its more screened forms. The end of such strife cannot be other than to destroy the cherished liberty. The dominating group will achieve the dominant benefit; or all will embroil the state in their dissensions.

Exactly such conflicts have centered of late around providing transportation to religious schools from public funds. The issue and the dissension work typically, in Madison's phrase, to "destroy that moderation and harmony which the forbearance of our laws to intermeddle with Religion, has produced amongst its several sects." This occurs, as he well knew, over measures at the very threshold of departure from the principle.

In these conflicts wherever success has been obtained it has been upon the contention that by providing the transportation the general cause of education, the general welfare of the individual will be forwarded; hence that the matter lies within the realm of public function, for legislative determination. State courts have divided upon the issue, some taking the view that only the individual, others that the institution receives the benefit. A few have recognized that this dichotomy is false, that both in fact are aided.

The majority here does not accept in terms any of those views. But neither does it deny that the individual or the school, or indeed both, are benefited directly and substantially. To do so would cut the ground from under the public function–social legislation thesis. On the contrary, the opinion conceded that the children are aided by being helped to get to the religious schooling. By converse necessary implication as well as by the absence of express denial, it must be taken to concede also that the school is helped to reach the child with its religious teaching. The religious enterprise is common to both, as is the interest in having transportation for its religious purposes provided.

Notwithstanding the recognition that this two-way aid is given and the absence of any denial that religious teaching is thus furthered, the Court concludes that the aid so given is not "support" of religion. It is rather only support of education as such, without reference to its religious content, and thus becomes public welfare legislation. To this elision of the religious element from the case is added gloss in two respects, one that the aid extended partakes of the nature of a safety measure, the other that failure to provide it would make the state unneutral in religious matters, discriminating against or hampering such children concerning public benefits all others receive.

As will be noted, the one gloss is contradicted by the facts of record and the other is of whole cloth with the "public function" argument's excision of the religious factor. But most important is that this approach, if valid, supplies a ready method for nullifying the Amendment's guaranty, not only for this case and others involving small grants in aid for religious education, but equally for larger ones. The only thing needed will be for the Court again to transplant the "public welfare–public function" view from its proper nonreligious due process bearing to First Amendment application, holding that religious education is not "supported" though it may be aided by the appropriation, and that the cause of education generally is furthered by helping the pupil to secure that type of training.

This is not therefore just a little case over bus fares. In paraphrase of Madison, distant as it may be in its present form from a complete establishment of religion, it differs from it only in degree; and is the first step in that direction. Today as in his time "the same authority which can force a citizen to contribute three pence only . . . for the support of any one religious establishment, may force him" to pay more; or "to conform to any other establishment in all cases whatsoever." And now, as then, "either . . . We must say, that the will of the Legislature is the only measure of their authority; and that in the plenitude of this authority, they may sweep away all our fundamental right; or, that they are bound to leave this particular right untouched and sacred."

The realm of religious training and belief remains, as the Amendment made it, the kingdom of the individual man and his God. It should be kept inviolately private, not "entangled . . . in precedents" or confounded with what legislatures legitimately may take over into the public domain:

V

No one conscious of religious values can be unsympathetic toward the burden which our constitutional separation puts on parents who desire religious instruction mixed with secular for their children. They pay taxes for others' children's education, at the same time the added cost of instruction for their own. Nor can one happily see benefits denied to children which others receive, because in conscience they or their parents for them desire a different kind of training others do not demand.

But if those feelings should prevail, there would be an end to our historic constitutional policy and command. No more unjust or discriminatory in fact is it to deny attendants at religious schools the cost of their transportation than it is to deny them tuitions, sustenance for their teachers, or any other educational expense which others receive at public cost. Hardship in fact there is which none can blink. But, for assuring to those who undergo it the greater, the most comprehensive freedom, it is one written by design and firm intent into our basic law.

Of course discrimination in the legal sense does not exist. The child attending the religious school has the same right as any other to attend the public school. But he foregoes exercising it because the same guaranty which assures this freedom forbids the public school or any agency of the state to give or aid him in securing the religious instruction he seeks.

Were he to accept the common school, he would be the first to protest the teaching there of any creed or faith not his own. And it is precisely for the reason that their atmosphere is wholly secular that children are not sent to public schools under the Pierce doctrine. But that is a constitutional necessity, because we have staked the very existence of our country on the faith that complete separation between the state and religion is best for the state and best for religion.

That policy necessarily entails hardship upon persons who forego the right to educational advantages the state can supply in order to secure others it is precluded from giving. Indeed this may hamper the parent and the child forced by conscience to that choice. But it does not make the state unneutral to withhold what the Constitution forbids it to give.

On the contrary it is only by observing the prohibition rigidly that the state can maintain its neutrality and avoid partisanship in the dissensions inevitable when sect opposes sect over demands for public moneys to further religious education, teaching or training in any form or degree, directly or indirectly. Like St. Paul's freedom, religious liberty with a great price must be bought. And for those who exercise it most fully, by insisting upon religious education for their children mixed with secular, by the terms of our Constitution the price is greater than for others.

The problem then cannot be cast in terms of legal discrimination or its absence. This would be true, even though the state in giving aid should treat all religious instruction alike. Thus, if the present statute and its application were shown to apply equally to all religious schools of whatever faith, yet in the light of our tradition it could not stand. For then the adherent of one creed still would pay for the support of another, the childless taxpayer with others more fortunate. Then too there would seem to be no bar to making appropriations for transportation and other expenses of children attending public or other secular schools, after hours in separate places and classes for their exclusively religious instruction. The person who embraces no creed also would be forced to pay for teaching what he does not believe. Again, it was the furnishing of "contributions of money for the propagation of opinions which he disbelieves" that the fathers outlawed. That consequence and effect are not removed by multiplying to all-inclusiveness the sects for which support is exacted. The Constitution requires, not comprehensive identification of state with religion, but complete separation.

VI

Short treatment will dispose of what remains. Whatever might be said of some other application of New Jersey's statute, the one made here has no semblance of bearing as a safety measure or, indeed, for securing expeditious conveyance. The transportation supplied is by public conveyance, subject to all the hazards and delays of the highway and the streets incurred by the public generally in going about its multifarious business.

Nor is the case comparable to one of furnishing fire or police protection, or access to public highways. These things are matters of common right, part of the general need for safety. Certainly the fire department must not stand idly by while the church burns. Nor is this reason why the state should pay the expense of transportation or other items of the cost of religious education.

Needless to add, we have no such case as Green v. Frazier, which dealt with matters wholly unrelated to the First Amendment, involving only situations where the "public function" issue was determinative.

I have chosen to place my dissent upon the broad ground I think decisive, though strictly speaking the case might be decided on narrower issues. The New Jersey statute might be held invalid on its face for the exclusion of children who attend private, profit-making schools. I cannot assume, as does the majority, that the New Jersey courts would write off this explicit limitation from the statute. Moreover, the resolution by which the statute was applied expressly limits its benefits to students of public and Catholic schools. There is no showing that there are no other private or religious schools in this populous district. I do not think it can be assumed there were none. But in the view I have taken, it is unnecessary to limit grounding to these matters.

Two great drives are constantly in motion to abridge, in the name of education, the complete division of religion and civil authority which our forefathers made. One is to introduce religious education and observances into the public schools. The other, to obtain public funds for the aid and support of various private religious schools. In my opinion both avenues were closed by the Constitution. Neither should be opened by this Court. The matter is not one of quantity, to be measured by the amount of money expended. Now as in Madison's day it is one of principle, to keep separate the separate spheres as the First Amendment drew them; to prevent the first experiment upon our liberties; and to keep the question from becoming entangled in corrosive precedents. We should not be less strict to keep strong and untarnished the one side of the shield of religious freedom than we have been of the other.

The judgment should be reversed.

APPENDIX

MEMORIAL AND REMONSTRANCE

AGAINST RELIGIOUS

ASSESSMENTS

To the Honorable the General Assembly

of

The Commonwealth of Virginia

A Memorial and Remonstrance.

We, the subscribers, citizens of the said Commonwealth, having taken into serious consideration, a Bill printed by order of the last

Session of General Assembly, entitled "A Bill establishing a provision for teachers of the Christian Religion," and conceiving that the same, if finally armed with the sanctions of a law, will be a dangerous abuse of power, are bound as faithful members of a free State, to remonstrate against it, and to declare the reasons by which we are determined. We remonstrate against the said Bill,

1. Because we hold it for a fundamental and undeniable truth, "that religion, or the duty which we owe to our Creator, and the manner of discharging it, can be directed only by reason and conviction, not by force or violence." The Religion then of every man must be left to the conviction and conscience of every man; and it is the right of every man to exercise it as these may dictate. This right is in its nature an unalienable right. It is unalienable; because the opinions of men, depending only on the evidence contemplated by their own minds, cannot follow the dictates of other men: It is unalienable also; because what is here a right towards men, is a duty towards the Creator. It is the duty of every man to render to the Creator such homage, and such only, as he believes to be acceptable to him. This duty is precedent both in order of time and degree of obligation, to the claims of Civil Society. Before any man can be considered as a member of Civil Society, he must be considered as a subject of the Governor of the Universe: And if a member of Civil Society, who enters into any subordinate Association, must always do it with a reservation of his duty to the general authority: much more must every man who becomes a member of any particular Civil Society, do it with a saving of his allegiance to the Universal Sovereign. We maintain therefore that in matters of Religion, no man's right is abridged by the institution of Civil Society, and that Religion is wholly exempt from its cognizance. True it is, that no other rule exists, by which any question which may divide a Society, can be ultimately determined, but the will of the majority; but it is also true, that the majority may trespass on the rights of the minority.

2. Because if religion be exempt from the authority of the Society at large, still less can it be subject to that of the Legislative Body. The latter are but the creatures and vicegerents of the former. Their jurisdiction is both derivative and limited: it is limited with regard to the co-ordinate departments, more necessarily is it limited with regard to the constituents. The preservation of a free government requires not merely, that the metes and bounds which separate each department of power may be invariably maintained; but more especially, that neither of them be suffered to overleap the great Barrier which defends the rights of the people. The Rulers who are guilty of such an encroachment, exceed the commission from which they derive their authority, and are Tyrants.

The People who submit to it are governed by laws made neither by themselves, nor by an authority derived from them, and are slaves.

3. Because, it is proper to take alarm at the first experiment on our liberties. We hold this prudent jealousy to be the first duty of citizens, and one of (the) noblest characteristics of the late Revolution. The freemen of America did not wait till usurped power had strengthened itself by exercise, and entangled the question in precedents. They saw all the consequences in the principle, and they avoided the consequences by denying the principle. We revere this lesson too much, soon to forget it. Who does not see that the same authority which can establish Christianity, in exclusion of all other Religions, may establish with the same ease any particular sect of Christians, in exclusion of all other Sects? That the same authority which can force a citizen to contribute three pence only of his property for the support of any one establishment, may force him to conform to any other establishment in all cases whatsoever?

4. Because, the bill violates that equality which ought to be the basis of every law, and which is more indispensable, in proportion as the validity or expediency of any law is more liable to be impeached. If "all men are by nature equally free and independent," all men are to be considered as entering into Society on equal conditions: as relinquishing no more and therefore retaining no less, one than another, of their natural rights. Above all are they to be considered as retaining an "equal title to the free exercise of religion according to the dictates of conscience." Whilst we assert for ourselves a freedom to embrace, to profess and to observe the Religion which we believe to be of divine origin, we cannot deny an equal freedom to those whose minds have not yielded to the evidence which has convinced us. If this freedom be abused, it is an offence against God, not against man: To God, therefore, not to men, must an account of it be rendered. As the Bill violates equality by subjecting some to peculiar burdens: so it violates the same principle, by granting to others peculiar exemptions. Are the Quakers and Mennonists the only sects who think a compulsive support of their religions unnecessary and unwarrantable? Can their piety alone be intrusted with the care of public worship? Ought their Religions to be endowed above all others? We think too favorably of the justice and good sense of these denominations, to believe that they either covet preeminencies over their fellow citizens, or that they will be seduced by them, from the common opposition to the measure.

5. Because the bill implies either that the Civil Magistrate is a competent Judge of Religious truth; or that he may employ Religion as an engine of Civil policy. The first is an arrogant pretension falsified

by the contradictory opinions of Rulers in all ages, and throughout the world: The second an unhallowed perversion of the means of salvation.

6. Because the establishment proposed by the Bill is not requisite for the support of the Christian Religion. To say that it is, is a contradiction to the Christian Religion itself; for every page of it disavows a dependence on the powers of this world: it is a contradiction to fact; for it is known that this religion both existed and flourished, not only without the support of human laws, but in spite of every opposition from them; and not only during the period of miraculous aid, but long after it had been left to its own evidence, and the ordinary care of Providence: Nay, it is a contradiction in terms; for a Religion not invented by human policy, must have pre-existed and been supported, before it was established by human policy. It is moreover to weaken in those who profess this Religion a pious confidence in its innate excellence, and the patronage of its Author; and to foster in those who still reject it, a suspicion that its friends are too conscious of its fallacies, to trust it to its own merits.

7. Because experience witnesseth that ecclesiastical establishments, instead of maintaining the purity and efficacy of Religion, have had a contrary operation. During almost fifteen centuries, has the legal establishment of Christianity been on trial. What have been its fruits? More or less in all places, pride and indolence in the clergy; ignorance and servility in the laity; in both, superstition, bigotry and persecution. Enquire of the Teachers of Christianity for the ages in which it appeared in its greatest lustre; those of every sect, point to the ages prior to its incorporation with Civil policy. Propose a restoration of this primitive state in which its Teachers depended on the voluntary rewards of their flocks; many of them predict its downfall. On which side ought their testimony to have greatest weight, when for or when against their interest?

8. Because the establishment in question is not necessary for the support of Civil Government. If it be urged as necessary for the support of Civil Government only as it is a means of supporting Religion, and it be not necessary for the latter purpose, it cannot be necessary for the former. If Religion be not within (the) cognizance of Civil Government, how can its legal establishment be said to be necessary to Civil Government? What influence in fact have ecclesiastical establishments had on Civil Society? In some instances they have been seen to erect a spiritual tyranny on the ruins of Civil authority; in many instances they have been seen upholding the thrones of political tyranny; in no instance have they been seen the guardians of the liberties of the people. Rulers who wished to subvert the public liberties, may have found an established clergy convenient auxiliaries. A just government, instituted

to secure and perpetuate it, needs them not. Such a government will be best supported by protecting every citizen in the enjoyment of his Religion with the same equal hand which protects his person and his property; by neither invading the equal rights by any Sect, nor suffering any Sect to invade those of another.

9. Because the proposed establishment is a departure from that generous policy which, offering an asylum to the persecuted and oppressed of every Nation and Religion, promised a lustre to our country, and an accession to the number of its citizens. What a melancholy mark is the Bill of sudden degeneracy? Instead of holding forth an asylum to the persecuted, it is itself a signal of persecution. It degrades from the equal rank of Citizens all those whose opinions in Religion do not bend to those of the Legislative authority. Distant as it may be, in its present form, from the Inquisition it differs from it only in degree. The one is the first step, the other the last in the career of intolerance. The magnanimous sufferer under this cruel scourge in foreign Regions, must view the Bill as a Beacon on our Coast, warning him to seek some other haven, where liberty and philanthropy in their due extent may offer a more certain repose from his troubles.

10. Because, it will have a like tendency to banish our Citizens. The allurements presented by other situations are every day thinning their number. To super-add a fresh motive to emigration, by revoking the liberty which they now enjoy, would be the same species of folly which has dishonoured and depopulated flourishing kingdoms.

11. Because, it will destroy that moderation and harmony which the forbearance of our laws to intermeddle with Religion, has produced amongst its several sects. Torrents of blood have been spilt in the old world, by vain attempts of the secular arm to extinguish Religious discord, by proscribing all difference in Religious opinions. Time has at length revealed the true remedy. Every relaxation of narrow and rigorous policy, wherever it has been tried, has been found to assuage the disease. The American Theater has exhibited proofs, that equal and complete liberty, if it does not wholly eradicate it, sufficiently destroys its malignant influence on the health and prosperity of the State. If with the salutary effects of this system under our own eyes, we begin to contract the bonds of Religious freedom, we know no name that will too severely reproach our folly. At least let warning be taken at the first fruit of the threatened innovation. The very appearance of the Bill has transformed that "Christian forbearance, love and charity," which of late mutually prevailed, into animosities and jealousies, which may not soon be appeased. What mischiefs may not be dreaded should this enemy to the public quiet be armed with the force of a law?

12. Because, the policy of the bill is adverse to the diffusion of

the light of Christianity. The first wish of those who enjoy this precious gift, ought to be that it may be imparted to the whole race of mankind. Compare the number of those who have as yet received it with the number still remaining under the dominion of false Religions; and how small is the former! Does the policy of the Bill tend to lessen the disproportion? No, it at once discourages those who are strangers to the light of (revelation) from coming into the Region of it; and countenances, by example the nations who continue in darkness, in shutting out those who might convey it to them. Instead of levelling as far as possible, every obstacle to the victorious progress of truth, the Bill with an ignoble and unchristian timidity would circumscribe it, with a wall of defence, against the encroachments of error.

13. Because attempts to enforce by legal sanctions, acts obnoxious to so great a proportion of Citizens, tend to enervate the laws in general, and to slaken the bands of society. If it be difficult to execute any law which is not generally deemed necessary or salutary, what must be the case where it is deemed invalid and dangerous? And what may be the effect of so striking an example of impotency in the Government, on its general authority?

14. Because a measure of such singular magnitude and delicacy ought not to be imposed, without the clearest evidence that it is called for by a majority of citizens: and no satisfactory method is yet proposed by which the voice of the majority in this case may be determined, or its influence secured. "The people of the respective counties are indeed requested to signify their opinion respecting the adoption of the Bill to the next Session of Assembly." But the representation must be made equal, before the voice either of the Representatives or of the Counties, will be that of the people. Our hope is that neither of the former will, after due consideration, espouse the dangerous principle of the Bill. Should the event disappoint us, it will still leave us in full confidence, that a fair appeal to the latter will reverse the sentence against our liberties.

15. Because, finally, "the equal right of every citizen to the free exercise of his Religion according to the dictates of conscience" is held by the same tenure with all our other rights. If we recur to its origin, it is equally the gift of nature; if we weigh its importance, it cannot be less dear to us; if we consult the Declaration of those rights which pertain to the good people of Virginia, as the "basis and foundation of Government," it is enumerated with equal solemnity, or rather studied emphasis. Either then, we must say, that the will of the Legislature is the only measure of their authority; and that in the plenitude of this authority, they may sweep away all our fundamental rights; or, that they are bound to leave this particular right untouched and sacred;

Either we must say, that they may control the freedom of the press, may abolish the trial by jury, may swallow up the executive and Judiciary Powers of the State; nay that they may despoil us of our very right of suffrage, and erect themselves into an independent and hereditary assembly; or we must say, that they have no authority to enact into law the Bill under consideration. We the subscribers say, that the General Assembly of this Commonwealth have no such authority; and that no effort may be omitted on our part against so dangerous an usurpation, we oppose to it, this remonstrance; earnestly praying, as we are in duty bound, that the Supreme Lawgiver of the Universe, by illuminating those to whom it is addressed, may on the one hand, turn their councils from every act which would affront his holy prerogative, or violate the trust committed to them; and on the other, guide them into every measure which may be worthy of his blessing, may redound to their own praise, and may establish more firmly the liberties, the prosperity, and the Happiness of the Commonwealth.

SUPPLEMENTAL APPENDIX A Bill Establishing A Provision for Teachers of the Christian Religion.

Whereas, the general diffusion of Christian knowledge hath a natural tendency to correct the morals of men, restrain their vices, and preserve the peace of society; which cannot be effected without a competent provision for learned teachers, who may be thereby enabled to devote their time and attention to the duty of instructing such citizens, as from their circumstances and want of education, cannot otherwise attain such knowledge; and it is judged that such provision may be made by the Legislature, without counteracting the liberal principle heretofore adopted and intended to be preserved by abolishing all distinctions of pre-eminence amongst the different societies or communities of Christians:

Be it therefore enacted by the General Assembly, that for the support of Christian teachers,—percentum on the amount, or—in the pound on the sum payable for tax on the property within this Commonwealth, is hereby assessed, and shall be paid by every person chargeable with the said tax at the time the same shall become due; and the Sheriffs of the several Counties shall have power to levy and collect the same in the same manner and under the like restrictions and limitations, as are or may be prescribed by the laws for raising the Revenues of this State.

And be it enacted, That for every sum paid, the Sheriff or Collector shall give a receipt, expressing therein to what society of Christians the person from whom he may receive the same shall direct the money to be paid, keeping a distinct account thereof in his books. The Sheriff of every County, shall, on or before the — day of — in every year, return to the Court, upon oath, two alphabetical lists of the payments to him made, distinguishing in columns opposite to the names of the persons who shall have paid the same, the society to which the money so paid was by them appropriated; and one column for the names where no appropriation shall be made. One of which lists, after being recorded in a book to be kept for that purpose, shall be filed by the Clerk in his office; the other shall by the Sheriff be fixed up in the Court-house, there to remain for the inspection of all concerned. And the Sheriff, after deducting five per centum for the collection, shall forthwith pay to such person or persons as shall be appointed to receive the same by the Vestry, Elders or Directors, however denominated of each such society, the sum so stated to be due to that society; or in default thereof, upon the motion of such person or persons to the next or any succeeding Court, execution shall be awarded for the same against the Sheriff and his security, his and their executors or administrators; provided that ten days previous notice be given of such motion. And upon every such execution, the Officer serving the same shall proceed to immediate sale of the estate taken, and shall not accept of security for payment at the end of three months, nor to have the goods forthcoming at the day of sale; for his better direction wherein, the Clerk shall endorse upon every such execution that no security of any kind shall be taken.

And be it further enacted, That the money to be raised by virtue of this Act, shall be by the Vestries, Elders, or Directors of each religious society, appropriated to a provision for a Minister or Teacher of the Gospel of their denomination, or the providing place of divine worship, and to none other use whatsoever; except in the denominations of Quakers and Mennonists, who may receive what is collected from their members and place it in their general fund, to be disposed of in a manner which they shall think best calculated to promote their particular mode of worship.

And be it enacted, That all sums which at the time of payment to the Sheriff or Collector may not be appropriated by the person paying the same, shall be accounted for with the Court in manner as by this Act is directed; and after deducting for his collection, the Sheriff shall pay the amount thereof (upon account certified by the Court to the Auditors of Public Accounts, and by them to the Treasurer) into the public Treasury, to be disposed of under the direction of the General Assembly, for the encouragement of seminaries of learning within the Counties whence such sums shall arise, and to no other use or purpose whatsoever.

This Act shall commence, and be in force, from and after the — day of —— in the year ——.

A Copy from the Engrossed Bill. John Beckley, C.H.D.

ILLINOIS ex rel. MCCOLLUM v. BOARD OF EDUCATION 333 US 203 (1948)

> "Here not only are the state's tax-supported public school buildings used for the dissemination of religious doctrines. The State also affords sectarian groups an invaluable aid in that it helps to provide pupils for their religious classes through use of the state's compulsory public school machinery. This is not separation of Church and State."
>
> Mr. Justice Black, for the Court

> "Separation means separation, not something less. Jefferson's metaphor in describing the relation between Church and State speaks of a 'wall of separation,' not of a fine line easily overstepped."
>
> Mr. Justice Frankfurter, concurring

> ". . . we are likely to make the legal 'wall of separation between Church and State' as winding as the famous serpentine wall designed by Mr. Jefferson for the University he founded."
>
> Mr. Justice Jackson, concurring

> "A rule of law should not be drawn from a figure of speech."
>
> "Devotion to the great principle of religious liberty should not lead us into a rigid interpretation of the constitutional guarantee that conflicts with the accepted habits of our people."
>
> Mr. Justice Reed, dissenting

A year after the Everson case the Court deals with the problem of "released-time" for religious education. Except for Justice Reed, the entire Court endorses the theory of "separation" as developed in the Everson case and applies it here to nullify an Illinois released time plan.

MR. JUSTICE BLACK DELIVERED THE OPINION OF THE COURT.

This case relates to the power of a state to utilize its tax-supported public school system in aid of religious instruction insofar as that power may be restricted by the First and Fourteenth Amendments to the Federal Constitution.

The appellant, Vashti McCollum, began this action for mandamus against the Champaign Board of Education in the Circuit Court of Champaign County, Illinois. Her asserted interest was that of a resident and taxpayer of Champaign and of a parent whose child was then enrolled in the Champaign public schools. Illinois has a compulsory education law which, with exceptions, requires parents to send their children, aged seven to sixteen, to its tax-supported public schools where the children are to remain in attendance during the hours when the schools are regularly in session. Parents who violate this law commit a misdemeanor punishable by fine unless the children attend private or parochial schools which meet educational standards fixed by the State. District boards of education are given general supervisory powers over the use of the public school buildings within the school districts.

Appellant's petition for mandamus alleged that religious teachers, employed by private religious groups, were permitted to come weekly into the school buildings during the regular hours set apart for secular teaching, and then and there for a period of thirty minutes substitute their religious teaching for the secular education provided under the compulsory education law. The petitioner charged that this joint public-school religious-group program violated the First and Fourteenth Amendments to the United States Constitution. The prayer of her petition was that the Board of Education be ordered to "adopt and enforce rules and regulations prohibiting all instruction in and teaching of all religious education in all public schools in Champaign District Number 71, . . . and in all public school houses and buildings in said district when occupied by public schools."

The board first moved to dismiss the petition on the ground that under Illinois law appellant had no standing to maintain the action. This motion was denied. An answer was then filed, which admitted that regular weekly religious instruction was given during school hours to those pupils whose parents consented and that those pupils were released temporarily from their regular secular classes for the limited purpose of attending the religious classes. The answer denied that this coordinated program of religious instruction violated the State or Federal Constitution. Much evidence was heard, findings of fact were made, after which the petition for mandamus was denied on the ground that the school's religious instruction program violated neither the federal nor state constitutional provisions invoked by the appellant. On appeal the State Supreme Court affirmed.

The appellee presses a motion to dismiss the appeal on several grounds, the first of which is that the judgment of the State Supreme Court does not draw in question the "validity of a statute of any State" as required by 28 U.S.C. 344(a). This contention rests on the admitted fact that the challenged program of religious instruction was not expressly authorized by statute. But the State Supreme Court has sustained the validity of the program on the ground that the Illinois statutes granted the board authority to establish such a program. This holding is sufficient to show that the validity of an Illinois statute was drawn in question within the meaning of 28 U.S.C. 344(a). A second ground for the motion to dismiss is that the appellant lacks standing to maintain the action, a ground which is also without merit. A third ground for the motion is that the appellant failed properly to present in the State Supreme Court her challenge that the state program violated the Federal Constitution. But in view of the express rulings of both state courts on this question, the argument cannot be successfully maintained. The motion to dismiss the appeal is denied.

Although there are disputes between the parties as to various inferences that may or may not properly be drawn from the evidence concerning the religious program, the following facts are shown by the record without dispute. In 1940 interested members of the Jewish, Roman Catholic, and a few of the Protestant faiths formed a voluntary association called the Champaign Council on Religious Education. They obtained permission from the Board of Education to offer classes in religious instruction to public school pupils in grades four to nine inclusive. Classes were made up of pupils whose parents signed printed cards requesting that their children be permitted to attend; they were held weekly, thirty minutes for the lower grades, forty-five minutes for the higher. The council employed the religious teachers at no expense to the school authorities, but the instructors were subject to the approval and supervision of the superintendent of schools. The classes were taught in three separate religious groups by Protestant teachers, Catholic priests, and a Jewish rabbi, although for the past several years there have apparently been no classes instructed in the Jewish religion. Classes were conducted in the regular classrooms of the school building. Students who did not choose to take the religious instruction were not released from public school duties; they were required to leave their classrooms and go to some other place in the school building for pursuit of their secular studies. On the other hand, students who were released from secular study for the religious instructions were required to be present at the religious classes. Reports of their presence or absence were to be made to their secular teachers.

The foregoing facts, without reference to others that appear in the record, show the use of tax-supported property for religious instruction and the close cooperation between the school authorities and the religious council in promoting religious education. The operation of the state's compulsory education system thus assists and is integrated with the program of religious instruction carried on by separate religious sects. Pupils compelled by law to go to school for secular education are released in part from their legal duty upon the condition that they attend the religious classes. This is beyond all question a utilization of the tax-established and tax-supported public school system to aid religious groups to spread their faith. And it falls squarely under the ban of the First Amendment (made applicable to the States by the Fourteenth) as we interpreted it in Everson v. Board of Education. There we said: "Neither a state nor the Federal Government can set up a church. Neither can pass laws which aid one religion, aid all religions, or prefer one religion over another. Neither can force or influence a person to go to or to remain away from church against his will or force him to profess a belief or disbelief in any religion. No person can be punished for entertaining or professing religious beliefs or disbeliefs, for church attendance or nonattendance. No tax in any amount, large or small, can be levied to support any religious activities or institutions, whatever they may be called, or whatever form they may adopt to teach or practice religion. Neither a state nor the Federal Government can, openly or secretly, participate in the affairs of any religious organizations or groups, and vice versa. In the words of Jefferson, the clause against establishment of religion by law was intended to erect 'a wall of separation between Church and State.' " The majority in the Everson case, and the minority . . . agreed that the First Amendment's language, properly interpreted, had erected a wall of separation between Church and State. They disagreed as to the facts shown by the record and as to the proper application of the First Amendment's language to those facts.

Recognizing that the Illinois program is barred by the First and Fourteenth Amendments if we adhere to the views expressed both by the majority and the minority in the Everson case, counsel for the respondents challenge those views as dicta and urge that we reconsider and repudiate them. They argue that historically the First Amendment was intended to forbid only government preference of one religion over another, not an impartial governmental assistance of all religions. In addition they ask that we distinguish or overrule our holding in the Everson case that the Fourteenth Amendment made the "establishment of religion" clause of the First Amendment applicable as a prohibition against the states. After giving full consideration to the arguments presented we are unable to accept either of these contentions.

To hold that a state cannot consistently with the First and Fourteenth Amendments utilize its public school system to aid any or all religious faiths or sects in the dissemination of their doctrines and ideals does not, as counsel urge, manifest a governmental hostility to religion or religious teachings. A manifestation of such hostility would be at war with our national tradition as embodied in the First Amendment's guaranty of the free exercise of religion. For the First Amendment rests upon the premise that both religion and government can best work to achieve their lofty aims if each is left free from the other within its respective sphere. Or, as we said in the Everson case, the First Amendment has erected a wall between Church and State which must be kept high and impregnable.

Here not only are the state's tax-supported public school buildings used for the dissemination of religious doctrines. The State also affords sectarian groups an invaluable aid in that it helps to provide pupils for their religious classes through use of the state's compulsory public school machinery. This is not separation of Church and State.

The cause is reversed and remanded to the State Supreme Court for proceedings not inconsistent with this opinion.

MR. JUSTICE FRANKFURTER DELIVERED THE FOLLOWING OPINION, IN WHICH MR. JUSTICE JACKSON, MR. JUSTICE RUTLEDGE AND MR. JUSTICE BURTON JOIN.

We dissented in Everson v. Board of Education, because in our view the Constitutional principle requiring separation of Church and State compelled invalidation of the ordinance sustained by the majority. Illinois has here authorized the commingling of sectarian with secular instruction in the public schools. The Constitution of the United States forbids this.

The case, in the light of the Everson decision, demonstrates anew that the mere formulation of a relevant Constitutional principle is the beginning of the solution of a problem, not its answer. This is so because the meaning of a spacious conception like that of the separation of Church from State is unfolded as appeal is made to the principle from case to case. We are all agreed that the First and the Fourteenth Amendments have a secular reach far more penetrating in the conduct of Government than merely to forbid an "established church." But agreement, in the abstract, that the First Amendment was designed to erect a "wall of separation between Church and State," does not preclude a clash of views as to what the wall separates. Involved is not only the Constitutional principle but the implications of judicial review in its enforcement. Accommodation of legislative freedom and Constitutional limitations upon that freedom cannot be achieved by a mere phrase. We cannot illuminatingly apply the "wall-of-separation" metaphor until we have considered the relevant history of religious education in America, the place of the "released time" movement in that history, and its precise manifestation in the case before us.

To understand the particular program now before us as a conscientious attempt to accommodate the allowable functions of Government and the special concerns of the Church within the framework of our Constitution and with due regard to the kind of society for which it was designed, we must put this Champaign program of 1940 in its historic setting. Traditionally, organized education in the Western world was Church education. It could hardly be otherwise when the education of children was primarily study of the Word and the ways of God. Even in the Protestant countries, where there was a less close identification of Church and State, the basis of education was largely the Bible, and its chief purpose inculcation of piety. To the extent that the State intervened, it used its authority to further aims of the Church.

The emigrants who came to these shores brought this view of education with them. Colonial schools certainly started with a religious orientation. When the common problems of the early settlers of the Massachusetts Bay Colony revealed the need for common schools, the object was the defeat of "one chief project of that old deluder, Satan, to keep men from the knowledge of the Scriptures."

The evolution of colonial education, largely in the service of religion, into the public school system of today is the story of changing conceptions regarding the American democratic society, of the functions of State-maintained education in such a society, and of the role therein of the free exercise of religion by the people. The modern public school derived from a philosophy of freedom reflected in the First Amendment. It is appropriate to recall that the Remonstrance of James Madison, an event basic in the history of religious liberty, was called forth by a proposal which involved support to religious education. As the momentum for popular education increased and in turn evoked strong claims for State support of religious education, contests not unlike that which in Virginia had produced Madison's Remonstrance appeared in various forms in other States. New York and Massachusetts provide famous chapters in the history that established dissociation of religious teaching from State-maintained schools. In New York, the rise of the common schools led, despite fierce sectarian opposition, to the barring of tax funds to church schools, and later to any school in which sectarian doctrine was taught. In Massachusetts, largely through the efforts of Horace Mann, all sectarian teachings were barred from the common school to save it from being rent by denominational conflict. The upshot of these controversies, often long and fierce, is fairly summarized by saying that long before the Fourteenth Amendment subjected the States to new limitations, the prohibition of furtherance by the State of religious instruction became the guiding principle, in law and feeling, of the American people. In sustaining Stephen Girard's will, this Court referred to the inevitable conflicts engendered by matters "connected with religious polity" and particularly "in a country composed of such a variety of religious sects as our country." That was more than one hundred years ago.

Separation in the field of education, then, was not imposed upon unwilling States by force of superior law. In this respect the Fourteenth Amendment merely reflected a principle then dominant in our national life. To the extent that the Constitution thus made it binding upon the States, the basis of the restriction is the whole experience of our people. Zealous watchfulness against fusion of secular and religious activities by Government itself, through any of its instruments but especially through its educational agencies, was the democratic response of the

American community to the particular needs of a young and growing nation, unique in the composition of its people. A totally different situation elsewhere, as illustrated for instance by the English provisions for religious education in State-maintained schools, only serves to illustrate that free societies are not cast in one mould. Different institutions evolve from different historic circumstances.

It is pertinent to remind that the establishment of this principle of separation in the field of education was not due to any decline in the religious beliefs of the people. Horace Mann was a devout Christian, and the deep religious feeling of James Madison is stamped upon the Remonstrance. The secular public school did not imply indifference to the basic role of religion in the life of the people, nor rejection of religious education as a means of fostering it. The claims of religion were not minimized by refusing to make the public schools agencies for their assertion. The non-sectarian or secular public school was the means of reconciling freedom in general with religious freedom. The sharp confinement of the public schools to secular education was a recognition of the need of a democratic society to educate its children, insofar as the State undertook to do so, in an atmosphere free from pressures in a realm in which pressures are most resisted and where conflicts are most easily and most bitterly engendered. Designed to serve as perhaps the most powerful agency for promoting cohesion among a heterogeneous democratic people, the public school must keep scrupulously free from entanglement in the strife of sects. The preservation of the community from divisive conflicts, of Government from irreconcilable pressures by religious groups, of religion from censorship and coercion however subtly exercised, requires strict confinement of the State to instruction other than religious, leaving to the individual's church and home, indoctrination in the faith of his choice.

This development of the public school as a symbol of our secular unity was not a sudden achievement nor attained without violent conflict. While in small communities of comparatively homogeneous religious beliefs, the need for absolute separation presented no urgencies, elsewhere the growth of the secular school encountered the resistance of feeling strongly engaged against it. But the inevitability of such attempts is the very reason for Constitutional provisions primarily concerned with the protection of minority groups. And such sects are shifting groups, varying from time to time, and place to place, thus representing in their totality the common interest of the nation.

Enough has been said to indicate that we are dealing not with a full-blown principle, nor one having the definiteness of a surveyor's metes and bounds. But by 1875 the separation of public education from Church entanglements, of the State from the teaching of religion, was firmly established in the consciousness of the nation. In that year President Grant made his famous remarks to the Convention of the Army of the Tennessee:

"Encourage free schools and resolve that not one dollar appropriated for their support shall be appropriated for the support of any sectarian schools. Resolve that neither the state nor the nation, nor both combined, shall support institutions of learning other than those sufficient to afford every child growing up in the land the opportunity of a good common school education, unmixed with sectarian, pagan, or atheistical dogmas. Leave the matter of religion to the family altar, the church, and the private school, supported entirely by private contributions. Keep the church and state forever separated."

So strong was this conviction, that rather than rest on the comprehensive prohibitions of the First and Fourteenth Amendments, President Grant urged that there be written into the United States Constitution particular elaborations, including a specific prohibition against the use of public funds for sectarian education, such as had been written into many State constitutions, By 1894, in urging the adoption of such a provision in the New York Constitution, Elihu Root was able to summarize a century of the nation's history: "It is not a question of religion, or of creed, or of party; it is a question of declaring and maintaining the great American principle of eternal separation between Church and State." The extent to which this principle was deemed a presupposition of our Constitutional system is strikingly illustrated by the fact that every State admitted into the Union since 1876 was compelled by Congress to write into its constitution a requirement that it maintain a school system "free from sectarian control."

Prohibition of the commingling of sectarian and secular instruction in the public school is of course only half the story. A religious people was naturally concerned about the part of the child's education entrusted "to the family altar, the church, and the private school." The promotion of religious education took many forms. Laboring under financial difficulties and exercising only persuasive authority, various denominations felt handicapped in their task of religious education. Abortive attempts were therefore frequently made to obtain public funds for religious schools. But the major efforts of religious inculcation were a recognition of the principle of Separation by the establishment of church schools privately supported. Parochial schools were maintained by various denominations. These, however, were often beset by serious handicaps, financial and otherwise, so that the religious aims which they represented found other directions. There were experiments with vacation schools, with Saturday as well as Sunday schools. They all fell short of their purpose. It was urged that by appearing to make religion a one-day-a-week matter, the Sunday school, which acquired national acceptance, tended to relegate the child's religious education, and thereby his religion, to a minor role not unlike the enforced piano lesson.

Out of these inadequate efforts evolved the weekday church school, held on one or more afternoons a week after the close of the public school. But children continued to be children; they wanted to play when school was out, particularly when other children were free to do so. Church leaders decided that if the weekday church school was to succeed, a way had to be found to give the child his religious education during what the child conceived to be his "business hours."

The initiation of the movement may fairly be attributed to Dr. George U. Wenner. The underlying assumption of his proposal, made at the Interfaith Conference on Federation held in New York City in 1905, was that the public school unduly monopolized the child's time and that the churches were entitled to their share of it. This, the schools should "release." Accordingly, the Federation, citing the example of the Third Republic of France, urged that upon the request of their parents children be excused from public school on Wednesday afternoon, so that the churches could provide "Sunday school on Wednesday." This was to be carried out on church premises under church authority. Those not desiring to attend church schools would continue their normal classes. Lest these public school classes unfairly compete with the church education, it was requested that the school authorities refrain from scheduling courses or activities of compelling interest or importance.

The proposal aroused considerable opposition and it took another decade for a "released time" scheme to become part of a public school system. Gary, Indiana, inaugurated the movement. At a time when industrial expansion strained the communal facilities of the city, Superintendent of Schools Wirt suggested a fuller use of the school buildings. Building on theories which had become more or less current, he also urged that education was more than instruction in a classroom. The school was only one of several educational agencies. The library, the playground, the home, the church, all have their function in the child's proper unfolding. Accordingly, Wirt's plan sought to rotate the schedules of the children during the school-day so that some were in class, others were in the library, still others in the playground. And some, he suggested to the leading ministers of the City, might be released to attend religious classes if the churches of the City cooperated and provided them. They did, in 1914, and thus was "released time" begun. The religious teaching was held on church premises and the public schools had no hand in the conduct of these church schools. They did not supervise the choice of instructors or the subject matter taught. Nor did they assume responsibility for the attendance, conduct or achievement of the child in a church school; and he received no credit for it. The period of attendance in the religious schools would otherwise have been a play period for the child, with the result that the arrangement did not cut into public school instruction or truly affect the activities or feelings of the children who did not attend the church schools.

From such a beginning "released time" has attained substantial proportions. In 1914–15, under the Gary program, 619 pupils left the public schools for the church schools during one period a week. According to responsible figures almost 2,000,000 in some 2,200 communities participated in "released time" programs during 1947. A movement of such scope indicates the importance of the problem to which the "released time" programs are directed. But to the extent that aspects of these programs are open to Constitutional objection, the more extensively the movement operates, the more ominous the breaches in the wall of separation.

Of course, "released time" as a generalized conception, undefined by differentiating particularities, is not an issue for Constitutional adjudication. Local programs differ from each other in many and crucial respects. Some "released time" classes are under separate denominational auspices, others are conducted jointly by several denominations, often embracing all the religious affiliations of a community. Some classes in religion teach a limited sectarianism; others emphasize democracy, unity and spiritual values not anchored in a particular creed. Insofar as these are manifestations merely of the free exercise of religion, they are quite outside the scope of judicial concern, except insofar as the Court may be called upon to protect the right of religious freedom. It is only when challenge is made to the share that the public schools have in the execution of a particular "released time" program that close judicial scrutiny is demanded of the exact relation between the religious instruction and the public educational system in the specific situation before the Court.

The substantial differences among arrangements lumped together as "released time" emphasize the importance of detailed analysis of the facts to which the Constitutional test of Separation is to be applied. How does "released time" operate in Champaign? Public School teachers distribute to their pupils cards supplied by church groups, so that the parents may indicate whether they desire religious instruction for their children. For those desiring it, religious classes are conducted in the regular classrooms of the public schools by teachers of religion paid by the churches and appointed by them, but, as the State court

250

found, "subject to the approval and supervision of the Superintendent." The courses do not profess to give secular instruction in subjects concerning religion. Their candid purpose is sectarian teaching. While a child can go to any of the religious classes offered, a particular sect wishing a teacher for its devotees requires the permission of the school superintendent "who in turn will determine whether or not it is practical for said group to teach in said school system." If no provision is made for religious instruction in the particular faith of a child, or if for other reasons the child is not enrolled in any of the offered classes, he is required to attend a regular school class, or a study period during which he is often left to his own devices. Reports of attendance in the religious classes are submitted by the religious instructor to the school authorities, and the child who fails to attend is presumably deemed a truant.

Religious education so conducted on school time and property is patently woven into the working scheme of the school. The Champaign arrangement thus presents powerful elements of inherent pressure by the school system in the interest of religious sects. The fact that this power has not been used to discriminate is beside the point. Separation is a requirement to abstain from fusing functions of Government and of religious sects, not merely to treat them all equally. That a child is offered an alternative may reduce the constraint; it does not eliminate the operation of influence by the school in matters sacred to conscience and outside the school's domain. The law of imitation operates, and nonconformity is not an outstanding characteristic of children. The result is an obvious pressure upon children to attend. Again, while the Champaign school population represents only a fraction of the more than two hundred and fifty sects of the nation, not even all the practicing sects in Champaign are willing or able to provide religious instruction. The children belonging to these non-participating sects will thus have inculcated in them a feeling of separatism when the school should be the training ground for habits of community, or they will have religious instruction in a faith which is not that of their parents. As a result, the public school system of Champaign actively furthers inculcation in the religious tenets of some faiths, and in the process sharpens the consciousness of religious differences at least among some of the children committed to its care. These are consequences not amenable to statistics. But they are precisely the consequences against which the Constitution was directed when it prohibited the Government common to all from becoming embroiled, however innocently, in the destructive religious conflicts of which the history of even this country records some dark pages.

Mention should not be omitted that the integration of religious instruction within the school system as practiced in Champaign is supported by arguments drawn from educational theories as diverse as those derived from Catholic conceptions and from the writings of John Dewey. Movements like "released time" are seldom single in origin or aim. Nor can the intrusion of religious instruction into the public school system of Champaign be minimized by saying that it absorbs less than an hour a week; in fact, that affords evidence of a design constitutionally objectionable. If it were merely a question of enabling a child to obtain religious instruction with a receptive mind the thirty or forty-five minutes could readily be found on Saturday or Sunday. If that were all, Champaign might have drawn upon the French system, known in its American manifestations as "dismissed time," whereby one school day is shortened to allow all children to go where they please, leaving those who so desire to go to a religious school. The momentum of the whole school atmosphere and school planning is presumably put behind religious instruction, as given in Champaign, precisely in order to secure for the religious instruction such momentum and planning. To speak of "released time" as being only half or three quarters of an hour is to draw a thread from a fabric.

We do not consider, as indeed we could not, school programs not before us which, though colloquially characterized as "released time," present situations differing in aspects that may well be constitutionally crucial. Different forms which "released time" has taken during more than thirty years of growth include programs which, like that before us, could not withstand the test of the Constitution; others may be found unexceptionable; we do not now attempt to weigh in the Constitutional scale every separate detail or various combination of factors which may establish a valid "released time" program. We find that the basic Constitutional principle of absolute separation was violated when the State of Illinois, speaking through its Supreme Court, sustained the school authorities of Champaign in sponsoring and effectively furthering religious beliefs by its educational arrangement.

Separation means separation, not something less. Jefferson's metaphor in describing the relation between Church and State speaks of a "wall of separation," not of a fine line easily overstepped. The public school is at once the symbol of our democracy and the most pervasive means for promoting our common destiny. In no activity of the State is it more vital to keep out divisive forces than in its schools, to avoid confusing, not to say fusing, what the Constitution sought to keep strictly apart. "The great American principle of eternal separation" —Elihu Root's phrase bears repetition—is one of the vital reliances of our Constitutional system for assuring unities among our people stronger than our diversities. It is the Court's duty to enforce this principle in its full integrity.

We renew our conviction that "we have staked the very existence of our country on the faith that complete separation between the state and religion is best for the state and best for religion." If nowhere else, in the relation between Church and State, "good fences make good neighbors."

MR. JUSTICE JACKSON, CONCURRING.

I join the opinion of Mr. Justice Frankfurter, and concur in the result reached by the Court, but with these reservations: I think it is doubtful whether the facts of this case establish jurisdiction in this Court, but in any event that we should place some bounds on the demands for interference with local schools that we are empowered or willing to entertain. I make these reservations a matter of record in view of the number of litigations likely to be started as a result of this decision.

A Federal Court may interfere with local school authorities only when they invade either a personal liberty or a property right protected by the Federal Constitution. Ordinarily this will come about in either of two ways:

First. When a person is required to submit to some religious rite or instruction or is deprived or threatened with deprivation of his freedom for resisting such unconstitutional requirement. We may then set him free or enjoin his prosecution. Typical of such cases was West Virginia State Board of Education v. Barnette. There penalties were threatened against both parent and child for refusal of the latter to perform a compulsory ritual which offended his convictions. We intervened to shield them against the penalty. But here, complainant's son may join religious classes if he chooses and if his parents so request, or he may stay out of them. The complaint is that when others join and he does not, it sets him apart as a dissenter, which is humiliating. Even admitting this to be true, it may be doubted whether the Constitution which, of course, protects the right to dissent, can be construed also to protect one from the embarrassment that always attends nonconformity, whether in religion, politics, behavior or dress. Since no legal compulsion is applied to complainant's son himself and no penalty is imposed or threatened from which we may relieve him, we can hardly base jurisdiction on this ground.

Second. Where a complainant is deprived of property by being taxed for unconstitutional purposes, such as directly or indirectly to support a religious establishment. We can protect a taxpayer against such a levy. This was the Everson Case as I saw it then and see it now; it was complained in that case that the school treasurer drew a check on public funds to reimburse parents for a child's bus fare if he went to a Catholic parochial school or a public school, but not if he went to any other private or denominational school. Reference to the record in that case will show that the School District was not operating busses, so it was not a question of allowing Catholic children to ride publicly owned busses along with others, in the interests of their safety, health or morals. The child had to travel to and from parochial school on commercial busses like other paying passengers, and all other school children, and he was exposed to the same dangers. If it could, in fairness, have been said that the expenditure was a measure for the protection of the safety, health or morals of youngsters, it would not merely have been constitutional to grant it; it would have been unconstitutional to refuse it to any child merely because he was a Catholic. But in the Everson Case there was a direct, substantial and measurable burden on the complainant as a taxpayer to raise funds that were used to subsidize transportation to parochial schools. Hence, we had jurisdiction to examine the constitutionality of the levy and to protect against it if a majority had agreed that the subsidy for transportation was unconstitutional.

In this case, however, any cost of this plan to the taxpayers is incalculable and negligible. It can be argued, perhaps, that religious classes add some wear and tear on public buildings and that they should be charged with some expense for heat and light, even though the sessions devoted to religious instruction do not add to the length of the school day. But the cost is neither substantial nor measurable, and no one seriously can say that the complainant's tax bill has been proved to be increased because of this plan. I think it is doubtful whether the taxpayer in this case has shown any substantial property injury.

If, however, jurisdiction is found to exist, it is important that we circumscribe our decision with some care. What is asked is not a defensive use of judicial power to set aside a tax levy or reverse a conviction, or to enjoin threats of prosecution or taxation. The relief demanded in this case is the extraordinary writ of mandamus to tell the local Board of Education what it must do. The prayer for relief is that a writ issue against the Board of Education "ordering it to immediately adopt and enforce rules and regulations prohibiting all instruction in and teaching of religious education in all public schools . . . and in all public school houses and buildings in said district when occupied by public schools." The plaintiff, as she has every right to be, is an avowed atheist. What she has asked of the courts is that they not only end the "released time" plan but also ban every form of teaching which suggests or recognizes that there is a God. She would ban all teaching of the Scriptures. She especially mentions as an example of invasion of her rights "having pupils learn and recite such statements as, 'The Lord is my Shepherd, I shall not want.'" And she objects to teaching that the King James version of the Bible "is called the Christian's Guide Book, the Holy Writ and the Word of God," and many other similar matters. This Court is directing the Illinois courts generally to sustain plaintiff's complaint without exception of any of these grounds of complaint, without discriminating between them and without laying down any standards to define the limits of the effect of our decision.

To me, the sweep and detail of these complaints is a danger signal which warns of the kind of local controversy we will be required to arbitrate if we do not place appropriate limitation on our decision and exact strict compliance with jurisdictional requirements. Authorities list 256 separate and substantial religious bodies to exist in continental United States. Each of them, through the suit of some discontented but unpenalized and untaxed representative, has as good a right as this plaintiff to demand that the courts compel the schools to sift out of their teaching everything inconsistent with its doctrines. If we are to eliminate everything that is objectionable to any of these warring sects or inconsistent with any of their doctrines, we will leave public education in shreds. Nothing but educational confusion and a discrediting of the public school system can result from subjecting it to constant law suits.

While we may and should end such formal and explicit instruction as the Champaign plan and can at all times prohibit teaching of creed and catechism and ceremonial and can forbid forthright proselyting in the schools, I think it remains to be demonstrated whether it is possible, even if desirable, to comply with such demands as plaintiff's completely to isolate and cast out of secular education all that some people may reasonably regard as religious instruction. Perhaps subjects such as mathematics, physics or chemistry are, or can be, completely secularized. But it would not seem practical to teach either practice or appreciation of the arts if we are to forbid exposure of youth to any religious influences. Music without sacred music, architecture minus the cathedral, or painting without the scriptural themes would be eccentric and incomplete, even from a secular point of view. Yet the inspirational appeal of religion in these guises is often stronger than in forthright sermon. Even such a "science" as biology raises the issue between evolution and creation as an explanation of our presence on this planet. Certainly a course in English literature that omitted the Bible and other powerful uses of our mother tongue for religious ends would be pretty barren.

And I should suppose it is a proper, if not an indispensable, part of preparation for a worldly life to know the roles that religion and religions have played in the tragic story of mankind. The fact is that, for good or for ill, nearly everything in our culture worth transmitting, everything which gives meaning to life, is saturated with religious influences, derived from paganism, Judaism, Christianity—both Catholic and Protestant—and other faiths accepted by a large part of the world's peoples. One can hardly respect a system of education that would leave the student wholly ignorant of the currents of religious thought that move the world society for a part in which he is being prepared.

But how one can teach, with satisfaction or even with justice to all faiths, such subjects as the story of the Reformation, the Inquisition, or even the New England effort to found "a Church without a Bishop and a State without a King," is more than I know. It is too much to expect that mortals will teach subjects about which their contemporaries have passionate controversies with the detachment they may summon to teaching about remote subjects such as Confucius or Mohamet. When instruction turns to proselyting and imparting knowledge becomes evangelism is, except in the crudest cases, a subtle inquiry.

The opinions in this case show that public educational authorities have evolved a considerable variety of practices in dealing with the religious problem. Neighborhoods differ in racial, religious and cultural compositions. It must be expected that they will adopt different customs which will give emphasis to different values and will induce different experiments. And it must be expected that, no matter what practice prevails, there will be many discontented and possibly belligerent minorities. We must leave some flexibility to meet local conditions, some chance to progress by trial and error. While I agree that the religious classes involved here go beyond permissible limits. I also think the complaint demands more than plaintiff is entitled to have granted. So far as I can see this Court does not tell the State court where it may stop, nor does it set up any standards by which the State court may determine that question for itself.

The task of separating the secular from the religious in education is one of magnitude, intricacy and delicacy. To lay down a sweeping constitutional doctrine as demanded by complainant and apparently approved by the Court, applicable alike to all school boards of the nation, "to immediately adopt and enforce rules and regulations prohibiting all instruction in and teaching of religious education in all public schools," is to decree a uniform, rigid and, if we are consistent, an unchanging standard for countless school boards representing and serving highly localized groups which not only differ from each other but which themselves from time to time change attitude. It seems to me that to do so is to allow zeal for our own ideas of what is good in public instruction to induce us to accept the role of a super board of education for every school district in the nation.

It is idle to pretend that this task is one for which we can find in the Constitution one word to help us as judges to decide where the secular ends and the sectarian begins in education. Nor can we find guidance in any other legal source. It is a matter on which we can find no law but our own prepossessions. If with no surer legal guidance we are to take up and decide every variation of this controversy, raised by persons not subject to penalty or tax but who are dissatisfied with the way schools are dealing with the problem, we are likely to have much business of the sort. And, more importantly, we are likely to make the legal "wall of separation between church and state" as winding as the famous serpentine wall designed by Mr. Jefferson for the University he founded.

MR. JUSTICE REED, DISSENTING.

The decisions reversing the judgment of the Supreme Court of Illinois interpret the prohibition of the First Amendment against the establishment of religion, made effective as to the states by the Fourteenth Amendment, to forbid pupils of the public schools electing, with the approval of their parents, courses in religious education. The courses are given, under the school laws of Illinois as approved by the Supreme Court of that State, by lay or clerical teachers supplied and directed by an interdenominational, local council of religious education. The classes are held in the respective school buildings of the pupils at study or released time periods so as to avoid conflict with recitations. The teachers and supplies are paid for by the interdenominational group. As I am convinced that this interpretation of the First Amendment is erroneous, I feel impelled to express the reasons for my disagreement. By directing attention to the many instances of close association of church and state in American society and by recalling that many of these relations are so much a part of our tradition and culture that they are accepted without more, this dissent may help in an appraisal of the meaning of the clause of the First Amendment concerning the establishment of religion and of the reasons which lead to the approval or disapproval of the judgment below.

The reasons for the reversal of the Illinois judgment, as they appear in the respective opinions may be summarized by the following excerpts. The opinion of the Court after stating the facts, says: "the foregoing facts, without reference to others that appear in the record, show the use of tax-supported property for religious instruction and the close cooperation between the school authorities and the religious council in promoting religious education. . . . And it falls squarely under the ban of the First Amendment (made applicable to the States by the Fourteenth) as we interpreted it in Everson v. Board of Education." Another opinion phrases it thus: "We do not now attempt to weigh in the Constitutional scale every separate detail or various combination of factors which may establish a valid 'released time' program. We find that the basic Constitutional principle of absolute separation was violated when the State of Illinois, speaking through its Supreme Court, sustained the school authorities of Champaign in sponsoring and effectively furthering religious beliefs by its educational arrangement." These expressions in the decisions seem to leave open for further litigation variations from the Champaign plan. Actually, however, future cases must run the gantlet not only of the judgment entered but of the accompanying words of the opinions. I find it difficult to extract from the opinions any conclusion as to what it is in the Champaign plan that is unconstitutional. Is it the use of school buildings for religious instruction; the release of pupils by the schools for religious instruction during school hours; the so-called assistance by teachers in handing out the request cards to pupils, in keeping lists of them for release and records of their attendance; or the action of the principals in arranging an opportunity for the classes and the appearance of the Council's instructors? None of the reversing opinions say whether the purpose of the Champaign plan for religious instruction during school hours is unconstitutional or whether it is some ingredient used in or omitted from the formula that makes the plan unconstitutional.

From the tenor of the opinions I conclude that their teachings are that any use of a pupil's school time whether that use is on or off the school grounds, with the necessary school regulations to facilitate attendance, falls under the ban. I reach this conclusion notwithstanding one sentence of indefinite meaning in the second opinion: "We do not consider, as indeed we could not, school programs not before us which, though colloquially characterized as 'released time,' present situations differing in aspects that may well be constitutionally crucial." The use of the words "cooperation," "fusion," "complete hands off," "integrate" and "integrated" to describe the relations between the school and the Council in the plan evidences this. So does the interpretation of the word "aid." The criticized "momentum of the whole school atmosphere," "feeling of separatism" engendered in the non-participating sects, "obvious pressure . . . to attend," and "divisiveness" lead to the stated conclusion. From the holding and the language of the opinions, I can only deduce that religious instruction of public school children during school hours is prohibited. The history of American education is against such an interpretation of the First Amendment.

The opinions do not say in words that the condemned practice of religious education is a law respecting an establishment of religion contrary to the First Amendment. The practise is accepted as a state law by all. I take it that when the opinion of the Court says that "The operation of the state's compulsory education system thus assists and is integrated with the program of religious instruction carried on by separate religious sects" and concludes "this is beyond all question a utilization of the tax-established and tax-supported public school system to aid religious groups to spread their faith," the intention of its author is to rule that this practice is a law "respecting an establishment of religion." That was the basis of Everson v. Board of Education. It seems obvious that the action of the School Board in permitting religious education in certain grades of the schools by all faiths did not prohibit the free exercise of religion. Even assuming that certain children who did not elect to take instruction are embarrassed to remain outside of the classes, one can hardly speak of that embarrassment as a prohibition against the free exercise of religion. As no issue of prohibition upon the free exercise of religion is before us, we need only examine the School Board's action to see if it constitutes an establishment of religion.

The facts, as stated in the reversing opinions, are adequately set out if we interpret the abstract words used in the light of the concrete incidents of the record. It is correct to say that the parents "consented" to the religious instruction of the children, if we understand "consent" to mean the signing of a card like the one in the margin. It is correct to say that "instructors were subject to the approval and supervision of the superintendent of schools," if it is understood that there were no definitive written rules and that the practice was as is shown in the excerpts from the findings below. The substance of the religious education course is determined by the members of the various churches on the council, not by the superintendent. The evidence and findings set out in the two preceding notes convince me that the "approval and supervision" referred to above are not of the teachers and the course of studies but of the orderly presentation of the courses to those students who may elect the instruction. The teaching largely covered Biblical incidents. The religious teachers and their teachings in every real sense, were financed, and regulated by the Council of Religious Education, not the School Board.

The phrase "an establishment of religion" may have been intended by Congress to be aimed only at a state church. When the First Amendment was pending in Congress in substantially its present form,

"Mr. Madison said, he apprehended the meaning of the words to be, that Congress should not establish a religion, and enforce the legal observation of it by law, nor compel men to worship God in any manner contrary to their conscience." Passing years, however, have brought about acceptance of a broader meaning, although never until today, I believe, has this Court widened its interpretation to any such degree as holding that recognition of the interest of our nation in religion, through the granting, to qualified representatives of the principal faiths, of opportunity to present religion as an optional, extracurricular subject during released school time in public school buildings, was equivalent to an establishment of religion. A reading of the general statements of eminent statesmen of former days, referred to in the opinions in this and Everson v. Board of Education, will show that circumstances such as those in this case were far from the minds of the authors. The words and spirit of those statements may be wholeheartedly accepted without in the least impugning the judgment of the State of Illinois.

Mr. Jefferson, as one of the founders of the University of Virginia, a school which from its establishment in 1819 has been wholly governed, managed and controlled by the State of Virginia, was faced with the same problem that is before this Court today: The question of the constitutional limitation upon religious education in public schools. In his annual report as Rector, to the President and Directors of the Literary Fund, dated October 7, 1822, approved by the Visitors of the University of whom Mr. Madison was one, Mr. Jefferson set forth his views at some length. These suggestions of Mr. Jefferson were adopted and ch.II, 1, of the Regulations of the University of October 4, 1824, provided that:

"Should the religious sects of this State, or any of them, according to the invitation held out to them, establish within, or adjacent to, the precincts of the University, schools for instruction in the religion of their sect, the students of the University will be free, and expected to attend religious worship at the establishment of their respective sects, in the morning, and in time to meet their school in the University at its stated hour."

Thus, the "wall of separation between church and State" that Mr. Jefferson built at the University which he founded did not exclude religious education from that school. The difference between the generality of his statements on the separation of church and state and the specificity of his conclusions on education are considerable. A rule of law should not be drawn from a figure of speech.

Mr. Madison's Memorial and Remonstrance against Religious Assessments relied upon by the dissenting Justices in Everson is not applicable here. Mr. Madison was one of the principal opponents in the Virginia General Assembly of A Bill Establishing a Provision for Teachers of the Christian Religion. The monies raised by the taxing section of that bill were to be appropriated "by the Vestries, Elders, or each religious society, . . . to a provision for a Minister or Teacher of the Gospel of their denomination, or the providing places of divine worship, and to none other use whatsoever. . . ." The conclusive legislative struggle over this act took place in the fall of 1785 before the adoption of the Bill of Rights. The Remonstrance had been issued before the General Assembly convened and was instrumental in the final defeat of the act which died in committee. Throughout the Remonstrance, Mr. Madison speaks of the "establishment" sought to be effected by the act. It is clear from its historical setting and its language that the Remonstrance was a protest against an effort by Virginia to support Christian sects by taxation. Issues similar to those raised by the instant case were not discussed. Thus, Mr. Madison's approval of Mr. Jefferson's report as Rector gives, in my opinion, a clearer indication of his views on the constitutionality of religious education in public schools than his general statements on a different subject.

This Court summarized the amendment's accepted reach into the religious field, as I understand its scope, in Everson v. Board of Education. The Court's opinion quotes the gist of the Court's reasoning in Everson. I agree as there stated that none of our governmental entities can "set up a church." I agree that they cannot "aid" all or any religions or prefer one "over another." But "aid" must be understood as a purposeful assistance directly to the church itself or to some religious group or organization doing religious work of such a character that it may fairly be said to be performing ecclesiastical functions. "Prefer" must give an advantage to one "over another." I agree that pupils cannot "be released in part from their legal duty" of school attendance upon condition that they attend religious classes. But as Illinois has held that it is within the discretion of the School Board to permit absence from school for religious instruction no legal duty of school attendance is violated. If the sentence in the first opinion, concerning the pupils' release from legal duty, is intended to mean that the Constitution forbids a school to excuse a pupil from secular control during school hours to attend voluntarily a class in religious education, whether in or out of school buildings, I disagree. Of course, no tax can be levied to support organizations intended "to teach or practice religion." I agree too that the state cannot influence one toward religion against his will or punish him for his beliefs. Champaign's religious education course does none of these things.

It seems clear to me that the "aid" referred to by the Court in the

Everson case could not have been those incidental advantages that religious bodies, with other groups similarly situated, obtain as a by-product of organized society. This explains the well-known fact that all churches receive "aid" from government in the form of freedom from taxation. The Everson decision itself justified the transportation of children to church schools by New Jersey for safety reasons. It accords with Cochran v. Louisiana State Board of Education, where this Court upheld a free textbook statute of Louisiana against a charge that it aided private schools on the ground that the books were for the education of the children, not to aid religious schools. Likewise the National School Lunch Act aids all school children attending tax exempt schools. In Bradfield v. Roberts, this Court held proper the payment of money by the Federal Government to build an addition to a hospital, chartered by individuals who were members of a Roman Catholic sisterhood, and operated under the auspices of the Roman Catholic Church. This was done over the objection that it aided the establishment of religion. While obviously in these instances the respective churches, in a certain sense, were aided, this Court has never held that such "aid" was in violation of the First or Fourteenth Amendments.

Well-recognized and long-established practice support the validity of the Illinois statute here in question. That statute, as construed in this case, is comparable to those in many states. All differ to some extent. New York may be taken as a fair example. In many states the program is under the supervision of a religious council composed of delegates who are themselves communicants of various faiths. As is shown by Bradfield v. Roberts, the fact that the members of the council have religious affiliation is not significant. In some, instruction is given outside of the school buildings; in others, within these buildings. Metropolitan centers like New York usually would have available quarters convenient to schools. Unless smaller cities and rural communities use the school building at times that do not interfere with recitations, they may be compelled to give up religious education. I understand that pupils not taking religious education usually are given other work of a secular nature within the schools. Since all these states use the facilities of the schools to aid the religious education to some extent, their desire to permit religious education to school children is thwarted by this Court's judgment. Under it, as I understand its language, children cannot be released or dismissed from school to attend classes in religion while other children must remain to pursue secular education. Teachers cannot keep the records as to which pupils are to be dismissed and which retained. To do so is said to be an "aid" in establishing religion; the use of public money for religion.

Cases running into the scores have been in the state courts of last resort that involved religion and the schools. Except where the exercises with religious significance partook of the ceremonial practice of sects or groups, their constitutionality has been generally upheld. Illinois itself promptly struck down as violative of its own constitution required exercises partaking of a religious ceremony. People ex el. Ring v. Board of Education. In that case compulsory religious exercises—a reading from the King James Bible, the Lord's Prayer and the singing of hymns—were forbidden as "worship services." In this case, the Supreme Court of Illinois pointed out that in the Ring case, the activities in the school were ceremonial and compulsory; in this, voluntary and educational.

The practices of the federal government offer many examples of this kind of "aid" by the state to religion. The Congress of the United States has a chaplain for each House who daily invokes divine blessings and guidance for the proceedings. The armed forces have commissioned chaplains from early days. They conduct the public services in accordance with the liturgical requirements of their respective faiths, ashore and afloat, employing for the purpose property belonging to the United States and dedicated to the services of religion. Under the Servicemen's Readjustment Act of 1944, eligible veterans may receive training at government expense for the ministry in denominational schools. The schools of the District of Columbia have opening exercises which "include a reading from the Bible without note or comment, and the Lord's prayer."

In the United States Naval Academy and the United States Military Academy, schools wholly supported and completely controlled by the federal government, there are a number of religious activities, Chaplains are attached to both schools. Attendance at church services on Sunday is compulsory at both the Military and Naval Academies. At West Point the Protestant services are held in the Cadet Chapel; at Annapolis only Protestant services are held on the reservation, midshipmen of other religious persuasions attend the churches of the city of Annapolis. These facts indicate that both schools since their earliest beginnings have maintained and enforced a pattern of participation in formal worship.

With the general statements in the opinions concerning the constitutional requirement that the nation and states, by virtue of the First and Fourteenth Amendments, may "make no law respecting an establishment of religion," I am in agreement. But, in the light of the meaning given to those words by the precedents, customs, and practices which I have detailed above, I cannot agree with the Court's conclusion that when pupils compelled by law to go to school for secular education are released from school so as to attend the religious classes, churches are unconstitutionally aided. Whatever may be the wisdom of the arrangement as to the use of the school buildings made with The Champaign Council of Religious Education, it is clear to me that past practice shows such cooperation between the schools and a non-ecclesiastical body is not forbidden by the First Amendment. When actual church services have always been permitted on government property, the mere use of the school buildings by a non-sectarian group for religious education ought not to be condemned as an establishment of religion. For a non-sectarian organization to give the type of instruction here offered cannot be said to violate our rule as to the establishment of religion by the state. The prohibition of enactments respecting the establishment of religion do not bar every friendly gesture between church and state. It is not an absolute prohibition against every conceivable situation where the two may work together any more than the other provisions of the First Amendment—free speech, free press—are absolutes. If abuses occur such as the use of the instruction hour for sectarian purposes, I have no doubt, in view of the Ring case, that Illinois will promptly correct them. If they are of a kind that tend to the establishment of a church or interfere with the free exercise of religion, this Court is open for a review of any erroneous decision. This Court cannot be too cautious in upsetting practices embedded in our society by many years of experience. A state is entitled to have great leeway in its legislation when dealing with the important social problems of its population. A definite violation of legislative limits must be established. The Constitution should not be stretched to forbid national customs in the way courts act to reach arrangements to avoid federal taxation. Devotion to the great principle of religious liberty should not lead us into a rigid interpretation of the constitutional guarantee that conflicts with accepted habits of our people. This is an instance where, for me, the history of past practices is determinative of the meaning of a constitutional clause not a decorous introduction to the study of its text. The judgment should be affirmed.

ZORACH v. CLAUSON 343 US 306 (1952)

"We are a religious people whose institutions presuppose a Supreme Being."

Mr. Justice Douglas, for the Court

"Before today, our judicial opinions have refrained from drawing invidious distinctions between those who believe in no religion and those who do believe. The First Amendment has lost much if the religious follower and the atheist are no longer to be judicially regarded as entitled to equal justice under law."

Mr. Justice Black, dissenting

> "As one whose children, as a matter of free choice, have been sent
> to privately supported Church schools, I may challenge the Court's
> suggestion that opposition to this plan can only be antireligious,
> atheistic, or agnostic. My evangelistic brethren confuse an objection
> to compulsion with an objection to religion."
>
> Mr. Justice Jackson, dissenting

A New York released-time program is sustained 6–3. The Court
does not repudiate the Everson and McCollum doctrines; rather, the
majority opinion states that "we follow the McCollum case," although
the dissenters have some doubts. Justice Jackson says that the McCollum
case has passed "like a storm in a teacup." Bitter feelings come to the
surface.

MR. JUSTICE DOUGLAS DELIVERED THE OPINION OF THE COURT.

New York City has a program which permits its public schools to
release students during the school day so that they may leave the school
buildings and school grounds and go to religious centers for religious
instruction or devotional exercises. A student is released on written request of his parents. Those not released stay in the classrooms. The
churches make weekly reports to the schools, sending a list of children
who have been released from public school but who have not reported
for religious instruction.

This "released time" program involves neither religious instruction
in public school classrooms nor the expenditure of public funds. All
costs, including the application blanks, are paid by the religious organizations. The case is therefore unlike McCollum v. Board of Education
which involved a "released time" program from Illinois. In that case
the classrooms were turned over to religious instructors. We accordingly
held that the program violated the First Amendment which (by reason
of the Fourteenth Amendment) prohibits the states from establishing
religion or prohibiting its free exercise.

Appellants, who are taxpayers and residents of New York City and
whose children attend its public schools, challenge the present law,
contending it is in essence not different from the one involved in the
McCollum case. Their argument, stated elaborately in various ways,
reduces itself to this: the weight and influence of the school is put
behind a program for religious instruction; public school teachers police
it, keeping tab on students who are released; the classroom activities
come to a halt while the students who are released for religious instruction are on leave; the school is a crutch on which the churches are
leaning for support in their religious training; without the cooperation
of the schools this "released time" program, like the one in the
McCollum case, would be futile and ineffective. The New York Court

of Appeals sustained the law against this claim of unconstitutionality. The case is here on appeal.

The briefs and arguments are replete with data bearing on the merits of this type of "released time" program. Views pro and con are expressed, based on practical experience with these programs and with their implications. We do not stop to summarize these materials nor to burden the opinion with an analysis of them. For they involve considerations not germane to the narrow constitutional issue presented. They largely concern the wisdom of the system, its efficiency from an educational point of view, and the political considerations which have motivated its adoption or rejection in some communities. Those matters are of no concern here, since our problem reduces itself to whether New York by this system has either prohibited the "free exercise" of religion or has made a law "respecting an establishment of religion" within the meaning of the First Amendment.

It takes obtuse reasoning to inject any issue of the "free exercise" of religion into the present case. No one is forced to go to the religious classroom and no religious exercise or instruction is brought to the classrooms of the public schools. A student need not take religious instruction. He is left to his own desires as to the manner or time of his religious devotions, if any.

There is a suggestion that the system involves the use of coercion to get public school students into religious classrooms. There is no evidence in the record before us that supports that conclusion. The present record indeed tells us that the school authorities are neutral in this regard and do no more than release students whose parents so request. If in fact coercion were used, if it were established that any one or more teachers were using their office to persuade or force students to take the religious instruction, a wholly different case would be presented. Hence we put aside that claim of coercion both as respects the "free exercise" of religion and "an establishment of religion" within the meaning of the First Amendment.

Moreover, apart from that claim of coercion, we do not see how New York by this type of "released time" program has made a law respecting an establishment of religion within the meaning of the First Amendment. There is much talk of the separation of Church and State in the history of the Bill of Rights and in the decisions clustering around the First Amendment. See Everson v. Board of Education; McCollum v. Board of Education. There cannot be the slightest doubt that the First Amendment reflects the philosophy that Church and State should be separated. And so far as interference with the "free exercise" of religion and an "establishment" of religion are concerned, the separation must be complete and unequivocal. The First Amendment within the scope of its coverage permits no exception; the prohibition is absolute. The First Amendment, however, does not say that in every and all respects there shall be a separation of Church and State. Rather, it studiously defines the manner, the specific ways, in which there shall be no concert or union or dependency one on the other. That is the common sense of the matter. Otherwise the state and religion would aliens to each other—hostile, suspicious, and even unfriendly. Churches could not be required to pay even property taxes. Municipalities would not be permitted to render police or fire protection to religious groups. Policemen who helped parishioners into their places of worship would violate the Constitution. Prayers in our legislative halls; the appeals to the Almighty in the messages of the Chief Executive; the proclamations making Thanksgiving Day a holiday; "so help me God" in our courtroom oaths—these and all other references to the Almighty that run through our laws, our public rituals, our ceremonies would be flouting the First Amendment. A fastidious atheist or agnostic could even object to the supplication with which the Court opens each session: "God save the United States and this Honorable Court."

We would have to press the concept of separation of Church and State to these extremes to condemn the present law on constitutional grounds. The nullification of this law would have wide and profound effects. A Catholic student applies to his teacher for permission to leave the school during hours on a Holy Day of Obligation to attend a mass. A Jewish student asks his teacher for permission to be excused for Yom Kippur. A Protestant wants the afternoon off for a family baptismal ceremony. In each case the teacher requires parental consent in writing. In each case the teacher, in order to make sure the student is not a truant, goes further and requires a report from the priest, the rabbi, or the minister. The teacher in other words cooperates in a religious program to the extent of making it possible for her students to participate in it. Whether she does it occasionally for a few students, regularly for one, or pursuant to a systematized program designed to further the religious needs of all the students does not alter the character of the act.

We are a religious people whose institutions presuppose a Supreme Being. We guarantee the freedom to worship as one chooses. We make room for as wide a variety of beliefs and creeds as the spiritual needs of man deem necessary. We sponsor an attitude on the part of government that shows no partiality to any one group and that lets each flourish according to the zeal of its adherents and the appeal of its dogma. When the state encourages religious instruction or cooperates with religious authorities by adjusting the schedule of public events to sectarian needs, it follows the best of our traditions. For it then respects the religious nature of our people and accommodates the public service to their spiritual needs. To hold that it may not would be to find in the Constitution a requirement that the government show a callous indifference to religious groups. That would be preferring those who believe in no religion over those who do believe. Government may not finance religious groups nor undertake religious instruction nor blend secular and sectarian education nor use secular institutions to force one or some religion on any person. But we find no constitutional requirement which makes it necessary for government to be hostile to religion and to throw its weight against efforts to widen the effective scope of religious influence. The government must be neutral when it comes to competition between sects. It may not thrust any sect on any person. It may not make a religious observance compulsory. It may not coerce anyone to attend church, to observe a religious holiday, or to take religious instruction. But it can close its doors or suspend its operations as to those who want to repair to their religious sanctuary for worship or instruction. No more than that is undertaken here.

This program may be unwise and improvident from an educational or a community viewpoint. That appeal is made to us on a theory, previously advanced, that each case must be decided on the basis of "our own prepossessions." See McCollum v. Board of Education. Our individual preferences, however, are not the constitutional standard. The constitutional standard is the separation of Church and State. The problem, like many problems in constitutional law, is one of degree.

In the McCollum case the classrooms were used for religious instruction and the force of the public school was used to promote that instruction. Here, as we have said, the public schools do no more than accommodate their schedules to a program of outside religious instruction. We follow the McCollum case. But we cannot expand it to cover the present released time program unless separation of Church and State means that public institutions can make no adjustment of their schedules to accommodate the religious needs of the people. We cannot read into the Bill of Rights such a philosophy of hostility to religion.

Affirmed.

MR. JUSTICE BLACK, DISSENTING.

Illinois ex rel. McCollum v. Board of Education held invalid as an "establishment of religion" an Illinois system under which school children, compelled by law to go to public schools, were freed from some hours of required school work on condition that they attend special religious classes held in the school buildings. Although the classes were taught by sectarian teachers neither employed nor paid by the state, the state did use its power to further the program by releasing some of the children from regular class work, insisting that those released attend the religious classes, and requiring that those who remained behind do some kind of academic work while the others received their religious training. We said this about the Illinois system:

"Pupils compelled by law to go to school for secular education are released in part from their legal duty upon the condition that they attend the religious classes. This is beyond all question a utilization of the tax established and tax-supported public school system to aid religious groups to spread their faiths. And it falls squarely under the ban of the First Amendment. . . ."

I see no significant difference between the invalid Illinois system and that of New York here sustained. Except for the use of the school buildings in Illinois, there is no difference between the systems which I consider even worthy of mention. In the New York program, as in that of Illinois, the school authorities release some of the children on the condition that they attend the religious classes, get reports on whether they attend, and hold the other children in the school building until the religious hour is over. As we attempted to make categorically clear, the McCollum decision would have been the same if the religious classes had not been held in the school buildings. We said:

"Here not only are the State's tax-supported public school buildings used for the dissemination of religious doctrines. The State also affords sectarian groups an invaluable aid in that it helps to provide pupils for their religious classes through the use of the State's compulsory school machinery. This is not separation of Church and State." McCollum thus held that Illinois could not constitutionally manipulate the compelled classroom hours of its compulsory school machinery so as to channel children into sectarian classes. Yet that is exactly what the Court holds New York can do.

I am aware that our McCollum decision on separation of church and state has been subjected to a most searching examination throughout the country. Probably few opinions from this Court in recent years have attracted more attention or stirred wider debate. Our insistence on "a wall between Church and State which must be kept high and impregnable" has seemed to some a correct exposition of the philosophy and a true interpretation of the language of the First Amendment to which we should strictly adhere. With equal conviction and sincerity, others have thought the McCollum decision fundamentally wrong and have pledged continuous warfare against it. The opinions in the court below and the briefs here reflect these diverse viewpoints. In dissenting today, I mean to do more than give routine approval to our McCollum decision. I mean also to reaffirm my faith in the fundamental philosophy expressed in McCollum and Everson v. Board of Education. That reaffirmance can be brief because of the exhaustive opinions in those recent cases.

Difficulty of decision in the hypothetical situations mentioned by the Court, but not now before us, should not confuse the issues in this case. Here the sole question is whether New York can use its compulsory education laws to help religious sects get attendants presumably too unenthusiastic to go unless moved to do so by the pressure of this state machinery. That this is the plan, purpose, design and consequence of the New York program cannot be denied. The state thus makes religious sects beneficiaries of its power to compel children to attend secular schools. Any use of such coercive power by the state to help or hinder some religious sects or to prefer all religious sects over nonbelievers or vice versa is just what I think the First Amendment forbids. In considering whether a state has entered this forbidden field the question is not whether it has entered too far but whether it has entered at all. New York is manipulating its compulsory education laws to help religious sects get pupils. This is not separation but combination of Church and State.

The Court's validation of the New York system rests in part on its statement that Americans are "a religious people whose institutions presuppose a Supreme Being." This was at least as true when the First Amendment was adopted; and it was just as true when eight justices of this Court invalidated the released time system in McCollum on the premise that a state can no more "aid all religions" than it can aid one. It was precisely because Eighteenth Century Americans were a religious people divided into many fighting sects that we were given the constitutional mandate to keep church and state completely separate. Colonial history had already shown that, here as elsewhere zealous sectarians entrusted with governmental power to further their causes, would sometimes torture, maim and kill those they branded "heretics," "atheists" or "agnostics." The First Amendment was therefore to insure that no one powerful sect or combination of sects could use political or governmental power to punish dissenters whom they could not convert to their faith. Now as then, it is only by wholly isolating the state from the religious sphere and compelling it to be completely neutral, that the freedom of each and every denomination and of all non-believers can be maintained. It is this neutrality the Court abandons today when it treats New York's coercive system as a program which merely "encourages religious instruction or cooperates with religious authorities." The abandonment is all the more dangerous to liberty because of the Court's legal exaltation of the orthodox and its derogation of unbelievers.

Under our system of religious freedom, people have gone to their religious sanctuaries not because they feared the law but because they loved their God. The choice of all has been as free as the choice of those who answered the call to worship moved only by the music of the old Sunday morning church bells. The spiritual mind of man has thus been free to believe, disbelieve, or doubt, without repression, great or small, by the heavy hand of government. Statutes authorizing such repression have been stricken. Before today, our judicial opinions have refrained from drawing invidious distinctions between those who believe in no religion and those who do believe. The First Amendment has lost much if the religious follower and the atheist are no longer to be judicially regarded as entitled to equal justice under law.

State help to religion injects political and party prejudices into a holy field. It too often substitutes force for prayer, hate for love, and persecution for persuasion. Government should not be allowed, under cover of the soft euphemism of "co-operation," to steal into the sacred area of religious choice.

MR. JUSTICE FRANKFURTER, DISSENTING.

By way of emphasizing my agreement with Mr. Justice Jackson's dissent, I add a few words.

The Court tells us that in the maintenance of its public schools, "(The State government) can close its doors or suspend its operations" so that its citizens may be free for religious devotions or instruction. If that were the issue, it would not rise to the dignity of a constitutional controversy. Of course a State may provide that the classes in its schools shall be dismissed, for any reason, or no reason, on fixed days, or for special occasions. The essence of this case is that the school system did not "close its doors" and did not "suspend its operations." There is all the difference in the world between letting the children out of school and letting some of them out of school into religious classes. If every one is free to make what use he will of time wholly unconnected from schooling required by law—those who wish sectarian instruction devoting it to that purpose, those who have ethical instruction at home, to that, those who study music, to that—then of course there is no conflict with the Fourteenth Amendment.

271

The pith of the case is that formalized religious instruction is substituted for other school activity which those who do not participate in the released-time program are compelled to attend. The school system is very much in operation during this kind of released time. If its doors are closed, they are closed upon those students who do not attend the religious instruction in order to keep them within the school. That is the very thing which raises the constitutional issue. It is not met by disregarding it. Failure to discuss this issue does not take it out of the case.

Again, the Court relies upon the absence from the record of evidence of coercion in the operation of the system. "If in fact coercion were used," according to the Court, "if it were established that any one or more teachers were using their office to persuade or force students to take the religious instruction, a wholly different case would be presented." Thus, "coercion" in the abstract is acknowledged to be fatal. But the Court disregards the fact that as the case comes to us, there could be no proof of coercion, for the petitioners were not allowed to make proof of it. Petitioners alleged that "The operation of the released time program has resulted and inevitably results in the exercise of pressure and coercion upon parents and children to secure attendance by the children for religious instruction." This allegation— that coercion was in fact present and is inherent in the system, no matter what disavowals might be made in the operating regulations— was denied by respondents. Thus were drawn issues of fact which cannot be determined, on any conceivable view of judicial notice, by judges out of their own knowledge or experience. Petitioners sought an opportunity to adduce evidence in support of these allegations at an appropriate trial. And though the courts below cited the concurring opinion in McCollum v. Board of Education to "emphasize the importance of detailed analysis of the facts to which the Constitutional test of Separation is to be applied," they denied that opportunity on the ground that such proof was irrelevant to the issue of constitutionality.

When constitutional issues turn on facts, it is a strange procedure indeed not to permit the facts to be established. When such is the case, there are weighty considerations for us to require the State court to make its determination only after a thorough canvass of all the circumstances and not to bar them from consideration. If we are to decide this case on the present record, however, a strict adherence to the usage of courts in ruling on the sufficiency of pleadings would require us to take as admitted the facts pleaded in the petitioners' complaint, including the fact of coercion, actual and inherent. Even on a more latitudinarian view, I cannot see how a finding that coercion was absent, deemed critical by this Court in sustaining the practice, can be made here, when petitioners were prevented from making a timely showing of coercion because the courts below thought it irrelevant.

The result in the McCollum case was based on principles that received unanimous acceptance by this Court, barring only a single vote. I agree with Mr. Justice Black that those principles are disregarded in reaching the result in this case. Happily they are not disavowed by the Court. From this I draw the hope that in future variations of the problem which are bound to come here, these principles may again be honored in the observance.

The deeply divisive controversy aroused by the attempts to secure public school pupils for sectarian instruction would promptly end if the advocates of such instruction were content to have the school "close its doors or suspend operation"—that is, dismiss classes in their entirety, without discrimination—instead of seeking to use the public schools as the instrument for security of attendance at denominational classes. The unwillingness of the promoters of this movement to dispense with such use of the public schools betrays a surprising want of confidence in the inherent power of the various faiths to draw children to outside sectarian classes—an attitude that hardly reflects the faith of the greatest religious spirits.

MR. JUSTICE JACKSON, DISSENTING.

This released time program is founded upon a use of the State's power of coercion, which, for me, determines its unconstitutionality. Stripped to its essentials, the plan has two stages, first, that the State compel each student to yield a large part of his time for public secular education and, second, that some of it be "released" to him on condition that he devote it to sectarian religious purposes.

No one suggests that the Constitution would permit the State directly to require this "released" time to be spent "under the control of a duly constituted religious body." This program accomplishes that forbidden result by indirection. If public education were taking so much of the pupils' time as to injure the public or the student's welfare by encroaching upon their religious opportunity, simply shortening everyone's school day would facilitate voluntary and optional attendance at Church classes. But that suggestion is rejected upon the ground that if they are made free many students will not go to the Church. Hence, they must be deprived of freedom for this period, with Church attendance put to them as one of the two permissible ways of using it.

The greater effectiveness of this system over voluntary attendance after school hours is due to the truant officer who, if the youngster fails to go to the Church school, dogs him back to the public schoolroom. Here schooling is more or less suspended during the "released time" so the nonreligious attendants will not forge ahead of the Churchgoing absentees. But it serves as a temporary jail for a pupil who will not go to Church. It takes more subtlety of mind than I possess to deny that this is governmental constraint in support of religion. It is as unconstitutional, in my view, when exerted by indirection as when exercised forthrightly.

As one whose children, as a matter of free choice, have been sent to privately supported Church schools, I may challenge the Court's suggestion that opposition to this plan can only be antireligious, atheistic, or agnostic. My evangelistic brethren confuse an objection to compulsion with an objection to religion. It is possible to hold a faith with enough confidence to believe that what should be rendered to God does not need to be decided and collected by Caesar.

The day that this country creases to be free for irreligion it will cease to be free for religion—except for the sect that can win political power. The same epithetical jurisprudence used by the Court today to beat down those who oppose pressuring children into some religion can devise as good epithets tomorrow against those who object to pressuring them into a favored religion. And, after all, if we concede to the State power and wisdom to single out "duly constituted religious" bodies as exclusive alternatives for compulsory secular instruction, it would be logical to also uphold the power and wisdom to choose the true faith among those "duly constituted." We start down a rough road when we begin to mix compulsory public education with compulsory godliness.

A number of Justices just short of a majority of the majority that promulgates today's passionate dialectics joined in answering them in Illinois ex rel. McCollum v. Board of Education. The distinction attempted between that case and this is trivial, almost to the point of cynicism, magnifying its nonessential details and disparaging compulsion which was the underlying reason for invalidity. A reading of the Court's opinion in that case along with its opinion in this case will show such difference of overtones and undertones as to make clear that the McCollum case has passed like a storm in a teacup. The wall which the Court was professing to erect between Church and State has become even more warped and twisted than I expected. Today's judgment will be more interesting to students of psychology and of the judicial processes than to students of constitutional law.

BURSTYN v. WILSON 343 US 495 (1952)

"It is not the business of government in our nation to suppress real or imagined attacks upon a particular religious doctrine, whether they appear in publications, speeches, or motion pictures."

Mr. Justice Clark, for the Court

"To criticize or assail religious doctrine may wound to the quick those who are attached to the doctrine and profoundly cherish it. But to bar such pictorial discussion is to subject non-conformists to the rule of sects."

Mr. Justice Frankfurter, concurring

"The Miracle," a film by Roberto Rossellini, was barred in New York as "sacrilegious." The Court here unanimously holds such censorship to be unconstitutional.

MR. JUSTICE CLARK DELIVERED THE OPINION OF THE COURT.

The issue here is the constitutionality, under the First and Fourteenth Amendments, of a New York statute which permits the banning of motion picture films on the ground that they are "sacrilegious." That statute makes it unlawful to "exhibit, or to sell, lease or lend for exhibition at any place of amusement for pay or in connection with any business in the state of New York, any motion picture film or reel (with specified exceptions not relevant here), unless there is at the time in full force and effect a valid license or permit therefor of the education department. . . ." The statute further provides:

"The director of the (motion picture) division (of the education department) or, when authorized by the regents, the officers of a local office or bureau shall cause to be promptly examined every motion picture film submitted to them as herein required, and unless such film or a part thereof is obscene, indecent, immoral, inhuman, sacrilegious, or is of such a character that its exhibition would tend to corrupt morals or incite to crime, shall issue a license therefor. If such director, or, when so authorized, such officer shall not license any film submitted, he shall furnish to the applicant therefor a written report of the reasons for his refusal and a description of each rejected part of a film not rejected in toto."

Appellant is a corporation engaged in the business of distributing motion pictures. It owns the exclusive rights to distribute throughout the United States a film produced in Italy entitled "The Miracle." On November 30, 1950, after having examined the picture, the motion picture division of the New York education department, acting under the statute quoted above, issued to appellant a license authorizing exhibition of "The Miracle," with English subtitles, as one part of a trilogy called "Ways of Love." Thereafter, for a period of approximately eight weeks, "Ways of Love" was exhibited publicly in a motion picture theater in

New York City under an agreement between appellant and the owner of the theater whereby appellant received a stated percentage of the admission price.

During this period, the New York State Board of Regents, which by statute is made the head of the education department, received "hundreds of letters, telegrams, post cards, affidavits and other communications" both protesting against and defending the public exhibition of "The Miracle." The Chancellor of the Board of Regents requested three members of the Board to view the picture and to make a report to the entire Board. After viewing the film, this committee reported to the Board that in its opinion there was basis for the claim that the picture was "sacrilegious." Thereafter, on January 19, 1951, the Regents directed appellant to show cause, at a hearing to be held on January 30, why its license to show "The Miracle" should not be rescinded on that ground. Appellant appeared at this hearing, which was conducted by the same three-member committee of the Regents which had previously viewed the picture, and challenged the jurisdiction of the committee and of the Regents to proceed with the case. With the consent of the committee, various interested persons and organizations submitted to it briefs and exhibits bearing upon the constitutional and statutory questions involved. On February 16, 1951, the Regents, after viewing "The Miracle," determined that it was "sacrilegious" and for that reason ordered the Commissioner of Education to rescind appellant's license to exhibit the picture. The Commissioner did so.

Appellant brought the present action in the New York courts to review the determination of the Regents. Among the claims advanced by appellant were (1) that the statute violates the Fourteenth Amendment as a prior restraint upon freedom of speech and of the press; (2) that it is invalid under the same Amendment as a violation of the guaranty of separate church and state and as a prohibition of the free exercise of religion; and, (3) that the term "sacrilegious" is so vague and indefinite as to offend due process. The Appellate Division rejected all of appellant's contentions and upheld the Regents' determination. On appeal the New York Court of Appeals, two judges dissenting, affirmed the order of the Appellate Division. The case is here on appeal.

As we view the case, we need consider only appellant's contention that the New York statute is an unconstitutional abridgment of free speech and a free press. In Mutual Film Corp. v. Industrial Commission, a distributor of motion pictures sought to enjoin the enforcement of an Ohio statute which required the prior approval of a board of censors before any motion picture could be publicly exhibited in the state, and which directed the board to approve only such films as it adjudged to be "of a moral, educational or amusing and harmless character." The statute was assailed in part as an unconstitutional abridgment of the freedom of the press guaranteed by the First and Fourteenth Amendments. The District Court rejected this contention, stating that the first eight Amendments were not a restriction on state action. On appeal to this Court, plaintiff in its brief abandoned this claim and contended merely that the statute in question violated the freedom of speech and publication guaranteed by the Constitution of Ohio. In affirming the decree of the District Court denying injunctive relief, this Court stated:

"It cannot be put out of view that the exhibition of moving pictures is a business pure and simple, originated and conducted for profit, like other spectacles, not to be regarded, nor intended to be regarded by the Ohio constitution, we think, as part of the press of the country or as organs of public opinion."

In a series of decisions beginning with Gitlow v. New York, this Court held that the liberty of speech and of the press which the First Amendment guarantees against abridgment by the federal government is within the liberty safeguarded by the Due Process Clause of the Fourteenth Amendment from invasion by state action. That principle has been followed and reaffirmed to the present day. Since this series of decisions came after the Mutual decision, the present case is the first to present squarely to us the question whether motion pictures are within the ambit of protection which the First Amendment, through the Fourteenth, secures to any form of "speech" or "the press."

It cannot be doubted that motion pictures are a significant medium for the communication of ideas. They may affect public attitudes and behavior in a variety of ways, ranging from direct espousal of a political or social doctrine to the subtle shaping of thought which characterizes all artistic expression. The importance of motion pictures as an organ of public opinion is not lessened by the fact that they are designed to entertain as well as to inform. As was said in Winters v. New York:

"The line between the informing and the entertaining is too elusive for the protection of that basic right (a free press). Everyone is familiar with instances of propaganda through fiction. What is one man's amusement, teaches another's doctrine."

It is urged that motion pictures do not fall within the First Amendment's aegis because their production, distribution, and exhibition is a large-scale business conducted for private profit. We cannot agree. That books, newspapers, and magazines are published and sold for profit does not prevent them from being a form of expression whose liberty is safeguarded by the First Amendment. We fail to see why operation for profit should have any different effect in the case of motion pictures.

It is further urged that motion pictures possess a greater capacity for evil, particularly among the youth of a community, than other modes of expression. Even if one were to accept this hypothesis, it does not follow that motion pictures should be disqualified from First Amendment protection. If there be capacity for evil it may be relevant in determining the permissible scope of community control, but it does not authorize substantially unbridled censorship such as we have here.

For the foregoing reasons, we conclude that expression by means of motion pictures is included within the free speech and free press guaranty of the First and Fourteenth Amendments. To the extent that language in the opinion in Mutual Film Corp. v. Industrial Commission, is out of harmony with the views here set forth, we no longer adhere to it.

To hold that liberty of expression by means of motion pictures is guaranteed by the First and Fourteenth Amendments, however, is not the end of our problem. It does not follow that the Constitution requires absolute freedom to exhibit every motion picture of every kind at all times and all places. That much is evident from the series of decisions of this Court with respect to other media of communication of ideas. Nor does it follow that motion pictures are necessarily subject to the precise rules governing any other particular method of expression. Each method tends to present its own peculiar problems. But the basic principles of freedom of speech and the press, like the First Amendment's command, do not vary. Those principles, as they have frequently been enunciated by this Court, make freedom of expression the rule. There is no justification in this case for making an exception to that rule.

The statute involved here does not seek to punish, as a past offense, speech or writing falling within the permissible scope of subsequent punishment. On the contrary, New York requires that permission to communicate ideas be obtained in advance from state officials who judge the content of the words and pictures sought to be communicated. This Court recognized many years ago that such a previous restraint is a form of infringement upon freedom of expression to be especially condemned. Near v. Minnesota. The Court there recounted the history which indicates that a major purpose of the First Amendment guaranty of a free press was to prevent prior restraints upon publication, although it was carefully pointed out that the liberty of the press is not limited to that protection. It was further stated that "the protection even as to previous restraint is not absolutely unlimited. But the limitation has been recognized only in exceptional cases." In the light of the First Amendment's history and of the Near decision, the State has a heavy burden to demonstrate that the limitation challenged here presents such an exceptional case.

New York's highest court says there is "nothing mysterious" about the statutory provision applied in this case: "It is simply this: that no religion, as that word is understood by the ordinary, reasonable person, shall be treated with contempt, mockery, scorn and ridicule. . . ." This is far from the kind of narrow exception to freedom of expression which a state may carve out to satisfy the adverse demands of other interests of society. In seeking to apply the broad and all-inclusive definition of "sacrilegious" given by the New York courts, the censor is set adrift upon a boundless sea amid a myriad of conflicting currents of religious views, with no charts but those provided by the most vocal and powerful orthodoxies. New York cannot vest such unlimited restraining control over motion pictures in a censor. Under such a standard the most careful and tolerant censor would find it virtually impossible to avoid favoring one religion over another, and he would be subject to an inevitable tendency to ban the expression of unpopular sentiments sacred to a religious minority. Application of the "sacrilegious" test, in these or other respects, might raise substantial questions under the First Amendment's guaranty of separate church and state with freedom of worship for all. However, from the standpoint of freedom of speech and the press, it is enough to point out that the state has no legitimate interest in protecting any or all religions from views distasteful to them which is sufficient to justify prior restraints upon the expression of those views. It is not the business of government in our nation to suppress real or imagined attacks upon a particular religious doctrine, whether they appear in publications, speeches, or motion pictures.

Since the term "sacrilegious" is the sole standard under attack here, it is not necessary for us to decide, for example, whether a state may censor motion pictures under a clearly drawn statute designed and applied to prevent the showing of obscene films. That is a very different question from the one now before us. We hold only that under the First and Fourteenth Amendments a state may not ban a film on the basis of a censor's conclusion that it is "sacrilegious."

Reversed.

MR. JUSTICE REED, CONCURRING IN THE JUDGMENT OF THE COURT.

Assuming that a state may establish a system for the licensing of motion pictures, an issue not foreclosed by the Court's opinion, our duty requires us to examine the facts of the refusal of a license in each case to determine whether the principles of the First Amendment have been honored. This film does not seem to me to be of a character that the First Amendment permits a state to exclude from public view.

MR. JUSTICE FRANKFURTER WHOM MR. JUSTICE JACKSON JOINS, CONCURRING IN THE JUDGMENT OF THE COURT; MR. JUSTICE BURTON, CONCURRED IN THE OPINION OF THE COURT, ALSO JOINS THIS OPINION.

A practised hand has thus summarized the story of "The Miracle": [1]

"A poor, simple-minded girl is tending a herd of goats on a mountainside one day, when a bearded stranger passes. Suddenly it strikes her fancy that he is St. Joseph, her favorite saint, and that he has come to take her to heaven, where she will be happy and free. While she pleads with him to transport her, the stranger gently plies the girl with wine, and when she is in a state of tumult, he apparently ravishes her. (This incident in the story is only briefly and discreetly implied.)

"The girl awakens later, finds the stranger gone, and climbs down from the mountain not knowing whether he was real or a dream. She meets an old priest who tells her that it is quite possible that she did see a saint, but a younger priest scoffs at the notion. 'Materialist!' the old priest says.

"There follows now a brief sequence—intended to be symbolic, obviously—in which the girl is reverently sitting with other villagers in church. Moved by a whim of appetite, she snitches an apple from the basket of a woman next to her. When she leaves the church, a cackling beggar tries to make her share the apple with him, but she chases him away as by habit and munches the fruit contentedly.

"Then one day, while tending the village youngsters as their mothers work at the vines, the girl faints and the women discover that she is going to have a child. Frightened and bewildered, she suddenly murmurs, 'It is the grace of God!' and she runs to the church in great excitement, looks for the statue of St. Joseph, and then prostrates herself on the floor.

"Thereafter she meekly refuses to do any menial work and the housewives humor her gently but the young people are not so kind. In a scene of brutal torment they first flatter and laughingly mock her, then they cruelly shove and hit her and clamp a basin as a halo on her head. Even abused by the beggars, the poor girl gathers together her pitiful rags and sadly departs from the village to live alone in a cave.

"When she feels her time coming upon her, she starts back towards the village But then she sees the crowds in the streets; dark memories haunt her; so she turns towards a church on a high hill and instinctively struggles towards it, crying desperately to God. A goat is her sole companion. She drinks water dripping from a rock. And when

<hr />

[1] Crowther, "The Strange Case of 'The Miracle,' " *Atlantic Monthly*, April 1951, pp. 35, 36-7.

she comes to the church and finds the door locked, the goat attracts her to a small side door. Inside the church, the poor girl braces herself for her labor pains. There is a dissolve, and when we next see her sad face, in close-up, it is full of a tender light. There is the cry of an unseen baby. The girl reaches towards it and murmurs, 'My son! My love! My flesh!' "

"The Miracle"—a film lasting forty minutes—was produced in Italy by Roberto Rossellini. Anna Magnani played the lead as the demented goat-tender. It was first shown at the Venice Film Festival in August, 1948, combined with another moving picture, "L'Umano Voce," into a diptych called "Amore." According to an affidavit from the Director of that Festival, if the motion picture had been "blasphemous" it would have been barred by the Festival Committee. In a review of the film in *L'Osservatore Romano,* the organ of the Vatican, its film critic, Piero Regnoli, wrote: "Opinions may vary and questions may arise—even serious ones—of a religious nature (not to be diminished by the fact that the woman portrayed is mad (because) the author who attributed madness to her is not mad). . . ." While acknowledging that there were "passages of undoubted cinematic distinction," Regnoli criticized the film as being "on such a pretentiously cerebral plane that it reminds one of the early d'Annunzio." The Vatican newspaper's critic concluded: "we continue to believe in Rossellini's art and we look forward to his next achievement." In October, 1948, a month after the Rome premiere of "The Miracle," the Vatican's censorship agency, the Catholic Cinematographic Centre, declared that the picture "constitutes in effect an abominable profanation from religious and moral viewpoints." By the Lateran agreements and the Italian Constitution the Italian Government is bound to bar whatever may offend the Catholic religion. However, the Catholic Cinematographic Centre did not invoke any governmental sanction thereby afforded. The Italian Government's censorship agency gave "The Miracle" the regular nulla osta clearance. The film was freely shown throughout Italy, but was not a great success. Italian movie critics divided in opinion. The critic for Il Popolo, speaking for the Christian Democratic Party, the Catholic party, profusely praised the picture as a "beautiful thing, humanly felt, alive, true and without religious profanation as someone has said, because in our opinion the meaning of the characters is clear and there is no possibility of misunderstanding." Regnoli again reviewed "The Miracle" for *L'Osservatore Romano.* After criticising the film for technical faults, he found "the most courageous and interesting passage of Rossellini's work" in contrasting portrayals in the film; he added: "Unfortunately, concerning morals, it is necessary to note some slight defects." He objected to its "carnality" and to the representation of illegitimate motherhood. But he did not suggest that the picture was "sacrilegious." The tone of Regnoli's critique was one of respect for Rossellini, "the illustrious Italian producer."

On March 2, 1949, "The Miracle" was licensed in New York State for showing without English subtitles. However, it was never exhibited until after a second license was issued on November 30, 1950, for the trilogy, "Ways of Love," combining "The Miracle" with two French films, Jean Renoir's "A Day in the Country" and Marcel Pagnol's "Jofroi." All had English subtitles. Both licenses were issued in the usual course after viewings of the picture by the Motion Picture Division of the New York State Education Department. The Division is directed by statute to "issue a license" unless (the) film or a part thereof is obscene, indecent, immoral, inhuman, sacrilegious, or is of such a character that its exhibition would tend to corrupt morals or incite to crime." The trilogy opened on December 12, 1950, at the Paris Theatre on 58th Street in Manhattan. It was promptly attacked as "a sacrilegious and blasphemous mockery of Christian religious truth" by the National Legion of Decency, a private Catholic organization for film censorship, whose objectives have intermittently been approved by various non-Catholic church and social groups since its formation in 1933. However, the National Board of Review (a non-industry lay organization devoted to raising the level of motion pictures by mobilizing public opinion, under the slogan "Selection Not Censorship") recommended the picture as "especially worth seeing." New York critics on the whole praised "The Miracle"; those who dispraised did not suggest sacrilege. On December 27 the critics selected the "Ways of Love" as the best foreign language film in 1950. Meanwhile, on December 23, Edward T. McCaffrey, Commissioner of Licenses for New York City, declared the film "officially and personally blasphemous" and ordered it withdrawn at the risk of suspension of the license to operate the Paris Theatre. A week later the program was restored at the theatre upon the decision by the New York Supreme Court that the City License Commissioner had exceeded his authority in that he was without powers of movie censorship.

Upon the failure of the License Commissioner's effort to cut off showings of "The Miracle," the controversy took a new turn. On Sunday, January 7, 1951, a statement of His Eminence, Francis Cardinal Spellman, condemning the picture and calling on "all right thinking citizens" to unite to tighten censorship laws, was read at all masses in St. Patrick's Cathedral.

The views of Cardinal Spellman aroused dissent among other devout Christians. Protestant clergymen, representing various denominations, after seeing the picture, found in it nothing "sacrilegious or immoral to the views held by Christian men and women," and with a few exceptions agreed that the film was "unquestionably one of unusual artistic merit."

In this estimate some Catholic laymen concurred. Their opinion is represented by the comment by Otto L. Spaeth, Director of the American Federation of Arts and prominent in Catholic lay activities:

"At the outbreak of the controversy, I immediately arranged for a private showing of the film. I invited a group of Catholics, competent and respected for their writings on both religious and cultural subjects. The essential approval of the film was unanimous.

"There was indeed 'blasphemy' in the picture—but it was the blasphemy of the villagers, who stopped at nothing, not even the mock singing of a hymn to the Virgin, in their brutal badgering of the tragic woman. The scathing indictment of their evil behaviour, implicit in the film, was seemingly overlooked by its critics."

William P. Clancy, a teacher at the University of Notre Dame wrote in *The Commonweal,* the well-known Catholic weekly, that "the film is not obviously blasphemous or obscene, either in its intention or execution." *The Commonweal* itself questioned the wisdom of transforming Church dogma which Catholics may obey as "a free act" into state-enforced censorship for all. Allen Tate, the well-known Catholic poet and critic, wrote: "The picture seems to me to be superior in acting and photography but inferior dramatically. . . . In the long run what Cardinal Spellman will have succeeded in doing is insulting the intelligence and faith of American Catholics with the assumption that a second-rate motion picture could in any way undermine their morals or shake their faith."

At the time "The Miracle" was filmed, all the persons having significant positions in the production—producer, director, and cast—were Catholics. Roberto Rossellini, who had Vatican approval in 1949 for filming a life of St. Francis, using in the cast members of the Franciscan Order, cabled Cardinal Spellman protesting against boycott of "The Miracle":

"In 'the Miracle' men are still without pity because they still have not come back to God, but God is already present in the faith, however confused, of that poor, persecuted woman; and since God is wherever a human being suffers and is misunderstood, 'The Miracle' occurs when at the birth of the child the poor, demented woman regains sanity in her maternal love."

In view of the controversy thus aroused by the picture, the Chairman of the Board of Regents appointed a committee of three Board members to review the action of the Motion Picture Division in granting the two licenses. After viewing the picture on Jan. 15, 1951, the committee declared it "sacrilegious." The Board four days later issued an order to the licensees to show cause why the licenses should not be cancelled in that the picture was "sacrilegious." The Board of Regents rescinded the licenses on Feb. 16, 1951, saying that the "mockery or profaning of these beliefs that are sacred to any portion of our citizenship is abhorrent to the laws of this great State." On review the Appellate Division upheld the Board of Regents, holding that the banning of any motion picture "that may fairly be deemed sacrilegious to the adherents of any religious group . . . is directly related to public peace and order" and is not a denial of religious freedom, and that there was "substantial evidence upon which the Regents could act."

The New York Court of Appeals, with one judge concurring in a separate opinion and two others dissenting, affirmed the order of the Appellate Division. After concluding that the Board of Regents acted within its authority and that its determination was not "one that no reasonable mind could reach," the majority held, first, that "sacrilegious" was an adequately definite standard, quoting a definition from Funk & Wagnalls' Dictionary and referring to opinions in this Court that in passing used the term "profane," which the New York court said was a synonym of "sacrilegious"; second, that the State's assurance "that no religion . . . shall be treated with contempt, mockery, scorn and ridicule . . . by those engaged in selling entertainment by way of motion pictures" does not violate the religious guarantee of the First Amendment; and third, that motion pictures are not entitled to the immunities from regulation enjoyed by the press, in view of the decision in Mutual Film Corp. v. Industrial Com. of Ohio. The two dissenting judges, after dealing with a matter of local law not reviewable here, found that the standard "sacrilegious" is unconstitutionally vague, and, finally, that the constitutional guarantee of freedom of speech applied equally to motion pictures and prevented this censorship. Both State courts, as did this Court, viewed "The Miracle."

Arguments by the parties and in briefs amici invite us to pursue to their farthest reach the problems in which this case is involved. Positions are advanced so absolute and abstract that in any event they could not properly determine this controversy. We are asked to decide this case by choosing between two mutually exclusive alternatives: that motion pictures may be subjected to unrestricted censorship, or that they must be allowed to be shown under any circumstances. But only the tyranny of absolutes would rely on such alternatives to meet the problems generated by the need to accommodate the diverse interests affected by the motion pictures in compact modern communities. It would startle Madison and Jefferson and George Mason, could they adjust themselves to our day, to be told that the freedom of speech which they espoused in the Bill of Rights authorizes a showing of "The Miracle" from windows facing St. Patrick's Cathedral in the forenoon of Easter Sunday, just as it would startle them to be told that any picture, whatever its theme and its expression, could be barred from being commercially exhibited. The general principle of free speech, expressed in the First Amendment as to encroachments by Congress, and included as it is in the Fourteenth Amendment, binding on the States, must be placed in its historical and legal contexts. The Constitution, we cannot recall too often, is an organism, not merely a literary composition.

If the New York Court of Appeals had given "sacrilegious" the meaning it has had in Catholic thought since St. Thomas Aquinas formulated its scope, and had sustained a finding by the Board of Regents that "The Miracle" came within that scope, this Court would have to meet some of the broader questions regarding the relation to the motion picture industry of the guarantees of the First Amendment so far as reflected in the Fourteenth. But the New York court did not define "sacrilegious" within such technical, Thomist limits, nor within any specific, or even approximately specified, limits. It may fairly be said that that court deemed "sacrilegious" a self-defining term, a word that carries a well-known, settled meaning in the common speech of men.

So far as the Court of Appeals sought to support its notion that "sacrilegious" has the necessary precision of meaning which the Due Process Clause enjoins for statutes regulating men's activities, it relied on this definition from Funk & Wagnalls' Dictionary: "The act of violating or profaning anything sacred." But this merely defines by turning an adjective into a noun and bringing in two new words equally undefined. It leaves wide open the question as to what persons, doctrines or things are "sacred." It sheds no light on what representations on the motion picture screen will constitute "profaning" those things which the State censors find to be "sacred."

To criticize or assail religious doctrine may wound to the quick those who are attached to the doctrine and profoundly cherish it. But to bar such pictorial discussion is to subject non-conformists to the rule of sects.

Even in Mutual Film Corp. v. Industrial Commission, it was deemed necessary to find that the terms "educational, moral, amusing or harmless" do not leave "decision to arbitrary judgment." Such general words were found to "get precision from the sense and experience of men." This cannot be said of "sacrilegious". If there is one thing that the history of religious conflicts shows, it is that the term "sacrilegious" if by that is implied offense to the deep convictions of members of different sects, which is what the Court of Appeals seems to mean so far as it means anything precisely—does not gain "precision from the sense and experience of men."

The vast apparatus of indices and digests, which mirrors our law, affords no clue to a judicial definition of·sacrilege. Not one case, barring the present, has been uncovered which considers the meaning of the term in any context. Nor has the practice under the New York law contributed light. The Motion Picture Division of the Education Department does not support with explanatory statements its action on any specific motion picture, which we are advised is itself not made public. Of the fifty-odd reported appeals to the Board of Regents from denials of licenses by the Division, only three concern the category "sacrilegious." In these cases, as in others under the Act, the Board's reported opinion confines itself to a bare finding that the film was or was not "sacrilegious," without so much as a description of the allegedly offensive matter, or even of the film as a whole to enlighten the inquirer. Well-equipped law libraries are not niggardly in their reflection of "the sense and experience of men," but we must search elsewhere for any which gives to "sacrilege" its meaning.

Sacrilege, as a restricted ecclesiastical concept, has a long history. Naturally enough, religions have sought to protect their priests and anointed symbols from physical injury. But history demonstrates that the term is hopelessly vague when it goes beyond such ecclesiastical definiteness and is used at large as the basis for punishing deviation from doctrine.

Etymologically "sacrilege" is limited to church-robbing: sacer, sacred, and legere, to steal or pick out. But we are told that "already in Cicero's time it had grown to include in popular speech any insult or injury to (sacred things)." "In primitive religions (sacrilege is) inclusive of almost every serious offence even in the fields now regarded as merely social or political. . . ." The concept of "tabu" in primitive society is thus close to that of "sacrilege." And in "the Theodosian Code the various crimes which are accounted sacrilege include—apostasy, heresy, schism, Judaism, paganism, attempts against the immunity of churches and clergy or privileges of church courts, the desecration of sacraments, etc., and even Sunday. Along with these crimes against religion went treason to the emperor, offences against the laws, especially counterfeiting, defraudation in taxes, seizure of confiscated property, evil conduct of imperial officers, etc." During the Middle Ages the Church considerably delimited the application of the term. St. Thomas Aquinas classified the objects of "sacrilege" as persons, places, and things. The injuries which would constitute "sacrilege" received specific and detailed illustration. This teaching of Aquinas is, I believe, still substantially the basis of the official Catholic doctrine of sacrilege. Thus, for the Roman Catholic Church, the term came to have a fairly definite meaning, but one, in general, limited to protecting things physical against injurious acts. Apostasy, heresy, and blasphemy coexisted as religious crimes alongside sacrilege; they were peculiarly in the realm of religious dogma and doctrine, as "sacrilege" was not. It is true that Spelman, writing "The History and Fate of Sacrilege" in 1632, included in "sacrilege" acts whereby "the very Deity is invaded, profaned, or robbed of its glory . . . In this high sin are blasphemers, sorcerers, witches, and enchanters." But his main theme was the "spoil of church lands done by Henry VIII" and the misfortunes that subsequently befell the families of the recipients of former ecclesiastical property as divine punishment.

To the extent that English law took jurisdiction to punish "sacrilege," the term meant the stealing from a church, or otherwise doing damage to church property. This special protection against "sacrilege," that is, property damage, was granted only to the Established Church. Since the repeal less than a century ago of the English law punishing "sacrilege" against the property of the Established Church, religious property has received little special protection. The property of all sects has had substantially the same protection as is accorded nonreligious property. At no time up to the present has English law known "sacrilege" to be used in any wider sense than the physical injury to church property. It is true that, at times in the past, English law has taken jurisdiction to punish departures from accepted dogma or religious practice or the expression of particular religious opinions, but never have these "offences" been denominated "sacrilege." Apostasy, heresy, offenses against the Established Church, blasphemy, profanation of the Lord's Day, etc., were distinct criminal offenses, characterized by Blackstone as "offenses against God and religion." These invidious reflections upon religious susceptibilities were not covered under sacrilege as they might be under the Court of Appeals' opinion. Anyone doubting the dangerous uncertainty of the New York definition which makes "sacrilege" overlap these other "offenses against religion," need only read Blackstone's account of the broad and varying content given each of these offenses.

A student of English lexicography would despair of finding the meaning attributed to "sacrilege" by the New York Court. Most dictionaries define the concept in the limited sense of the physical abuse of physical objects. The definitions given for "sacrilege" by two dictionaries published in 1742 and 1782 are typical. Bailey's defined it as "the stealing of sacred things, Church Robbing; and alienation to laymen, and to profane and common Purposes, of what was given to religious Persons, and to pious Uses." Barclay's said it is "the crime of taking any thing dedicated to divine worship, or profaning any thing sacred," where "to profane" is defined "to apply any thing sacred to common uses. To be irreverent to sacred persons or things." The same dictionaries defined "blasphemy," a peculiarly verbal offense, in much broader terms than "sacrilege," indeed in terms which the New York court finds encompassed by "sacrilegious." For example, Barclay said "blasphemy" is "an offering some indignity to God, any person of the Trinity, any messengers from God, his holy writ, or the doctrines of revelation." It is hardly necessary to comment that the limits of this definition remain too uncertain to justify constraining the creative efforts of the imagination by fear of pains and penalties imposed by a necessarily subjective censorship. It is true that some earlier dictionaries assigned to "sacrilege" the broader meaning of "abusing Sacraments or holy Mysteries," but the broader meaning is more indefinite, not less. Noah Webster first published his American Dictionary in 1828. Both it and the later dictionaries published by the Merriam Company, Webster's International Dictionary and Webster's New International Dictionary, have gone through dozens of editions and printings, revisions and expansions. In all editions throughout 125 years, these American dictionaries have defined "sacrilege" and "sacrilegious" to echo substantially the narrow, technical definitions from the earlier British dictionaries collected in the Appendix.

The New York Court of Appeals' statement that the dictionary "furnishes a clear definition," justifying the vague scope it gave to "sacrilegious," surely was made without regard to the lexicographic history of the term. As a mater of fact, the definition from Funk & Wagnalls' used by the Court of Appeals is taken straight from 18th Century dictionaries, particularly Doctor Johnson's. In light of that history it would seem that the Funk & Wagnalls' definition uses "sacrilege" in its historically restricted meaning, which was not, and could hardly have been, the basis for condemning "The Miracle." If the New York court reads the Funk & Wagnalls' definition in a broader sense, in a sense for which history and experience provide no gloss, it inevitably left the censor free to judge by whatever dogma he deems "sacred" and to ban whatever motion pictures he may assume would "profane" religious doctrine widely enough held to arouse protest.

Examination of successive editions of the *Encyclopaedia Britannica* over nearly two centuries up to the present day gives no more help than the dictionaries. From 1768 to the eleventh edition in 1911, merely a brief dictionary-type definition was given for "sacrilege." The eleventh edition, which first published a longer article, was introduced as follows: "the violation or profanation of sacred things, a crime of varying scope in different religions. It is naturally much more general and accounted more dreadful in those primitive religions in which cultural objects play so great a part, than in more highly spiritualized religions where they tend to disappear. But wherever the idea of sacred exists, sacrilege is possible." The article on "sacrilege" in the current edition of the *Encyclopaedia Britannica* is substantially the same as that in the 1911 edition.

History teaches us the indefiniteness of the concept "sacrilegious" in another respect. In the case of most countries and times where the concept of sacrilege has been of importance, there has existed an established church or a state religion. That which was "sacred," and so was protected against "profaning," was designated in each case by ecclesiastical authority. What might have been definite when a controlling church imposed a detailed scheme of observances becomes impossibly confused and uncertain when hundreds of sects, with widely disparate and often directly conflicting ideas of sacredness, enjoy, without discrimination and in equal measure, constitutionally guaranteed religious freedom. In the Rome of the late emperors, the England of James I, or the Geneva of Calvin, and today in Roman Catholic Spain, Mohammedan Saudi Arabia, or any other country with a monolithic religion, the category of things sacred might have clearly definable limits. But in America the multiplicity of the ideas of "sacredness" held with equal but conflicting fervor by the great number of religious groups makes the term "sacrilegious" too indefinite to satisfy constitutional demands based on reason and fairness.

If "sacrilegious" bans more than the physical abuse of sacred persons, places, or things, if it permits censorship of religious opinions, which is the effect of the holding below, the term will include what may be found to be "blasphemous." England's experience with that treacherous word should give us pause, apart from our requirements for the separation of Church and State. The crime of blasphemy in Seventeenth Century England was the crime of dissenting from whatever was the current religious dogma. King James I's "Book of Sports" was first required reading in the churches; later all copies were consigned to the flames. To attack the mass was once blasphemous; to perform it became so. At different times during that century, with the shifts in the attitude of government towards particular religious views, persons who doubted the doctrine of the Trinity (e.g., Unitarians, Universalists, etc.) or the divinity of Christ, observed the Sabbath on Saturday, denied the possibility of witchcraft, repudiated child baptism or urged methods of baptism other than sprinkling, were charged as blasphemers, or their books were burned or banned as blasphemous. Blasphemy was the chameleon phrase which meant the criticism of whatever the ruling authority of the moment established as orthodox religious doctrine. While it is true that blasphemy prosecutions have continued in England—although in lessening numbers—into the present century, the existence there of an established church gives more definite contours to the crime in England than the term "sacrilegious" can possibly have in this country. Moreover, the scope of the English common-law crime of blasphemy has been considerably limited by the declaration that "if the decencies of controversy are observed, even the fundamentals of religion may be attacked," a limitation which the New York court has not put upon the Board of Regents' power to declare a motion picture "sacrilegious."

In Cantwell v. Connecticut, Mr. Justice Roberts, speaking for the whole Court, said: "In the realm of religious faith, and in that of political belief, sharp differences arise. In both fields the tenets of one man may seem the rankest error to his neighbor." Conduct and beliefs dear to one may seem the rankest "sacrilege" to another. A few examples suffice to show the difficulties facing a conscientious censor or motion picture producer or distributor in determining what the New York statute condemns as sacrilegious. A motion picture portraying Christ as divine—for example, a movie showing medieval Church art—would offend the religious opinions of the members of several Protestant denominations who do not believe in the Trinity, as well as those of a non-Christian faith. Conversely, one showing Christ as merely an ethical teacher could not but offend millions of Christians of many denominations. Which is "sacrilegious"? The doctrine of transubstantiation, and the veneration of relics or particular stone and wood embodiments of saints or divinity, both sacred to Catholics, are offensive to a great many Protestants, and therefore for them sacrilegious in the view of the New York court. Is a picture treating either subject, whether sympathetically, unsympathetically, or neutrally, "sacrilegious"? It is not a sufficient answer to say that "sacrilegious" is definite because all subjects that in any way might be interpreted as offending the religious beliefs of any one of the 300 sects of the United States are banned in New York. To allow such vague, undefinable powers of censorship to be exercised is bound to have stultifying consequences on the creative process of literature and art—for the films are derived largely from literature. History does not encourage reliance on the wisdom and moderation of the censor as a safeguard in the exercise of such drastic power over the minds of men. We not only do not know but cannot know what is condemnable by "sacrilegious." And if we cannot tell, how are those to be governed by the statute to tell?

It is this impossibility of knowing how far the form of words by which the New York Court of Appeals explained "sacrilegious" carries the proscription of religious subjects that makes the term unconstitutionally vague. To stop short of proscribing all subjects that might conceivably be interpreted to be religious, inevitably creates a situation whereby the censor bans only that against which there is a substantial outcry from a religious group. And that is the fair inference to be drawn, as a matter of experience, from what has been happening under the New York censorship. Consequently the film industry, normally not guided by creative artists, and cautious in putting large capital to the hazards of courage, would be governed by its notions of the feelings likely to be aroused by diverse religious sects, certainly the powerful ones. The effect of such demands upon art and upon those whose function is to enhance the culture of a society need not be labored.

To paraphrase Doctor Johnson, if nothing may be shown but what licensors may have previously approved, power, the yea or nay saying by officials, becomes the standard of the permissible. Prohibition through words that fail to convey what is permitted and what is prohibited for want of appropriate objective standards, offends Due Process in two ways. First, it does not sufficiently apprise those bent on obedience of law of what may reasonably be foreseen to be found illicit by the law-enforcing authority, whether court or jury or administrative agency. Secondly, where licensing is rested, in the first instance, in an administrative agency, the available judicial review is in effect rendered inoperative. On the basis of such a portmanteau word as "sacrilegious," the judiciary has no standards with which to judge the validity of administrative action which necessarily involves, at least in large measure, subjective determinations. Thus, the administrative first step becomes the last step.

From all that has been said one is compelled to conclude that the term "sacrilegious" has come down the stream of time encrusted with a specialized, strictly confined meaning, pertaining to things in space not things in the mind. The New York Court of Appeals did not give the term this calculable content. It applied it to things in the mind, and things in the mind so undefined, so at large, as to be more patently in disregard of the requirement for definiteness, as the basis of proscriptions and legal sanctions for their disobedience, than the measures that were condemned as violative of Due Process in United States v. L. Cohen Grocery Co.; Small Co. v. American Sugar Refining Co.; Connaly v. General Constr. Co.; Winters v. New York; Kunz v. New York. This principle is especially to be observed when what is so vague seeks to fetter the mind and put within unascertainable bounds the varieties of religious experience.

KEDROFF v. SAINT NICHOLAS CATHEDRAL
344 US 94 (1952)

> "This controversy concerning the right to use St. Nicholas Cathedral is strictly a matter of ecclesiastical government, the power of the Supreme Church Authority of the Russian Orthodox Church to appoint the ruling hierarch of the archdiocese of North America."
>
> Mr. Justice Reed, for the Court

> "The fear, perhaps not wholly groundless, that the loyalty of its citizens might be diluted by their adherence to a church entangled in antagonistic political interests, reappears in history as the ground for interference by civil government with religious attachments."
>
> Mr. Justice Frankfurter, concurring

> "I shall not undertake to wallow through the complex, obscure and fragmentary details of secular and ecclesiastical history, theology, and canon law in which this case is smothered. To me, whatever the canon law is found to be and whoever is the rightful head of the Moscow patriarchate, I do not think New York law must yield to the authority of a foreign and unfriendly state masquerading as a spiritual institution."
>
> Mr. Justice Jackson, dissenting

Even here, the communist menace raises its head. The dispute is over the control of St. Nicholas Cathedral. New York took control away from the Moscow hierarchy, but the Supreme Court regarded this as an improper state intervention in religious affairs. (Parts of the opinion are omitted.)

MR. JUSTICE REED DELIVERED THE OPINION OF THE COURT.

The right to the use and occupancy of a church in the city of New York is in dispute.

The right to such use is claimed by appellee, a corporation created in 1925 by an act of the Legislature of New York, for the purpose of acquiring a cathedral for the Russian Orthodox Church in North America as a central place of worship and residence of the ruling archbishop "in accordance with the doctrine, discipline and worship of the Holy Apostolic Catholic Church of Eastern Confession as taught by the holy scriptures, holy tradition, seven ecumenical councils and holy fathers of that church."

The corporate right is sought to be enforced so that the head of the American churches, religiously affiliated with the Russian Orthodox Church, may occupy the Cathedral. At the present time that head is the Metropolitan of All America and Canada, the Archbishop of New York Leonty, who like his predecessors was elected to his ecclesiastical office by a sobor of the American churches.

That claimed right of the corporation to use and occupancy for the archbishop chosen by the American churches is opposed by appellants who are in possession. Benjamin Fedchenkoff bases his right on an appointment in 1934 by the Supreme Church Authority of the Russian Orthodox Church, to wit, the Patriarch locum tenens of Moscow and all Russia and its Holy Synod, as Archbishop of the Archdiocese of North America and the Aleutian Islands. The other defendant-appellant is a priest of the Russian Orthodox Church, also acknowledging the spiritual and administrative control of the Moscow hierarchy.

Determination of the right to use and occupy Saint Nicholas depends upon whether the appointment of Benjamin by the Patriarch or the election of the Archbishop for North America by the convention of the American churches validly selects the ruling hierarch for the American churches. The Court of Appeals of New York, reversing the lower court, determined that the prelate appointed by the Moscow ecclesiastical authorities was not entitled to the Cathedral and directed the entry of a judgment that appellee corporation be reinvested with the possession and administration of the temporalities of St. Nicholas Cathedral. This determination was made on the authority of Article 5-C of the Religious Corporations Law of New York, against appellants' contention that this New York statute, as construed, violated the Fourteenth Amendment to the Constitution of the United States . . .

Article 5-C was added to the Religious Corporations Law of New York in 1945 and provided both for the incorporation and administration of Russian Orthodox churches. Clarifying amendments were added in 1948. The purpose of the article was to bring all the New York churches, formerly subject to the administrative jurisdiction of the Most Sacred Governing Synod in Moscow or the Patriarch of Moscow, into an administratively autonomous metropolitan district. That district was North American in area, created pursuant to resolutions adopted at a sobor held at Detroit in 1924. This declared autonomy was made effective by a further legislative requirement that all the churches formerly administratively subject to the Moscow synod and patriarchate should for the future be governed by the ecclesiastical body and hierarchy of the American metropolitan district. The foregoing analysis follows the interpretation of this article by the Court of Appeals of New York, an interpretation binding upon us.

Article 5-C is challenged as invalid under the constitutional prohibition against interference with the exercise of religion. The appellants' contention, of course, is based on the theory that the principles of the First Amendment are made applicable to the states by the Fourteenth.

The Russian Orthodox Church is an autocephalous member of the Eastern Orthodox Greek Catholic Church. It sprang from the Church of Constantinople in the Tenth Century. The schism of A.D. 1054 split the Universal Church into those of the East and West. Gradually self-government was assumed by the Russian Church until in the Sixteenth Century its autonomy was recognized and a Patriarch of Moscow appeared. For the next one hundred years the development of the church kept pace with the growth of power of the Czars but it increasingly became a part of the civil government—a state church. Throughout that period it also remained a hierarchical church with a Patriarch at its head, governed by the conventions or sobors called by him. However, from the time of Peter the Great until 1917 no sobor was held. No patriarch ruled or was chosen. During that time the church was governed by a Holy Synod, a group of ecclesiastics with a Chief Procurator representative of the government as a member.

Late in the Eighteenth Century the Russian Church entered the missionary field in the Aleutian Islands and Alaska. From there churches spread slowly down the Pacific Coast and later, with the Slavic immigration, to our eastern cities, particularly to Detroit, Cleveland, Chicago, Pittsburgh and New York. The character of the administrative unit changed with the years as is indicated by the changes in its name. In 1904 when a diocese of North America was created its first archbishop, Tikhon, shortly thereafter established himself in his seat at Saint Nicholas Cathedral. His appointment came from the Holy Synod of Russia as did those of his successors in order Platon and Evdokim. Under those appointments the successive archbishops occupied the Cathedral and residence of Saint Nicholas under the administrative authority of the Holy Synod.

In 1917 Archbishop Evdokim returned to Russia permanently. Early that year an All Russian Sobor was held, the first since Peter the Great. It occurred during the interlude of political freedom following the fall of the Czar. A patriarch was elected and installed—Tikhon who had been the first American Archbishop. Uncertainties as to the succession to and administration of the American archbishopric made their appearance following this sobor and were largely induced by the almost contemporaneous political disturbances which culminated swiftly in the Bolshevik Revolution of 1917. The Russian Orthodox Church was drawn into this maelstrom. After a few years the Patriarch was imprisoned. There were suggestions of his counterrevolutionary activity. Church power was transferred, partly through a sobor considered by many as non-canonical to a Supreme Church Council. The declared reforms were said to have resulted in a "Living Church" or sometimes in a "Renovated Church." Circumstances and pressures changed. Patriarch Tikhon was released from prison and died in 1925. He named three bishops as locum tenens for the patriarchal throne. It was one of these, Sergius, who in 1933 appointed the appellant Benjamin as Archbishop. The Church was registered as a religious organization under

Soviet law in 1927. Thereafter the Russian Church and the Russian State approached if not a reconciliation at least an adjustment which eventuated by 1943 in the election of Sergius, one of the bishops named as locum tenens by Tikhon, to the Patriarchate. The Living or Renovated Church, whether deemed a reformed, a schismatic or a new church, apparently withered away. After Sergius' death a new patriarch of the Russian Orthodox Church, Alexi, was chosen Patriarch in 1945 at Moscow at a sobor recognized by all parties to this litigation as a true sobor held in accordance with the church canons.

The Russian upheaval caused repercussions in the North American Diocese. That Diocese at the time of the Soviet Revolution recognized the spiritual and administrative control of Moscow. White Russians, both lay and clerical, found asylum in America from the revolutionary conflicts, strengthening the feeling of abhorrence of the secular attitude of the new Russian Government. The church members already here, immigrants and native-born, while habituated to look to Moscow for religious direction, were accustomed to our theory of separation between church and state. The Russian turmoil, the restraints on religious activities and the evolution of a new ecclesiastical hierarchy in the form of the "Living Church," deemed noncanonical or schismatic by most churchmen, made very difficult Russian administration of the American diocese. Furthermore, Patriarch Tikhon, on November 20, 1920, issued Decision No. 362 relating to church administration for troublesome times. This granted a large measure of autonomy, when the Russian ruling authority was unable to function, subject to "confirmation later to the Central Church Authority when it is reestablished." Naturally the growing number of American-born members of the Russian Church did not cling to a hierarchy identified with their country of remote origin with the same national feeling that moved their immigrant ancestors. These facts and forces generated in America a separatist movement. [omission] From those circumstances it seems clear that the Russian Orthodox Church was, until the Russian Revolution, an hierarchical church with unquestioned paramount jurisdiction in the governing body in Russia over the American Metropolitanate. Nothing indicates that either the Sacred Synod or the succeeding Patriarchs relinquished that authority or recognized the autonomy of the American church. The Court of Appeals decision proceeds, we understand, upon the same assumption. That court did consider "whether there exists in Moscow at the present time a true central organization of the Russian Orthodox Church capable of functioning as the head of a free international religious body." It concluded that this aspect of the controversy had not been sufficiently developed to justify a judgment upon that ground.

THE RELIGIOUS CORPORATIONS LAW

—The New York Court of Appeals depended for its judgment, refusing recognition to Archbishop Benjamin, the appointee of the Moscow Hierarchy of the Russian Orthodox Church, upon Article 5-C of the Religious Corporations Law . . . Certainly a legislature is free to act upon such information as it may have as to the necessity for legislation. But an enactment by a legislature cannot validate action which the Constitution prohibits, and we think that the statute here in question passes the constitutional limits. We conclude that Article 5-C undertook by its terms to transfer the control of the New York churches of the Russian Orthodox religion from the central governing hierarchy of the Russian Orthodox Church, the Patriarch of Moscow and the Holy Synod, to the governing authorities of the Russian Church in America, a church organization limited to the diocese of North America and the Aleutian Islands. This transfer takes place by virtue of the statute. Such a law violates the Fourteenth Amendment. It prohibits in this country the free exercise of religion. Legislation that regulates church administration, the operation of the churches, the appointment of clergy, by requiring conformity to church statutes "adopted at a general convention (sobor) held in the City of New York on or about or between October fifth to eighth, nineteen hundred thirty-seven, and any amendments thereto," prohibits the free exercise of religion. Although this statute requires the New York churches to "in all other respects conform to, maintain and follow the faith, doctrine, ritual, communion, discipline, canon law, traditions and usages of the Eastern Confession (Eastern Orthodox or Greek Catholic Church)," their conformity is by legislative fiat and subject to legislative will. Should the state assert power to change the statute requiring conformity to ancient faith and doctrine to one establishing a different doctrine, the invalidity would be unmistakable.

Although 5 of the Religious Corporations Law had long controlled religious corporations, the Court of Appeals held that its rule was not based on any constitutional requirement or prohibition. Since certain events of which the Court took judicial notice indicated to it that the Russian Government exercised control over the central church authorities and that the American church acted to protect its pulpits and faith from such influences, the Court of Appeals felt that the Legislature's reasonable belief in such conditions justified the State in enacting a law to free the American group from infiltration of such atheistic or subversive influences.

This legislation, Art. 5-C, in the view of the Court of Appeals, gave the use of the churches to the Russian Church in America on the theory that this church would most faithfully carry out the purposes of the religious trust. Thus dangers of political use of church pulpits would be minimized. Legislative power to punish subversive action cannot be doubted. If such action should be actually attempted by a cleric, neither his robe nor his pulpit would be a defense. But in this case no problem of punishment for the violation of law arises. There is no charge of subversive or hostile action by any ecclesiastic. Here there is a transfer by statute of control over churches. This violates our rule of separation between church and state. That conclusion results from the purpose, meaning and effect of the New York legislation stated above, considered in the light of the history and decisions considered below.

[omission]

This controversy concerning the right to use St. Nicholas Cathedral is strictly a matter of ecclesiastical government, the power of the Supreme Church Authority of the Russian Orthodox Church to appoint the ruling hierarch of the archdiocese of North America. No one disputes that such power did lie in that Authority prior to the Russian Revolution.

Watson v. Jones, although it contains a reference to the relations of church and state under our system of laws, was decided without depending upon prohibition of state interference with the free exercise of religion. It was decided in 1871, before judicial recognition of the coercive power of the Fourteenth Amendment to protect the limitations of the First Amendment against state action . . . The opinion radiates, however, a spirit of freedom for religious organizations, an independence from secular control or manipulation, in short, power to decide for themselves, free from state interference, matters of church government as well as those of faith and doctrine. Freedom to select the clergy, where no improper methods of choice are proven, we think, must now be said to have federal constitutional protection as a part of the free exercise of religion against state interference.

Legislative Power.—The Court of Appeals of New York recognized, generally, the soundness of the philosophy of ecclesiastical control of church administration and polity but concluded that the exercise of that control was not free from legislative interference. That Court presented forcefully the argument supporting legislative power to act on its own knowledge of "the Soviet attitude toward things religious." It was said:

"The Legislature realized that the North American church, in order to be free of Soviet interference in its affairs, had declared its temporary administrative autonomy in 1924, pursuant to the ukase of 1920, while retaining full spiritual communion with the patriarchate, and that there was a real danger that those properties and temporalities long enjoyed and used by the Russian Orthodox Church worshippers in this State would be taken from them by the representatives of the patriarchate."

[omission]

In upholding the validity of Article 5-C, the New York Court of Appeals apparently assumes Article 5-C does nothing more than permit the trustees of the Cathedral to use it for services consistent with the desires of the members of the Russian Church in America. Its reach goes far beyond that point. By fiat it displaces one church administrator with another. It passes the control of matters strictly ecclesiastical from one church authority to another. It thus intrudes for the benefit of one segment of a church the power of the state into the forbidden area of religious freedom contrary to the principles of the First Amendment. Such prohibition differs from the restriction of a right to deal with Government allowed in Douds, in that the Union in the Douds Case had no such constitutionally protected right. New York's Article 5-C directly prohibits the free exercise of an ecclesiastical right, the Church's choice of its hierarchy. [omission]

The record before us shows no schism over faith or doctrine between the Russian Church in America and the Russian Orthodox Church. It shows administrative control of the North American Diocese by the Supreme Church Authority of the Russian Orthodox Church, including the appointment of the ruling hierarch in North America from the foundation of the diocese until the Russian Revolution. We find nothing that indicates a relinquishment of this power by the Russian Orthodox Church.

Ours is a government which by the "law of its being" allows no statute, state or national, that prohibits the free exercise of religion. There are occasions when civil courts must draw lines between the responsibilities of church and state for the disposition or use of property. Even in those cases when the property right follows as an incident from decisions of the church custom or law on ecclesiastical issues, the church rule controls. This under our Constitution necessarily follows in order that there may be free exercise of religion.

The decree of the Court of Appeals of New York must be reversed, and the case remanded to that court for such further action as it deems proper and not in contravention of this opinion.

MR. JUSTICE FRANKFURTER, CONCURRING.

Let me put to one side the question whether in our day a legislature could, consistently with due process, displace the judicial process and decide a particular controversy affecting property so as to decree that

A not B owns it or is entitled to its possession. Obviously a legislature would not have that power merely because the property belongs to a church.

In any event, this proceeding rests on a claim which cannot be determined without intervention by the State in a religious conflict. St. Nicholas Cathedral is not just a piece of real estate. It is no more that than is St. Patrick's Cathedral or the Cathedral of St. John the Divine. A cathedral is the seat and center of ecclesiastical authority. St. Nicholas Cathedral is an archiepiscopal see of one of the great religious organizations. What is at stake here is the power to exercise religious authority. That is the essence of this controversy. It is that even though the religious authority becomes manifest and is exerted through authority over the Cathedral as the outward symbol of a religious faith.

The judiciary has heeded, naturally enough, the menace to a society like ours of attempting to settle such religious struggles by state action. And so, when courts are called upon to adjudicate disputes which, though generated by conflicts of faith, may fairly be isolated as controversies over property and therefore within judicial competence, the authority of courts is in strict subordination to the ecclesiastical law of a particular church prior to a schism. This very limited right of resort to courts for determination of claims, civil in their nature, between rival parties among the communicants of a religious faith is merely one aspect of the duty of courts to enforce the rights of members in an association, temporal or religious, according to the laws of that association.

Legislatures have no such obligation to adjudicate and no such power. Assuredly they have none to settle conflicts of religious authority and none to define religious obedience. These aspects of spiritual differences constitute the heart of this controversy. The New York legislature decreed that one party to the dispute and not the other should control the common center of devotion. In doing so the legislature effectively authorized one party to give religious direction not only to its adherents but also to its opponents.

The arguments by which New York seeks to justify this inroad into the realm of faith are echoes of past attempts at secular intervention in religious conflicts. It is said that an impressive majority both of the laity and of the priesthood of the old local church now adhere to the party whose candidate New York enthroned, as it were, as Archbishop. Be that as it may, it is not a function of civil government under our constitutional system to assure rule to any religious body by a counting of heads. Our Constitution does assure that anyone is free to worship according to his conscience. A legislature is not free to vest in a schismatic head the means of acting under the authority of his old church, by affording him the religious power which the use and occupancy of St. Nicholas Cathedral make possible.

Again, it is argued that New York may protect itself from dangers attributed to submission by the mòther church in Moscow to political authority. To reject this claim one does not have to indulge in the tendency of lawyers to carry arguments to the extreme of empty formal logic. Scattered throughout the country there are religious bodies with ties to various countries of a world in tension—tension due in part to shifting political affiliation and orientation. The consideration which permeates the court's opinion below would give each State the right to assess the circumstances in the foreign political entanglements of its religious bodies that make for danger to the State, and the power resting on plausible legislative findings, to divest such bodies of spiritual authority and of the temporal property which symbolizes it.

Memory is short but it cannot be forgotten that in the State of New York there was strong feeling against the Tsarist regime at a time when the Russian Church was governed by a Procurator of the Tsar. And when Mussolini exacted the Lateran Agreement, argument was not wanting by those friendly to her claims that the Church of Rome was subjecting herself to political authority. The fear, perhaps not wholly groundless, that the loyalty of its citizens might be diluted by their adherence to a church entangled in antagonistic political interests, reappears in history as the ground for interference by civil government with religious attachments. Such fear readily leads to persecution of religious beliefs deemed dangerous to ruling political authority. It was on this basis, after all, that Bismarck sought to detach German Catholics from Rome by a series of laws not too different in purport from that before us today. The long, unedifying history of the contest between the secular state and the church is replete with instances of attempts by civil government to exert pressure upon religious authority. Religious leaders have often made gestures of accommodation to such pressures. History also indicates that the vitality of great world religions survived such efforts. In any event, under our Constitution it is not open to the governments of this Union to reinforce the loyalty of their citizens by deciding who is the true exponent of their religion.

Finally, we are told that the present Moscow Patriarchate is not the true superior church of the American communicants. The vicissitudes of war and revolution which have beset the Moscow Patriarchate since 1917 are said to have resulted in a discontinuity which divests the present Patriarch of his authority over the American church. Both parties to the present controversy agree that the present Patriarch is the legitimately chosen holder of his office, and the account of the proceedings and pronouncements of the American schismatic group so indicate.

Even were there doubt about this it is hard to see by what warrant the New York Legislature is free to substitute its own judgment as to the validity of Patriarch Alexi's claim and to disregard acknowledgment of the present Patriarch by his coequals in the Eastern Confession, the Patriarchs of Constantinople, Alexandria, Antioch, and Jerusalem, and by religious leaders throughout the world, including the present Archbishop of York.

These considerations undermine the validity of the New York legislation in that it enters the domain of religious control barred to the States by the Fourteenth Amendment.

MR. JUSTICE JACKSON, DISSENTING.

[omission]

. . . I greatly oversimplify the history of this controversy to indicate its nature rather than to prove its merits. This Cathedral was incorporated and built in the era of the Czar, under the regime of a state-ridden church in a church-ridden state. The Bolshevik Revolution may have freed the state from the grip of the church, but it did not free the church from the grip of the state. It only brought to the top a new master for a captive and submissive ecclesiastical establishment. By 1945, the Moscow patriarchy had been reformed and manned under the Soviet regime and it sought to re-establish in other countries its prerevolutionary control of church property and its sway over the minds of the religious. As the Court's opinion points out, it demanded of the Russian Church in America, among other things, that it abstain "from political activities against the U.S.S.R." The American Cathedral group, along with others, refused submission to the representative of the Moscow Patriarch, whom it regarded as an arm of the Soviet Government. Thus, we have an ostensible religious schism with decided political overtones.

If the Fourteenth Amendment is to be interpreted to leave anything to the courts of a state to decide without our interference, I should suppose it would be claims to ownership or possession of real estate within its borders and the vexing technical questions pertaining to the creation, interpretation, termination, and enforcement of uses and trusts, even though they are for religious and charitable purposes. This controversy, I believe, is a matter for settlement by state law and not within the proper province of this Court. [omission]

The Court holds, however, that the State cannot exercise its reserved power to control this property without invading religious freedom, because it is a Cathedral and devoted to religious uses. I forbear discussion of the extent to which restraints imposed upon Congress by the First Amendment are transferred against the State by the Fourteenth Amendment beyond saying that I consider that the same differences which apply to freedom of speech and press are applicable to questions of church and state.

It is important to observe what New York has not done in this case. It has not held that Benjamin may not act as Archbishop or be revered as such by all who will follow him. It has not held that he may not have a Cathedral. Indeed, I think New York would agree that no one is more in need of spiritual guidance than the Soviet faction. It has only held that this cleric may not have a particular Cathedral which, under New York law, belongs to others. It has not interfered with his or anyone's exercise of his religion. New York has not outlawed the Soviet-controlled sect nor forbidden it to exercise its authority or teach its dogma in any place whatsoever except on this piece of property owned and rightfully possessed by the Cathedral Corporation.

The fact that property is dedicated to a religious use cannot, in my opinion, justify the Court in sublimating an issue over property rights into one of deprivation of religious liberty which alone would bring in the religious guaranties of the First Amendment. I assume no one would pretend that the State cannot decide a claim of trespass, larceny, conversion, bailment or contract, where the property involved is that of a religious corporation or is put to religious use, without invading the principle of religious liberty.

Of course, possession of the property will help either side that obtains it to maintain its prestige and to continue or extend its sway over the minds and souls of the devout. So would possession of a bank account, an income-producing office building, or any other valuable property. But if both claimants are religious corporations or personalities, can not the State decide the issues that arise over ownership and possession without invading the religious freedom of one or the other of the parties?

Thus, if the American group, which owns the title to the Cathedral, had by force barred Benjamin from entering it physically, would the Court say it was an interference with religious freedom to entertain and decide his ejectment action? If state courts are to decide such controversies at all instead of leaving them to be settled by a show of force, is it constitutional to decide for only one side of the controversy and unconstitutional to decide for the other? In either case, the religious freedom of one side or the other is impaired if the temporal goods they need are withheld or taken from them.

As I have earlier pointed out, the Soviet Ecclesiast's claim, denial of which is said to be constitutional error, is not that this New York property is impressed with a trust by virtue of New York law. The claim is that it is impressed with a trust by virtue of the rules of the Russian Orthodox Church. This Court so holds.

302

I shall not undertake to wallow through the complex, obscure and fragmentary details of secular and ecclesiastical history, theology, and canon law in which this case is smothered. To me, whatever the canon law is found to be and whoever is the rightful head of the Moscow patriarchate, I do not think New York law must yield to the authority of a foreign and unfriendly state masquerading as a spiritual institution. (See "The Soviet Propaganda Program," Staff Study No. 3, Senate Subcommittee on Overseas Information Programs of the United States, 82nd Cong. 2d Sess.)

I have supposed that a State of this Union was entirely free to make its own law, independently of any foreign-made law, except as the Full Faith and Credit Clause of the Constitution might require deference to the law of a sister state or the Supremacy Clause require submission to federal law. I do not see how one can spell out of the principles of separation of church and state a doctrine that a state submit property rights to settlement by canon law. If there is any relevant inference to be drawn, I should think it would be to the contrary, though I see no obstacle to the state allowing ecclesiastical law to govern in such a situation if it sees fit . . .

FOWLER v. RHODE ISLAND   345 US 67 (1953)

"Baptist, Methodist, Presbyterian, or Episcopal ministers, Catholic priests, Moslem mullahs, Buddhist monks, could all preach to their congregations in Pawtucket's parks with impunity. But the hand of the law would be laid on the shoulder of a minister of this unpopular group for performing the same function."

Mr. Justice Douglas, for the Court

A case of discrimination against Jehovah's Witnesses.

MR. JUSTICE DOUGLAS DELIVERED THE OPINION OF THE COURT.

The City of Pawtucket, Rhode Island, has an ordinance which reads as follows:

"Sec. 11. No person shall address any political or religious meeting in any public park; but this section shall not be construed to prohibit any political or religious club or society from visiting any public park in a body, provided that no public address shall be made under the auspices of such club or society in such park."

Jehovah's Witnesses, a religious sect, assembled in Slater Park of Pawtucket for a meeting which at the trial was conceded to be religious in character. About 400 people attended, 150 being Jehovah's Witnesses. Appellant is a minister of this sect, residing in Arlington, Mass.

He was invited to Pawtucket as a visiting minister to give a talk before the Pawtucket congregation of Jehovah's Witnesses. Appellant accepted the invitation, attended the meeting in the park, and addressed it over two loud speakers. It was a quiet, orderly meeting with no disturbances or breaches of the peace whatsoever.

Appellant's address was entitled "The Pathway to Peace." He discussed the futility of efforts being made to establish peace in the world. And then, according to his uncontradicted testimony he "launched forth into the scriptural evidence to show where we were on the string of time; that we had reached the end of this wicked system of things." Appellant had been talking only a few minutes when he was arrested by the police and charged with violating the ordinance set forth above. He was tried and found guilty over objections that the ordinance as so construed and applied violated the First and the Fourteenth Amendments of the Constitution. He was fined $5. His conviction was affirmed by the Rhode Island Supreme Court . . . The case is here on appeal.

Davis v. Massachusetts, decided in 1897, sustained a conviction of a man for making a speech on the Boston Commons in violation of an ordinance that forbade the making of a public address there without a permit from the mayor. Much of the oral argument and most of the briefs have been devoted on the one hand to a defense of the Davis Case and on the other hand to an attack on it. Analyses of subsequent decisions have been submitted in an effort either to demonstrate that the Davis Case is today good law, or to show that it has been so qualified as no longer to have any vitality. We are invited by appellant to overrule it; we are asked by respondent to reaffirm it.

We put to one side the problems presented by the Davis Case and its offspring. For there is one aspect of the present case that undercuts all others and makes it necessary for us to reverse the judgment. As we have said, it was conceded at the trial that this meeting was a religious one. On oral argument before the Court the Assistant Attorney General further conceded that the ordinance, as construed and applied, did not prohibit church services in the park. Catholics could hold mass in Slater Park and Protestants could conduct their church services there without violating the ordinance. Church services normally entail not only singing, prayer, and other devotionals but preaching as well. Even so, those services would not be barred by the ordinance. That broad concession, made in oral argument, is fatal to Rhode Island's case. For it plainly shows that a religious service of Jehovah's Witnesses is treated differently than a religious service of other sects. That amounts to the state preferring some religious groups over this one. In Niemotko v. Maryland, we had a case on all fours with this one. There a public park, open to all religious groups, was denied Jehovah's Witnesses because of the dislike which the local officials had of these people and their views. That was a discrimination which we held to be barred by the First and Fourteenth Amendments.

Appellant's sect has conventions that are different from the practices of other religious groups. Its religious service is less ritualistic, more unorthodox, less formal than some. But apart from narrow exceptions not relevant here (Reynolds v. United States, Davis v. Beason), it is no business of courts to say that what is a religious practice or activity for one group is not religion under the protection of the First Amendment. Nor is it in the competence of courts under our constitutional scheme to approve, disapprove, classify, regulate, or in any manner control sermons delivered at religious meetings. Sermons are as much a part of religious service as prayers. They cover a wide range and have as great a diversity as the Bible or other Holy Book from which they commonly take their texts. To call the words which one minister speaks to his congregation a sermon, immune from regulation, and the words of another minister an address, subject to regulation, is merely an indirect way of preferring one religion over another. That would be precisely the effect here if we affirmed this conviction in the face of the concession made during oral argument. Baptist, Methodist, Presbyterian, or Episcopal ministers, Catholic priests, Moslem mullahs, Buddhist monks could all preach to their congregations in Pawtucket's parks with impunity. But the hand of the law would be laid on the shoulder of a minister of this unpopular group for performing the same function.

The judgment is reversed and the cause is remanded to the Supreme Court of Rhode Island for proceedings not inconsistent with this opinion.

Reversed.

Mr. Justice Frankfurter concurs in the opinion of the Court, except insofar as it may derive support from the First Amendment. For him it is the Equal-Protection-of-the-Laws Clause of the Fourteenth Amendment that condemns the Pawtucket ordinance as applied in this case.